Understanding Multiculturalism

Austrian and Habsburg Studies

General Editor: Gary B. Cohen

Published in Association with the Center for Austrian Studies, University of Minnesota

Volume 1
Austrian Women in the Nineteenth and Twentieth Centuries: Cross-Disciplinary Perspectives
Edited by David F. Good, Margarete Grandner, and Mary Jo Maynes

Volume 2
From World War to Waldheim: Culture and Politics in Austria and the United States
Edited by David F. Good and Ruth Wodak

Volume 3
Rethinking Vienna 1900
Edited by Steven Beller

Volume 4
The Great Tradition and Its Legacy: The Evolution of Dramatic and Musical Theater in Austria and Central Europe
Edited by Michael Cherlin, Halina Filipowicz, and Richard L. Rudolph

Volume 5
Creating the Other: Ethnic Conflict and Nationalism in Habsburg Central Europe
Edited by Nancy M. Wingfield

Volume 6
Constructing Nationalities in East Central Europe
Edited by Pieter M. Judson and Marsha L. Rozenblit

Volume 7
The Environment and Sustainable Development in the New Central Europe
Edited by Zbigniew Bochniarz and Gary B. Cohen

Volume 8
Crime, Jews and News: Vienna 1890–1914
Daniel Mark Vyleta

Volume 9
The Limits of Loyalty: Imperial Symbolism, Popular Allegiances, and State Patriotism in the Late Habsburg Monarchy
Edited by Laurence Cole and Daniel L. Unowsky

Volume 10
Embodiments of Power: Building Baroque Cities in Europe
Edited by Gary B. Cohen and Franz A. J. Szabo

Volume 11
Diversity and Dissent: Negotiating Religious Differences in Central Europe, 1500–1800
Edited by Howard Louthan, Gary B. Cohen, and Franz A. J. Szabo

Volume 12
"Vienna Is Different": Jewish Writers in Austria from the Fin de Siècle to the Present
Hillary Hope Herzog

Volume 13
Sexual Knowledge: Feeling, Fact and Social Reform in Vienna, 1900–1934
Britta McEwen

Volume 14
Journeys Into Madness: Mapping Mental Illness in the Austro-Hungarian Empire
Edited by Gemma Blackshaw and Sabine Wieber

Volume 15
Territorial Revisionism and the Allies of Germany in the Second World War: Goals, Expectations, Practices
Edited by Marina Cattaruzza, Stefan Dyroff, and Dieter Langewiesche

Volume 16
The Viennese Cafe and Fin-de-Siecle Culture
Edited by Charlotte Ashby, Tag Gronberg, and Simon Shaw-Miller

Volume 17
Understanding Multiculturalism: The Habsburg Central European Experience
Edited by Johannes Feichtinger and Gary B. Cohen

Understanding Multiculturalism

The Habsburg Central European Experience

Edited by

Johannes Feichtinger
and
Gary B. Cohen

berghahn
NEW YORK · OXFORD
www.berghahnbooks.com

First edition published in 2014 by
Berghahn Books
www.berghahnbooks.com

© 2014 Johannes Feichtinger and Gary B. Cohen

All rights reserved. Except for the quotation of short passages
for the purposes of criticism and review, no part of this book
may be reproduced in any form or by any means, electronic or
mechanical, including photocopying, recording, or any information
storage and retrieval system now known or to be invented,
without written permission of the publisher.

Library of Congress Cataloging-in-Publication Data

Understanding multiculturalism: the Habsburg Central European experience / edited by Johannes Feichtinger and Gary B. Cohen.
  pages cm. — (Austrian and Habsburg studies ; volume 17)
  Includes bibliographical references and index.
  ISBN 978-1-78238-264-5 (hardback : alk. paper) — ISBN 978-1-78238-265-2 (ebook)
 1. Austria—Ethnic relations—History. 2. Europe, Central—Ethnic relations—History. 3. Multiculturalism—Austria—History. 4. Multiculturalism—Europe, Central—History. 5. National characteristics, Austrian. 6. National characteristics, Central European. I. Feichtinger, Johannes, editor of compilation. II. Cohen, Gary B., 1948– editor of compilation.
  DB47.U64 2014
  305.8'009436—dc23   2013023149

British Library Cataloguing in Publication Data

A catalogue record for this book is available from the British Library

Printed on acid-free paper
ISBN: 978-1-78238-264-5 hardback
ISBN: 978-1-78238-265-2 ebook

Contents

List of Tables and Figures ... vii

Preface ... ix

Introduction. Understanding Multiculturalism:
The Habsburg Central European Experience ... 1
Johannes Feichtinger and Gary B. Cohen

Section I. Identity Formation in Multicultural Societies

1. Heterogeneities and Homogeneities: On Similarities
and Diversities ... 17
Anil Bhatti

2. *Mestizaje* and Hybrid Culture: Toward a Transnational
Cultural Memory of Europe and the Development of Cultural
Theories in Latin America ... 47
Michael Rössner

3. Do Multiple Languages Mean a Multicultural Society?
Nationalist "Frontiers" in Rural Austria, 1880–1918 ... 61
Pieter M. Judson

Section II. The Dynamics of Multicultural Societies, Politics, and the State

4. Multiculturalism, Polish Style: Glimpses from the Interwar Period ... 85
Patrice M. Dabrowski

5. Multiculturalism against the State: Lessons from Istria ... 101
Pamela Ballinger

6. Migration in Austria: An Overview of the 1920s to 2000s ... 122
Michael John

SECTION III. IDENTITIES EXPRESSED, NEGOTIATED, AND CHALLENGED IN MULTICULTURAL SETTINGS

7. The Slice of Desire: Intercultural Practices versus National Loyalties in the Peripheral Multiethnic Society of Central Europe at the Beginning of the Twentieth Century 161
   Oto Luthar

8. On "Neighbors" and "Strangers": The Literary Motif of "Central Europe" as *Lieu de Mémoire* 174
   Andrei Corbea-Hoisie

9. Culture as a Space of Communication 187
   Moritz Csáky

Selected Bibliography 209

Notes on Contributors 233

Index 237

Tables and Figures

Tables

6.1. Place of Birth, Residents of Vienna, Language of Everyday Use, Religion, 1923–34 — 130

6.2. Population Born Outside Austria by Province, 1951–2001 — 139

6.3. Population in Austria, 1 January 2011, by Nationality and Birth — 144

Figures

6.1. Workforce in Austria by Nationality, 1963–2006 — 138

7.1. Recipe for *Preznic* from a Manuscript Cookbook by Marija Hujs, in the possession of Oto Luthar — 171

World." The research group brought together twenty scholars from Austria, Germany, Hungary, India, Slovenia, Switzerland, Ukraine, the United Kingdom, and the United States. The present volume grew out of an extended period of scholarly discussions and exchanges among members of that group.

The editors are grateful to all who participated in the research project during the intervening years. We thank the nine authors of chapters in this volume in particular for their patient and dedicated work. The whole venture was only possible due to the generous support of the Institute of Culture Studies and Theatre History of the Austrian Academy of Sciences, the University of Minnesota Center for Austrian Studies, and the Rockefeller Foundation and its Bellagio Center. We are especially grateful for the careful editorial work performed by a succession of research assistants at the Center for Austrian Studies, including Anne Carter, Joshua Kortbein, Mollie Madden, Kevin Mummey, Sharon Park, Lisa Peschel, Barbara Reiterer, Eric Roubinek, and Edward Snyder. Finally, we are happy to thank Marion Berghahn, Ann Przyzycki DeVita, Adam Capitanio, and their colleagues at Berghahn Books for their care, understanding, and dedication to the best traditions of independent scholarly publishing in bringing the preparation of this book to a happy conclusion as a volume in the series *Austrian and Habsburg Studies*.

Johannes Feichtinger and Gary B. Cohen
Vienna and Minneapolis, August 2013

INTRODUCTION
Understanding Multiculturalism:
The Habsburg Central European Experience

Johannes Feichtinger and Gary B. Cohen

Today, after decades of linking the concept of multiculturalism to a call for tolerance of cultural heterogeneity, societies are subjecting multiculturalism to close scrutiny. In countries of culturally mixed populations, society commonly viewed the entire idea of multiculturalism as a mandate to protect minorities and guarantee them individual and collective rights. If, in the decades following the political upheavals of 1968, the commitment to multiculturalism was perceived as a liberal manifesto, multiculturalism in the post-9/11 era is under attack for its relativizing, particularist, essentializing, and potentially divisive implications.

Under the cover of multiculturalism, new injustices might be permitted—as, for example, if permission were granted to Muslims in Europe to have sharia govern familial and communal relations. Multiculturalism celebrates diversity while at the same time permitting different cultural camps within a given society to ascribe to "the others" a specific linguistic, ethnic, or religious identity and origin, thereby limiting them in terms of the "defining culture"—and implicitly circumscribing their role in that society. One notes here a distinct odor of patronizing protectionism and tolerance, but also one of distance from the culture of "the others." The multicultural respect for their distinctiveness comes along with a claim of its own superiority. In other words, multiculturalism in this view easily becomes a concealed, inverted, self-referential form of racism, a "racism of distancing oneself."[1] In a recent review of studies on the challenges to contemporary polities of dealing justly with diverse populations, Timothy Garton Ash found that programs and policies of multiculturalism have so often produced contradictory, illiberal results that, with respect to normative political theory and public policy, the term itself "should be consigned to the dustbin of history."[2]

In the realm of nation-state policy, multiculturalism results from a strategy adopted by the governments of nation-states to solve problems created by cultural diversity and is now, under postnational conditions, subject to particularly severe criticism. The initial introduction of legislation to assure the political rights of those persons whose language, religion, race, or place of origin differ from that of the national majority was well received. Given the postnational condition proclaimed today, however, people have become increasingly aware of how such well-meaning measures also abetted a policy of classifying individuals into presumably homogeneous groups along ethnic, linguistic, or religious lines and denying ambiguity or indifference, in order to create subordinate units manageable for the dominant groups of society.

In the Anglo-American world, multiculturalism implies the political will to include, recognize, and represent ethnically diverse groups living together in single nation-states. As shown in the following chapters, in other parts of the world multiculturalism as a political doctrine has often turned step-by-step from an integrative practice into an ideology that aimed at keeping the groups separate from each other and from the majority. Since multiculturalism in continental Europe typically stands for the idea of peaceful coexistence of ethnic groups in single political units without allowing them to intermingle, right-wing political activists in several Central European countries have been using multiculturalism as a tool for consolidating the established power relationships between majorities and minorities. Today—or today again—minority populations fear that their own distinctive culture may fall victim to a uniformly imposed dominant culture. It must not be ignored, however, that from the political perspective, the views of the late eighteenth-century German idealist thinker Johann Gottfried Herder still strongly influence today's nationally encoded and territorialized understanding of cultural identity—one people (*Volk*), one language, one state.

Beyond these contemporary political conflicts but inspired by the challenges they pose, this book offers a scholarly discussion of multiculturalism whose results might then be fruitfully applied to contemporary political questions. For purposes of this book, we use the notion of multiculturalism as a delimited analytic tool of historical inquiry, and we consider the term to be appropriate as a category of scholarly description and analysis of the social conditions characteristic of societies that comprise culturally heterogeneous individuals and communities. They live together in spaces confined by politically established frontiers characterized by uncontrollable crossings and interactions in the practices of everyday life that are culturally encoded in multiple ways. Thus, we understand multiculturalism within the framework of this pluralistic cultural experience, without presupposing any necessary dominant or leading culture or any necessary direction for the development of relations and contacts between the various cultures.

Habsburg Central Europe may be regarded, as Moritz Csáky argues, as a "laboratory" for the pluricultural experience—to use a descriptive term without the exclusionary and essentialist assumptions that "multiculturalism" often carries in political contexts—in which processes significant for the globalized character of society in the twenty-first century can be usefully explored. This volume identifies and examines historical practices for dealing with the challenges of linguistic diversity, pluriculturality, and hyphenated identities that currently confront Europe and the world, and hopes to make a significant contribution to a more enlightened and fruitful approach to this critical problem confronting modern society.

Since we do not want to reproduce the logic of nationalist politics in the late Habsburg Empire in our analysis, we employ the notion of multiculturalism for historical inquiry descriptively and analytically. Or, to put it more explicitly, since it is the main goal of this volume to understand the manifestations of multiculturalism in Habsburg Central Europe, we have to formulate a new methodological approach, beyond any simple or static political notions of multiculturalism, which will allow us to capture cultural diversity more appropriately and precisely by defining culture as fragmented, multivalent, and fluid. This approach allows us to explore—paraphrasing Anil Bhatti's words in this volume—how Habsburg Central European society was structured with respect to culture; that is to say, it was and still is characterized by more fluid, communicatively open pluricultural conditions, instead of bounded, fixed ones. To grasp these structures in analytical terms, the authors of this book strive to define and use more elaborate categories than "multilinguality," "multinationality," or "multiethnicity," which do not encompass but rather typically obstruct the highly complex and dynamic cultural phenomena in question. However, since multiculturalism as a concept and a set of realities was and still is politically, and in consequence socially, relevant in the whole Central European area, multiculturalism is the focal point and object of study for our book, though that term in itself does not provide the theoretical approach and conceptual framework for our work.

Multiculturalism and Habsburg Central Europe

In this volume, multiculturalism will be revisited through the prism of the Habsburg Central European historical experience. If the experience of heterogeneity, whether in the form of multilinguality, multinationality, multiethnicity, differing administrative and legal structures, or different religions, has been the norm in Habsburg Central Europe and beyond for centuries, does such pluralism make a region multicultural? Or to put a finer point on the question, what political agenda may be hidden behind the apparently naive but common labeling of societies as multinational rather than multicultural? If one follows convention and labels the Habsburg Monarchy as multinational, multilingual, or multiethnic, the scholar not only runs the risk of retaining an implicit political dimension, but also of reproducing in the analysis the very nationalism our volume seeks to overcome. In recent writings the renowned Austrian historian Gerald Stourzh shows that in the late nineteenth century national politics increasingly promoted what he calls an "ethnicizing process" that tended to deemphasize not only the legal position and political roles of imperial Austria's historical provinces but also of the individual person as a "citizen of the state"—replacing the position of the individual as a citizen equal before the law with the criterion of individuals' national or ethnic belonging. The citizen of the state became a member of a nationally defined group officially termed a "nationality" (*Nationalität*) or later, a "national group," (in German, *Volksgruppe*). In this view the Habsburg Monarchy gradually turned from an empire encompassing several historic kingdoms and many provinces into a multinational, multiethnic, and multilingual state in which each nationality increasingly favored the ideal of national belonging now understood in ethnic terms, with both the central authorities and protagonists of the national movements within the monarchy promoting linguistic purity and monolingualism, and instruments of governance increasingly focused on the various nationalities.[3]

The historical region we focus on, and that we call Habsburg Central Europe, can be defined as a geographic designation or as a heuristic concept. For decades, this designation stood for the whole Austro-Hungarian Monarchy and, after World War I and the treaties of St. Germain and Trianon in 1919/20, for the successor states. Later on—after much scholarly reflection on the German imperialist concept of *Mitteleuropa* (Central Europe)—many observers included Germany and other adjacent countries in the scheme of Central Europe.[4] In this volume we define Central Europe in terms of the legacy of Habsburg Central Europe, not geographically in the framework of *Mitteleuropa*. Our concept of Central Europe is predefined in two main categories: first, a structural one, which Moritz Csáky terms the "pluralities," constituted by the rich experience of linguistic, cultural, and ethnic diversity within the region and the adoption at various times of Spanish, Italian, French, and Ottoman styles in the arts, music, and cuisine, as well as in practices of everyday life; and second, one of values and practice, that is, certain distinct traditions and correlate actions that were generated by shared social and historical developments. Over time, both categories experienced significant shifts in meaning.

The entire social area we call Habsburg Central Europe was under significant pressure from broader mechanisms of political and social change. The political change from the estates-based state of the early seventeenth century to the absolutist state and finally to the constitutional state after 1848 and 1867 offered new social and economic opportunities for individuals and social groups and entailed at the same time considerable risks for other people, while cultural heterogeneity proved a far more constant characteristic of these societies.

The phenomenon of Habsburg Central Europe at issue here should be viewed as a dynamic structure of culturally variegated social areas affected by processes of demarcation and exchange, including in particular the use of shared symbols. This interactive area expanded or contracted in size over the centuries, and thus Belgrade in Serbia at the time of the wars of Ottoman imperial expansion from the fifteenth through the eighteenth centuries CE was just as much a part of Habsburg Central Europe as was Leipzig, a city that, though also not part of the Habsburg Monarchy, enjoyed intellectual exchange with both Prague and Vienna during the eighteenth-century Enlightenment. One can say much the same about Breslau/Wrocław after Prussia took most of Silesia from the Habsburgs in the 1740s, and the entire province of Lombardy in northern Italy contributed culturally to Habsburg Central Europe from the time of the War of Spanish Succession just after 1700 to the Italian Risorgimento of the mid-nineteenth century. Ultimately, we note that the Habsburg Monarchy was indeed only one part—albeit a highly significant one—of the larger concept of Habsburg Central Europe.

Differences and Identities

Scholarly writers of the nineteenth century bore witness to the characteristic prenational cultural constitution of the Habsburg Monarchy. They described the Austro-Hungarian Monarchy as a "state of contrast,"[5] in which *no* single province was inhabited only by members of one cultural or ethnic group or one religious denomination, speaking only one language. History shows that diversity as a lived and intensely debated experience does not, in defiance of all differences, necessarily articulate itself in divisive terms. In this regard the Habsburg Monarchy serves as an excellent case in point.

The intricate experience of Habsburg Central Europe lends itself particularly well to establishing a model for coping with the challenges of modern cultural heterogeneity, as the chapters presented in this volume show. It is now generally accepted that cultural differences often serve social and political functions of constituting identity. Those functions result from processes of signification that articulate or even establish specific power relationships. Stuart Hall argues that the postulation of difference serves as the distinctive feature of the very symbolic order, which we choose to call culture.[6] Recent studies have abandoned the nineteenth-century notion of culture as a homogenizing, unifying force, authenticated by an individual and unique past and kept alive by the imagined national tradition of the people.[7] Nowadays, culture is conceptualized as a system of orientation, helping to constitute identity by means of differentiation but always in flux. Thus, cultures are no longer regarded as "things with mind,"[8] but as preemptive, arbitrary, fragile, and historical. If cultures are not conceptualized in this contingent and mutable way, identities are inevitably essentialized. It is the intention of this volume to reflect on and critique the still-common reification of cultures. The Austrian physicist and philosopher Ernst Mach once noted that identities were in fact names, makeshifts, and remedies that allow a temporary orientation, and that they are strongly shaped by the difference from that which they are not. Mach used here the phrase "by the environment" (*durch die Umgebung*) in asserting that identities are more intensely affected by demarcation from their immediate surroundings than by any inherent "psychological identity" (*psychische Identität*).[9]

Our approach strives to portray cultural, and in consequence social, differences and identities as two sides of the same coin: neither is conceptualized as static, deeply rooted, and intrinsically authentic. In contrast to earlier theological, philosophical, or biological conceptualizations, identities are now understood as fragile, provisional, continually rebuilt, and constantly shifting—as unstable interfaces evolving in a dialogue between similarity and difference under specific conditions of power. They are no longer viewed as quintessentially constant in times of change. The contemporary theoretical approach recognizes and heightens awareness of the historically experienced differences leading to different expressions of collective identity, be it regional, social, religious. However, differences also have the potential to increase discrepancies between cultures, as well as to stimulate or support challenges to asymmetrical balances of power.

Epistemological Implications of the Nationalization Process

In the Habsburg Monarchy after the mid-nineteenth century, nationalist activists exploited the many manifest heterogeneities for their own purposes. In order to establish the very nations they claimed to represent, nationalist movements made culture an inherent part of geography and territory. They exaggerated differences and nationalized identity in bi- or multilingual communities by using language as a differentiating feature. Nationalists perceived homogeneity in the use of language as the ideal model of political unity and state organization. Teachers, journalists, and artists supported the nationalization process, which included, for example, performances of "national" vehicles in the "national" language in opera houses, theaters, and other public venues. Nationalist activists used public spaces as stages during the late nineteenth century for inventing, spreading, and enforcing national identities by generating so-called ethnic differences and presenting national communities as immutable natural phenomena. In the scholarly sphere, historiography, language, literature, law studies, and other disciplines played their part by subjecting inquiry and conceptualizations to the national master narrative. Nationalists worked assiduously to enforce national loyalties and to combat ethnic and national indifference, ambiguity, and mutability in the population and then fostered narratives that denied or minimized the existence of indifference and mutability.[10] The development of the nationalist master narrative also affected the construction of collective memory, especially the building of historical traditions, which is still the case. If history writing in and about Habsburg Central Europe interprets cultural differences in society only as a result of nationalist endeavors, this might signify that it still operates within the national narrative initially defined by the activists of the nineteenth century. One might thus easily ignore the daily practice of individuals' identification with various contradictory nonnational narratives, which later were wrongly understood as being national.

National identity is, according to the Cambridge historian Peter Burke, "clearly an important field of study, and it has received a good deal of attention recently, from sociologists and social historians alike." Burke finds it self-evident that "even in the modern world of nations it is obvious enough that other types of cultural identity remain significant: regional identities, ethnic identities, civic identities, and religious identities, to say nothing of gender, of family, or of clerical or noble identities (whether or not these should be described in terms of 'class')." "This multiplicity, when it is recognized," Burke concludes, "is sometimes perceived as a 'postmodern' phenomenon." However, for him, "there seems to be nothing uniquely postmodern, or even modern, about it." He evaluates these older definitions of identity (which include hyphenated identities) rather as persistent "rivals to national identity."[11] They are still present, but in the process of memorization they have become distorted. Thanks to the well-meaning efforts of the experts on tradition building—who so often turned identity and memory into a vast monoculture of "methodological nationalism"[12]—as well as to the many proponents of multiculturalism caught in national identity traps, potentially enriching differences and confrontations were transformed into situations of insurmountable opposition, boundaries were drawn, and parallel societies created.

The significance of the present volume lies in its theoretical approach. It analyzes and critiques those existing theoretical presuppositions, which scholars still hold even though they have been proven inadequate to the understanding of multicultural phenomena such as nation-based concepts of identity building. This volume advances the development of more productive transdisciplinary approaches to cultural diversity. The point of departure is the Habsburg Central European experience of diversity—and from this point the volume will develop its theme, transcending the Western perspective, on the one hand, by extending the horizon of empirical analysis of cultural pluralism to India and South America and, on the other hand, by clarifying conceptions from this perspective. In doing this, the volume advances the ongoing efforts to break through nation-based concepts of multiculturalism, identity, and difference and directly addresses the question of how we can best understand the social, political, and cultural realities of culturally heterogeneous societies.

For the authors of this volume, identity formation can be explained only by means of appreciating and analyzing the development of the discourse and social or political performance of identity under particular historical conditions, as well as the capturing in that discourse of memories of prior historical experiences. Memories provide important means for the constitution of identity. Memory is no longer defined as a given point of departure; it can serve multiple meanings and is continuously being transformed in processes of recoding. Over time, new protagonists accentuate new differences or recalibrate old ones to build new collective identities. This volume offers a subtler and more nuanced analysis of the role of memory in the elaboration of discourses of identity, such as in historiography and tradition building, than is possible in conventional discussions of identity. The latter adopt nationalist narratives all too easily and try to connect contemporary identity to a distant, imagined historical moment, in the process of which they become caught in the trap of methodological nationalism by employing the conceptualizations of nineteenth-century nationalists as categories of analysis and then explaining collective identities in complex cultural milieus from an at base nationalist perspective. In the early twentieth century Austrian intellectuals heavily criticized the destructive effects they anticipated from the application of the nationality principle to the heterogeneous state. As an antidote, figures such as Otto Bauer, Karl Renner, and Hans Kelsen elaborated theories of how to put national autonomy into practice with guarantees for the rights and freedoms of individual members of minority communities that were to be grounded in a "personality principle" or "rule of law" rather than in distinct territorial bases. However, also acting politically, they were not always able to transcend the habits of thought of nationalist politics. It is significant that a scholar such as Ephraim Nimni still labels Otto Bauer as one of "the precursors of multiculturalism," since drawing this very connection offers—from our pluricultural point of view—evidence for the methodological nationalism that the authors of this volume seek to overcome.[13]

One must also note that the more national criteria are used to explain social processes of pre- or postnational conditions, the more fallacious such reasoning becomes. Before the late eighteenth century neither national nor ethnic categories were articulated in intellectual or popular discourse. Yet if they still play a role in describing social processes after the twentieth century, they do not meet the needs of the "post-national constellation," as Jürgen Habermas has termed it.[14] Continuing to think within the constraints of national and ethnic categories leads to ignoring the connected and shared histories inherent in political, social, and economic practices, or to ignoring other cultural identities based on class, region, and gender, which, Peter Burke and others argue, frequently rival powerful national identities.

Goals

This volume addresses substantive questions of global importance: the chapters explore strategies of collective identity formation in the past and present in culturally diverse frameworks that recognize the claims of difference, while at the same time they are able to rise above the ethnic, racial, and/or cultural demarcations induced and reinforced by the nation-state. Taking Habsburg Central Europe as a point of departure, the contributors to this volume offer a substantial modification of the nation-based concept of identity. If contemporary political actors across Europe want to avoid following the old paths charted by nationalist identity policy in attempting to construct a distinct European identity, they should be prepared to develop new approaches while increasing awareness of the lingering effects of nineteenth-century concepts. This volume reconceptualizes various understandings of identity and concepts of the coexistence of culturally diverse populations within states while jettisoning the methodological nationalism characteristic of many contributions to the field. We want to analyze and understand the different manifestations of multiculturalism as a political strategy or discourse with which new boundaries of inclusion or exclusion were drawn, and as a mode of understanding and practice used by social actors for coping with diversity. The value added by the pluricultural point of view is that attributed differences may be valued by analysts as long as they are considered for what they are, namely, identity-constituting features, established in specific power relationships, but with no ontological status or value as such. Furthermore, we note that our scholarly approach to multicultural manifestations differs from both multiculturalism and ethnopluralism as political conceptions. On the one hand, it is distinct from the former, which has commonly served as a state-directed or politically induced concept of cultural diversity that tends to view cultures as monolithic blocks and calls for diversity while at the same time trying to reify and possibly also degrade "the other." On the other hand, ethnopluralism refers to a culture of perceived autochthonous and allochthonous ethnic groups. The modern concept of ethnopluralism has much in common with—as well as many significant differences from—the multiculturalism so cherished by left-wing liberals: both recognize culture as essence. However, by seemingly defending cultural disparity, ethnopluralism is able to veil its, at base, racist character—a fact that we ignore at our peril.

The respect that most modern societies demand be shown for the identity of other cultural groups calls for attentiveness to the differences between them and is expressed in the motto "unto each people its own." This concept—clearly analogous to the "separate but equal" explanation and defense of segregation—plays directly into the hands of those political powers that seem to accept the inevitability of cultural diversity, while at the same time engineering its protection. Thus, they are able to defend the distinct lines of ethnic segregation that they draw in order to show who, in fact, is in charge of the situation. Preserving diversity is not an obligation, and other measures similar to those described above should be recognized for what they are: an attack on human rights. Understanding multiculturalism within the framework of cultural diversity is an important endeavor of contemporary scholarship. Pluriculturality—as elaborated in this volume by Anil Bhatti—meets the epistemological requirements for historical inquiry. In this perspective culture is conceptualized as a meshwork of similarities and differences that describes ongoing processes both of negotiation, transfer, and translation and of marking the boundaries of which everyday life consists. Identifications do not emerge from multicultural coexistence but from cross-cultural exchange and shifting demarcations.

If we want to understand multiculturalism in the Habsburg Central European experience, we must recognize its cultural coding in multiple ways rather than simply designating the region as multicultural. No rigid conceptual approaches have been imposed on the authors, so as not to impoverish the different analytical approaches, or to reify the research strategies as they are represented in the following chapters. The authors critically scrutinize the deployment of multiculturalism as a political strategy and scholarly category, taking a nonessentialist notion of culture and a dynamic understanding of the role of memory as a point of departure in the elaboration of discourses of identity. Since this book proposes new interpretations of the Habsburg Central European multicultural experience, it is also necessary to assess that experience from a wider perspective.

The book begins in the first section with several approaches to understanding processes of identity formation in culturally diverse societies, with comparisons of the Central European experience to other parts of the world. Anil Bhatti's chapter on India and Michael Rössner's on Latin America are particularly instructive. They bring in the global dimension by comparing ways of dealing with cultural diversity in East and West with the Habsburg Central European case, about which both scholars are well informed. Bhatti and Rössner show that national self-understanding in Habsburg Central Europe never became as essentialist as in India (Hinduness, *Hindutva*), Latin America (ethnic mix, *Mestizaje*), and colonizing Europe (e.g., Germanness, Britishness, Frenchness), and that Indian and Latin American postcolonial theory offer new concepts and approaches (e.g., palimpsest, rhizome, hybridity) for understanding the pluricultural phenomena in Habsburg Central Europe beyond the nationally encoded concept of multiculturalism.

In Habsburg Central Europe, the practices of everyday life were shaped by both nationalist doctrines of national homogeneity and a reality of striking heterogeneity (language, confession, culture) and multiple identities. Rounding out the first section, Pieter Judson's chapter warns against adopting what Jeremy King has termed an "ethnicist approach,"[15] confusing those who spoke a language with those who felt a belonging to a nation defined by the use of that language. National loyalties were never as deeply rooted as were other forms of self-identification (e.g., religion). If one ignores these realities, the analytical use of multiculturalism might simply presume the existence of separate ethnic cultures, defined on the basis of language use. In multilingual communities, the choice to use *one* or another language did not necessarily evidence a defined national loyalty but rather often a situational strategy to increase one's life chances in given social circumstances. Thus, Judson asks: did Imperial Austria's multilingual composition make its society in fact multicultural? Or vice versa: does the multiculturalist's approach not simply validate in retrospect the social boundaries that the national activists had once created? If in everyday life few such boundaries had actually existed, Judson asks with good cause how and why these societies came to be understood and analyzed overwhelmingly in nationalist terms.

The chapters in the second section of the book raise questions about the dynamics of multicultural societies and the relationship to politics and the state. Patrice Dabrowski and Pamela Ballinger identify in their chapters different forms of political action that arise out of multicultural circumstances. Dabrowski examines the critical impact of multiculturalism on nation building in the inclusive interwar Poland. In the reestablished Polish state, the traditional understanding of the Polish nation, meaning the noble class, clashed with new ethnolinguistic conceptions. Multiculturalist approaches to the nation challenged the integralist nationalist view that acknowledged ethnic, linguistic, and cultural diversity in regional areas but still insisted on a common loyalty to a Polish nation-state. In her main example, Dabrowski shows the efforts made to present the Hutsuls, highlanders on Poland's southern borders, as a culturally distinct community. For political, cultural, and economic reasons, they were exhorted to maintain their nativeness when integrating into the modern state. Pamela Ballinger analyzes how people in Istria, a small peninsula that was divided in 1991 between Slovenia and Croatia, used claims for multiculturalism as a political instrument "against the state." Her chapter critically examines the recent policy, discourses, and practices of multiculturalism in Istria. Multiculturalism there has been presented in its recent political form against the nationalist Croatian state. However, the Istrian regionalist project has adopted many of the limitations of a state-sponsored system of ethnonational identity politics derived from the previous Habsburg and Yugoslav incarnations of political multiculturalism. In particular, the tradition of understanding identity as dominantly marked by linguistic difference remains present in the Istrian way of acting with cultural plurality and practicing ethnic diversity. Dabrowski and Ballinger consider multiculturalism as Pieter Judson does, more or less as a nationalist invention, albeit from different perspectives.

Migration in the twentieth century has continuously reinforced multicultural realities in the daily life of the Austrian Republic, even if the dominant political forces have often tried to ignore those circumstances. Michael John's chapter reminds us that Austria since 1918 has been in fact a "land of immigration," made up of people with different cultural backgrounds. In contrast to Istria, however, multiculturalism is not an issue of formal government policy in contemporary Austria, even though political forces have repeatedly debated the impact of cultural diversity. There has been a huge influx of immigrants, and although many have acquired citizenship, large numbers do not have the minority rights that the six constitutionally recognized, relatively small autochthonous ethnic minorities possess. To a great extent the people of the Austrian Republic appear to have forgotten the great waves of migration in the old empire, and that part of their history has ceased to be an integral part of their collective self-understanding.

The chapters in the final section of the book examine how people in the former Habsburg lands have expressed and negotiated identities in the complex multicultural settings in which they have lived. Oto Luthar, Andrei Corbea-Hoisie, and Moritz Csáky each reply to the questions raised by Pieter Judson in his own way: Luthar with a microhistorical approach, Corbea-Hoisie with a community study, and Csáky with a macrohistorical synthesis. All three focus on the practices of dealing with cultural heterogeneity, which do not necessarily efface differences but rather permit and retain them. Oto Luthar discusses the development of intercultural practices in the Slovenian region of Prekmurje, located in the multilingual triangle of Austria, Croatia, and Hungary. The author offers two revealing documents about everyday experience: a poor but educated soldier's diary, written in three languages, and a handwritten multilingual cookbook. Nationalist activists insisted on language use as essential in defining distinct national communities, but Luthar's documents demonstrate the contingent use of particular languages, depending on momentary circumstances, by individuals who, in fact, defined their loyalties in varying ways. Luthar argues that the polyglot mode of remembering and sharing particular kinds of expertise was a usual practice of everyday communication and intercultural cohabitation in a nationalizing society, even while it was becoming more and more ethnically divided. Corbea-Hoisie uses multiculturalism as an analytic category for describing its expression in Bukovina (today in northeastern Romania). Here the imported urban culture of German and Jewish settlers clashed with the practices of the autochthonous population. From the late nineteenth century neighborhoods changed at an accelerated rate and locals came into conflict with in-migrants, who gained and maintained supremacy. The gap between the metropolitan center and regional periphery grew continuously, dividing society along social, ethnic, and confessional lines. The new strange neighbors became targets of national protest, occasionally ending in violence. Ultimately, the Bukovinian model of multiculturalism stood for suppression, a life in conflict and hostile coexistence, missing any intercultural encounter—the never-accomplished ideal that Corbea-Hoisie illustrates with two fictional wet nurses, Gregor von Rezzori's Kassandra and Aharon Applefeld's Katerina. Moritz Csáky opposes and transcends the multicultural approach that perpetuates categories that nationalists have introduced in their elusive quest for a coherent national culture. He presents an analytic model to historicize the nationalists' projects of cultural homogenization by deconstructing the categories that continue to inform historiography and cultural memory. He reappraises cultural heterogeneity as the ordinary state of life, stimulating communication and offering modes of transcultural interaction. From this point of view, Habsburg Central Europe may be regarded as a "laboratory" in which processes emerged that have global relevance today.

The chapters presented in this book offer a nuanced analysis of the multifaceted cultural experience that took place in the Habsburg Monarchy and beyond. The authors respond to the question of how social spaces that are culturally coded in multiple ways can be described historically without lapsing into the categories once introduced to justify the separation of groups that were consigned to a nation, an ethnicity, or a singular culture. In the long run, the book might stimulate reflection upon what the uncritical adoption of politically exploited notions can tell us today about how we approach history, even if we only try to understand multiculturalism in a territory we now call "Habsburg Central Europe."

Notes

1. Slavoj Žižek, *Ein Plädoyer für die Intoleranz* (Vienna, 1998), 70–71.
2. Timothy Garton Ash, "Freedom and Diversity: A Liberal Pentagram for Living Together," *New York Review of Books* 59, no. 18 (22 November 2012): 33.
3. See, e.g., Gerald Stourzh, "Ethnic Attribution in Late Imperial Austria: Good Intentions, Evil Consequences (1994)," in *From Vienna to Chicago and Back: Essays on Intellectual History and Political Thought in Europe and America,* ed. Gerald Stourzh (Chicago, 2007), 157–76; Gerald Stourzh, *Die Gleichberechtigung der Nationalitäten in der Verfassung und Verwaltung Österreichs 1848–1918* (Vienna, 1985).
4. See Friedrich Naumann, *Mitteleuropa* (Berlin, 1915).
5. Friedrich Umlauft, *Die Oesterreichisch-Ungarische Monarchie: Geographisch-statistisches Handbuch mit besonderer Rücksicht auf die politische und Kultur-Geschichte für Leser aller Stände* (Vienna, 1876), 1–4.
6. Stuart Hall, "The Spectacle of the 'Other,'" in *Representation: Cultural Representations and Signifying Practices,* ed. Stuart Hall (London, 1997), 236: "The argument here is that culture depends on giving things meaning by assigning them to different positions within

a classificatory system. The marking of 'difference' is thus the basis of that symbolic order which we call culture."
7. See Katherine Verdery, *Transylvanian Villagers: Three Centuries of Political, Economic, and Ethnic Change* (Berkeley, CA, 1984); Rogers Brubaker, *Ethnicity without Groups* (Cambridge, MA, 2004); Rogers Brubaker et al., eds., *Nationalist Politics and Everyday Ethnicity in a Transylvanian Town* (Princeton, NJ, 2008).
8. Michael Herzfeld, *Anthropology: Theoretical Practice in Culture and Society* (Oxford, 2001), 28.
9. Ernst Mach, "Auszüge aus den Notizbüchern 1871–1910," in *Ernst Mach: Werk und Wirkung,* ed. Rudolf Haller and Friedrich Stadler (Vienna, 1998), 180.
10. On national indifference, see the conceptual discussion in Tara Zahra, "Imagined Non-Communities: National Indifference as a Category of Analysis," *Slavic Review* 69 (Spring 2010): 93–119; James Bjork, *Neither German nor Pole: Catholicism and National Indifference in a Central European Borderland* (Ann Arbor, MI, 2008); see also the local studies of the Habsburg Monarchy by Gary B. Cohen, *The Politics of Ethnic Survival,* 2nd ed., rev. (West Lafayette, IN, 2006), 18–40, 75–83; Pieter M. Judson, *Guardians of the Nation: Activists on the Language Frontiers of Imperial Austria* (Cambridge, MA, 2006), passim; Jeremy King, *Budweisers into Czechs and Germans: A Local History of Bohemian Politics, 1848–1948* (Princeton, NJ: Princeton University Press, 2002), passim. Gerald Stourzh offers critical reservations regarding "national indifference" in "The Ethnicizing of Politics and 'National Indifference' in Late Imperial Austria," in *Der Umfang der österreichischen Geschichte: Ausgewählte Studien 1990–2010* (Vienna, 2011), 283–323.
11. Peter Burke, "Language and Identity in Early Modern Italy," in *The Art of Conversation* (Cambridge, 1993), 66–67.
12. On "methodological nationalism" see Anthony D. Smith, *Nationalism in the Twentieth Century* (New York, 1979).
13. Ephraim J. Nimni, "Introduction for the English-Reading Audience," in *Otto Bauer: The Question of Nationalities and Social Democracy,* ed. Ephraim J. Nimni (Minneapolis, 2000), xvii.
14. Jürgen Habermas, *Die postnationale Konstellation: Politische Essays* (Frankfurt, 1998).
15. Jeremy King, "The Nationalization of East Central Europe: Ethnicism, Ethnicity, and Beyond," in *Staging the Past: The Politics of Commemoration in Habsburg Central Europe, 1848 to the Present,* ed. Nancy Wingfield and Maria Bucur (West Lafayette, IN, 2001), 112–52.

Section I

Identity Formation in Multicultural Societies

Chapter 1

HETEROGENEITIES AND HOMOGENEITIES
On Similarities and Diversities

Anil Bhatti

Introduction

It is useful to remember that we seem to have come a long way from the vision of tolerant, flexible societies characterized by interpretative openness with a distrust of dogmatic purity in matters concerning languages, religions, and social codes. The sympathetic attitude to possibilities of cultural metamorphoses and experimental transformations (Goethe's "The Metamorphosis of Plants," Kafka's "Metamorphosis") emerged as a vision of the Enlightenment, various socialist movements, and anticolonial and antifascist struggles, and was temporarily revived by the international student movements of the previous century. Little of this seems to remain today. Far from generating a creative polycentric society in which the recognition of difference becomes an integral part of the richness and plenitude of involved coexistence, today's liberal, multicultural state has been shown in fact to move almost in the opposite direction, nurturing rigid difference, freezing boundaries, and becoming a helpless witness to vicious outbreaks of sudden racial violence. The view that liberal multiculturalism has led to the creation of parallel societies in Europe and put a premium on retaining alterity/otherness/foreignness is now commonplace.

Instead of reducing cultural distance, the recognition of otherness simultaneously seeks to freeze it in its otherness. We are witnessing the weakening of the gains of secularism and democracy in our societies, which are increasingly undergoing a spurious classification of the population into homogenized groups along social, religious, and linguistic lines. Democracy today, as indeed other projects concerned with the transition from feudal, patriarchal, exploitative societies to more liberating forms of human organization and greater freedom, remains an unfinished project.

The context for my remarks is, of course, the crises in societies that are undergoing rapid transition as a result of migrations, economic liberalization, and the growing disaffection with the nation-state and its inability to solve the problems of unemployment and the consequent marginalization of large sections of the population as expendable.

We are in a period of transition without the settled formulae of earlier periods of our several histories. But we can at least hope that the centrality of the search for human emancipation and freedom is maintained. There is also disaffection with the idea of the nation, which in today's world is increasingly enmeshed in international interests of finance capital and has lost its anti-imperialist edge. Religious fundamentalism and ethnicism are symptoms of our crisis. In India, as a pluricultural, multireligious state, there is an exploitation of religion, and this threatens the secularism that was one of the most significant achievements of the anticolonial struggle. But this is coupled with the rhetoric of tolerance and diversity. If diversity is only legitimist then it does not threaten the present system of power and exploitation.[1] This can lead to the struggle for monopolizing representation and the legitimization to be *the* representative in liberal societies with multicultural social situations. Recognition is no longer important. The right to be considered *the* representative in a power game within society becomes a deeply antidemocratic feature of the multicultural society that solves problems by exporting them into the patriarchies of communities defined in terms of religion or so-called ethnicity.[2]

In any case, the uncritical move from respect to recognition in cultural matters only underscores the liberal dilemma of trying to solve a problem by identifying an appropriate negotiating partner who becomes the sole representative of a particular group. In the multicultural power game the struggle is not over the right to be recognized but rather over the right to be the exclusive representative. We have gone beyond tolerance and are dealing now with questions of power and contested spaces.

The perspective of the construction of a polycentric world also implies that we realize we do not necessarily have a conflict of cultures as bounded domains but tensions between different visions of societies and futures cutting across cultures. Questions of ethics are involved here. But we are sometimes blocked by the assumption that the hermeneutics of understanding and the dialogical path are imperative when it comes to dealing with such tensions and that the aim of dialogues is consensus. Perhaps one should consider the possibility of a kind of "nonconsensual ethics" that would enable us to register "multicultural differences and multiple narratives" without lapsing into a hard substantive relativism.[3] This also implies that we constantly have to negotiate the difficult terrain between the Universalists and those whom Goethe called the Singularists,[4] and situate ourselves in a field of consciously paradoxical, and perhaps ironic, praxes characterized by another of Goethe's maxims, where we act as pantheists in our scientific research, polytheists as poets, and ethically as monotheists.[5]

The point is that we emphasize the simultaneity of this manifold praxis. This allows us to propose a methodological preference for the conceptualization of pluriculturality as the condition characterized by shared, overlapping, and interconnected cultural fields and historical experiences in complex societies. It was part of the colonial ideology to demarcate cultures and create borders and boundaries. The countermovement is to see them as enmeshed. The use of the term "pluricultural" seeks to convey this.

We could suggest that the unprogrammed, self-organized emergence of a pluricultural, urban society could be seen as a process of interaction and exchange leading to ever-new variations of interlinked and connected cultures through which we become multilingual residents of polyglot cities in pluricultural states. To use an ironic phrase from Heimito von Doderer about fin de siècle Vienna, a kind of polyglot preparedness (*polyglotte Bereitwilligkeit*) also characterizes the language disposition or habitus of the pluricultural situation in the large urban centers in the postcolonial world.[6] Polyglot and pluricultural spaces could then be alternatives to our contemporary parallel societies or melting pots.

If the phase in which a comfortable and politically correct affirmation of segregationist multiculturalism was dominant is over, we are now forced to fall back on historical experience and present contingencies and remember that complex, pluricultural, multinational states are endangered states. In Europe, historical formations, characterized by pluricultural communication (as against merely multicultural coexistence), that could have been usefully compared to postcolonial India, such as the Habsburg Monarchy, lost out against the romantic idea associated with Herder of the bond between language, people (*Volk*), and nation becoming as congruent as possible in that social form of organization called a nation-state. The ideology of this kind of homogenization also meant that older traditions of communicative multilingualism and diversity in Europe (the medieval, Renaissance, and Baroque periods)[7] were devalued. They fell under the spurious categorization of modern/premodern. Recovering the memory of these traditions is a significant activity in contemporary scholarship and sociocultural praxis. What can be the significance of referring to such an archive? Quite simply, Europe's progress toward a multilingual, multireligious, pluricultural formation, and its memories of past pluricultural spaces in Central Europe (Habsburg Monarchy, Yugoslavia), can become part of a comparative field of study with other non-European societies like India or Africa where experiences of diversities abound, with all their contradictions. The explicit assumption is that neither are prescriptive models for the other because the corresponding historical trajectories were, of course, very different. Asymmetries abound. But at the same time we should remember that these different regions were strongly interconnected and that there is a shared though certainly not necessarily harmonious history of Europe and the former colonized world.[8] This involves references to some key problems concerning questions of heterogeneity and homogeneity, and more urgently the play between similarity and difference, as these emerge in the discursive field of contemporary discussions.

How, in fact, can and should large pluricultural states work? This is India's continuing problem and will be Europe's question. The important point is not how Austria, Germany, or France, for instance, become pluricultural, but rather how the incorporation of traditional national states into the larger entity of Europe manages to deal with diversity that is articulated in divisive cultural terms. Or, in other words, how will the culturalization of difference as a divisive move affect the establishment and maintenance of pluricultural conditions that should supposedly lead to greater freedoms? In the following remarks I would like to sketch some aspects of these considerations in the form of short vignettes.

Contemporary Social and Cultural Transformations

We could look upon contemporary international developments as fields of social and cultural transformations, which are characterized by two moments. On the one hand, relatively homogeneous societies are developing into more complex societal formations. On the other hand, existing complex, heterogeneous societies are being subjected to tensions that continually threaten their heterogeneity. This rephrases what Goethe once referred to in the context of his idea of metamorphosis as the tension between a "vis centrifuga" and a "vis centripeta," both of which are forces that work simultaneously in nature.[9]

The process of European integration may be looked upon as an example of the first type of transformation process creating greater heterogeneity. Units that were organized as nation-states are slowly being incorporated into larger transnational units.[10] Large-scale migrations and globalizing processes are leading to long-term societal transformations. In spite of great internal diversity within the nations of Europe, it would still be reasonably correct to say that the formation of Europe envisions a process of coming closer to the kind of diversity that characterizes India or most African and South Asian states; namely, heterogeneous formations with multiplicities of webs of languages and cultural and religious practices with varying degrees of intensity spread across a large territory.

On the other hand, in a counterprocess, traditionally pluricultural countries like India, which seemed to have muddled through (*fortwursteln* in the Habsburg Monarchy) to an uneasy functional balance, are now increasingly being subjected to fundamentalist pressures that would logically lead to more and more rigid forms of homogeneous organization of sociocultural and political units, which may of course coexist in a form of liberal apartheid. Here we could remember the collapse of the Habsburg Monarchy. The end of Yugoslavia would be a more drastic contemporary reminder of this type of process.

Religions, language, and "ethnicity" (a colonial term) are the usual and most obvious fields of analysis here. One could ask in general: What are the tensions surrounding the inscription of social structures, family, law, religion, and language in order to maintain complex structures or to destroy them? How do fields of identification like region, social milieu, religion, or language get mobilized in transformation processes? Discussing culture and diversity implies a discussion about the renegotiations of the coordinates of possible life-worlds. Questions of power, freedom, and autonomy are involved. The tension between old and new, between continuity and rupture, lead to various kinds of anxieties, and these are not the same and do not have the same reasons everywhere. When do temples, synagogues, churches, or mosques lose their place in our landscapes and cityscapes? Or, to put it differently, when do changing power equations lead to demands for their construction? The historicity of landscapes and their changing physiognomies through architectural developments require renewed concretization.[11]

Our topic is complicated by historical and spatial factors. The European experience is uneven. There is a difference between the debate in countries with a long colonial heritage, like France and Great Britain, and those with a briefer, active colonial past, like Germany. Yet again, there is a difference between Germany and Austria, if Austria chooses to reflect on the experience of its pluricultural Austro-Hungarian past. For instance, the distinguished jurist Hans Kelsen thought that it was unreal to base the theory of the state on any sociobiological or sociopsychological contexts, given the composition of the Austria state with its many racial, linguistic, and religious groups. To that extent his pure theory of law, he thought, was a specifically Austrian theory.[12] And it is not without significance that one of the few reflections on the nationality question under conditions of diversity emerged out of this experience in the writings of Otto Bauer and other Austro-Marxists and their disputes with Lenin.

Then again, there are significant differences in the accumulated historical experience of dealing with migration, racism, and assimilation and the rhetoric and reality of inclusion/exclusion, authenticity, and so on within the European ambit. England and Germany draw upon different resources when it comes to dealing with the postcolonial order. This may well go back to different ways in which the heritage of the Roman Empire manifested itself in Europe in the nineteenth century. Herder looked upon the Reformation as the marker of the great division among the peoples of Europe. Madame de Staël observed that the Germanic peoples were educated and formed by Christianity, whereas the Latin peoples of Europe inherited their training in trade and commerce from the Roman experience.[13] This could be further extrapolated to the dividing lines created by the Reformation between an older dichotomy between Roman and Germanic orders.

This by no means ignores the real divisions in mutual perceptions and cleavages concerning the European experience so clearly articulated by the Hungarian writer Peter Nadas, who drew from the recent experience of Yugoslavia to comment on Europe. His comments should be seen in the context of other Hungarian and East European articulations.[14] Calling, ironically, for the creation of the "first Great European Encyclopedia," a "three dimensional mental map of Europe," Nadas revived memories of more recent empires:

> the war launched against Yugoslavia, the democratic states of Europe reached a horrible, unvarnished moment of self-recognition. After a ten-year delay, they had to acknowledge that, on account of their own traditions, constraints, needs, and pressures, they were unable to avoid the utopia of full European integration (with the painful consequences that would entail) but unable to attain it either. Societies of very different mentality have found themselves, since that time, directly confronted with one another—and with their own selves.
>
> At the sight of one another's acts, they are at a loss to understand. Nor do they understand even what they fail to understand about themselves and so are, a priori, incapable of genuine integration.

Continuing, Nadas noted how an experience of exercising colonial power manifests itself as the criteria for internal European difference:

> There is a strong mental dividing line between monarchies and republics. There is an even more significant line of fracture between colonial powers and those European nationalities and states that never had colonies, or none of importance, or else themselves chafed along under colonial repression. Within the former group, there is a momentous difference between those that relinquished their colonies, or allowed them to be lost with little resistance, and those that fought with brutal means to hang on to them. Today the former colonial powers form the trunk of the European Community. It could hardly be otherwise, as the administration of Europe is graspable only for those with the experience of empire. These days, the colonial basis of the European Community is not determined primarily by the weight of artistic and material values that derive from several centuries of trading in human beings, enslaving human beings, and plundering the world (though naturally, there is all of that, too), but by the vast knowledge that derives from the experience of several centuries of governing foreign worlds. That knowledge has given to those societies a disciplined internal structure, an exceptional self-discipline that, in all likelihood, is possessed by none but the Spanish, the French, the Dutch, and the British.

Nadas may well have articulated a Central European perspective, and his concluding concern was with the uses of this privileged knowledge and experience and how it is linked to the failure in Yugoslavia: "From the perspective of the European Community as a whole, it is not a trivial question whether such knowledge is of a reflective and humane kind. In the Bosnian war, it seemed unreflective, crude, and bestial."[15]

Nation Formation in Europe and Herder's Views

The accuracy of Nadas's diagnosis need not concern us here. The significance of the Hungarian writer's observation lies in the reminder we get about the internal differences in the European tradition. The process of nation formation in Europe was a contradictory process in which heterogeneity and internal consolidation often coexisted in a state of tension. As a result of a questionable and abbreviated extrapolation of the European process of nation formation in the eighteenth and nineteenth centuries, fundamentalist thought today favors organizations that are as homogeneous as possible with regard to language, ethnicity, and religion. This in itself is not the explosive point. What is important is the assumption that this is the "natural" form of organization of nation-states. The concept of minorities results from this, and thereafter the negotiation of minority rights (civil rights, religious rights) is established.

Significantly, it was Johann Gottfried Herder—the misuse of his concept of *Volk* has done so much damage—who presupposed a mixing of races as a precondition for the process of nation formation in Europe. In his great work, "Ideas on the Philosophy of the History of Humanity" (1784), he indeed pointed out that drastic migrations and intermingling of peoples characterized the prehistory of Europe, and without this process of amalgamation the "General Spirit of Europe" (*Allgemeingeist Europas*) could hardly have been awakened. Writing in 1784, he emphasized the unique historical significance of such a mixing of peoples taking place then in Europe. Migrations had led to changes in manners and mores, moderating and changing old racial characteristics.[16]

The whole point, however, of Herder's remarkable insight was to then go on to affirm that the historical retention of this diversity would be unnatural and therefore wrong. Assimilation and amalgamation are indeed the necessary and natural part of the prehistory of a historical process leading to increasing orders of complexity. But this is precisely why organizational solutions have to be found to deal with this process as one enters the modern age. In Herder's thought, the most natural social order would be one that corresponds to a plan of nature. Since nature produces families in order to ensure the survival of the species, the most natural order was that of an organic family. Since the modern nation was to mirror this order, the most natural state would be an organic state in which one *Volk* with one national character would exist and develop independently. It is this perspective that also leads to Herder's anticolonialism and his espousal of cultural tolerance. Because colonialism led to an unnatural expansion of states and an unnatural and "wild" intermingling of the human species and nations under one scepter, colonialism in Herder's eyes was, in the modern era, against the plan of nature. If there is such a thing as an enlightened and liberal philosophy of segregation, Herder's thought would lead to it. In fact, as already suggested, multiculturalism essentially goes back to this principle of liberal segregation. I need not point out here how fraught with problems such a perspective is and how vulnerable it is to a distortion through notions of racial hegemony and ghettoization, and how fragile the dividing line would be between liberal segregation and racist apartheid.

Herder's remarkable historical achievement is indeed to affirm the variety and diversity in creation and also to celebrate it. But at the same time he tends to freeze this diversity into multiple parallel worlds with an internal logic of organic growth. Respect and noninterference characterize his attitude, which therefore also means surrendering these diverse formations to their own internal structures of power and domination. Although on the face of it this is an attractive gesture of equality among cultures, it is also deeply ahistorical, since it ignores the factual structures of international domination. Herder's moral point of view is sympathetic, but it also leads to a noble form of distancing that legitimizes itself as democratic noninterference. Herder's reflections on alien people in Europe and on European colonialism are in many ways prophetically topical for contemporary discussions.[17] There are ambivalences in his recovery of those whom he calls the dormant peoples (*schlafende Völker*)[18] from Eastern Europe, including the advocacy of their internal right to cultural self-determination. This stands in sharp contrast to the modern movement toward greater interconnectedness and permeability with lines of critique and solidarity across cultures. This point was already clear to Friedrich Schlegel, who criticized Herder for accepting a cultural status quo and implicitly denying the possibility of comparing different times and peoples.[19]

Only later did Wilhelm von Humboldt and Goethe establish the dialectical link between a common human spirit, difference, and similarity. The impoverishment through homogenization becomes acutely apparent when one contrasts it with the impulses leading to the development of a humanist perspective that emerged out of the self-contradictions of European expansion and colonialism.

Goethe, for instance, stressed that all must be equal in society and that society cannot but be founded on the concept of equality and not of freedom.[20] Goethe writes that equality is something the individual wants to find in society. The *sittlich,* moral freedom, to subordinate myself (if I may/wish) is something I bring with me. Therefore, the society I enter must offer me equality. Society can only add that it hopes that I may be free. I should therefore willingly and out of an exercise of reasonable will (*vernünftiger Wille*) renounce my privileges. But this does not amount to the erasure of difference. Rather, it indicates a move toward a new order that is nondichotomous. It is a process, transforming all who are involved, and this is different from a hegemonic concept of culture

(*Leitkultur*), which divides society into a majority with many minorities who are tolerated, but not as equal partners. Their rights are a condescending, generous concession. The notion of a *Leitkultur* to which all are assimilated is different from the Goethean process of cultural transformation, which involves all members of the society.

It has been pointed out that Herder's thought, which emphasized the presence of discrete but equal units, could not have led to a supranational perspective of a dynamic process like *Weltliteratur*.[21] The importance of Goethe's insight here lies in the emphasis he placed on the growing rapidity of communication and commercial activity that would make the process of *Weltliteratur* "inevitable," a perspective that Marx and Engels highlighted later. Even if Goethe—thinking quite dialectically—otherwise saw the negative and "velociferous" principle at work in history, which brings velocity, and Lucifer on one plane as a metaphor for capitalism, he does accept the principle of the "progress of the human race." Goethe's thought developed a global perspective in the nineteenth century by foreseeing wide-ranging prospects of growing international human relationships. He looked at this development very favorably, and in a well-known conversation with Eckermann welcomed the growing contact between the French, English, and Germans, through which a mutual process of self-correction could commence. Goethe saw that the advantage of an emerging future world literature lay in this emancipatory effect.[22]

Thinking about Nation Formation in Central Europe and India

The difficulties in Central Europe with coming to terms with diversity and the existence of large states; the revolutionary struggle in Russia and the breakup of the Austro-Hungarian Monarchy; the establishment of small nation-states in Europe and the anticolonial struggle—all these give us the themes that still preoccupy us.[23] The problem has been articulated from different, politically divergent points of view. For instance, Hugo von Hofmannsthal evoked the idea of fluid borders from a conservative point of view to emphasize the specificity of supranational Austria at a time when the idea of the nation had gripped Central Europe, threatening to eclipse heterogeneity. Despite deep political and artistic differences between their respective positions, Hofmannsthal's opinions, James Joyce's reflections on Ireland during his sojourn in Trieste, Robert Musil's critical remarks on nationalism, and Rabindranath Tagore's speeches on the problem of colonialism and nationalism have nevertheless an intellectual affinity without any direct influences, and they form an intellectual constellation.[24]

In the context of the anticolonial freedom struggle in India, Tagore was aware of some of the problems relevant for discussions on diversity. Recognizing structural parallels between India and Europe, he wrote in 1919 that India's problem was "the problem of the world in miniature. India is too vast in its area and too diverse in its races. It is many countries packed in one geographical receptacle. It is just the opposite of what Europe truly is: namely, one country made into many."[25] There is a curiously Herderian ring in the reference to Europe, but Tagore was mainly concerned with India's two interconnected problems. One was the freedom from external bondage (colonialism) and the other was the internal impermeability of caste and class barriers, which prevented the formation of a liberating heterogeneity in India. With idealistic fervor, he writes:

> An almost impossible task has been set to India by her Providence, a task given to no other great countries in the world. Among her children and her guests differences in race and language, religion and social ideals are as numerous as great, and she has to achieve the difficult unity which has to be true in spite of the separateness that is real. The best and greatest of her sons have called us in immortal words to realize the unity of souls in all human beings and thus fulfill the highest mission of our history; but we have merely played with their words, and we have rigidly kept apart man from man, and class from class, setting up permanent barriers of indignity between them. We remained unconscious of the suicidal consequence of such divisions, so long as we lay stationary in the torpor of centuries, but when the alien world suddenly broke upon our sleep and dragged us on in its impetus of movement, our disjointed heterogeneity set up in its lumbering unwieldiness an internal clash and crush and unrhythmic stagger which is both ludicrous and tragic at the same moment.[26]

Tagore undoubtedly casts the problem in an idealistic, heroic mode, deriving from the "ludicrous and tragic" stage presence of India the exceptional task, which then also becomes a responsibility of a transformation with universal implications. But if we resist being distracted by his idealistic vocabulary we can interpret his remarks as suggesting that preindependence India could be looked upon as a "result" (*Resultat,* in the philosophical sense) of two simultaneous processes: the political struggle against colonialism and the social struggle for emancipation from a largely feudal order. Indeed, the unity of freedom from external domination (anticolonialism) and the liberation from inner repression (historical reforms within India) were at the core of Tagore's admittedly idealistic vision of a new formation of India in a universal context. This is linked to his perhaps overly optimistic view that scientific progress was leading to a greater unity of the world and, therefore, that national history was becoming universal history. Tagore repeatedly emphasized that race, language, religion, and the caste system were the divisive factors of India's "disjointed heterogeneity." Liberation from external bondage and inner pacification lay in overcoming social oppression while retaining heterogeneity. The caste system, with its immovable walls, provided the negative advantage of peace and order but not the positive possibilities of free movement and expansion.[27] India's impossible task was to achieve a substantial, true unity in spite of the real division of its population.[28]

For Tagore, freedom and liberation meant the search for principles in which the "spirit of India" could be realized.[29] These principles could not be found in "commercialism" and nationalism but in universalism. The goal is not only "self-determination, but self-conquest and self-dedication."[30] This was also the basis of his rejection of nationalism as "the collective Egotism of the whole nations."[31] In a formulation reminiscent of Grillparzer's well-known epigram in which we progress from humanity through nationality to bestiality, Tagore thought that the "demonic spirit of nationalism" generated a "harvest of suspicion, hatred and inhospitable exclusiveness."[32] Tagore's cosmopolitan, antinational attitude is characteristic of a kind of romantic anticapitalism. In many ways it reminds us of similar traditions of discussion around cosmopolitanism, world citizenship *(Weltbürgertum)*, and the nation-state, which formed an integral part of German and Central European thought in the nineteenth century.[33]

In 1923 Tagore remarked that the end of the war had led neither to a reduction of borders in Europe nor to an end of nationalisms. Instead of coming together, there was a greater fragmentation of the people of Europe. Referring to the widespread metaphor of Austro-Hungary as a peoples' dungeon *(Völkerkerker)*, he noted that the small nations had broken their bonds and were happy with their separate existence. Suppressed difference is explosive, he wrote. But his remarks also showed that he was increasingly wary of homogenizing ethnic solutions to problems of national self-determination, which had emerged through the American President Wilson's plan for reorganizing the map of Europe. Tagore's initial enthusiasm for Wilson's plan gave way to disillusionment when it became clear that President Wilson's advocacy of self-determination did not extend to the colonized world. The precondition for a harmonious unity was the recognition of the differences of the constituting parts. This is why Tagore's plea against nationalism was coupled with a plea for the recognition of internal difference.[34] This is also linked to the insight into the historical process leading to the greater interconnectedness of the world. Tagore thought that if India's problem of internal difference—which was frozen through caste stratification—could be overcome, it would become a model for the international problem of diversity. We are far from that, of course.

However idealistic Tagore's position may have been,[35] he was posing problems similar to those that had been discussed from a different vantage point by socialists and Marxists at the end of the nineteenth century in the "multinational empires of Europe" regarding the relation between the large state and its culturally heterogeneous elements and the question of defending class interests while recognizing national cultural specificities.[36]

As already mentioned, Otto Bauer and Karl Renner wrote with great perspicacity on the question of retaining and nurturing cultural diversity within the parameters of a multinational state. In a sense, the Austro-Marxists were countering the Herderian drive toward the small, homogenized nation-state. But Bauer's position also had the drawback of essentializing culture and underestimating the importance of establishing lines of solidarity, which cut through cultural units. This position also devalues transcultural connections and does not pay sufficient attention to the multiple affiliations citizens have in complex societies. In effect, it privileges culture as a guarantor of belonging, giving it a central place through uncritical affirmation instead of problematizing its role in society.

As Lenin wrote at that time, shortly before World War I, "advocacy of 'cultural-national autonomy' . . . divides the nations." We then have segregated homogenized units, which in fact undermine the lines of communication and solidarity that exist across cultural boundaries, and the "millions and thousands of millions of economic, legal, and social bonds." By dividing nations along lines of cultural homogeneity, and particularly in matters concerning education, we ignore the material factor of economic communication. This predictably reinforces the inequality among the supposed nationalities in a multinational state by freezing them in an ascribed identity.[37]

In today's contexts, cultural autonomy is increasingly a demand for religious segregation, and from my point of view it seems that the demand for cultural autonomy raised by Bauer would indeed lead to parallel societies. But the relevance of the Austro-Marxist position does not lie in the answers, but in the fact that they posed a question that is becoming increasingly relevant. Were the comparatively small size and the unevenness of the socioeconomic structures of Austro-Hungary limiting factors? Anticolonial movements emphasized the need for large states, not least as a means of building up viable units of resistance against imperialism. In spite of internal differences, therefore, such movements were inclusivist and emphasized the lines of solidarity within the anti-imperialist movement. Conservative factions, however, preferred homogenized nations in which essentialized foundational myths were instrumentalized. Samir Amin has reminded us of essentialist Arab notions of Arabness (*al uruba*) analogous to Britishness, Englishness, or Germanness. Since this was not possible on the basis of ethnicity alone, Islam was seen as being an integral part of Arabness, and thus the bridge to Islamic fundamentalism could be built. *Négritude* in Africa (and in the Caribbean) and, more recently, *Hindutva* in India are other examples.[38]

Polyglossia and Heterogeneity

Language is a field where questions of heterogeneity and homogeneity are often articulated particularly clearly. The myth of the Tower of Babel, it has been often suggested, works as a foundational text of European culture and its language ideology. One can read this myth as an expression of the monosemic opposition to polysemy and as a narrative against the heterogeneity of languages. In this myth the unity of language was good, paradisiacal, "normal." Multiplicity of language was bad, abnormal; it was punishment and loss of the original paradisiacal unity and the true original words.[39] All attempts to view linguistic diversity as positive were doomed to failure from this point of view. With the rise of the nation-state, monoglossia remained privileged in the European imagination as the ideal, and this was reflected in colonial ideology, which looked upon the bewildering variety of languages in other parts of the world as a form of chaos requiring taming through the drive toward classification.

It is against the background of this ideology of a natural and organic order that we can understand the nineteenth-century colonial drive toward classification and schematization constructed out of chaos leading to the achievement of something like a *colonial competence* with which the material world, now so suddenly at the disposal of the colonial powers, could be controlled and administered.

The colonial model, based on domination, control, and exploitation, views complexity as a chaos that does not submit easily to regulation. India's linguistic complexity, for instance, was domesticated under colonialism by an extraordinary development of classificatory and taxonomic energy. In learning to speak as a colonial power and developing a colonial competence, the systematic codification of modern Indian languages and dialects was necessary. Since language and translation are important instruments of power, a certain type of language ideology developed that ignored real, overlapping forms of communication in favor of abstract linguistic classification. The colonial system destroyed pluralities of social communication and replaced them with linguistic classification. Grierson's *Linguistic Survey of India* is a monument to this classificatory energy, which also signaled the triumph of a specific colonial epistemology. Languages as classified systems became autonomous and, therefore, negotiable among classes and communities of people who claimed to represent them. It then became part of the self-interest of the representatives of the new classified order and its beneficiaries to sustain the autocratically imposed system of classification and impart to it the status of being real and natural. This holds good for the classification of the caste system, too.[40]

In the Indian subcontinent, as well as in Europe, the creation of homogenized nations after the two World Wars has decisively shaped history, turning our age into one of migration and demarcations through borders. And, indeed, the rejection of hard borders and boundaries may well be the signature of pluricultural positions.[41]

Sensitivity toward polyglossia in Europe emerged from multilingual states, and it is in this context that Joseph Hammer-Purgstall's remarkable speech on polyglossia or multilingualism deserves to be read.[42] Significantly, this speech was delivered in 1852, on the eve of the festival of Pentecost —the actual festival of polyglossia ("des eigentlichen Festes der *Polyglottie* oder Vielsprachigkeit"), as Hammer-Purgstall calls it, thus placing it as the countermyth to the Tower of Babel. The Orientalist Hammer-Purgstall, whose translations of Oriental texts played an important role in the rise of German and Austrian Oriental studies (Goethe's Oriental studies and the *West-östlicher Divan* profited from his work) was also the first president of the Austrian Academy of Sciences and spoke on the occasion with suitable authority. The speech begins with a brief overview of multilingualism, or more accurately polylingualism, in the post-Napoleonic era. In a very Goethean formulation, Hammer-Purgstall links this polylingualism (*Vielsprachigkeit*) with the development of traffic and commerce among peoples in war and peace and through the mutual influence of their literatures. The justifiable, jealous desire to protect and develop the mother tongue does not, in Hammer-Purgstall's view, contradict the spread of multilingualism. On the contrary, it furthers plurilingual situations and acts against the domination of one single world language.[43]

In the context of European concerns, Hammer-Purgstall clearly favors linguistic diversity over the hierarchization of languages. The rule of one world language can only be a transitory moment in the plurilingual vision. In fact, a world language can only be seen as a transitory phase (*Übergangsperiode*) in world history, which evolves through increasing interconnectedness and greater intimate commerce among peoples and exchange of goods and ideas stimulated by industrial development.

Hammer-Purgstall's speech is an early and rare example where the polyglossia of the East (*Morgenland*) is looked upon favorably. It does not proceed from the privileged position of monolingualism and is, of course, addressed to the educated (*gebildet*) people of Europe, to those who were, as he says, in a position to understand at least three languages without necessarily being fluent in all. It is noteworthy that Hammer-Purgstall emphasizes that plurilingualism is not the same as fluency. This is indeed seen by him as a European goal. This is also the backdrop for his variation of the idea of a multilingual commitment to Austria. One progresses toward becoming what he calls a complete Austrian by progressively understanding more languages of the monarchy.[44]

It is important that Hammer-Purgstall emphasizes the function of understanding languages without necessarily being able to speak them. In a plurilingual situation, the participants would be able to understand the languages used in public and speak in those they feel they can use. A plurilingual community is characterized by a fair chance that everybody understands to some extent what everybody else says.

Much of this is relevant today. The contemporary intermingling of peoples and the exchange of commodities and ideas speak against the ideology of a reductive bilingualism. This is emerging in Europe today, through which the richness of the polyglot linguistic landscape of Europe is reduced to the knowledge of a "first language" (or "mother tongue") and English alone. Instead of looking upon the liberating potential of opening up multiple lifeworlds through many languages, the technocratic drive enthrones a bilateral simplification on an otherwise multilateral situation. Or, it creates the condition for the dominance of a power-based monolingualism based on new class divisions, privileges, and forms of inclusion and exclusion.

Although Hammer-Purgstall was sensitive to the polyphonic texture of polyglossia, he also wrote against what he called linguistic mixing (*Sprachmengerei*) and for retaining the purity of the individual voice in a harmonious configuration.[45] Today we would look upon purity and overlapping in language differently, as will be discussed below. Hammer-Purgstall's remarks may, however, be read as an expression of the realization that plurilingualism is more than polyglot competence. It requires a different *attitude* to language. Language competence, purity of usage, and social communication is delinked from the substantive and expressive notion of language. The Heideggerian sense of being in the language, of language as a House or Abode of Being (*Haus des Seins*), is demystified. There is *less* of the pathos-driven drive to situate language, communication, and creativity in the substantive mystique of a mother tongue in the pluricultural situation. Implicitly, at least, this also deconstructs the nineteenth-century dominant discourse of an organic connection between monolingualism and authenticity.

Hammer-Purgstall's reservations against *Sprachmengerei*, or language mixing, may also be related to the fact that large urban centers and large-scale industrial migration were only gradually becoming significant in the Austro-Hungarian Monarchy of those times.[46] However, migration was already an essential part of the linguistic landscape of Vienna in the later nineteenth century, during Hugo von Hofmannsthal's times. Hofmannsthal found a felicitous expression for Austrian colloquial speech in Vienna as being the most mixed (*gemengteste*) among "all German languages," the language of the culturally richest and most mixed of all worlds.[47]

It is noteworthy that Hofmannsthal looked upon this mixed colloquial language so favorably. Many Indian thinkers also articulated their opposition to an attitude of purism in language matters during this period. Jawaharlal Nehru was against homogenization in the sensitive issue of language: "Purists object to the use of foreign words, but I think they make a great mistake, for the way to enrich our language is to make it flexible and capable of assimilating words and ideas from other languages."[48] In Nehru's case, this was also a result of his awareness of the situation of the colonial, which he formulated in terms anticipating contemporary postcolonial culture theory:

> I have become a queer mixture of the East and West, out of place everywhere, at home nowhere. . . . They are both part of me, and though they help me in both the

East and the West, they also create in me a feeling of spiritual loneliness not only in public activities but in life itself. I am a stranger and alien in the West. I cannot be of it. But in my own country also, sometimes, I have an exile's feeling.[49]

Already in 1918 Tagore had recognized that Hindi was best suited for the communicative functions of a national language for an independent India. Writing to Gandhi he said: "Of course Hindi is the only possible national language for inter-provincial intercourse in India." But more importantly, he was against a "communal bias" in Hindi, which "must truly represent the double current of Sanskrit and Persian literatures that have been working side by side for the last many centuries and must *boldly enfranchise* all the words that have been naturalized by long use."[50]

However, the actual practice of language development in the Indian subcontinent in the twentieth century did precisely the opposite. It tore apart the common fabric of the secular, ecumenical, communicative medium Hindi/Urdu along religious lines of Hindu/Muslim, which contributed to the ideology of partition. This was one of the reasons behind Nehru's criticism of the misuse of the term "culture" and the supposed incommensurability or antagonism between Muslim "culture" and Hindu "culture." Writing during the Indian freedom struggle, Nehru pointed out: "The inevitable deduction from this is (although it is not put baldly) that the British must remain in India for ever and ever to hold the scales and mediate between the two 'cultures.'" He also thought that the inflationary use of the culture argument was outdated. "The day of even national cultures is rapidly passing and the world is becoming one cultural unit."[51]

Today, India's linguistic diversity and complexity remains as part of a general fuzzy cultural, social, and religious practice (as distinct from precepts) resisting the homogenization of classificatory order. The information collected by the anthropological survey of India, according to which more than 65 percent of India's so-called communities are bilingual and many are multilingual, comes as no surprise. This is normal, but fundamentalists polemicize against this, and instead of looking upon multilingualism as a sign of cultural enrichment they see in it the loss of authenticity or a loss of substance (*Substanzverlust*).

In this connection, a brief characterization of the type of functioning performative multilingualism in India, with the simultaneous presence of many languages in the immediate lifeworld, may be useful. It is difficult to define, and a behaviorist model of "code switching" would hardly help in comprehending it. There is no mechanical switch that is turned on and off in plurilingual situations. There are more helpful metaphors. Many languages coexist and merge, float, and glide into each other. Writing with reference to an Austro-Hungarian background, Moritz Csáky captures the way multilingual lifeworlds constitute themselves. He writes about how he had learned from childhood to move between many languages. Parents, relations, and playmates created many overlapping circles of communicative behavior that cannot be simply categorized in terms of ethnicity or different sociocultural classes. They were an early example of how natural this has become in an epoch of migration, interconnectedness, mobility, and globalized communication.[52]

These are lines that could also easily refer to India. Languages in plurilingual situations become part of a repertoire that one can draw upon depending on the situation. And, as in all repertoires, the relative competence in each component can vary, and again, depending on the requirement and circumstances, it can be refined and improved upon. There can also be an element of play in this. It seems to me that we are dealing in cases like India with a question of linguistic disposition (or habitus, a term I am skeptical about since it is linked to an institution), as if a multilingual competence creates a metalinguistic level of reference that makes communication sufficiently possible, or, as the case may be, allows for an oblique, polyvalent communication. Perhaps one could use a musical metaphor to comprehend multilingualism. The ability to deal with musical material allows a musician to play freely. The musician can improvise, create variations, change styles and tonalities. Multilingualism is something similar. It allows one to function with a language repertoire in an environment where the purity of essentialized language is not privileged. All attempts to sabotage multilingual situations (movements for linguistic purification) wish to establish homogenized languages that can negotiate between one's "own" language and "foreign" languages. The relationship between languages in a multilingual repertoire is not the relationship between a mother tongue and foreign languages. German or French can be foreign languages in India, but in a polyglot city like Delhi the relationship between the Indian languages Hindi, Urdu, Punjabi, English, Bengali, etc., is not that between foreign languages. This is a historical consequence in India and is related to the shared history of colonialism. In Europe, the Habsburg model, the only historical model that could have been compared to India, lost out against the romantic model influenced by the (probably partially biased) reception of Herder, which preferred the unity of language, *Volk,* and nation.

Against this background, Jacques Derrida's contemporary paradoxes on monolingualism ("Yes, I have only one language but it is not mine"; "We always speak only one language. We never speak only one language") are enlightening. If I take a position where I am ready to state that my language does not belong to me in the sense that it is not my property (*Eigentum*), then I indicate an interest in crossing borders. In Derrida's words,

> For these phenomena that interest me are precisely those that blur these boundaries, cross them, and make their historical artifice appear, also their violence, meaning the relations of force that are concentrated there and actually capitalize themselves there interminably. Those who are sensitive to all stakes of "creolization," for example, assess this better than others.[53]

We could understand this in Wilhelm von Humboldt's perspective. The expansion of the simultaneous usage of different languages (*der gleichzeitige Gebrauch verschiedener Sprachen*) enriches the languages themselves and is beneficial for thought and fluency.[54] The gesture is against the tyranny of monolingualism established under homogenization.

Homogenization versus Pluriculturalism

The Goethean perspective of *Weltliteratur* was renewed during the anticolonial struggle in India by Tagore, who coined the corresponding Indian term *vishwasahitya*. This was a perspective for a larger emancipative project with a strong universalist claim. The particularities of India, Europe, and the world emphasized the need for such a perspective. Opposition to this emerged from fundamentalist positions.

Fundamentalism in India inherited the ideological drive toward demarcation and creating boundaries and borders from colonialism and channeled it toward religious homogeneity. Fundamentalism seeks to replace the pluralist praxis of religions in India and the syncretic traditions in Hinduism, which has many diverse forms, by creating a monolithic bloc with a textual base ("syndicated Hinduism" is Romila Thapar's well-known phrase for it) that then marginalizes or patronizes other religions in India, like Islam or Christianity, by stamping them as foreign and therefore implying that they are unauthentic.[55] In the invidious logic of this "therefore" lies the threat to a secular India, which means a threat to its pluralistic form of inclusive diversity, anchored in its constitution.[56] In a sense what we are increasingly being threatened with is historically evolved "natural" (*naturwüchsig*) diversity being replaced by the ideologically posited naturalness of monochromatic forms. The logic of homogenization was perhaps propounded most succinctly by the German legal thinker Carl Schmitt, whose study of constitutional law (*Verfassungslehre*) in 1928 treats homogeneity of the *Volk* (not of humanity) as the basis for the relationship between ruler and ruled.[57] The ground for homogenization may vary, and race, color, and religion are the usual candidates, but homogenization establishes substantive equality as the basic precondition of Schmitt's conception of democracy, which was influential in formulating the ideology of the fascist German state. It also forms the basis for the distinction between clearly marked and defined systems of "friend" and "enemy" in Schmitt's political philosophy. Fundamentalisms today have inherited this dubious legacy of inclusion and exclusion. Current affirmations of Britishness, *Leitkultur* (a thinly veiled euphemism for *Deutschtum,* or Germanness), and *Hindutva* (Hinduness) are variations of the same theme.

Hindu nationalism, as it was codified by Vinayak D. Savarkar around 1923, coalesced racial, geographical, and cultural meanings of Hindu, *Hindutva*

(Hinduness), and *Hindudom* (analogue of Christendom)[58] in order to follow a strategy of inclusion and exclusion. Everybody is a Hindu who accepts the geographic entity of India ("from the Indus to the seas") as his/her motherland and the fount of his/her own religion. This automatically excludes Christians and Muslims, whose religions originated outside of India.[59]

In our context it is interesting to note that Savarkar rejected pluricultural concepts of the state by referring to the Habsburg Monarchy. The end of that empire was to him a stern warning against all attempts to unite heterogeneous peoples into "such hotch-potch nations." Without cultural, racial, or historical "affinities," the common will to be a nation was lacking.[60] His ideal was homogeneous national units like England, France, Germany, Italy, or Portugal, where, he thought, "organic affinities" existed.[61] Homogeneity for Savarkar became a marker for exclusion and contrast. For him, Hindus were homogeneous in spite of internal differentiation. In contrast, "non-Hindu people," in his terminology, were "on the whole more inclined to identify themselves and their interests with Muslims outside India than Hindus [*sic*] who lived next door, like Jews in Germany."[62] This is a most revealing example, written at a time when the Jews were being excluded from being a neighbor in Germany.

For Savarkar *Hindutva* became the basis for the *substanzielle Gleichartigkeit* (substantial racial sameness) of the people in the sense of Carl Schmitt.[63] This involves the marginalization of syncretic traditions of the people, the breaking up of existing structures of pluricultural communication and the erecting of borders and boundaries, and the instrumentalization of tradition for political power. We have, then, an Indian variant of a *Leitkultur*.

As against the ideology of the "natural," homogenized order, the consciously secular postcolonial state dispenses with its legitimatization through the appeal to any transcendental "natural" order. Secularism is a conscious utopian construct.[64] It dispenses with the tribal principle that bonds through race, religion, and language, and this explains its vulnerability and its fragility. It is highly dependent on the success of modern democratic institutions functioning in an intact manner. It is the political way of dealing with and sustaining pluriculturalism. This also marks the attempt to create a pluricultural society (*Gesellschaft*), as opposed to a religious community (*Gemeinschaft*).[65]

Secularism is a project of the postcolonial Indian state, a utopian goal, which is directed against linear processes of religious homogenization. I think there is a striking similarity here to Hannah Arendt's lines written in 1947:

> Culture is by definition secular. It requires a kind of broadmindedness of which no religion will ever be capable. . . . Although culture is "hospitable" we should not forget that neither religion nor ideologies will, nor ever can, resign themselves to being only parts of a whole. The historian, though hardly ever the theologian, knows that secularization is not the ending of religion.[66]

India's Cultural Palimpsest

The distinguished scholar D. D. Kosambi once called India a country of long survivals. Jawaharlal Nehru tried to capture the linguistic and cultural complexity of India, its diversity and unity, by using the image of a palimpsest, which negates the essentialization imposed by authenticity and origins. The validity of the palimpsest lies in its totality and not in any particular layer. In 1946, India appeared to him like an

> ancient palimpsest on which layer upon layer of thought and reverie had been inscribed, and yet no succeeding layer had completely hidden or erased what had been written previously. All of these exist together in our conscious or subconscious selves, though we may not be aware of them, and they had gone to build up the complex and mysterious personality of India.[67]

This image of the palimpsest, which Victor Hugo also used for Europe,[68] is admittedly idealistic, but it corresponds in many ways with the notion of "nonsynchronous simultaneity" (*Gleichzeitigkeit des Ungleichzeitigen*), which Ernst Bloch formulated in the context of his study of fascism in "Erbschaft unserer Zeit" (Heritage of Our Times) in 1935. In a palimpsest, the layering can be seen as a form of enrichment, which leads to the dominance of the multiple. Any attempt to ascribe authenticity to one particular layer, to some mythical "urtext," leads to an impoverishment because it destroys the totality of the process of inscription. In any case, the original layer would logically have to be an empty surface. Thus, fundamentalists affirm the doctrine of complete erasure, of tabula rasa, in order to ensure the ascendancy of homogenization against the presence of the pluricultural. The desire for the authentic and the corresponding search for "urtexts" and roots generate strong tensions in the pluricultural formation.

Culture theory is strongly linked to finding appropriate metaphors for its concerns, and here botany seems to prevail.[69] The metaphor of "root" leads to thinking in dichotomizing categories like the self and the other, between which relations are created in the act of hermeneutic understanding. This is certainly an important operation, and perhaps genuinely monolingual and monocultural nations, if there are any, have no other choice. But the world is rather spread out in multilingual and pluricultural formations, which, in addition, are strongly interlinked. Perhaps Tagore's metaphor, which anticipates the use of the metaphor of the rhizome in contemporary culture theory, is apt here: "I would rather insist on the inexhaustible variety of the human race, which does not grow straight up, like a palmyra tree, on a single stem, but like a banian tree spreads itself in ever-new trunks and branches."[70]

The rhizome is characterized by heterogeneity, and for Deleuze and Guattari its ability to create free (arbitrary) relationships between very diverse areas was crucial.[71] Trees and roots steer toward one point. They characterize homogeneity. The rhizome, in contrast, multiplies and diversifies its various roots. This is why it is particularly suitable as a metaphor to characterize pluricultural situations and heterogeneous relationships. It is, of course, important to emphasize that multilingual and pluricultural spaces are not yet pacified societies. We have not yet achieved that kind of utopia of freedom. The consequences for our awareness of space and territory undergo a transformation as a result of this process.

Already in 1935, in "Erbschaft dieser Zeit," Bloch polemicized against Spengler's use of *Kulturraum* and *Kulturkreis* and against the forceful disruption of history (*Zersprengung der Geschichte*) in Karl Mannheim's use of the concept of structure in sociology.[72] More emphatically, Bloch later opposed the geographism (*Geographismus*) in theories based on the notion of a *Kulturkreis* in order to search for a space-time union (*Raum-Zeit-Union*), which would avoid a dichotomization of space and time. Time, he wrote, is only manifest through something that is happening and only there where something happens.[73] Bloch was looking for an "elastic" concept of space and time in order to overcome rigidity (*Starre*).

Geographism, Bloch pointed out, has a complementary relationship to linear historicism (*geradlinigen Historismus*). The aporia of historicism is linked to the difficulty of accommodating and depicting the vast non-European historical material in an axis of world history, which deals with past cultures like Babylon and ancient Egypt and has as its goal the European present. Cultures like China and India, which do not belong only to the historical past, do not seem to find a proper place therein. Geographism casts this non-European world into individual *Kulturräume,* gives them their own internal logic and lets them coexist without interlinkages. This form of bordering (*Grenzziehung*) effectively domesticates the complexity of world historical contexts.

For Bloch, dialectical space-time thought operates with a spatial addition or supplement (*Zuschuss*) in the historical time line (*historische Zeitlinie*). This makes it possible to depict many simultaneous, neighboring, related moments in the process of history. We can project a polyphonic arrangement or topography (*vielstimmige Topisierung*), and this is not the same as a periodization, because it is situated in what Bloch calls the spatiotemporal *Multiversum* of cultures.[74] Spengler's *Kulturgärten* (cultural gardens) and *Kulturseelen* (cultural souls) exist unmediated. They are cultural monads, cultural windowless souls with no connection to each other or to nature but with inwardly reflecting mirrors. *Kulturkreise* can then be accommodated in the unlimited space available to us as parallel worlds but at the price of obliterating the overarching historical processes. We have disconnected autonomous worlds in place of connected histories. In order, however, to comprehend the process of history, we would require the mediation with man and labor (as the continuous material of history), as also with nature as that other continuum within which this history is placed.

It seems to me that this problem of mediation is also the major concern of some variants of contemporary geography and geopolitics, which wish to make a differentiated concept of space that would be dynamic, politically progressive, and thus productive. Space becomes a social construct. Spatial relations and processes are looked upon as social relationships, which adopt a certain geographical form. If space is socially constructed, the social sphere is also spatially constructed. The spatial results from a complex meshing of local and global relations characterized by simultaneity (corresponding to Bloch's *Gleichzeitigkeit*). As in Bloch's thought, concepts of contemporary physics are used in culture theory today to emphasize the relational nature of space-time.[75] This kind of radical geography can then situate power relations in a space-time context and can therefore develop perspectives on migration and mobility that go beyond static binaries (self-other, *Eigen-Fremd*, center-periphery, north-south, east-west, etc.). In the long term, this is predicated toward transnational and transcultural analytic frameworks, which look upon global migration in the context of unequal power relations. This also destabilizes static notions of national identities and makes it possible for us to question the productivity of notions like identity for comprehending contemporary praxis.

In Bloch's words, the *Multiversum* of culture expresses the incompleteness of the *Humanum*. The only tolerant point of time, which is utopian tolerant, lies in its ever-growing incorporation of nations and national cultures in the humanist camp. Bloch reminds us that for Hegel the *whole of history* was "progress in the consciousness of freedom."[76] This *Humanum* is comprehensive enough in the real possibilities of the intended goal (*Zielinhalt*) to encompass *all* movements and forms of human cultures in the *Miteinander* (togetherness) of different times. Thus, one can say as a result of a realistic view of the shared history of colonialism and freedom struggles that "[t]he western concept of progress implied in its revolutions *no* European (and, indeed also *no* Asian or African) point, but *another* better world."[77] The world-historical perspective implies a rejection of parallel and organically authentic logics of separated historical trajectories. Instead, Bloch's perspective reinforces the polycentricity of pluricultural shared histories in which the plurality ensures the retention of multiple but deeply interconnected, interwoven paths of world history, which, as Bloch emphasizes, remains an experiment.

Similarity: Concluding Remarks

In conclusion, I would like to take up a point made by Samir Amin and suggest that complex societies could be characterized by the relationships and tensions between various semiautonomous logics of socially determining factors such as politics, economy, culture, and religion. The specific logic and internal dynamics of these factors put their stamp on the heterogeneous shape of society.[78] Autonomy, as Brecht has reminded us, is not autarchy. One could consider it the utopian goal of society to balance out these divergent logics in the interest of a plural society. This means that there are always different ways and routes through which such balances can be achieved.

Homogenization means ultimately giving one of these logics complete primacy, and cultural homogenization does this by exclusively privileging religion and culture within the context of power. Other logics are subordinated to this power. This is a process of staggering simplification of complexity. The defense of heterogeneity means that we do not grant to the differentiating features of homogenization (race, ethnicity, religion, and language) any substantial ontological status that could lead to divisive criteria for the formation of social organization forms such as nations. Distinguishing features (*Unterscheidungsmerkmale*) need not necessarily become marks of separation (*Trennungsmerkmale*). We have a right to be different, but must also realize that antidemocratic practices flourish under the mantel of the right to diversity. It is therefore correct to demand that the right to diversity and alterity must be coupled with the "right to be similar."[79] Similarity (*Ähnlichkeit*) is different from the demand for generic sameness (*Gleichartigkeit*). It is the process toward equality.

This could be formulated in Wittgenstein's terms. He writes that we can expand our concept of number

> as in spinning a thread we twist fiber on fiber. And the strength of the thread does not reside in the fact that a fiber runs through its whole length, but in the overlapping of many fibers. But if someone wished to say: "There is something common to all these constructions—namely the disjunction of all their common properties"—I should reply: Now you are only playing with words. One might as well say: "Something runs through the whole thread—namely the continuous overlapping of those fibers."[80]

This is remarkably reminiscent of Joyce's vision of Ireland:

> Our civilization is a vast fabric, in which the most diverse elements are mingled, in which Nordic aggressiveness and Roman Law, the new bourgeois conventions and the remnant of a Syriac religion are reconciled. In such a fabric, it is useless to look for a thread that may have remained pure and virgin without having undergone the influence of a neighbouring thread.[81]

In this sense, pluricultural and heterogeneous societies can be viewed as complex webs and palimpsests of overlapping similarities.[82] Similarity (*Ähnlichkeit*) with diversity would then be the goal of the historical process based on a universalist humanist perspective. It is based on solidarity, which ignores particularist bondings in order to project a pluricultural society of communication characterized by fuzzy borders and transcended boundaries. We could indeed see the signature of the pluricultural form of life in the affirmation of *similarity in diversity* (and *not* unity in diversity) as against the absolutization through identity or difference.[83] The affirmation of similarity would help us to defend secular, democratic principles. Only objects, frozen in time and space, can be identical and remain the same. Processes involving individuals and their social configurations, alliances, and allegiances explore ranges of similarities emphasizing the fluidity of borders and the fuzziness of identities. These processes lead to social and cultural weaves (*Gewebe*). It would be more important now to assess the nature of the weave (and the process of weaving) achieved as an outcome of the tension between processes of creating heterogeneities and homogeneities.

Instead of bounded *multicultural* conditions we could say that in such situations more fluid, communicatively open *pluricultural* conditions characterize society.[84] The goal is to establish lines of solidarity across cultures, opening them up to visions of new possibilities of transformation rather then freezing them into systems of bounded recognition. The dichotomizing hermeneutics of difference is replaced in such situations by an attitude of praxis, which does not remain at the level of only trying to understand each other but tries to move on to ways of arriving at sets of communicative practices in order to find a more acceptable and indeed more radical common solution to our societal problems. Postcolonial thought in this vein treats social complexity as something positive that has to be nurtured. We could then say that in complex situations it is more important for the time being to cultivate the operative art of just getting along with each other than to insist on a hermeneutic of understanding based on the creation of a dichotomy of self and other. One could even suggest that complex, pluricultural, heterogeneous societies allow us to develop a *habitus* based on the principle of hermeneutic abstinence, which sharpens a sense of similarities. This kind of awareness helps us to resist the drive that leads us toward the constant construction and interpretation of difference. Similarity, it should be emphasized, is not sameness, and it is in the dialectic of similarity and diversity that the productive potential of pluricultural formations can be nurtured.[85]

This perspective is predicated on the assumption that contemporary societies are transitional societies, and, therefore, the dialectic of similarity and diversity includes the perspective of latency (Bloch) and an awareness of the possibility of the development of revolutionary conjunctures leading to radical transformations.

Notes

1. Prabhat Patnaik, *The Retreat to Unfreedom: Essays on the Emerging World Order* (New Delhi, 2003); Prabhat Patnaik, "The Ideological Hegemony of Finance Capital," in *Re-envisioning Socialism* (New Delhi, 2011); Samir Amin, "Economic Globalism and Political Universalism: Conflicting Issues," *Journal of World-Systems Research* 6, no. 3 (Fall/Winter 2000): 581–622.

2. See also Shaheen Sardar Ali, "Religious Pluralism, Human Rights and Muslim Citizenship in Europe: Some Preliminary Reflections on an Evolving Methodology for Consensus," in *Religious Pluralism and Human Rights in Europe: Where to Draw the Line*, ed. Titia Leonon and J. E. Goldschmidt (Antwerp, 2007), 57–79; Levent Tezcan, "Operative Kultur und die Subjektivierungsstrategien in der Integrationspolitik," in *Wider den Kulturzwang: Migration, Kulturalisierung und Weltliteratur*, ed. Özkan Ezli et al. (Bielefeld, 2009), 47–80.
3. Christine Battersby, *The Sublime, Terror and Human Difference* (London, 2007), 41. See also Margaret Chatterjee, *Hinterlands and Horizons: Excursions in Search of Amity* (Lanham, MD, 2002).
4. Johann Wolfgang von Goethe, "Maximen und Reflexionen," in *Goethes Werke*, Hamburger Edition, vol. 12, ed. Erich Trunz (Munich, 1981), 380–81 (remarks 124 and 125). See also Johann Wolfgang von Goethe, *Goethes Anschauen der Welt: Schriften und Maximen zur wissenschaftlichen Methode*, compiled and with an afterword by Ekkehard Krippendorff (Frankfurt, 1994), 33.
5. Johann Wolfgang von Goethe, *Goethes Werke*, vol. 12 (Munich, 1981), 372 (remark 49). See also Hans Blumenberg, *Arbeit am Mythos* (Frankfurt, 1996), 585ff.
6. Heimito von Doderer, *Die Wasserfälle von Slunj: Roman* (Munich, 1963), 324.
7. For India and Pakistan, see Robert D. King, *Nehru and the Language Politics of India* (Delhi, 1998); Tariq Rahman, *Language and Politics in Pakistan* (Karachi, 2003); Tariq Rahman, *From Hindi to Urdu: A Social and Political History* (Delhi, 2011). For Europe, see Ernst Kantorowicz, *Kaiser Friedrich der Zweite* (Düsseldorf, 1973), 1st ed. published in 1927; Christiane Maass and Anette Volmer, eds., *Mehrsprachigkeit in der Renaissance* (Heidelberg, 2005); Italo Michele Battafarano, "Bilingualismus und Simultaneum: Marginalia zu einem aktuellen Problem, dass vor mehr als drei Jahrhunderten im barocken Sulzbach schon gelöst wurde," *Morgen-Glantz: Zeitschrift der Christian Korr von Rosenroth-Gesellschaft* 10 (2000): 333–46.
8. Earlier remarks on these questions have been published as: Anil Bhatti, "Kulturelle Vielfalt und Homogenisierung," in *Habsburg Postcolonial: Machtstrukturen und kollektives Gedächtnis*, ed. Johannes Feichtinger et al. (Innsbruck, 2003), 55–68. For further literature, see Sanjay Subhramanyam, "Connected Histories: Notes towards a Reconfiguration of Early Modern Eurasia," *Modern Asian Studies* 31, no. 3 (1997): 735–61; C. A. Bayley, *Imperial Meridian: The British Empire and the World, 1780–1830* (London, 1989); Horst Turk et al., *Kulturelle Grenzziehungen im Spiegel der Literaturen: Nationalismus, Regionalismus, Fundamentalismus* (Göttingen, 1998); Moritz Csáky and Klaus Zeyringer, eds., *Ambivalenz des kulturellen Erbes: Vielfachkodierung des historischen Gedächtnisses: Paradigma* (Innsbruck, 2000); Moritz Csáky, *Das Gedächtnis der Städte: Wien und die urbanen Milieus in Zentraleuropa* (Vienna, 2010); Johannes Feichtinger and Peter Stachel, eds., *Das Gewebe der Kultur: Kulturwissenschaftliche Analysen zur Geschichte und Identität Österreichs in der Moderne* (Innsbruck, 2001); Dipesh Chakrabarty, *Provincializing Europe: Postcolonial Thought and Historical Difference* (New Delhi, 2001; Princeton, 2000); Wolfgang Müller-Funk, Peter Plener, and Clemens Ruthner, eds., *Kakanien Revisited: Das Eigene und das Fremde der österreichisch- ungarischen Monarchie* (Tübingen, 2002); Sebastian Conrad and Shalini Randeria, eds., *Jenseits des Eurozentrismus: Postkoloniale Perspektiven in den Geschichts- und Kulturwissenschaften* (Frankfurt, 2002). See also www.kakanien.ac.at.
9. Johann Wolfgang von Goethe, "Zur Naturwissenschaft im allgemeinen," in *Goethes Werke*, Hamburger Edition, vol. 13, ed. Erich Trunz (Munich, 1981), 35.
10. This, of course, is different from the nineteenth-century vision of a *Staatenverbund*, for which the nation-state was a precondition. It is also different from the romantic notion of being national and universal. For this see Friedrich Meinecke, *Weltbürgertum und Nationalstaat*, edited and with an introduction by Hans Herzfeld (Munich, 1962).

11. For some important points, see Ernst Bloch, *Tübinger Einleitung in die Philosophie,* vol. 2 (Frankfurt, 1969), 129. The problem is relevant for the discussion concerning "Gestalt."
12. Mathias Jestaedt with the Hans Kelsen-Institut, eds., *Hans Kelsen im Selbstzeugnis: Sonderpublikation anlässlich des 125: Geburtstages von Hans Kelsen am 11. Oktober 2006* (Tübingen, 2006), 62. The theme is also present in Ernest Gellner, *Language and Solitude* (Cambridge, 1998), with reference to Wittgenstein and Malinowski. See also Johannes Feichtinger, *Wissenschaft als reflexives Projekt: Von Bolzano über Freud zu Kelsen: Österreichische Wissenschaftsgeschichte 1848–1938* (Bielefeld, 2010); Johannes Feichtinger, "Europa, quo vadis? Zur Erfindung eines Kontinents zwischen transnationalem Anspruch und nationaler Wirklichkeit," in *Europa—geeint durch Werte? Die europäische Wertedebattenauf dem Prüfstand der Geschichte,* ed. Moritz Csáky and Johannes Feichtinger (Bielefeld, 2007), 19–44. Feichtinger draws attention to Freud and Ernst Mach in addition to Kelsen in a similar connection, relating the pluricultural situation of the Habsburg Monarchy to the style of theory that emerges in it. See also Karl Acham, ed., *Geschichte der österreichischen Humanwissenschaften,* vol. 5, *Sprache, Literatur und Kunst* (Vienna, 2003), 43; Karl Acham, "Volk, Nation, Europa—bezogen auf ältere und neuere Formen Österreichs und des Österreichischen," in *Volk—Nation—Europa: Zur Romantisierung und Entromantisierung politischer Begriffe,* ed. Alexander von Bormann (Würzburg, 1998), 245–62.
13. See Horst Turk, "Am Ort des Anderen: Natur und Geschichte in Herders Nationenkonzept," in *Unerledigte Geschichten: Der literarische Umgang mit Nationalität und Internationalität,* ed. Gesa von Essen and Horst Turk (Göttingen, 2000), 442.
14. Margit Köves, "Jumping on to the Moving Train: Hungarian Responses to European Integration," in *Yearbook of the Goethe Society of India,* ed. Rajendra Dengle (New Delhi, 2005), 35–53.
15. Péter Nádas, "The Citizen of the World and the Buck Goat," trans. Tim Wilkinson, *Common Knowledge* 11, no. 1 (Winter 2005): 8–17, http://muse.jhu.edu/login?uri=/journals/common_knowledge/v011/11.1nadas.html.
16. "In keinem Weltheil haben sich die Völker so vermischt, wie in Europa: in keinem haben sie so stark und oft ihre Wohnplätze, und mit denselben ihre Lebensart und Sitten verändert.... Durch hundert Ursachen hat sich im Verfolg der Jahrhunderte die alte Stammesbildung mehrerer Europäischen Nationen gemildert und verändert; ohne welche Verschmelzung der Allgemeingeist Europa's schwerlich hätte erweckt werden mögen." Johann Gottfried Herder, *Ideen zur Philosophie der Geschichte der Menschheit* (Frankfurt, 1989), 287.
17. Johann Gottfried Herder, "Bekehrung der Juden," in *Adrastea,* ed. Günter Arnold (Frankfurt, 2000), 628–42.
18. Among Austro-Marxists, Karl Renner also spoke of the "people without history." For a general critique of this notion, see Eric Wolf, *Europe and the People Without History* (Berkeley, CA, 1982).
19. Friedrich Schlegel, "Herder's Humanitätsbriefe: 7. und 8. Sammlung," in *Friedrich Schlegel: Kritische Ausgabe,* vol. 2, ed. Ernst Behler (Munich, 1967), 54. See also Fritz Wefelmeyer, "Glück und Aporie des Kulturtheoretikers: Zu Johann Gottfried Herder und seiner Konzeption der Kultur," in *Naturplan und Verfallskritik: Zu Begriff und Geschichte der Kultur,* ed. Helmut Brackert and Fritz Wefelmeyer (Frankfurt, 1984), 94–121.
20. Johann Wolfgang von Goethe, "Maximen und Reflexionen," in *Goethes Werke,* Hamburger Edition, vol. 12, ed. Erich Trunz (Munich, 1981), 380–81 (remarks 124 and 125).
21. See Wefelmeyer, "Glück und Aporie des Kulturtheoretikers," 94–121.
22. See the relevant passages of Goethe's most important statements about *Weltliteratur* in *Goethes Werke,* vol. 12 (Munich, 1981), 361–64. See also Hendrik Birus, "The Goethean

Concept of World and Comparative Literature," *Comparative Literature and Culture* 2, no. 4 (2000): 1090, http://dx.doi.org/10.7771/1481-4374.

23. See Michael Adas, "Contested Hegemony: The Great War and the Afro-Asian Assault on the Civilising Mission Ideology," *Journal of World History* 15, no. 1 (2003): 31–63, http://www.historycooperative.org/journals/jwh/15.1/adas.html. For the European context, see Sigrid Thieleking, *Weltbürgertum: Kosmopolitische Idee in Literatur und politischer Publizistik seit dem achtzehnten Jahrhundert* (Munich, 2000), 84–123; Andrea Albrecht, *Kosmopolitismus: Weltbürgerdiskurse in Literatur, Philosophie und Publizistik um 1800* (Berlin, 2005).

24. See especially James Joyce, "Ireland, Island of Saints and Sages (1907)," in *The Critical Writings of James Joyce*, ed. Ellsworth Mason and Richard Ellmann (New York, 1972), 165–66; Hugo von Hofmannsthal, "Die Österreichische Idee," in *Gesammelte Werke in zehn Einzelbänden* [IX] : *Reden und Aufsätze II: 1914–1924* (Frankfurt, 1977), 456; Robert Musil, "Nation als Ideal und Wirklichkeit (1921)," in *Robert Musil, Tagebücher, Aphorismen, Essays und Reden* (Hamburg, 1955), 607–22; Rabindranath Tagore, *Nationalism* (Delhi, 2009), originally published in 1917.

25. Rabindranath Tagore, "Nationalism in India," in *Between Tradition and Modernity: India's Search for Identity: A Twentieth Century Anthology*, ed. Fred Dallmayr and G. N. Devy (New Delhi, 1998), 84.

26. Rabindranath Tagore, "The Message of the Forest," in *The English Writings of Rabindranath Tagore*, vol. 3, *A Miscellany*, ed. Sisir Kumar Das (New Delhi, 1996), 400. See also *The Mahatma and the Poet: Letters and Debates between Gandhi and Tagore 1915–1941*, compiled and edited by Sabyasachi Bhattacharya (New Delhi, 1997).

27. Sisir Kumar Das, ed., *The English Writings of Rabindranath Tagore*, vol. 3, *A Miscellany* (New Delhi, 1996), 200.

28. Rabindranath Tagore, "The Way to Unity," in Das, *A Miscellany*, 400.

29. Ibid.

30. Ibid. See also Peter Stachel, "Übernationales Gesamtstaatsbewusstsein in der Habsburgermonarchie: Zwei Fallbeispiele," *Kakanien Revisited* (2002): 1–8, http://www.kakanien.ac.at/beitr/fallstudie/PstachelI.pdf; Acham, "Volk, Nation, Europa," 245–62.

31. Rabindranath Tagore, "The Union of Cultures (1921)," in Das, *A Miscellany*, 436.

32. Rabindranath Tagore, "International Relations (1924)," in Das, *A Miscellany*, 472. Cf. Franz Grillparzer's epigram from 1849, "Der Weg der neuern Bildung/Geht/Von Humanität/Durch Nationalität/Zur Bestialität," in *Franz Grillparzer, Sämtliche Werke*, vol. 1, ed. Peter Frank and Karl Pörnbacher (Munich, 1960), 500.

33. See Friedrich Meinecke, *Weltbürgertum und Nationalstaat*, ed. Hans Herzfeld (Munich, 1962), originally published in 1908. I am, of course, referring to Meinecke's classical study as part of the tradition that it seeks to analyze.

34. Ibid., 459.

35. Samir Amin, *Capitalism in the Age of Globalization: The Management of Contemporary Society* (London, 1977; New Delhi, 1977), 86: "Faced with the reality of national identities, yet concerned to insist upon class interests, socialists have defended positions which, though not always politically effective in the short term, have been noble, worthy and in advance of the times. I am thinking here of the attitudes of the socialist movement within the multinational empires of Europe: the Austro-Marxists of the Austro-Hungarian Empire and the Bolsheviks of the Russian Empire. The Austro-Marxists wanted to save the large state, but by reconstructing it on the basis of recognition of ethnic, religious and national differences as democratically legitimate."

36. Ibid. See also Tom Bottomore and Patrick Goode, *Austro-Marxism* (Oxford, 1978); *Austromarxistische Positionen*, ed. Gerald Mozetič (Vienna, 1983); Günther Sandner,

"Zwischen Anerkennung und Differenz: Die Nationalitätentheorien von Karl Renner und Otto Bauer im Kontext," in *Eigene und andere Fremde: "Postkoloniale" Konflikte im europäischen Kontext,* ed. Wolfgang Müller-Funk and Brigitte Wagner (Vienna, 2005), 20–104.
37. Quoted from *Lenin on Language* (Moscow, 1983), 126ff. See also V. I. Lenin, *Collected Works,* vol. 19 (Moscow, 1977), 503–7.
38. Amin, *Capitalism in the Age of Globalization,* 86–87.
39. Jürgen Trabant, *Mithridates im Paradies: Kleine Geschichte des Sprachdenkens* (Munich, 2003), 21; Arno Borst, *Der Turmbau zu Babel: Geschichte der Meinungen über Ursprung und Vielfalt der Sprachen und Völker* (Stuttgart, 1957–1963; reprinted in Munich in 1995). See also Wilfried Seipel, ed., *Der Turmbau zu Babel: Ursprung und Vielfalt von Sprache und Schrift, Ausstellungskatalog des Kunsthistorischen Museums Wien* (Vienna, 2003).
40. Bernhard Cohn, "The Command of Language and the Language of Command," in *Subaltern Studies IV,* ed. Ranajit Guha (Delhi, 1985), 276–329; C. A. Bayly, *Empire and Information: Intelligence Gathering and Social Communication in India, 1780–1870* (Cambridge, 1996), 298; Anil Bhatti, "Sprache, Übersetzung, Kolonialismus," in *Kulturelle Identität: Deutschindische Kulturkontakte in Literatur, Religion und Politik,* ed. Horst Turk and Anil Bhatti (Berlin, 1997), 3–19; Tariq Rahman, *Language and Politics in Pakistan*; Alok Rai, *Hindi Nationalism* (Delhi, 2001).
41. Hofmannsthal, "Die Österreichische Idee," 456.
42. Joseph Freiherr von Hammer-Purgstall, *Vortrag über die Vielsprachigkeit: Festvortrag zur feierlichen Eröffnungssitzung der kaiserl: Akademie der Wissenschaften* (Vienna, 1852), 87–100.
43. Ibid., 92.
44. Ibid., 96.
45. Ibid., 97.
46. See Csáky and Zeyringer, *Ambivalenz des kulturellen*; Csáky, *Das Gedächtnis der Städte.*
47. Hugo von Hofmannsthal, "Unsere Fremdwörter," in *Gesammelte Werke in zehn Einzelbänden* [IX]: *Reden und Aufsätze II: 1914–1924,* ed. Bernd Schoeller and Rudolf Hirsch (Frankfurt, 1979), 363. Emphasis added.
48. Jawaharlal Nehru, *An Autobiography* (New Delhi, 1989), 469, 1st ed. published in London in 1936.
49. Ibid., 596. Nehru anticipates the position of "in-between," theorized later especially by Homi Bhaba.
50. Rabindranath Tagore, "National Language of India," in Das, *A Miscellany,* 736–37. Emphasis added.
51. Nehru, *An Autobiography,* 456.
52. Csáky, *Das Gedächtnis der Städte,* 302–3.
53. Jacques Derrida, *Monolingualism of the Other: Or the Prosthesis of Origin,* trans. Patrick Mensah (Palo Alto, CA, 1998), 9.
54. Wilhelm von Humboldt, "Ueber die Verschiedenheiten des menschlichen Sprachbaues [1827–1829]," in *Werke in fünf Bänden: Bd. III: Schriften zur Sprachphilosophie,* ed. Andreas Flitner and Klaus Giel, 3rd ed. (Darmstadt, 1963), 144–367.
55. M. T. Ansari, ed., *Secularism, Islam and Modernity: Selected Essays of Alam Khundmiri,* with an introduction by the editor (New Delhi, 2001), 280–81.
56. See, among others, Gyanendra Pandey, *The Construction of Communalism in Colonial North India* (Delhi, 1992); Christophe Jaffrelot, *Les nationalistes hindous* (Paris, 1993), published in English as *The Hindu Nationalist Movement and Indian Politics, 1925 to the 1990s* (London, 1996); K. N. Pannikar, *Culture, Ideology, Hegemony: Intellectuals and Social Consciousness in Colonial India* (New Delhi, 1995); Peter Van de Veer, *Religious Nationalism: Hindus and Muslims in India* (Delhi, 1996); Partha Chatterjee, ed., *Wages of Freedom: Fifty Years of the*

Indian Nation-State (Delhi, 1998); Romila Thapar, *History and Beyond* (New Delhi, 2000); Prabhat Patnaik, *The Retreat to Unfreedom: Essays on the emerging World Order* (New Delhi, 2003).
57. See Carl Schmitt, *Verfassungslehre*, 4th ed. (Berlin, 1965), 228–30; Carl Schmitt, *Staat, Bewegung, Volk: Die Dreigliederung der politischen Einheit* (Hamburg, 1933), 42–46.
58. See Jaffrelot, *Les nationalistes hindous*.
59. Vinayak D. Savarkar, "Some of the Basic Principles and Tenets of the Hindu Movement," as quoted in Dallmayr and Devy, *Between Tradition and Modernity*, 115.
60. Ibid., 116.
61. Ibid., 116.
62. Ibid., 117.
63. See Schmitt, *Verfassungslehre*, 228–30; Schmitt, *Staat, Bewegung, Volk*, 42–46.
64. "Secularism" in the Indian context does not imply opposition to religion. It is characterized by equidistance and corresponds to what "civil society" means in some Arab states.
65. A distinction already made popular in 1887 by the sociologist Tönnies. See Ferdinand Tönnies, *Gemeinschaft und Gesellschaft* (Darmstadt, 1991).
66. Hannah Arendt, "Creating a Cultural Atmosphere," in *The Jew as Pariah: Jewish Identity and Politics in the Modern Age*, ed. Ron H. Feldman (New York, 1978), 92; Hannah Arendt, "Aufklärung und Judenfrage," in *Hannah Arendt: Die Verborgene Tradition: Acht Essays* (Frankfurt, 1976), 108–26.
67. Jawaharlal Nehru, *The Discovery of India* (New Delhi, 1997), 59.
68. Victor Hugo, *Betrachtungen zur Geschichte*, as quoted in Paul Michael Lützeler, ed., *Europa: Analysen und Visionen der Romantiker* (Frankfurt, 1982), 442.
69. See Franco Moretti, "Conjectures on World Literature," *New Left Review* 1 (January/February 2000): 54–68.
70. Rabindranath Tagore, "The Message of the Forest," in Das, *A Miscellany*, 399.
71. Gilles Deleuze and Felix Guattari, *A Thousand Plateaus: Capitalism and Schizophrenia*, trans. Brian Masumi (London, 1988), 15.
72. Ernst Bloch, *Erbschaft dieser Zeit* (Frankfurt, 1979), 323.
73. Ernst Bloch, *Tübinger Einleitung in die Philosophie* (Frankfurt, 1964), 176.
74. Ibid., 175.
75. See, for instance, Doreen Massey, "Politics and Space/Time," in *Place and the Politics of Identity*, ed. Michael Keith and Steve Pile (London, 1993), 156; David Morley and Kevin Robins, *Spaces of Identity: Global Media, Electronic Landscapes and Cultural Boundaries* (London, 1995); Jennifer Hyndman, "Border Crossings," *Antipode* 29, no. 2 (1997): 149–76. Radical geography has, as is well-known, been proposed by Michel Foucault. See Michel Foucault, *Power/Knowledge: Selected Interviews and Other Writings*, ed. Colin Gordon (Sussex, 1980), 63–77; Jeremy W. Crampton and Stuart Elden, eds., *Space, Knowledge and Power: Foucault and Geography* (Aldershot, 2007). A recent useful collection is Jörg Dünne and Stephan Günzel, eds., *Raumtheorie: Grundlagentexte aus Philosophie und Kulturwissenschaften* (Frankfurt, 2006).
76. Bloch, *Tübinger Einleitung in die Philosophie*, 169. Emphasis added.
77. Ibid., 200. Emphasis added.
78. Samir Amin, *Spectres of Capitalism: A Critique of Current Intellectual Fashions* (New Delhi, 1999), 42.
79. Ibid., 91.
80. Ludwig Wittgenstein, *Philosophische Untersuchungen*, 3rd ed. (Frankfurt, 1975), 58 (remark 67). Translation taken from http://www.voidspace.org.uk/psychology/wittgenstein/eight.shtml (accessed 3 December 2010).
81. Joyce, "Ireland, Island of Saints and Sages (1907)," 165–66.

82. Wittgenstein, *Philosophische Untersuchungen,* 57 (remark 66) and 77 (remark 76).
83. Perhaps Goethe's *West-östlicher Divan* may be the poetic model here. For this and further references to Goethe scholarship, see Anil Bhatti, "'. . . zwischen zwei Welten schwebend . . .': Zu Goethes Fremdheitsexperiment im West-östlichen Divan," in *Goethe: Neue Ansichten,* ed. Hans-Jörg Knobloch und Helmut Koopmann (Würzburg, 2007), 103–21. http://www.goethezeitportal.de/fileadmin/PDF/kk/df/postkoloniale_studien/bhatti_divan.pdf. Similarities are also an underlying theme in Salman Rushdie's work. Referring to his novel *The Enchantress of Florence* (2008), Rushdie states in an interview that "[t]here are ideas which grew up in the West, and in a slightly different form they grew up as well in the East; the idea of freedom, of open discourses, of tolerance, of sexual freedom even to the level of hedonism. . . . So to say that we must now consider them to be culturally specific . . . is a denial of human nature." See the review of the novel by Joyce Carol Oates, *New York Review of Books* 55, no. 10 (12 June 2008).
84. See Csáky and Zeyringer, *Ambivalenz des kulturellen Erbes,* 31–34; Feichtinger and Stachel, *Das Gewebe der Kultur*; Csáky, *Das Gedächtnis der Städte.*
85. Similarity or *Ähnlichkeit* in German are terms that are linked variously to Walter Benjamin's writings and to Wittgenstein's *Philosophische Untersuchungen* (Philosophical Investigations). One can also go back to Leibniz and remember Goethe's approval of thinking in analogies. See Anil Bhatti et al., "Ähnlichkeit: Ein kulturtheoretisches Paradigma," *Internationales Archiv für Sozialgeschichte der deutschen Literatur* 3, no. 1: 261–75.

Chapter 2

MESTIZAJE AND HYBRID CULTURE
Toward a Transnational Cultural Memory of Europe and the Development of Cultural Theories in Latin America

Michael Rössner

Over the past twenty years we have all experienced the hopes and disappointments, the enthusiasm and discouragement, that accompanied the development of a European spirit, a European conscience, or, in the parlance of official documents, a common identity. Born out of the ruins of World War II, sustained by economic success, and driven by the euphoria that marked the end of the continent's division in 1989, this common European identity seemed almost a reality. Today, more than two decades and two accession stages later, after the inglorious demise of the European Constitution in the French and Dutch referendums, it seems further from our grasp than ever before. Instead of witnessing a "European" identity building, we observe on a daily basis how our media and politicians are exploiting the short-time advantages of blaming the "Brussels bureaucrats" for every single problem we have to face in everyday life, thus creating a "populist," nationalistic renaissance and building their own identities as heroic fighters for a national identity opposed to the European "Moloch." This short-sighted behavior has created an atmosphere in which it is difficult to develop a common identity; when politicians go to Brussels to discuss guidelines for our common future, they are expected to come home "successful" in their negotiations, that is to say, to come home with an arrangement that allows their country to pay less, disregard common rules, or benefit from special treatment. All these trends have led to the most spectacular manifestation of popular dissent: the refusal by two of the founding partners of the European Union in 2005 to accept the common constitution, which would have strengthened democracy, but not on a national level.

It is perhaps no coincidence that the problems encountered by Europe's common identity originated in countries with a long tradition of *national* (i.e., centralist) identity *and* a tradition of colonial dominance over other continents. It seems to me that the nation-building processes that began earlier on and more exclusively (in France, for instance, whose tradition of a strong national identity has overlapped and blanketed regional and even individual identities), those bolstered by the familiar and widely described identity-building processes of colonial rule ("us and the *Other*"),[1] have given rise to problems in adapting to a new situation, one where Europe cannot simply remain an administrative entity with a free trade zone if it wishes to go on playing a key role in the world. It appears that former "centers" of colonial empires, which went through early nation-building processes before engaging in colonial imperialism, are more reluctant to fuse and/or confuse their national identities in the context of a wider European identity than others. Viewed in this light, Britain's "special role" within the European Union appears as just one more example of this rule.

Obviously, the Habsburg Central European experience is quite different. There nation building took place, if at all, only in the nineteenth and twentieth centuries. Previous unification stages were driven mainly by religion and were far more regional in scope. The Habsburg Monarchy was far from achieving even the religious unity to which it aspired, and ethnic or linguistic unity was nonexistent, even at the local level. Prague and Bratislava, and also nineteenth-century Budapest, as multilingual capitals, are good examples of this nonhomogeneous reality.

In the last quarter of the nineteenth century, however, nation building in Habsburg Central Europe (based on linguistic criteria and the establishment of the corresponding narratives) began to gather pace dramatically, leading to the creation of nation-states after World War I, which in some cases, such as Czechoslovakia or Yugoslavia, proved to be artificially founded nations. Nationalism, halted during the Cold War initially by communist internationalism, which emerged soon enough as merely colonialism in disguise, quickly returned to fill the ideological void after 1989. We have since experienced many examples of a new form of nation building, one that begins with a strong expression of "European feelings" and the desire to become a member of the European Union as soon as possible before gradually turning into the assertion of that nation's claim to its own "national identity," one opposed to Brussels's "colonialist" bureaucratic spirit. And yet, there is no denying the long tradition of togetherness in the sometimes chaotic, overlapping atmospheres of Habsburg Central European regions, and it might be possible to recover that togetherness—which has never been harmonious, but rather merely negotiations in progress—and to use it to create something that could replace the concept of a European identity erroneously conceived on the model of national identity.

In our search for theoretical models capable of describing such a dynamic and relational concept of identity, it seems only natural to look at the American experience of identities in progress created out of the cohabitation of different ethnicities, religions, and linguistic communities. Indeed, if a "European spirit" was ever going to emerge, then surely it would have to have been in the Americas, where a single European national culture could no longer be ascribed to the local populations, even though they were predominantly European in origin. This paradigm is perhaps even stronger in Latin America, which not only maintained greater spiritual ties to Europe, but also a degree of cohabitation with its indigenous cultures, a situation that led inevitably to experiences of "hybridity *avant la lettre*" already during the colonial period. By the time Latin American states achieved their independence from Spain, we again encountered a situation where "Europeanness" became a virtual reality far sooner than in Europe, that is, during the first half of the nineteenth century, a time when Latin American countries sought to conceive of their identity no longer on the basis of their Hispanic roots but by creating an alternative between American *barbarie* and European *civilización*, whereby European stood for a mixture of British (political and technical) modernity and French cultural *raffinement*.

This is especially the case of Domingo Faustino Sarmiento, the Argentine essayist and later president, who in 1845 coined the phrase "civilización y barbarie" in a famous essay on a gaucho warlord, Juan Facundo Quiroga, which was written in Chilean exile and directed against the brutal regime of dictator Juan Manuel Rosas, himself a gaucho warlord. In Sarmiento's work, the "European" *civilización* is contrasted with both Native American savageness (of the Indians and the *gaucho-mestizos*) and Spanish medieval brutality (the spirit of the Inquisition tribunals, but also the "African elements" in Spanish identity, as he calls them).[2] It is obvious that Sarmiento's sympathy is with the "European" model, and the same holds true for his entire generation, not only in Argentina but also almost everywhere among the intelligentsia of the former Spanish American colonies. It was so influential that we even find it in twentieth-century literature, such as in Rómulo Gallegos's famous novel *Doña Bárbara* (1929), where the protagonist represents the spirit of "barbarie" and is defeated by youth and "civilization" represented by Santos Luzardo.[3] However, it is quite obvious that such a Europeanness, corresponding simply to "modernity" and Enlightenment values in a dominantly French and British context, is far removed from the "dynamic and relational" identity concept we are seeking. Sarmiento and his fellow intellectuals in South America at that time conceived a European identity to suit their needs, serving the myths of progress and civilization they defended against the representatives of traditional *cacique* structures.

However, this was only the first step in a discussion that must include the developments that took place in Europe, where ideas of national unity and purity became more and more popular. These ideas led to the creation of new nation-states (Germany and Italy) and to continual unrest in Habsburg Central European areas, where the creation of such pure nation-states seemed—and indeed was—impossible without the violence that later occurred in the twentieth century under the name of ethnic cleansing. Nineteenth-century nationalism, combined with the aggressive imperialism and/or colonialism of even smaller nations, made it even more difficult for a common European identity to emerge; indeed, it led to the creation of a series of imaginary "supranations" with nationalist or even racist roots: pan-Slavism, pan-Germanism, and the idea of a union of Latin cultures opposed to the Anglo-Saxon and Germanic cultures.

In the second half of the century a newfound solidarity between the ex-colonies and Spain, a spirit of "Latinness" (derived from French essayists such as Ernest Renan), took hold in the former Spanish colonies. It was founded on the wave of massive immigration, essentially from Italy, that surged across Latin America and on the growing fear of US domination following the 1898 Spanish-American war. This mind-set, formed in Paris, contrasted the "Latin cultures" and the "Anglo-Saxon cultures," creating an identity model that compensated for French feelings of *décadence* in the face of the British Empire's dominance and the growing power of the new German Reich; it also quite suited the emotions felt by Latin Americans. Latin American cultural philosophers now perceived their identity in terms of a "European" America that had to be "Latin-based," as opposed to the purely materialistic culture in the North (i.e., the United States). One of the fiercest defenders of these theories, José Enrique Rodó from Uruguay, found those two cultures ideally personified in the two spirits that appear on the island of Shakespeare's *The Tempest*. In his essay "Ariel" (1900), the idealistic, generous, intellectual "spirit of the air" Ariel (which represents European-influenced Latin American culture and is still based on Sarmiento's "European values") contrasts with the barbarian, rich, and powerful spirit of North America represented by Caliban, the spirit of the earth.[4] The fact that such Latinness is rooted in Europe was further demonstrated by the "pilgrimage" that Rodó made to Rome in order to retrace his "Latin roots." In any case, his essay again created a continental identity that became overwhelmingly popular among intellectuals of at least two generations from Mexico to Argentina, and it was not until the period of the famous "boom" and the Cuban Revolution that Rodó's scheme was definitively overthrown.[5]

It may seem curious that Latin Americans were developing pan-European cultural models such as these at precisely the same time that Europeans were adopting a clearly nationalistic approach and setting the stage for World War I. These European cultural models were, however, only partial ones, excluding Eastern Europe, Habsburg Central Europe, and Northern Europe; and they were falsely homogeneous models that within Latin American societies led to the exclusion of subordinate cultures, that is, African American and indigenous cultures—an exclusion that, at least on a symbolic level, ended only with the twentieth century's conception of an ethnic (and cultural) mix (*mestizaje*) as a new symbol of identity.

In simpler terms, we could say that in the discourse on Latin American cultural identity, the concepts of Europeanness predominant in the nineteenth-century discussion were replaced in the twentieth century by a genuine mixed identity based on the ethnic, but also spiritual, fusion of European and indigenous races and cultures. This revaluation of the *mestizo* was not entirely new; indeed, it has a colonial prologue. In early seventeenth-century Peru, Garcilaso de la Vega el Inca, the son of a Spanish nobleman and an Incan princess, conceived the notion of a "fusion of two Histories" and therefore two nobilities, two historical sources of rights by a *translatio imperii*, two "Romes" as he calls it (Rome and Cuzco), which would find its symbolic—and real—manifestation in the physical body of *mestizo* people such as himself. In his *Comentarios reales*, he calls for the derogative term *mestizo* to be rehabilitated:

> The children of Spaniards by Spanish women born there are called *criollos* or *criollas*, implying that they were born in the Indies. The name was invented by the Negroes, as its use shows. They use it to mean a Negro born in the Indies, and they devised it to distinguish those who come from this side and were born in Guinea from those born in the New World, since the former are held in greater honor and considered to be of higher rank because they were born in their own country, while their children were born in a strange land. The parents take offense if they are called *criollos*. The Spaniards have copied them by introducing this word to describe those born in the New World, and this way both Spaniards and Guinea Negroes are called *criollos* if they are born in the New World. The Negro who arrives there from the Old World is called Negro or Guineo. The child of a Negro by an Indian woman or of an Indian and a Negro woman is called *mulato* or *mulata*. Their children are called *cholos,* a word from the Windward Islands: it means a dog, but is not used for a thoroughbred dog, but only for a mongrel cur: the Spaniards use the word in a pejorative and vituperative sense. The children of Spaniards by Indians are called *mestizos,* meaning that we are a mixture of the two races. The word was applied by the first Spaniards who had children by Indian women, and because it was used by our fathers, as well as on account of its meaning, I call myself by it in public and am proud of it, though in the Indies, if a person is told: "You're a mestizo" or "he's a mestizo," it is taken as an insult.[6]

Clearly, Inca Garcilaso was an exception: as the son of a Spanish nobleman, he took the name of his uncle, the famous Renaissance poet Garcilaso de la Vega; he lived and worked in Spain, and his idea of merging two equivalent—or almost equivalent—traditions had no chance of succeeding in his native Peru, where the opposite trend—that is, the elimination of Inca structures—predominated throughout the seventeenth century, and even more so after Peruvian independence.[7] The triumph of the European Enlightenment further reduced the chances of peripheral, non-European discourses entering into a dialogue with mainstream, *ratio*-based thinking.

However, during the twentieth century, the symbol of identity Inca Garcilaso had created was soon in high demand. Its stronghold was to be found in Mexico, combined with the myth of the Mexican Revolution, which, in fact, was more a succession of civil wars leading to the long-lasting one-party rule of the Partido Revolucionario Institucional than a revolution in the European sense. But by then it could be presented as the heroic birth of a homogeneous nation that united all ethnic groups to form a new identity, and as such the Mexican Revolution found its way into the arts, above all in the famous *murales* by Diego Rivera, José Clemente Orozco, David Alfaro Siqueiros, and others. This new identity—be it Mexican or Latin American—was even conceived in racial terms, as a "superhuman mixed race" proclaimed by the minister of education and essayist José Vasconcelos in his book *La raza cósmica* (The Cosmic Race, 1925). In it, he posited the concept of what he called "aesthetic eugenics," whereby the most beautiful and fit of the Spanish, Anglo-Saxon, black, and Indian races would meld and produce a futuristic "cosmic race," while "pure races"—recognizing their inferiority—would voluntarily refrain from procreation and die out.[8] What Vasconcelos proclaimed—and, in a milder, more spiritual form, the Argentinian essayist Ricardo Rojas (*Eurindia*, 1924)[9]— went against the European mainstream of the 1930s in which the "purity of races" became a political goal. Yet in some ways this "crossbreeding" ideology followed the same principles: for Vasconcelos, the perfect fusion of European and non-European races takes the place of the "pure" Aryan or other race, and it must impose itself and eliminate all other races merely on the strength of its higher aesthetic value. *Mestizaje* is, therefore, conceived as a result, not as a process, as a perfect fusion that eliminates all other existing races. Paradoxically, the perfect *mestizaje* ideology produces the same outcome as racial ideologies in Europe: the elimination of others and the creation of a "pure" (albeit mixed) *mestizo* race.

Mestizaje became a more spiritual concept of identity with what is referred to as the 1960s "boom" in Latin American literature, a concept no longer related directly to ethnic or racial realities. Even intellectuals from countries where the entire indigenous culture and population had been exterminated were able to embrace this magical realist concept as an identity trait for the entire Latin American continent. And they did. As exemplary representatives of such an exclusively spiritual concept—one that was used in the context of dependency theory—one might mention the La Plata–based Uruguayan writers Eduardo Galeano (*Las Venas abiertas de América Latina*, 1971) and Mario Benedetti (*Letras del continente mestizo*, 1967).

For many years, this essentialist concept of *mestizaje* served not only as an internal symbol of identity, but also as a commercial label to promote Latin American culture in Europe in the postcolonial era with obvious colonialist economic traits, as I have pointed out elsewhere.[10] In a literature initially marketed in post-1968 Europe and the United States, "Europeanness" became a kind of pejorative label used to distinguish *mestizaje*-oriented "real Latin American literature," which had to be about indigenous people and the revolution, from politically incorrect "Europe-oriented" authors, such as Jorge Luis Borges in Argentina. However, in the 1980s and later, it became increasingly obvious that this "genuine Latin American literature" was an export product that merely served the exotic dreams of frustrated post-1968 Europeans; it had, in fact, lost touch with the reality of Latin American societies, excluding their marginalized indigenous cultures, living in sprawling megacities and burdened by economic problems and the overwhelming influence of US media in the context of dictatorial regimes.

By the 1970s Latin American cultural theory (and in the 1990s, Latin American literature, too) had emancipated itself not only from these essentialist myths but also from the cultural theory models of the center (Europe and the United States), and developed new creative theories based on poststructuralist concepts by Deleuze (mapping, rhizome) and Derrida (dissemination), and Foucault's theory of discourse. Anticipating Bhabha's concept of hybridity, these theorists invoked, for instance, cultural "heterogeneity" and a "multiplicity of logics," which questioned the essentialist ideas as *one* reason, *one* modernity, or even *one mestizaje*. This movement was shared by new groups of literary authors protesting against the *macondismo,* the image of the continent created by writers of magical realism, authors who became well-known internationally through groups such as McOndo or Crack in the late 1990s.

On both theoretical and literary grounds, Latin American identities therefore no longer appear as a fusion of ethnic and cultural identities, but rather as a marketplace of negotiations between various overlapping and sometimes intertwined social, ethnic, religious, or cultural groups with a lack of linearity in space and time. This is an image that I think closely resembles what the Habsburg Central European situation was like before the century of ethnic cleansing, and in some aspects still is. However, this "marketplace of negotiations," both here and there, has been made to look as if it is lagging behind in relation to the "project of modernity" presented by the so-called center. It may well be, however—and I think Viennese culture around 1900 is a good example of this—that real dynamism stems not from the centers but from the tensions created by the simultaneity of the nonsimultaneous in so-called peripheral areas.

Indeed, another parallel, specifically with regard to the situation in Habsburg Central Europe, is the dynamics of peripheral cultures. Latin America's struggle to join the universe of discourse began in the sixteenth and early seventeenth centuries and continued into the twentieth century. It has led to a rhizomic situation of overlapping discourses and aesthetics, a patchwork culture with highly original structures of communication between small groups of intellectuals on the one hand (meeting in coffeehouses, for instance)[11] and an open-field structure (to use Pierre Bourdieu's terminology) on the other, in which elite and popular cultures are not as far apart as they were in Bourdieu's object of investigation, that is, late nineteenth-century France. After the period of essentialist proclamation of *mestizaje* as a symbol of its identity and its quest for global human development, Latin America's cultural theory over the past few decades has become more modest and more open-minded: with its conceptual innovations in media culture, hybridity, and fragmentation, it might go some way toward describing similar situations in Central Europe, too. If, at the fall of the Iron Curtain, it seemed there would be only one model of modernity (as appears to be the case also in the political discourse of the "war between cultures"), Latin American thinkers since the 1980s have concluded that "by reaching the hegemony, Western culture has simultaneously lost the monopoly of modernity" (to quote the Chilean sociologist José Joaquín Brunner in 1985).[12] Brunner, therefore, also refutes the myth of a paradise lost of "original purity and authenticity" and evokes for Latin American culture the image of a "broken mirror" reflecting myriad facets of popular and high-brow culture, of commercial and folklore culture, without any possibility of structuring or "ordering" them to achieve progress, a goal, or at least one particular direction.

Similarly, the Colombian media scientist Jesús Martín-Barbero preaches "de-totalization," replacing the search for a national or continental identity with a conflictive relationship between historical and contemporary elements in a "third space," an "in-between," operating a "de-territorialization" (Deleuze) of peripheral folklore or popular culture elements as a whole and their "re-territorialization" in the center.[13]

New Latin American cultural theory is international and transdisciplinary: the Argentine critic Beatriz Sarlo first investigated the coexistence of various stages of development in Latin American "modern" societies in her study on Buenos Aires culture in the 1920s and 1930s ("a peripheral modernity");[14] Argentine-born Mexican anthropologist Néstor García Canclini introduced the concept of hybridity (*culturas híbridas*)[15] to describe a cultural situation created by the new communication technologies, a new entwinement of public and private sectors in the urban space, and by what he calls the "deterritorialization of symbolic processes." Already in the preceding generation, Latin American philosophers such as Leopoldo Zea had declared a "spiritual independence" from the European tradition of thinking, creating a Latin American school of philosophy aimed at "transcending Occidental logocentrism by means of dialogue."[16]

So in a nutshell, we could synthesize the main trends in Latin American cultural theory as follows:

1. There is no possibility of nation building molded on the example of "pure" Western European nations; there is no longer *one* model of modernity,

civilization, or development. Not even the essentialization of mixture (*mestizaje*) can be used as a substitute for lost purity, even though this had been the "continental identity model" for at least five decades during the twentieth century.
2. Consequently, there are no "developed" or "developing" societies, merely civilizations characterized by the concurrence of fragments that can be seen—subject to the observer's position—as the simultaneity of the non-simultaneous; this concurrence cannot be conceived as harmonious but more or less as a conflictive negotiation of culture conceived not as a state but as a process.
3. In this process, cultural memories have an important role, but again, they are part of a conflictive negotiation, not a harmonizing unification into a kind of national or supranational collective, static identity.

If we are to try out these principles as a basis for developing a European identity model, then we must accept the fact that we have lost the "goal" of progress; in return, we have gained space in which to negotiate our cultural identities. We can no longer accept linear concepts of development—be they Marxist or democratic—toward one (central) model of culture—and that may be the parallel with postcolonial thinkers within US academia. As for Europe, it will be important not only to "include" the new members of the European Union and candidate members, ordering them to align themselves with the development models, but to open up to all the elements—historical and contemporary—of its heterogeneous, impure richness of culture. The conception of European identity as a supranational identity (that is to say, a fusion of national identities) definitely seems foredoomed. I am afraid we shall have to accept the marketplace, or *piazza,* as the Italians say.

As the Latin American example shows, this is not equivalent to some essentialist model of fusion, amalgamation, or mixture, a form of European *mestizaje* that might even be regarded as the ethnic outcome of European migrations following the freedom of settlement or contacts created by exchange programs for students and young people such as Erasmus, Leonardo, and others. The marketplace is not a static, homogeneous unit; it is a dynamic entity of negotiating people from different parts whose common identity stems precisely from what they do: for many centuries they have had the tradition of coming together and negotiating (obviously not in the economic sense). It is this tradition that shapes their common character, not some obscure metaphysical basis. But are there traces of a conception such as this in the Habsburg Central European tradition? After all, we cannot presume to deduce new concepts of European identity purely from Latin American models. In fact, I believe we can find similar elements of identity formed through an awareness of togetherness in many instances in the Habsburg Monarchy after 1815, when (linguistic) nation building began and many people were forced to reflect on their (in-between) condition. Some years ago the Institute of Culture Studies and Theatre History of the Austrian Academy of Sciences organized a conference on the "Baroque as *lieu de mémoire*," reflecting on the role of the Austrian and Central European Baroque (always bearing in mind that the term itself was invented in the nineteenth century) in the collective memory of people living in this geographical area, and I had the occasion to point out some interesting parallels with the situation in Latin America.[17] In fact, Latin American writers, too, have oscillated between the concepts of *mestizaje*, translated in the aesthetic formulas of "magical realism" (*realismo mágico* or *lo real maravilloso americano*) and a notion of "Baroque" as a genuine expression of Latin American identity. The Cuban novelist Alejo Carpentier, who coined the phrase "real maravilloso americano," even postulated a certain synonymy between the two concepts: "And why is Latin America the promised land of the baroque? Because all symbiosis, all *mestizaje*, gives rise to baroqueness."[18]

On the other hand, there is no denying the fact that the Baroque style in architecture must be seen as one of the common characteristics of Central European countries, a fact that led to the adoption of the Baroque as the "Austrian national style" in the last decades of the Habsburg Monarchy.[19] It is also interesting to note that in those same years, the concept of *mestizo* appeared polemically in the discussion of Austrian identity. In his book *Österreichischer Genius* (1906), which looks at the "Baroque" character of the Viennese, the famous critic Hermann Bahr cites the invectives used against Viennese people, who are called *Mestizzos* and *Mischlinge* (crossbreeds) because they "only ever do things in half measures, they are only playing, everything is just fun and games for them."[20]

Indeed, after Austria's defeat in the war against Prussia in 1867, when the Habsburg Central European giant was forced to find a new collective identity, a narrative opposed to the German nationalist narrative, *mestizaje* concepts appeared in various publications, whether of a scientific or literary nature. In 1883, for instance, the scholar Friedrich Umlauft referred to the Austro-Hungarian Monarchy as "the most variegated mixture of ethnicities you are likely to find in Europe," not only because of the fact that, at that time and by his definition of "nations," there were "twelve different nationalities" with "five different religions" within its territory, but also because of the "entwined territorial realities" that led to "strange mixtures," rather than the peoples referred to living in "rigidly enclosed and separated areas."[21]

We find an analogous objective in the major identity-building project of these years, the *Kronprinzenwerk* initiated by the emperor's son Rudolf in 1885, which was aimed at showcasing the variety of landscapes, climates, religions, and ethnicities of the monarchy.[22] However, the prologue insists less on the mixtures (obviously because of Hungary's opposition to recognizing the ethnic heterogeneity of their territory) than on interdependence, presenting the purpose of the twenty-four planned volumes thus: to show the "advantages and particularities of the various ethnographical [*sic*] groups and their reciprocal and material interdependence."[23]

Hugo von Hofmannsthal, in trying to find an identity for the small new state that had survived World War I and had to be contrasted with a pan-German linguistic identity, even dared to compare this "mixed" Austrian identity with identities in the Americas: "there is in our national character, both the German and the Slavic, a great deal of the young and the untapped, and here again can be heard the idea of a European America."[24] However, these trends have always been defensive in nature, emerging from a context of growing nationalism and the establishment of myths of ethnic purity and racism, but also from a context of geopolitical "rights" to territories founded in historical claims (a concept that remains to this day, as the example of Kosovo shows). While parallels with Latin American trends are evident, there is never a comprehensive essentialist myth of "Habsburg Central European crossbreeding" that could have served as the basis for a concept of identity. On the other hand, such myths have a tendency to appear as counterdiscourses once national (or supranational) unities have been realized—let us cite the example of Istria trying to find a different transnational identity within the new national state of Croatia or the trends toward creating a Habsburg Central European identity in Ukraine's Lviv, as opposed to Eastern Ukraine (and its purer Slavic identity).[25] But counterdiscourses are counterdiscourses—they never became as essentialist and homogeneous as the *mestizaje* discourse was in Latin America during the "boom" years of Latin American literature.

And so it would seem that it might be possible to pass directly from the Habsburg Central European discourses to the period of critically balanced representation of hybrid cultural situations as we have found it in the new theory discourses in Latin America. In fact, even the results of modern historical investigation of Habsburg Central Europe reveal a hybrid cultural situation and do not shy away from using the term *mestizaje*, as Csáky, Feichtinger, Karoshi, and Munz have done in the prologue to their volume *Pluralitäten, Heterogenitäten, Differenzen* (2004):

> [S]traight away, therefore, hybrid relations (creolization, mestizaje, crossover) also dominated the scene. This confusion manifested itself in social reality in, amongst others, the fact that for a long time there was no compulsory model of individual cultural belonging: neither "either-or" identities nor "single" identities.[26]

This situation of neither/nor, of nondecision in a transitional situation, obviously invites us to refer to poststructuralistic and even postcolonial theories. It is perhaps not a sheer coincidence that Jean-François Lyotard located the first instances of the "delegitimization" of what he calls the *grands récits* in 1900 Vienna and Habsburg Central Europe,[27] and that it has become more and more acceptable to apply—judiciously adapted—postcolonial theories to the analysis of Habsburg Central European literature and cultural phenomena,[28] a fact that seems to constitute another parallel with the Latin American development in cultural theory.

But let us return to our starting point. We have been searching for ways of conceiving transnational, hybrid, mixed identities within a defined territory—that is, Europe—and looking for potential models in Latin American and Central European culture. As always, we did not find a patent remedy ready to be applied; however, we did encounter a number of pitfalls we need to avoid. We said that it was obvious that Europe cannot be conceived merely as an accumulation of national identities; on the other hand, our research has shown that it is not possible to conceive it in the opposite sense either, that is to say, through an essentialist myth of a *mestizo* identity that would amalgamate all European ethnicities, religions, and regional particularities into a single European spirit based on common values and a common history. If the Habsburg Central European and Latin American experiences can teach us anything, then surely it must be that we need to find a situation of neither/nor, as discussed above; an identity in progress, one that has no fixed roots, no center or origin, but consists of multiple—rhizomatic—relations between the various ethnic, linguistic, religious, and social groups that cannot be separated other than by force.

Perhaps we should refer back to the definition of identity given by Robert Musil in his famous novel *The Man Without Qualities* (1931) and his "Kakanian" identity, that is to say, the identity forged during the last years of the Austro-Hungarian Monarchy. There he explains that all men have multiple identities, that they have a series of at least nine "characters" that determine their affiliation to various groups; for Kakanians, such an identity is dominated by a tenth "character," the "trace" of passing through the other nine, a "passive Phantasie unausgefüllter Räume" that allows one the freedom to do anything, with one exception: "to take seriously what the other nine characters do"—a void center, therefore, or a space of negotiation that is not overly influenced by the essentialist pretensions of these other characters.

If we learn to accept this situation, we might be able to develop a form of Europeanness that is *inclusive* and not *exclusive,* based on Habsburg Central European experiences of many years ago, a time before Europe was visited by nightmares of national grandeur and ethnic purity. Latin America's new willingness to embrace and exploit a hybrid peripheral situation could provide the impulse to consider European identity no longer as an amalgamation of "pure" national identities but as a means of addressing its incongruities.

Notes

1. It is, therefore, perhaps no coincidence either that, in his famous study, Said contemplates exclusively French and British Orientalism and completely ignores the rather important

traditions of Central European Orientalism represented, among others, by Joseph Freiherr von Hammer-Purgstall and his followers. Edward Said, *Orientalism* (London, 1978).
2. Domingo Faustino Sarmiento, *Facundo: Civilización y Barbarie*, published in *El Progreso* (Santiago, 1845).
3. See Karl Hölz, *Das Fremde, das Eigene, das Andere: Die Inszenierung kultureller und geschlechtlicher Identität in Lateinamerika* (Berlin, 1998).
4. José Enrique Rodó, *Ariel* (Montevideo, 1900).
5. See Robert Fernández Retamar, *Calibán* (Mexico City, 1971).
6. Garcilaso de la Vega el Inca, *Royal commentaries of the Incas and general history of Peru*, Part I (Indianapolis, 2006), 88.
7. See Raquel Chang-Rodríguez, "Coloniaje y conciencia nacional: Garcilaso de la Vega Inca y Felipe Guamán Poma de Ayala," *Caravelle: Cahiers du monde hispanique et luso-brésilien* 38 (1982): 29–43; Aurelio Miro Quesada Sosa, "El Inca Garcilaso de la Vega: El mestizaje racial y cultural," in *Encuentro de dos mundos*, ed. Germán Peralta Rivera (Lima, 1991), 27–49.
8. José Vasconcelos, *La Raza Cósmica: Misión de la raza iberoamericana. Notas de viajes a la América del Sur* (Mexico, 1948), 41.
9. Ricardo Rojas, *"Eurindia. Ensayo de estética sobre las culturas americanas,"* (Buenos Aires, 1951).
10. Michael Rössner, "Ein Blick auf Weltordnungen und Zwischenwelten vom 16. bis zum 20. Jahrhundert," in Alfonso de Toro, ed., *Andersheit: Von der Eroberung bis zu New World Borders: das Eigene und das Fremde: Globalisierungs-und Hybriditätsstrategien in Lateinamerika* (Hildesheim, 2008), 41–60.
11. See Michael Rössner, ed., *Literarische Kaffeehäuser: Kaffeehausliteraten* (Vienna, 1999).
12. José Joaquín Brunner, *Un espejo trizado: Ensayos sobre cultura y políticas culturales* (Santiago de Chile, 1988).
13. See Jesús Martín-Barbero, *De los medios a las mediaciones: Comunicación, cultura y hegemonía* (Mexico City, 1987), published in English as *Communication, Culture, and Hegemony: From the Media to Mediations*, trans. Elizabeth Fox and Robert A. White, with an introduction by Philip Schlesinger (London, 1993).
14. See Beatriz Sarlo, *Una modernidad periférica: Buenos Aires 1920 y 1930* (Buenos Aires, 1988).
15. See Néstor García Canclini, *Culturas híbridas: Estrategias para entrar y salir de la modernidad* (Mexico City, 1990).
16. See Leopoldo Zea, *En torno a una filosofía americana* (Mexico, 1945), 17 and passim.
17. See Michael Rössner, "Barock als Element mitteleuropäischer und lateinamerikanischer Identität—Überlegungen zur Konstruktion und 'Innenausstattung' von Gedächtnisorten," in *Barock: Ein Ort des Gedächtnisses. Interpretament der Moderne/Postmoderne*, ed. Moritz Csáky, Federico Celestini, and Ulrich Tragatschnig (Vienna, 2007), 47–64.
18. Alejo Carpentier, "The Baroque and the Marvelous Real," in *Magical Realism: Theory, History, Community*, ed. Lois Parkinson Zamora and Wendy B. Faris (Durham, NC, 1995), 89–108. First published as "Lo barroco y lo real maravilloso," in *Rázon de ser* (Caracas, 1976). See also Cesar Augusto Salgado, "Hybridity in New World Baroque Theory," in *The Journal of American Folklore* 112, no. 445 (Summer 1999): 316–31.
19. See Peter Stachel, "Alfred Ilg und die 'Erfindung' des Barocks als österreichischer 'Nationalstil,'" in Csáky, Celestini, and Tragatschnig, *Barock*, 101–51.
20. See Hermann Bahr, *Österreichischer Genius* (Vienna, 1906), 112.
21. Friedrich Umlauft, *Die Österreichisch-Ungarische Monarchie: Geographisch-statistisches Handbuch mit besonderer Rücksicht auf politische und Cultur-Geschichte* (Vienna, 1883), 2.
22. Rudolf, Crown Prince of Austria, ed., *Die Oesterreichisch-Ungarische Monarchie in Wort und Bild: Auf Anregung und unter Mitwirkung weiland seiner kaiserl. und königl. Hoheit des durchlauchtigsten Kronprinzen Erzherzog Rudolf begonnen, fortgesetzt unter dem Protectorate*

Ihrer kaiserl. und königl. Hoheit der durchlauchtigsten Frau Kronprinzessin-Witwe Erzherzogin Stephanie, 24 vols. (Vienna, 1886–1902).
23. Rudolf, Crown Prince of Austria, "Einleitung," in Rudolf, ed., *Die Österreichisch-Ungarische Monarchie in Wort und Bild,* vol. 1 (Vienna, 1886), 5.
24. Hugo von Hofmannsthal, "Wir Österreicher und Deutschland," in *Gesammelte Werke,* vol. 2, *Reden und Aufsätze,* ed. Bernd Schoeller and Rudolf Hirsch (Frankfurt, 1979), 394.
25. See Pamela Ballinger, *History in Exile: Memory and Identity at the Borders of the Balkans* (Princeton, NJ: 2002); Jurko Prochasko, "Die Sarmatische Zivilisation," in *Sarmatische Landschaften: Nachrichten aus Litauen, Belarus, der Ukraine, Polen und Deutschland,* ed. Martin Pollack (Frankfurt, 2005), 233–48.
26. See Moritz Csáky et al., "Pluralitäten, Heterogenitäten, Differenzen. Zentraleuropas Paradigmen für die Moderne," in *Kultur—Identität—Differenz: Wien und Zentraleuropa in der Moderne,* Gedächtnis—Erinnerung—Identität 4, ed. Moritz Csáky, Astrid Kury, and Ulrich Tragatschnig (Innsbruck, 2004), 20.
27. Jean-François Lyotard, *La condition postmoderne* (Paris, 1979), 121–22.
28. See Johannes Feichtinger, Ursula Prutsch, and Moritz Csáky, eds., *Habsburg Postcolonial: Machtstrukturen und kollektives Gedächtnis,* Gedächtnis—Erinnerung—Identität 2 (Innsbruck, 2003); Clemens Ruthner, "'K.(u.)K. Postcolonial?' Für eine neue Lesart der österreichischen (und benachbarter) Literatur/en," in *Kakanien Revisited: Das Eigene und das Fremde (in) der österreichisch-ungarischen Monarchie,* Kultur—Herrschaft—Differenz 1, ed. Wolfgang Müller-Funk, Peter Plener, and Clemens Ruthner (Tübingen, 2002), 93–103.

Chapter 3

Do Multiple Languages Mean a Multicultural Society?
Nationalist "Frontiers" in Rural Austria, 1880–1918

Pieter M. Judson

At the turn of the last century, Czech, German, Slovene, and Italian nationalist activists worked hard to delineate the social and cultural boundaries they claimed separated their national communities from each other in the western regions of Imperial Austria where more than one language was spoken. Their ambivalent and often frustrating experiences suggest that beliefs about national difference actually had to be imported to these rural regions. In many localities where pluricultural practices had long characterized daily life, local perceptions of difference did not always rest on the experience of different language usage, nor did such differences by themselves produce conflict.[1] Rural life in Austria certainly had its share of social conflicts, but those conflicts were not often produced by a prior sense of belonging to one nation or another or by a sense of profound victimization based on one's own language use. Nor does the evidence suggest that local differences in language use had traditionally led to skirmishes within rural communities in multilingual regions.[2] Activists' assertions about the profound nationalist significance of linguistic differences did not reflect deeply rooted cultural conflict or even significant local power differentials between alleged national groups in the rural world. In fact, nationalist claims ran counter to the logic of local social practice in such regions. Instead of giving political voice to existing cultural differences in rural Austria, as nationalists claimed they did, their rhetoric constituted an attempt to *create* new social boundaries in multilingual communities precisely where few such boundaries had traditionally existed.

The cumulative effect over time of repeated nationalist campaigns, the proliferation of nationalist media, and the increased presence of nationalist organizations did produce a normalization of nationalist discourses in rural communities, just as they had in urban centers of the monarchy. There is no question that in the early twentieth century nationalist views not only suffused debate in local elected or administrative institutions but also shaped the attitudes of local elites: writers, applied artists, engineers, and pub owners (to name a few) in rural regions of Habsburg Central Europe. Local populations, in turn, often learned to use the rhetoric of nation during the interwar period in order to legitimize their particular demands on the state. Whether these populations became nationalized in the ways hoped for by nationalist activists, however, remains far less clear. The very fact that individuals and communities increasingly turned opportunistically to nationalist rhetoric as an instrument to advance different agendas suggests that at least until the mid-twentieth century, nationalist loyalties were never as deeply rooted as were other social and cultural forms of self-identification, such as religious or regional ones.

Social scientists and historians who examine the twentieth-century histories of multilingual regions of Central and Eastern Europe frequently see the situation much differently, often presuming that linguistic diversity in the region actually signified the presence of different cultures. These alleged language-based cultures, so the story goes, eventually produced different national societies in the twentieth century. This presumption greatly underestimates the enormous labor undertaken by nineteenth- and twentieth-century local nationalist activists to realize this outcome, and it greatly overestimates the degree to which this national outcome was actually obtained. According to such narratives, language use assumes a significant quality of individuation, serving as a marker to define communities, rather than being a contingent instrument whose purpose is communication. The fact that more than one language was spoken in a given rural region does not mean that each language constituted an identity that even loosely defined a group.[3] Following recent work by sociologist Rogers Brubaker, this chapter argues that instead of eliding language-based identities with the people who used those languages, we should understand them primarily as situational means of communication in rural Austria among people whose level of education rarely went beyond primary schooling. Those languages may well have served as the ideological bases for mass national group identities during the nineteenth century, but it would be a mistake to confuse those who spoke a language with those who belonged to a nation defined by the use of that language. As we know from Gary Cohen's pioneering work on Czech and German speakers in nineteenth-century Prague, the choice to identify with one language community or another among the lowest classes of society in multilingual settings depended crucially on the existence of language-based social networks and institutions in communities and neighborhoods. German-speaking workers who moved to predominantly Czech-speaking neighborhoods, for example, often came to use the Czech language (thereby "becoming" Czechs in the eyes of nationalists), unless some local social institution offered them a different option. More and more frequently, it was nationalist neighborhood organizations that tried to offer such options to immigrants, enabling them to join in local social life without having to learn a different language. Not surprisingly, however, this nationalist option of not having to learn the "other" language could often produce the opposite effect: the desire to have one's children learn both languages to give them even more options in the future. Functional bilingualism was not necessarily a remnant of a premodern age but rather a situational strategy meant to increase one's life chances in a given society.[4]

The ethnicist approach, as Jeremy King dubbed scholars' confusion of language use with group solidarity, has also predisposed scholars to refer to Austrian society as "multicultural," less in its descriptive sense then in a troubling analytic one.[5] It is clearly true that people spoke different languages in several regions of the empire. But does the use of several languages make a society in fact multicultural? In using this term analytically scholars imagine that the use of different languages in Austrian society implies the existence of separate ethnic cultures, defined and differentiated primarily on the basis of language use. Given this assumption about Austrian society, the challenge to imperial institutions is usually understood as a search for the right set of administrative and legal structures to accommodate the different ethnic groups who lived, not in separate territories, but often dispersed among each other. This way of understanding Austrian society results less from the reality of multilanguage usage but more from the claims made by nationalists themselves that such differences were significant for most Austrians. The ability of nationalist parties and movements to dominate political agendas and rhetoric at every level of administration and government made it appear as if Austrian society indeed consisted of self-defined national cultures, each seeking a fair degree of political autonomy for itself and each asserting its right to equal treatment from the state. While there were certainly many nationalists to be found in Austrian society, there is less evidence for the existence of the mass nations in whose name the nationalists claimed to speak, especially when we examine the rural world.

The power of nationalist rhetoric at every level of politics was not a product of some kind of reality of conflicting nations. On the contrary, as some scholars have recently argued, nationalist politics functioned to constitute the very nations it claimed to represent. The increasing predominance of specifically nationalist conflict in Austrian political life was also a product of the particular political opportunities Austria's constitutional structure offered its citizens for political activism. The constitutional clauses that articulated the fundamental equality of language use were, like many constitutional clauses, at once sweeping in the scope of their basic promise and vague about the specific realms of public life or the extent to which they could be applied. This gap created considerable space for activism among political groups eager to extend and broaden the application of those constitutional guarantees. Nationalist parties pursued agendas that cast the equality of language use in public life as a symbol for several popular and populist causes. Without such equality in this or that realm of public life, how could a people develop to its fullest extent? Nationalist parties built their programs around achieving or protecting the rights of certain languages in different regions (e.g., the rights of individuals to use their language in communications with the state administration, the need for provincial administrators to have a working knowledge of those languages, the provision of adequate schooling in those languages, first at the primary and middle level, later at the secondary and university level, the provision of bilingual street or railway signs, and so on).[6] Still another influential set of Austrian laws also helped nationalist parties to build constituencies and power bases around questions of local rights to determine many practical matters of language use. Strong communal autonomy laws assigned many (but not all) local administrative functions to village, municipal, and regional councils directly elected by local voters. This, too, made it easier for nationalist parties to assert their social, economic, and political programs in terms of the extension or protection of the national language at the local level.[7]

If political and legal structures helped make nationalism a prime issue in the development of mass politics, several historians have also pointed out an important internal function of nationalist rhetoric in the development of popular political parties in Austria. In the 1880s and 1890s, nationalist rhetoric became more radical in tone and substance, making it appear increasingly unlikely that different nationalist movements could find common ground with each other in the maintenance of an Austrian state. Yet as these historians point out, this radicalizing dimension had far less to do with irreconcilable conflicts among alleged nations and everything to do with struggles internal to expanding political movements. By the 1880s, staking out an uncompromisingly radical nationalist position had become an effective strategic means to burnish one's own political credentials at the expense of a rival's credibility *within* a nationalist party. Much of the nationalist rhetoric about difference, which scholars view as proof of irreconcilable conflict among nations, was in fact directed inward to the national community itself rather than outward against the national enemy.[8]

In rural Austria nationalists often found it necessary to do more for the local public than simply specify the alleged differences that separated various nations. They worked hard to make concepts of cultural difference relevant to rural Austrians in multilingual communities, struggling to give meaning to the national community itself. Local nationalists often found it as difficult to disseminate a coherent set of national values and cultural practices within their communities as it was to create effective and lasting stereotypes about national others. Belonging to a nation meant not only sharing a common linguistic heritage but also adhering to a set of standard norms in behavior. As arbiters of those norms, nationalist activists assigned themselves considerable influence in local communities to determine appropriate behavior. What happened, however, when alleged members of a national community refused to live up to its norms, or even rejected its relevance to their lives? As we will see, the very tensions created by the demands of nationalist ideologies on the one hand and people's lived social experience on the other helped to radicalize nationalist activists. It also made local people aware of the considerable opportunities nationalist discourses and practices offered them as they attempted to navigate the changing and often confusing terrain of a modernizing world. When local people adopted elements of nationalist reasoning to advance their own agendas, however, they did not necessarily become nationalists themselves. They merely recognized the opportunities nationalist language afforded them to pursue their interests more effectively.

New Forms of Activism

In the mid-nineteenth century, nationalist activism had remained largely confined to urban spaces and to middle-class people. Early nationalist associations were linked closely to political movements and institutions that tended to be dominated by better-educated and moneyed elites. Associations generally attracted those people to their ranks who had the right to vote in municipal or regional elections, still a relatively small percentage of the male population in Austria. Early nationalist associations promoted political reform programs, such as greater political autonomy for a given region, the legitimation of a particular vernacular language in administrative practice, or the creation of more cultural and educational institutions to serve speakers of a particular language. The public settings where nationalist activism took place also remained highly limited in scope, as did Austrian political life in general: the imperial parliament, the provincial diets, and the municipal councils. In some cities nationalist political rhetoric reached broader social milieus, especially given the democratizing influence of the expanding media and its coverage of domestic politics during this period. Nevertheless, nationalist political leaders tended to treat the broader masses more as a passive audience for their political rhetoric, rather than as partners in the promotion of reform. At election time the enfranchised might ratify the positions articulated by political leaders, but their participation in the nationalist movement did not extend much further than this. Similarly, nationalist ideologies during this period focused more generally on the history and high cultural accomplishments of the nation as a justification for broadening or protecting a language's status in public life, rather than on more populist or democratic qualities.

As I have argued elsewhere, German nationalist efforts in this period tended to be limited to statements of cultural superiority grounded in historical, literary, and artistic achievements.[9] These assertions produced a sense of nation defined by an objectively advanced culture of science and the arts, one that remained theoretically open to all those who sought higher levels of education and self-cultivation. Early German nationalist politicians in Austria associated themselves with the mission of the central state and played down the notion that the German nation might have a set of specific interests that diverged from the interests of the whole. For this reason, German nationalism did not associate itself with a particular set of territories in Austria, for example, but instead saw itself as a broad and dominant cultural force throughout the monarchy, committed to maintaining the power and prestige of the central state. Czech nationalism, by contrast, associated itself closely with the historic crown lands of Bohemia and Moravia. Locating national identity firmly in a revived Czech language and in the cultural renaissance that language had experienced in the nineteenth century, Czech nationalists argued strongly for territorial autonomy in those regions where they believed their nation constituted a majority of the people. Czech nationalists asserted their own cultural superiority over their German neighbors, figuring the latter historically as interlopers and foreign colonists, and attributing a democratic impulse to their own traditions of political culture.[10] The point is that early on both nationalist movements, as different as they were in their ideological particulars, nevertheless focused their energies on mobilizing the small political classes and cultural elites for their programs. Neither movement sought broad political input or support from the peasantry or working classes, for example, nor felt particularly compelled to mobilize a mass base for its efforts.

The character of these nationalist movements began to change radically (the Czech movement in the 1860s and 1870s, the German movement in the 1870s and 1880s, and the Slovene movement in the 1890s) as more Austrians gradually became enfranchised and political survival required the mobilization of as many supporters as possible at all levels of society. The most important transformations involved the character of nationalist organizational activism. The 1880s saw the founding of several nationalist associations whose aims moved well beyond explicitly political issues to transform society broadly through new forms of educational, economic, and social activism. The Czech, German, and Slovene school associations (Matice česká in 1880, Deutscher Schulverein in 1880, and Družba Ciril-Metod in 1885, respectively) are fine examples of this new direction. These associations raised considerable funds to build private, so-called minority schools in areas where Czech-, German-, or Slovene-speaking children constituted such a small minority in the local population that they had no access to state schooling in their own language. The school associations went well beyond traditional goals of representing national interests in the public sphere of politics. They sought to mobilize populations previously outside the world of politics—especially women—by creating ways for them to participate actively in national life. They were also among the first organizations to pay close attention to the distinctive and different needs of rural and urban communities. The school associations raised prodigious sums of money, but, perhaps equally important, they found ways to mobilize people at almost every level of society to participate in some small way in national life, generally through local social activities, nationalist rituals, and through incessant fund-raising efforts. The school associations painted a zero-sum picture in which a victimized nation threatened by demographic attrition through assimilation required new efforts to retain its most vulnerable members, those at the bottom of society whose dependence made them helpless to withstand the denationalizing efforts of cruel bosses, manipulative landlords, and influential schoolteachers. These lower classes—and especially their children—were in danger of losing their very nationality, and activism must find ways to fortify their national will.[11]

The school associations were soon followed by other kinds of nationalist associations that focused their efforts on strengthening the economic and demographic position of their nation at the local level. The Böhmerwaldbund, the four regional Czech nationalist associations in Bohemia, and the Südmark all sought to maintain and expand the local position of the nations in whose interests they claimed to work, offering their less affluent conationals financial credits, job training, adult education, small local libraries, festivals, and a regular social life organized around national identity. Because these associations were categorized as nonpolitical, they could legally mobilize women into their ranks. Soon many women joined, developing new forms of activism and often creating separate women's branches. Probably the most successful aspect of this transformation involved the adaptation of essentially consumerist tactics to nationalist needs. Just as the proliferation of consumer advertising in public tended to blur the older belief in a separate private sphere, so too did nationalist activists develop tactics to make national identity into an all-consuming element of personal self-identification, something that would operate at all times and not simply when the individual was acting as citizen.

The 1880s and 1890s had witnessed a fundamental transformation of the nature and scope of nationalist activism, from a narrowly and politically based elite phenomenon to one that sought to mobilize many more social groups and to influence every conceivable realm of life, especially areas previously regarded as private and thus off-limits to activism. These new nationalist associations also received considerable support from an expanding regional print media in the 1890s that catered to increasing numbers of people in more out-of-the-way regions. As we will see, newspapers were critical allies of the nationalist movements, especially those newspapers that framed local and international events in a particularly nationalist rhetoric. Newspapers not only confirmed, reinforced, and normalized nationalist interpretations of the news, but they also lavished attention on the activities of the nationalist associations, making their activism a legitimate form of news and elevating their social and cultural importance for local communities. Nationalist organizations also published their own illustrated magazines, journals, and popular farmers' almanacs. They reported on detailed elements of the nationalist struggle, interspersing news items with entertaining literary works of nationalist fiction and poetry, works that emphasized themes of national difference and the necessity of separation. The magazines also welcomed readers' own shared experiences of the national struggle, and their editors worked creatively to involve more and more aspects of personal life in the greater drama of the nation. In particular, they attempted to influence several kinds of consumer habits on a trial and error basis, such as shopping preferences (boycotts were technically illegal), hiring practices, summer vacation options, and real estate transactions.

Still another technical development that strongly shaped the options pursued by nationalist activists was the institution of the decennial census. In 1880, the same year that saw the founding of the Czech and German school associations, the Austrian government undertook the first regular census that attempted to measure language use in the empire. The Austrian constitution did not recognize nations as legitimate actors in the law,[12] and the government determined after lengthy internal debate to query respondents about their language of daily use rather than about their national identity or even their mother tongue. The state's insistence that respondents report only a single language of daily use made the census blind to the extent of regional bilingualism, a fact that further complicates matters for historians.[13] Nationalist activists in Austria had, of course, urged categories like mother tongue or nationality on the government instead of language of daily use, but they, too, were silent about the census's inability to measure bilingualism, a phenomenon they preferred to ignore and hoped would die out.[14] Whatever their reservations, nationalists of all stripes immediately treated this decennial census as a critical weapon in their arsenal, refusing to accept that language of daily use measured anything other than national belonging.[15]

The decennial census strongly influenced nationalist activism in several key ways. It helped to produce a growing territorialization of nations within the empire because it enabled activists for the first time to plot their alleged demographic strengths and weaknesses geographically. If the use of one language had made inroads at the expense of another in the past ten years, for example, it was now easy to say exactly where that erosion had taken place. Especially in the case of German nationalists who had previously identified themselves with the state as a whole, the census outcome radically altered perceptions of the German nation's position in the empire. German nationalists spoke increasingly of particular territories rather than of the state as a whole, and they now worked to create a perception among people of the fundamental similarity that linked various and diverse German-speaking populations from Vorarlberg in the west to Bukovina in the east, from Silesia in the north to Bosnia in the south. At the same time, the census results also lent a greater legitimacy to the kind of territorial-based claims for national political autonomy long advocated by Czech nationalists, who tied their social advancement specifically to the increased use of their language in the public life of Bohemia and Moravia. If Czech were the language spoken by a great majority of Bohemians and Moravians, then Czech should take its place beside German as an official administrative language for those provinces as well.[16] Czech speakers should have equal—if not greater—access to secondary- and university-level education in their own language as German speakers in Bohemia and Moravia did. The Kingdom of Bohemia should be understood as a fundamentally Czech national kingdom within the larger Habsburg imperial framework, albeit one that also housed a German-speaking minority. Equally importantly, however, what Czech nationalists viewed as the regional particularist attitudes that often characterized politics in neighboring Moravia should give way to a broader common Czech nationalist identity.

It is worth considering for a moment the question of what exactly was being depicted when nationalists mapped their nations onto specific territories, especially in a linguistically diverse society like Austria. When nationalists used the census results to plot what they considered to be the exact boundaries of their nations, a critical slippage occurred between their own understanding of what it meant to use a language, and the alleged national self-identification of those who reported one language or another in the census. Nationalists, of course, claimed that the mapping of languages portrayed graphically the national loyalties of the individuals who inhabited various territories, loyalties expressed to census takers. Did the reporting of language on the census really constitute a confession of deeper national loyalty? To nationalists, the very fact of different language usage proved the coexistence of separate and distinct cultures—in fact, of nations. Nevertheless, we should remember that those who did the actual reporting might well have harbored a very different understanding of the significance of language use. Language maps based crudely on the results of the imperial census continue to serve as powerful tools that can legitimate and normalize the alleged existence of nations in Central and Eastern Europe around 1900.

Not surprisingly, the nationalists' fascination with the census drew their attention to those locales where their numbers could potentially be improved upon or might suffer decline. The census, and the territorialization of the nation it had helped to produce, thus also helped create the concept of the language frontier, a conceptual border region where people who spoke different languages lived in close proximity to each other. Such regions swiftly became the objects of increased nationalist attention, especially in election years or when the census was taken. Nationalists soon measured the effectiveness of their long-term efforts according to the outcomes of the decennial census or of local election results precisely in those regions that they had identified as language frontiers.

The Language Frontier

> From time immemorial, the Bjelounka [river] had served as a clear frontier between the Czech and the German people, between the Slavic lowlands and the [German] highlands. The triangle that it formed with the Elbe and with the border [to the north] was so completely German, that even the boatmen didn't know how to say water in Slavic. He could not even order a beer on the other bank of the river except in German. To the north the German region stretched as far as the border, while to the south, Blatna's tollhouse was the last piece of German soil; even the [statue of] St. John Nepomuk on the bridge would have spoken Czech, if silence had not been his lot.
>
> Fritz Mauthner, *Der letzte Deutsche von Blatna*[17]

As an ideological construct, illustrated by the above quotation from Fritz Mauthner's 1913 novel, the concept of a language frontier embodied the nationalist belief in the existence of national communities separated by recognizable differences. According to nationalist logic, in places where the use of different languages bordered each other, larger national differences between them ought to be most striking. And yet, when they encountered the reality of life in such regions, nationalists often fretted that the frontiers between nations were in fact dangerously porous. Inhabitants of such regions seemed not to notice that they belonged to different nations, and they rarely engaged consistently in self-conscious practices of national separation. The nationalist use of the term language frontier to describe places where two languages were spoken often served to produce the very effect that it was understood to describe in the first place: a border between two distinct cultures. The use of the term was also part of a larger strategy meant to change the very ways in which people thought about themselves, their homes, and their communities, rather than a way of actually describing them. It offered nationalists a means to create a negative sense of multiculturalism in regions where linguistic differences had not previously conveyed significant cultural difference. The nationalist mission in such regions was the creation of greater local consciousness about national identity and the strengthening of boundaries between nations.

Plenty of literary, journalistic, and political writings already portrayed Austria as culturally divided into several nations, each defined primarily by its different language. But these mainly literary or political efforts conveyed stories about generally distant and abstract situations to their readers, most of whom were, in any case, already convinced nationalists. The challenge to nationalists in the 1880s and 1890s, however, was twofold: (1) to make the language frontier real to its inhabitants and (2) to involve people who lived in more linguistically homogeneous regions more fully in nationalist efforts in frontier regions, especially through financial and volunteer efforts.

A classic example of this attempt to increase popular interest in the obscure language frontiers and their fate was German nationalist demographer Johann Zemmrich's 1902 study of language use in Bohemian society.[18] At the outset, Zemmrich tried to draw his readers' attention away from the obvious nationalist battles that dominated the imperial parliament, seeking to direct it instead to the little-known rural regions he referred to as "language frontiers." It was in these peasant villages, he claimed, that neighboring nations literally jostled up against each other. These unknown and peripheral language frontiers served as the crucial setting for the "little nationalist wars fought daily from village to village," conflicts whose outcome would allegedly determine the ultimate fates of Austria's nations. Zemmrich's description of the rural language frontier conjures an image of tectonic plates and the slowly changing continental fault lines their friction inexorably creates. For him, the nationality conflict in Bohemia, and indeed elsewhere in Austria, had to be understood as a long-term war between spatially defined entities that struggled for control of the liminal zones where they actually bordered each other.

The quality of this national war also had to be understood as different from that of other conflicts. This war was not limited to the realm of politics. It could and should be observable in the most personal of choices, in the context of family life, and even occasionally expressed through the individual's private desires. Consciousness of this war ought to dominate all the various social interactions that made up daily life. And, as we have seen with the census, Zemmrich emphasized a belief that territory won or lost could easily be mapped, that the spatial element in this war actually represented the choices made by individual people, people who were either won or lost to the nation. So Zemmrich's work not only brought the language frontier to German nationalist readers elsewhere in the monarchy, but it also tried to make activists as well as inhabitants of the language frontier regions aware that their every action contained in it a particularly national significance.

If the writings of activists like Zemmrich made the local rural aspects of the nationalist struggle more immediate to urban readers in Vienna, Prague, Graz, or Ljubljana, they also suggested specific forms of activism that would be effective in helping rural people in such regions to act more in the interests of their nation. Zemmrich believed, for example, that the presence of a trusted and authoritative individual in a small rural community (such as a nationalist schoolteacher) made a crucial difference in alerting local peasants to the nationalist implications of their daily decisions. From examples of the censuses of 1880, 1890, and 1900 he sought to show that precisely in areas where activists had managed to maintain a strong presence, losses had been stopped and some gains had been posted.[19] Slovene nationalist A. Beg, who spent several years evaluating the national strengths and weaknesses of Slovene-speaking communities on the Slovene-Italian-German language frontiers, commented repeatedly on the critical importance that an influential local organizer could play in creating and strengthening nationalist consciousness. Beg attributed the relative strength of German nationalism in the region precisely to the efforts of "a small number of innkeepers, railway employees and gendarmes." At the same time he also noted the promising examples of a local Slovene nationalist schoolteacher who had recently founded a choral society, and another who had created a local credit fund.[20] Czech nationalist František Joklík, too, argued that "the local branches of our national unions [in Moravia] owe their existence in the countryside mainly to the activities of teachers."[21]

Nevertheless, the very importance of such white-collar organizers frustrated activists, who hoped that peasants themselves might assume a leading role in nationalist activism. German nationalist activist Viktor Heeger, who researched many of the same regions as the Slovene nationalist Beg, complained in 1905 that "only occasionally do some real natives show up [to my presentations] ... hardly ever farmers or workers. Of the thirty or so people who attend, hardly more than five actually grew up in the place. The rest are all new arrivals, namely, the civil servant, the physician, the lawyer, the teacher, etc."[22] Clearly, the question that continued to haunt nationalist activists well into the twentieth century was how to combat what they viewed as rural apathy, the tendency of peasants and rural villagers to ignore alleged national differences in their social lives.

Indifference to Nation Figured in Terms of Rural Backwardness

When nationalists traveled from the cities to the countryside, as they increasingly did in the 1890s, they often expressed surprise that the nationalist conflicts that they took for granted in Austrian cities and towns did not extend to Austria's rural districts. To them, it seemed as if the country population had not yet caught up to its urban counterparts in its appreciation for the fundamental importance of nationalist conflict to political and social life. Not only that, but early nationalist organizing efforts in rural Austria had largely also failed to establish a successful long-term presence. When the first nationalists arrived in rural out-of-the-way-villages, essentially as outsiders, and attempted to organize the locals into bourgeois forms of association, local apathy often appeared to doom these early efforts. Nationalists noted that even associations that managed to establish themselves in rural regions in the 1880s and 1890s tended to stagnate within a few years, to lose members, and, most importantly, to stop holding meetings. Many local branches of their associations, complained nationalists, existed only on paper.[23]

If nationalist activists reluctantly admitted to themselves the hurdles they faced in building their movements in rural regions, they nevertheless continued to disseminate a public message to their urban followers that praised the peasant as a hearty repository of national virtue. Untainted by urban life (and the degeneracy its leisure activities imparted to the poor), the unspoiled peasant family allegedly embodied the best qualities of the nation. If we confine our analysis to works of nationalist fiction from the period, from almanac stories to novels, we indeed encounter an often-flattering picture of the peasant. The broader function of this enduring image may have had more to do with nationalist concern about the evils of urban life and the specific antiurban values they hoped to propagate as national ones than with any knowledge or experience of rural life. It was only in the pages of organizational reports and occasionally in association magazines that nationalists allowed themselves to wrestle openly with the awkward gap that separated pleasing fantasies from frustrating facts. As writers like Zemmrich pointed out, untutored peasants often intermarried with members of other nations, they sometimes sought bilingual education for their children, they remained depressingly ignorant of their own precious national identity, and they could not be relied upon to act according to nationalist principles, especially at election or census time. These complaints are echoed in associational reports of peasant ingratitude for nationalist support, peasant indifference to nationalist organizational efforts, and even peasant opposition to nationalist community initiatives, such as the founding of new schools.

The only plausible explanation nationalists could find for such behavior lay in the profound ignorance and the relative economic, social, and cultural backwardness they believed characterized rural life. Experiencing rural Austria primarily in terms of this perceived backwardness, nationalists expected that only a vigorous modernization program could create fertile conditions for their message. Uneducated peasants had allegedly become habituated to a life of ignorance and blind obedience to institutions like the church and the nobility. This particular perception of rural life as fundamentally backward caused nationalists to deploy weapons and techniques of mobilization with overtly pedagogic functions. Nationalists of all stripes believed that they would have to use tools of enlightenment—especially the models offered by the secular school system—to bring rural Austrians into a new era. Only then could they learn to value their national identities.

Despite the belief that Austrian rural society was backward, that society was in fact changing rapidly by 1900, especially in the western regions of the empire. Nationalists by themselves could have hardly made any impact on rural communities in the early years of the twentieth century without the revolutionary transformations that were being delivered by new systems of compulsory education and teacher training, the rapid increase in transportation and communications networks, and the state's increasing obligation to raise the social and economic conditions in which its citizens lived. When nationalists decided to bring modernity to rural Austria as a precondition for rooting their organizations, they built on and adapted for themselves several of the institutions that were in fact already transforming rural society. The most important of these, as mentioned above, was the school system.

Viewing education, broadly conceived, as the linchpin of their efforts, activists developed nationalist pedagogies not only to help rural Austrians understand their critical place in their nation's life but also to improve the quality of their lives in economic and cultural terms, and according to their urban, bourgeois, and nationalist standards. As we have already seen, early populist nationalist activism originated with the idea of building and maintaining private minority schools that would educate children in their national language and prevent the evil of denationalization. Within those schools children (and their parents) were constantly reminded of the importance of their language and national identity to their lives. Their reading exercises, the games they played, the wall decorations they saw, the school festivals they participated in each reiterated the importance of national identity, of national heritage, and of the differences that separated nations. And if this were not enough, schools also frequently offered peasant children free meals or gifts of clothing, shoes, books, and toys at Christmas, designed in part to win them and their parents to the nationalist cause. Nationalist associations often treated the local schoolteacher in military terms as a leader on the front line of the nationalist war. They often paid teachers a salary bonus for their service in difficult frontier situations where they might be subjected to threats of national violence. Indeed, teachers in language frontier regions often received a bonus when they took on diverse extra responsibilities in the community besides simply teaching its children.

The teachers' role in building local national society expanded on their core educational functions in the classroom. Nationalist teachers in Bohemia and Moravia also served as librarians for the local people's libraries that offered entertaining and educational nationalist fare to their clients. Rural schoolteachers often served as informal loan officers for local nationalist credit unions in some regions, or as the organizers of reading societies, discussion clubs, adult education groups, lecture series, and patriotic nationalist public celebrations. When local nationalists raised a monument to Jan Hus or Joseph II, for example, the schoolteacher often led the consecration ritual, explaining to onlookers the significance of the national figure whose stone likeness would now dominate the village square. Provincial nationalist organizations also attempted to strengthen their local rural branches by combining them into formal networks so that they could both reinforce each other's activism and create a sense of a broader community that linked local villages in a regional identity. Many associations hired traveling teachers, for example, men who traveled regularly from village to village in a given region, holding lectures and workshops on both nationalist and economic themes, and reporting to their employers on the national conditions they encountered in each locality. All of these pedagogical exercises aimed to mobilize as many local villagers as possible for nationalist events, to reinforce fundamental concepts of national difference that allegedly separated peoples, and to make those differences visible in daily life.

Because activists frequently framed their nationalization efforts in rural Austria in terms of rural modernization and education, they attributed their organizational failures to peasants' backwardness and not to the possibility that rural social life itself demanded precisely the kind of bilingual cultural skills and strategies that nationalists deplored. In other words, nationalists convinced themselves that any peasant resistance to strict nationalization had more to do with peasant backwardness than with the attractiveness of an alternative and nonnationalist approach to rural life. For this reason, too, nationalists in rural Austria focused considerable effort on changing the daily life habits and attitudes of the people who allegedly already belonged to the nation. The peasant way of life may have offered a model of virtue for nationalists when they considered the ills of modern urban life, but very often nationalists felt the need to teach rural Austrians how to be modern Czechs, Germans, or Slovenes, not simply by encouraging belief in national differences. Nationalists frequently complained about rural people's ignorance of what were essentially bourgeois practices and bourgeois standards of behavior in daily life.

This assertion of rural failure often extended beyond nationalists' frustration about peasant indifference, ignorance, or poor standards of hygiene. Nationalists themselves remained highly conflicted about their specific aims when they encountered rural Austrians. The encounter often forced nationalists to adopt a pragmatic approach that contradicted their most cherished beliefs about the very meanings of nation and community. If their goal was to produce higher numbers at census time by consolidating national communities and preventing the loss of members to the other side, then who exactly constituted the local targets of the nationalists' activism? Was it perhaps those individuals who were especially vulnerable to the blandishments of the other side? Or was it those individuals who identified with the other side but who could possibly be wooed away? Nationalists always claimed to be consolidating their own nations, and they claimed that the differences between nations were so great as to make it obvious just who belonged to which side. In the context of village life, however, nationalists acted with a kind of opportunistic panache that completely belied their confident assertions of insurmountable difference among nations. As Tara Zahra has pointed out, much nationalist activism, especially that targeted at children, involved persuading nationally unaffiliated people simply to join a nation in the first place. Although their rhetoric focused on the pronounced and obvious differences that separated nations, the nationalists' practices often treated those alleged differences as if they were negligible. If a German-speaking farmer could be won to the Slovene national community, for example, so much the better for the nationalist cause. When it came to practical strategies, nationalists tacitly abandoned their belief in self-evident national differences based on culture, language use, or even descent.

In villages or regions where people traditionally practiced bilingualism, for example, it was hard for nationalists to say where one nation—or even one language—stopped and another started. Territory can at least be marked off on a map; corralling people into a group defined by the beholder and not by those assumed to be its members is a far more difficult challenge. In the first place, it was often hard to point to any significant cultural differences that separated those who spoke different languages in rural villages, either because many people spoke both languages or because all the villagers shared a similar way of life, participated together in the local economy, and shared similar forms of religion and sociability that were not based completely on language use. Even in regions where villages tended to organize themselves more by dominant language, there was plenty of interaction, both personal and social, with neighboring villages.[24]

Nationalists justified the potential confusion that could ensue when the same person who might appear to be a national enemy in one context became a potential recruit in another context by referring to two popular tropes, one based on peasant powerlessness and the other on peasant ignorance. The first of these tropes invoked ideas of forced denationalization. The allegedly real members of one nation had been forced by circumstances beyond their control to switch nations and, therefore, could legitimately be won back to their original and authentic national community, even if they spoke the other language and appeared to belong to the other nation. Nationalists repeatedly invoked this explanation after World War I to explain why census statistics suggested that populations had changed rapidly from one linguistic identity to another.[25] The second of these tropes invoked the older recourse to the high degree of ignorance that nationalists believed characterized rural society, which we have already seen. Peasants ignorant of the significance of nation had reported the wrong language without understanding the terrible consequences of such a choice.

If rural people often appeared unwilling to commit themselves to national communities, or to change their allegiance from one nation to another, why should we conclude that their behavior was produced either by forced denationalization or by the power of so-called traditional or antimodern loyalties, as nationalists at the time did? For the same reasons, we should not easily conclude that when rural people made use of modern nationalist discourses to address administrative or governmental institutions, this signified their successful nationalization. Rather, it may be that as such people were increasingly confronted with state demands for outward adherence to national communities (especially after 1918), people learned to use the language demanded of them by the state in order to articulate their demands on that state more effectively. In the interwar period nationalists appeared finally to have succeeded in nationalizing rural populations. But they still found themselves confronted by individual and community challenges to national categorization that often referred specifically to prewar legal precedents and belief in rights of self-determination. Both of these phenomena demonstrate that local rural people could use nationalist rhetoric to speak back to the state when they felt their own right to make certain social choices—such as how to school their children—was being taken away from them, as indeed it often was.[26] They also illustrate the degree to which such people continued to treat adherence to a national community as an issue of opportunity rather than as an issue of internal belief, in the way that adherence to a religious community might have been experienced.

Conclusions

By 1900, nationalist claims about the profound cultural differences that allegedly characterized people who spoke different languages had increasingly come to dominate media, political debate, judicial arguments, and administrative practice in Imperial Austria. After 1918, the successor states would build on this foundation, adopting harsh nationalizing policies that attempted to remove any element of individual choice from the issue. At the same time, however, many forms of self-identification in multilingual rural regions continued to contradict the presumptions that underlay the powerful nationalist discourses of difference. The ongoing efforts by activists to establish national differences based on language use and cultural norms within allegedly nationally homogeneous communities met with ambivalent and often opportunistic responses among local populations. Individuals frequently refused to identify themselves firmly with one national community or another, or they used nationalist conflict opportunistically to tack between different groups, hoping to achieve particular social aims for themselves and their families.

The apparent disconnect between the totalizing demands of a nationalist worldview and local attitudes toward national belonging suggest the possibility of very different yet simultaneous readings of local events and incidents. What looked like a nationalist incident to some observers, for example, may have had very little to do with national concerns to others. Scholars, journalists, and politicians have tended to valorize fundamentally nationalist approaches to local society, seeing the nationalization of communities as an inexorable and largely successful project—indeed, as a necessary component of modernization processes. Even when they recognize the constructed nature of national communities, many scholars nevertheless imply that constructed national cultural identities were rooted in the allegedly significant social experience of different language use. These scholars miss the point that even the people who rejected national identities for themselves often learned to assume national identities situationally, in order to operate in a world where nationalist discourse and nationalist categories increasingly offered the most effective forms of negotiation.

There remains one further and significant point to consider in this reflection on the analytic disadvantages of understanding Imperial Austria as a multicultural society. The correlation that scholars often make between nationalizing projects and modernizing projects to which I alluded in the above analysis should cause us to question our reflexive association of power differentials with different national groups in Imperial Austria. Efforts to analyze Austrian culture and society using postcolonial theory, for example, frequently seek to locate the ways in which some cultures exercised hegemony over others, or some cultures imagined their relation to others, specifically in colonial terms. Much of the evidence for this kind of interpretation derives from literary and journalistic texts that employ powerful metaphors of colonialism to assert their authors' cultural legitimacy. Analysis of those texts can provide a wealth of information about important popular attitudes toward issues of cultural differences, yet we should remember the highly limited nature of what they can tell us about social life. Because we have so few historical sources about rural social attitudes, it is tempting to allow literary texts to stand uncritically for social phenomena.[27]

While power differentials may have privileged knowledge of some languages over others, especially in the first half of the nineteenth century, we should never confuse the privileges attached to *literacy* in a given language with the actual *speakers* of that language. Some of those speakers, after all, may themselves have only achieved rudimentary levels of literacy, and therefore no access to the kind of prestige that nationalist writers claimed for their cultures. In the nineteenth century, literacy in the German language, for example, might provide an individual with several social and educational opportunities that were unavailable to those who were not literate in the language, such as study at a gymnasium, a university, or a career in certain branches of the civil service or the military. Still, this privilege did not attach to German speakers as such, many of whom were barely literate peasants with no access to the social privileges that allegedly attached to "their culture." It is one thing to speak of the nationalist presumptions that governed political and cultural life in Austria's political institutions or press. It is quite another to project those assumptions onto populations that may not have shared a sense that nation was an important factor in their social lives. Is it useful, for example, to speak of the cultural privileges allegedly accorded to some language groups over others, or to characterize the relations between language groups themselves as hegemonic in nature, when many members of allegedly privileged groups remained incapable of accessing that privilege? Should we speak instead of hegemonic social groups in Austrian society, not necessarily defined by nation, groups such as "the educated," "the educators," "the agents of an expanding economy," or "the administrators of an expanding state structure?" If any cultures in Austria embodied hegemonic—or imperial—attitudes toward rural Austrians, it was these.

Similarly, historians should not confuse the impulse toward cultural homogenization brought by modern forms of communication, social organization, and education in late nineteenth-century Austria with assimilation to allegedly hegemonic nations. The kind of cultural homogenization produced by the late nineteenth-century transformation of rural Austrian society encouraged assimilation to urban bourgeois models of behavior, and it also aided the nationalists' work to create a rising sense of national identity, whether Czech, German, Slovene, or other. But this increasing homogenization did not simply produce a growing awareness of ethnic differences, as if those differences had only needed the drive toward homogenization to be recognized for what they really were.[28] Nationalists' efforts, in tandem with broader processes of cultural homogenization like expanded literacy or access to media, constituted ethnic differences. Ethnic differences were therefore largely an effect, not a cause, of nationalist activism.

If nationalists struggled to establish a sense of cultural difference among inhabitants of multilingual rural regions of the empire, then we may also have to question whether our own understanding of that society as multicultural holds much relevance for historical analysis. Austrians may have perceived local cultural differences in far different terms than those which nationalists wanted. Religious diversity, for example, was often a far better predictor of local perceptions of cultural difference in rural Austria than was linguistic diversity, a fact that frustrated Czech, German, and Slovene nationalists, whose communities were usually not defined by distinctive religious practices. And if Austrians did not necessarily see their own social and power relations as defined mainly by linguistic difference the way their political leaders, journalists, and poets did, can we truly treat Austria as that kind of multicultural society? Should we not rather ask how and why these societies came to be understood and analyzed overwhelmingly in these terms? Nationalists may well have understood the language frontier as the site of intercultural diversity and coexistence, but did the villagers see their communities in these terms? Whatever linguistic differences may in fact have characterized the populations of these regions, this diversity did not always produce a perception of distinct cultures among their local inhabitants.

Notes

1. Anil Bhatti, "Kulturelle Vielfalt und Homogenisierung," in *Habsburg Postcolonial Machtstrukturen und kollektives Gedächtnis*, ed. Johannes Feichtinger, Ursula Prutsch, and Moritz Csáky (Vienna, 2003), 55–68. Bhatti defines pluricultural character in terms of strategies, rather than outcomes, of daily life interactions.

2. In the eastern crown lands of Imperial Austria (Galicia, Bukovina), religious differences created more of a sense of distinct local cultures, but even there shared local cultural commonalities may often have outweighed specific differences in language use or religious practice when it came to loyalty and self-identification.
3. Rogers Brubaker, "Ethnicity without Groups," in *Ethnicity without Groups* (Cambridge, MA, 2004), 7–27.
4. Gary B. Cohen, *The Politics of Ethnic Survival: Germans in Prague, 1861–1914*, 2nd ed., rev. (West Lafayette, IN, 2006), esp. 75–83.
5. Jeremy King, "The Nationalization of East-Central Europe: Ethnicism, Ethnicity, and Beyond," in *Staging the Past: The Politics of Commemoration in Habsburg Central Europe, 1848 to the Present*, ed. Maria Bucur and Nancy Wingfield (West Lafayette, IN, 2001), 112–52.
6. Gerald Stourzh, *Die Gleichberechtigung der Nationalitäten der Verfassung und Verwaltung Österreichs, 1848–1918* (Vienna, 1985); Hannelore Burger, *Sprachenrecht und Sprachgerechtigkeit im österreichischen Unterrichtswesen 1867–1918* (Vienna, 1995).
7. Jiří Klabouch, *Die Gemeindeselbstverwaltung in Österreich, 1848–1918* (Vienna, 1968); Werner Ogris, "Die Entwicklung des österreichischen Gemeinderechts im 19. Jahrhundert," in *Die Städte Mitteleuropas im 19. Jahrhundert*, ed. Wilhelm Rausch (Linz, 1983), 85–90; Josef Redlich, *Das Wesen der österreichischen Kommunal-Verfassung* (Leipzig, 1910).
8. Catherine Albrecht, "The Rhetoric of Economic Nationalism in the Bohemian Boycott Campaigns of the Late Habsburg Monarchy," *Austrian History Yearbook* 32 (2001): 47–67; T. Mills Kelly, "'Taking It to the Streets': Czech National Socialists in 1908," *Austrian History Yearbook* 29 (1998): 93–112; Jeremy King, *Budweisers into Czechs and Germans: A Local History of Bohemian Politics 1848–1948* (Princeton, NJ, 2002), 62–147; Pieter M. Judson, *Exclusive Revolutionaries: Liberal Politics, Social Experience, and National Identity in the Austrian Empire, 1848–1914* (Ann Arbor, MI, 1996), 223–65.
9. Judson, *Exclusive Revolutionaries*, 1–164.
10. Peter Bugge, "Czech Nation-Building, National Self Perception and Politics 1780–1914" (PhD diss., University of Aarhus, 1994). A superb analysis of the development and character of territorial thinking in Czech nationalist movements is Peter Haslinger, *Nation und Territorium in tschechischen politischen Diskurs 1880–1938* (Munich, 2010).
11. On nationalism, schools, and children, see Tara Zahra, *Kidnapped Souls: National Indifference and the Battle for Children in the Bohemian Lands, 1900-1948* (Ithaca, NY, 2008).
12. Most German liberals regarded the clause guaranteeing equality of language use in their 1867 constitution as a guarantee of basic civil rights for groups of individuals and not as a way to give constitutional standing to so-called nations. Implicit in this reading was a belief that while local or domestic relations might be transacted in a vernacular language, more serious public transactions would take place in German. The liberal state would sanction equality among Austria's languages in primary school education, while giving Austrians who spoke all languages the opportunity to pursue secondary or university education in German. The German liberal authors of Austria's 1867 constitution believed that this would have the effect of diminishing nationalist conflict over time. This was not to be the case. Instead, every nationalist movement in post-1867 Austria organized its political agenda primarily around achieving linguistic parity for itself in education, in provincial administration, and in the judiciary.
13. Jeremy King attributes the latter decision to the influence of a resolution at the 1872 International Statistical Congress held in St. Petersburg. Although delegates from the Habsburg Monarchy at the congress opposed the claim that language use was a proxy for nationality, they nevertheless agreed to the single language principle in order to make Cisleithania's statistics comparable with those of other states. King, *Budweisers*, 58–59.

14. The Hungarian government took a different approach to the phenomenon of bilingualism. In some censuses, bilingualism was reported as a way to measure the progress of the Magyar language in regions where other languages had predominated.
15. The best general work on the imperial census is Emil Brix, *Die Umgangssprachen in Altösterreich zwischen Agitation und Assimilation: Die Sprachenstatistik in den zisleithanischen Volkszählungen 1880 bis 1910* (Vienna, 1982). Cohen offers an excellent analysis of the census using specific examples from Prague, *Politics of Ethnic Survival*, 65–104. See also Stourzh, *Gleichberechtigung*.
16. In the 1880 census 37.17 percent of Bohemians reported their language of daily use as German and 62.79 percent as Czech. For Moravia, the statistics were 29.38 percent German and 70.41 percent Czech, while in Silesia 48.91 percent reported German, 22.95 percent Czech, and 28.13 percent Polish. For Styria, 67 percent reported German and 32.74 percent Slovene, and in Tyrol 54.39 percent reported German and 45.44 percent reported Italian. In the city of Trieste, Italian was reported by 73.76 percent, while 21.79 percent reported Slovene and 4.27 percent reported German. In Cisleithania as a whole, 36.75 percent reported German as their language of daily use, 23.77 percent reported Czech, 14.86 percent reported Polish, 12.81 percent reported Ruthene (Ukrainian), 5.23 percent reported Slovene, and 3.07 percent reported Italian. See "Tabelle 1, Die Bevölkerung der Kronländer Cisleithaniens nach der Nationalität und nach der Umgangssprache 1851–1910" in Adam Wandruscka and Peter Urbanitsch, eds., *Die Habsburger Monarchie 1848–1918*, vol. 3, *Die Völker des Reiches* (Vienna, 1980), 138–39.
17. Fritz Mauthner, *Der letzte Deutsche von Blatna* (Berlin: Ullstein & Co., 1913), 22–23.
18. Johann Zemmrich, *Sprachgrenze und Deutschtum in Böhmen* (Braunschweig: F. Vieweg und Sohn, 1902).
19. Ibid., 7–10.
20. "Slowenische Grenzbeschreibungen und Anklage," in *Mitteilungen des Vereins Südmark* (Graz, 1913), 443.
21. František Joklík, *O poměrech českého národního školství a učitelstva v kralovství českem* (Prague, 1900), 129.
22. "Bericht des Wanderlehrers V. Heeger," in *Mitteilungen des Vereines Südmark* (Graz, 1905–6), 26.
23. Several association magazines complained of rural branches that did not send their dues to the executive with any regularity and did not report holding annual meetings or local activities such as lectures, festivals, or even social events like trips. See Pieter M. Judson, *Guardians of the Nation: Activists on the Language Frontiers of Imperial Austria* (Cambridge, MA, 2006), 72–74.
24. See the project results of the Austrian and Czech coproject "Verfeindete Brüder an der Grenze: Südböhmen/Südmähren/Waldviertel/Weinviertel: Die Zerstörung der Lebenseinheit 'Grenze' 1938 bis 1945," led by Hanns Haas (University of Salzburg); Petr Lovoziuk, "Karlov/Libindsorf: A Village in Discourse, a Discourse in a Village: Preliminary Research Report," *Fieldwork and Local Communities: Prague Occasional Papers in Ethnology* 7 (2005): 146–73; Peter Mähner, "Grenze als Lebenswelt: Gnadlersdorf (Hnanice), ein südmährisches Dorf an der Grenze," in *Grenze im Kopf: Beiträge zur Geschichte der Grenze in Ostmitteleuropa*, ed. Peter Haslinger (Vienna, 1999), 67–102.
25. Such arguments were striking in the case of postwar census data both for parts of Yugoslavia (Slovenia) that had formerly been part of the Austrian province of Styria and for the Austrian provinces of Carinthia and Styria. In both cases, postwar census numbers for minority populations differed drastically from prewar statistics.
26. For an excellent analysis of this kind of behavior as it was broadly manifested in the interwar period, see Tara Zahra's analysis of court cases produced by the Czechoslovakian census of

1921 in *Kidnapped Souls,* chap. 4. Zahra has recently argued in an important theoretical work that historians should in general take seriously such forms of indifference to nationhood, seeing them—as much as nationalism and nationhood—as constituting a legitimate category for scholarly analysis. Tara Zahra, "Imagined Noncommunities: National Indifference As a Category of Analysis," *Slavic Review* 69, no. 1 (Spring 2010): 93–119.
27. See, for example, Karl-Markus Gauss, *Ins unentdeckte Österreich: Nachrufe und Attacken* (Vienna, 1998).
28. Johannes Feichtinger, "Habsburg (Post)-colonial: Anmerkungen zur Inneren Kolonisierung in Zentraleuropa," in Feichtinger, Prutsch, and Csáky, *Habsburg Postcolonial,* 19.

Section II

THE DYNAMICS OF MULTICULTURAL SOCIETIES, POLITICS, AND THE STATE

Chapter 4

MULTICULTURALISM, POLISH STYLE
Glimpses from the Interwar Period

Patrice M. Dabrowski

Although the subject of multiculturalism has gained currency in recent times, particularly among those working on the Habsburg lands, the multicultural approach (albeit not labeled as such) is hardly new to Polish historiography. Certainly those familiar with the *longue durée* of this "heart of Europe" know that, historically, the very definition of what it meant to be Polish reflected the multicultural approach laid out by the editors of the present volume, who define multiculturalism as a "mode of understanding and practice used by social actors for coping with diversity."[1] In the early modern period the nation could be equated with the approximately 8 percent of the population that was the nobility (a much larger percentage than was found in Western Europe). More importantly, "Polish" noblemen hailed from varying ethnic backgrounds: Lithuanian, Belarusian, Ruthenian/Ukrainian, German, even Tatar, as well as Polish. What brought them together was a sense of estate loyalty, not any loyalty based on religion or language. What cemented them within the state was their sense of belonging to the "noble nation," which in those days ruled Poland—more accurately entitled the Commonwealth of Two Nations, Polish and Lithuanian (in the West usually termed the Polish-Lithuanian Commonwealth), a state that was even more of an ethnic and religious mosaic than these titles imply—much more than did the elective monarchy that followed the death of the last Jagiellon in the late sixteenth century. The noted intellectual historian Andrzej Walicki has argued, contra Hans Kohn and others, that Poland in this period was characterized by a civic nationalism much like the nations of Western Europe, and not the ethnic nationalism generally associated with Central and Eastern Europe.[2]

Furthermore, an elaborate myth was constructed to explain the distinctiveness of the nobility—that is, not vis-à-vis ethnic groups but vis-à-vis the other estates dwelling within the borders of the Commonwealth: burghers, Jews, the vast peasantry. Beginning in the sixteenth century, noblemen began to claim that the nobility of the Commonwealth was descended from the ancient Sarmatians. This, of course, was a gross error, but it was a useful fiction, in keeping with Renan's famous statement that getting things wrong is part of being a nation. These noble Sarmatians attributed their privileged status to the fact that, like the ancient Sarmatians before them, they were the defenders of their country's borders. Better to convince them of this link to this ancient past, these early modern Sarmatians imitated Oriental dress and ultimately turned away from the West. The assumption was that everything Polish was best—nay, perfect: their form of government, their "golden liberty," and the like. This multinational estate identity has been called the first Polish national identity, although to be sure others would argue that it is premature to talk of a national identity before the modern age.[3]

I bring up this Sarmatian myth because the idea of useful fictions figures in the present chapter, which is based upon early findings from a current research project of mine concerning Polish attitudes toward the Carpathian Mountains and their indigenous inhabitants.[4] These findings come not from the Habsburg period, more often identified with multiculturalism (as in this volume), but rather from the interwar period. To be sure, one could write a good deal about the peculiar Habsburg multiculturalism as it played out in Galicia.[5] What I would like to do in this chapter, though, is not to choose examples from this period of Habsburg multiculturalism but rather to delve into a little-known example from a much more stridently national period, the interwar years, with the assumption that this example might speak better to contemporary concerns.

The interwar period surely was a much more modern—certainly more challenging—time than the Habsburg period, or the age of the Commonwealth before it. It was an age characterized by the striving of nations to construct uniform nation-states out of the sundry-colored building blocks accorded them by the Paris Peace Conference. Different views of the Polish state and nation emerged, views at odds with each other, as personified by the leaders of the two basic camps, Roman Dmowski and Józef Piłsudski.[6] Whereas Dmowski and his National Democrats saw the Polish nation as the overweening good and sought to turn the Second Republic into a true nation-state, Piłsudski's vision of Poland was more closely aligned to the old Commonwealth, and he placed the state above the nation. Indeed, Piłsudski maintained—much as d'Azeglio reportedly did in the Italian case—that it was the state that would make the nation, not the other way around.[7]

That there were attempts at fostering multicultural approaches in the interwar period may come as a surprise to some. The interwar period in Poland was not known for its ethnic toleration. The country's minorities faced many hurdles, despite their being given full rights of citizenship under the law. In *Nationalism Reframed,* Rogers Brubaker used interwar Poland as an example of a "nationalizing" state, that is, one in which a weak ethnic majority seeks to transform its state into a genuine nation-state.[8] Thus, what can possibly be learned from the Second Republic that might teach us something positive about multiculturalism and how to deal with diversity?

One example of multiculturalism in interwar Poland was discussed several years ago by Timothy Snyder. The province of Volhynia represented a major experiment in Polish multiculturalism following the coup d'état of Józef Piłsudski in 1926. The newly appointed governor of the province, Henryk Józewski, shared Piłsudski's view of the multicultural state and the type of progress that should be made under Polish rule. "Józewski . . . was under no illusions that modernization led by the Polish state would create a province that was ethnically Polish. Indeed, he desired no such outcome. He took for granted that modernity must be multinational."[9] That is, he shared the view of yet another Piłsudski-ite, Tadeusz Hołówko, who wrote:

> It is not a matter of whether there be Poles or Belarusians or Ukrainians in the borderlands, but rather that the frontier of the Polish state be simultaneously the frontier of western culture, that . . . all . . . feel that they are children of one great family of western nations and that the Republic is the state that brought them all up in the common western culture.[10]

The borderlands would themselves prove crucial in this regard. Snyder weaves quotations of Józewski into his own assessment of the particular view of Polishness held by Piłsudski's men of trust, like Józewski:

> Polishness itself was an activity rather than a state of being, and Polishness could only prosper at the margin, on the frontier, where it could attract others and learn from them. The very "essence" of Polishness was "the emergence of Poland in non-Polish environments." The political task was "state assimilation," to be understood "not as denationalization, but as a creative process of mutual interpenetration."[11]

The approach to Polishness of these early twentieth-century men seems quite modern and Brubakeresque, with Polishness being seen in fluid, relational, and processual terms.[12] The real "Poland" was to transcend the narrow borders of ethnolinguistic definition.

Such were the multicultural views of Henryk Józewski. He strove to foster his vision of Poland in the experiment that characterized his term as provincial governor in the province of Volhynia (1928–38). This experiment came under question after Piłsudski's death brought to power others who preferred unambiguously to strengthen Polishness—understood in ethnic, not statist, terms—in the province.

Yet Volhynia is not the experiment I intend to explore in this chapter. My own example from the interwar period is related, if somewhat differently motivated. As in the case of Volhynia, it, too, had an aspect of strategic thinking (after all, we are dealing with the borderlands of the Polish Second Republic). The region in question possessed other strengths: climatic, touristic, civilizational—strengths that encouraged a broad range of actors to support its native diversity.

This region was part of an even more challenging multinational borderland, one that had been part of Galicia before the Great War: Eastern Galicia. Unlike Volhynia, Eastern Galicia had been home to a growing Ukrainian national sentiment at the fin de siècle. The transformation of Ruthenians into Ukrainians is beyond the scope of this chapter. Suffice it to say that national consciousness-raising, although not universal, was certainly more widespread in Eastern Galicia prior to World War I than in the lands that had been under Russian control, such as Volhynia. At the same time, within Eastern Galicia there were pockets of peasants who did not yet conceive of themselves as national beings. Some of these were found in the highland regions.

One such group with a regional identity was the fascinating and exotic people known as the Hutsuls. They lived in the Hutsul region (Pol. Huculszczyzna, Ukr. Hutsul'shchyna), also known as Czarnohora/Chornohora. Czarnohora was the remotest corner of Eastern Galicia. Part of the Stanisławów Province, it lay between the Prut and Czeremosz Rivers and bordered on both interwar Czechoslovakia and Romania. This backward and isolated region of interwar Poland abounded in natural beauty: it featured primeval forests, chiseled cliffs, cascading waterfalls, and fast-flowing streams leading into the more temperate lowlands, where orchards and vineyards flourished. The high uplands were peppered with verdant, rich pastures, where the Hutsul menfolk spent the summer months as nomadic shepherds with their cattle, sheep, and horses. Yet the region was also famous as a haven for highland brigands, who preyed on travelers until the Habsburgs' harsh reprisals against them made brigandage less attractive. It should be added that this remote corner of the interwar Polish state was one of its most ethnically diverse regions: in addition to Hutsul highlanders, Poles, Ukrainians, Jews, Germans, Armenians, and Roma could also be found in various parts of the highland borderland.

Although they lived in relative isolation, the Hutsuls had managed to entice a wide range of visitors to the region.[13] They had made their name as talented artisans since Habsburg times, creating elaborately carved and encrusted woodworking, woolen *lizhnyky* (blankets) and kilims, and imaginatively painted pottery. The artistically inclined Hutsuls were unquestionably the best—certainly the most colorfully—dressed peasants of Galicia. In addition to their work in the highland pastures, they could be found in the forests working as lumberjacks, or atop rafts of logs being transported along the Czeremosz (Cheremosh) River into the lowlands. Their preferred means of transport were the small Hutsul horses known for their surefootedness and reliability. In sum, the Hutsuls were a feisty and freedom-loving people, very much a people of the mountains.

From the description of both region and people, it is not hard to imagine that this region, despite its general inaccessibility, held great promise as a tourist destination.[14] Indeed, the Carpathian Mountains were being "discovered" in this way, particularly during the interwar period.[15] The effect of this "discovery" on the heterogeneous highland borderlands is worth pondering. For what would happen to the indigenous folk once masses of tourists started to pour in? Would this result in the kind of modernity that, as Gellner has argued, would make people national? Would Hutsuls begin to see themselves as Ukrainians, given their shared Greek Catholic religion and East Slavic dialect, and in the process define themselves in opposition to Polishness? Would they come to see themselves as members of the Polish state, much as Józewski had envisaged for the Volhynians: to encounter "Poland" at the margins, contribute something of themselves both to Polishness and to the state in general? Or would they—as Dmowski and his National Democrats would wish—become assimilated into the Polish nation, more narrowly defined?

These were burning questions in the early 1930s, questions that were addressed—if indirectly—by a new organization: the Society of Friends of the Hutsul Region (Towarzystwo Przyjaciół Huculszczyzny). Founded in the second half of 1933, this was no mere alpine society or *Heimatskunde* (Pol. *krajoznawstwo*, Ukr. *krajeznavstvo*) club. Rather, it had support from the highest echelons of the Polish government (although, unfortunately, the full extent of this connection may never be known, given the destruction of the relevant archives in World War II). This is demonstrated by the fact that the first president of the organization was Brigadier General Tadeusz Kasprzycki, who at the time was deputy minister for military affairs. The connection between Kasprzycki and the Polish leader Piłsudski was hardly insignificant: already as a twenty-three-year-old lieutenant Kasprzycki had been chosen by Piłsudski to lead the first foray of Polish soldiers into Russian Poland in August 1914.[16] One thus assumes that the general was close to the First Marshal—and likely acted with his approval. What it most certainly meant is that the organization had greater access, through its highly placed head, to funding and support in Warsaw—something very important, given the centralization of power in the interwar period.

This military connection would have other implications for the organization and the way it gained greatest resonance. The society organized a large annual public event in the region, the Hutsul Route March, an occasion for lowlanders to travel to the highlands and come to an appreciation of the land and people. Formally entitled the March along the Hutsul Route of the Second Brigade of the Polish Legions (Marsz Huculskim Szlakiem Drugiej Brygady Legionów Polskich), it commemorated an event of special importance to relations between Hutsuls and Poles. This was the fact that, during World War I, they had both fought a common enemy together. In the words of a report on the society, "The history of the Second Brigade—in its most essential moment, for through battles, fights, through the graves of Carpathian soldiers . . . is connected with the Hutsul land and with the Hutsuls, who in a . . . relatively significant number served in the Second Brigade."[17] Apparently a whole company of Hutsuls was formed during the winter of 1914/15, when the Polish Legions were in the Carpathians. Some Hutsuls likewise helped out with reconnaissance or by serving as guides for the troops.

Yet in many ways, this interwar vision of Polish-Hutsul brotherhood is doubtless more mythic than real. Although a number of Hutsuls joined the Polish Legions to fight the Russians, enlisting on the spot as World War I raged in their homeland—the account of one of the recruits was later published in *Żołnierz Polski* (Polish Solider)[18]—there is no reason to assume that all Hutsuls who ended up in the Second Brigade truly wished to be there together with the Poles. Nor was it at all certain, much less likely, that they were—as interwar Polish publications repeatedly stated—fighting for *Polish* independence. Recall that, although this company of Hutsuls was part of the Polish Legions, the latter were still very much part of the Austro-Hungarian Army. Was there any reason, thus, for Hutsuls not to wish to defend their country—their land—against foreign incursion? Indeed, they could be completely indifferent, or even negatively inclined, toward the Polish desire for independence. It was actually likely that many Hutsuls were opposed, as the pro-Ukrainian Radical Party that had gained influence in the region in the first decades of the twentieth century, saw the Poles of Galicia as their foe. Thus, this Polish interpretation—that Hutsuls had voluntarily joined the common fight, against Russia, for Polish independence—may have been more wishful thinking than a reflection of the reality circa 1914/15.

It was a useful fiction, nonetheless, for interwar Poland—the most promising way to write the Hutsuls into Polish history. That Hutsuls happened to have enlisted in the Second Brigade of the Polish Legions made it possible to create a myth of the common struggle for Polish independence.[19] This interpretation made it seem that, unlike the Ukrainians of the lowlands, Hutsul highlanders might be more favorably disposed toward the Polish state—certainly (and this was repeatedly stressed by highland activists) a Polish state that would do what was within its power to improve the lives of the Hutsuls.

The creation of the myth of the common struggle for Polish independence was likewise facilitated by the fact that the Hutsuls in some ways more closely resembled the Polish nobility of old than did their Ukrainian brethren of the lowlands. They certainly did not act like run-of-the-mill peasants: Hutsuls traditionally bore arms, were an equestrian people, and comported themselves with a *dignitas* rarely found in folk populations. In many ways, they seemed more like the Poles imagined themselves to be. To be sure, this purported closeness was also attributed to the mixed heritage of the Hutsuls—they were considered to be a composite of Polish, Ukrainian, and Wallachian stock and thus were "free of the artificially cultivated neo-Ukrainian chauvinism."[20] Therefore, an opportunity existed to drive a wedge between Hutsuls and Ukrainians—certainly to keep the former from becoming the latter—while strengthening bonds between Hutsuls and Poles.

The nature of the Hutsul Route March suggests that the event was full of lessons for Poles as well as Hutsuls. This was not an event designed simply to impress the Hutsuls with the deeds of the World War I generation, to demonstrate that their efforts were appreciated. For that, a commemorative session, with a solemn trip to the local cemetery, might have sufficed. Instead, men—soldiers, Hutsuls, and civilians, all together—were to revisit the conditions of war in a three-day cross-country ski competition, with a shooting component as well. Teams ("patrols") of four competitors apiece, representing military formations, Hutsul villages, or ski or sports clubs, made their way across the rugged terrain, with all but the captain of each team obliged to shoot at the designated targets. The patrols were also required to bring back some earth from beneath the Legionnaires' Cross at the mountain pass known as Legionnaires' Pass. Although the Hutsul Route March was not a reenactment of any particular battle, it echoed elements of the war while providing a living memorial to the past and directions for the future. The event was under the patronage of Marshal Piłsudski himself, demonstrating high-placed support for its aims.

The Hutsul Route March was supposed to infuse new generations of Poles—and Hutsuls—with purpose, encouraging them to dedicate themselves to ensuring a strong future for the new state. In the words of Kasprzycki, "New generations, who come forth with the destiny of consolidating the achieved State—must turn their thoughts toward deeds of the past, which teach [the need for] . . . energy in striving for a goal, for solidaristic work in a team, where each must forget about himself, ready to evoke the greatest energy for the common good." This deed of the past was to be an example for those who made the trip now to this remote region, those who had returned "to a people and a land, where the Carpathian brigade found heart and help in difficult moments and bloody battles."[21]

Former legionnaires were included in the Hutsul Route March. Doubtless few of these men now participated in the actual march (although, of names mentioned, Brigadier General Tadeusz Malinowski, who had served in the Second Brigade during World War I, did traverse the route, albeit not as a member of a team).[22] Rather, they were assembled into a branch of the Society of Friends of the Hutsul Region, the so-called Legionnaires Club, based in the village of Żabie.[23] It turns out that a number of legionnaires had ended up settling in the Hutsul region, and they were ready to work toward the improvement of living conditions for the people who had once fought alongside them and helped them.

Among other things, they sought to identify those Hutsuls who had enlisted in the Polish Legion during the war or assisted the armed forces.

Yet not all the activities of the Society of Friends of the Hutsul Region bore the imprint of the military. The four main aims of the society make this clear. They emphasize the society's desire: (1) to coordinate the methodical economic and cultural development of the Hutsul region; (2) to protect those characteristics of the region that comprised its distinctiveness; (3) to utilize, in a rational way, the "climatic values" of the Hutsul region to improve the "social hygiene" of the state; and (4) to oversee and develop—again, in rational fashion—the Hutsul region as a center for tourism, summer, and health resorts.[24] To this end, the Society of Friends of the Hutsul Region would coordinate the work of all institutions and individuals seeking to improve the Hutsul region and assist in their development, serve as an intermediary to the authorities and advocate on the region's behalf, and generally promote the "Hutsul question" in myriad ways.[25]

The wording of the statute makes clear the special value that Czarnohora had for the interwar Polish state: it was a "valuable component in the sum of the natural and spiritual riches of the Polish Republic."[26] In other words, this was no simple "Polska B"—second-class Poland. Rather, this periphery of the interwar Polish state had much to offer those at the center: cultural distinctiveness and exoticism, a restorative climate, and opportunities to profit from them. It was the goal of the society to encourage those outside the region to avail themselves of this peculiar reservoir of values: physical, climatic, even (according to the quotation above) spiritual.

Other branches of the Society of Friends of the Hutsul Region demonstrate the range of concerns of the region's "friends" and suggest that the distinct culture of the region and people was being valued. There were a number of specialized sections—eight, to be exact—founded at the very outset. The Legionnaires Club, which gathered Poles and Hutsuls together, has already been mentioned. There was also a Scouts Club. It was assumed that organized youth—particularly during winter and summer vacations—could provide a ready source of assistance with the various programs of the Society of Friends of the Hutsul Region, so many members of which lived in Warsaw or otherwise were located far from the highlands. In the summer of 1933, when the society was first conceived, scouts were already sent to the Hutsul region. Among other things, they engaged in educational, cultural, and charitable activities in the region and established relationships with individual Hutsul families.[27]

Other sections of the organization had their base not in the region but in Warsaw: they were run by specialists in the given field and designed to further the region in different ways. One of the most important fields of activity for the society, already mentioned in the four main aims cited earlier, was the promotion of tourism. Tourism was understood in the broader Polish definition of including (or even primarily referring to) hiking, that is, touring on foot. This, of course, was most appropriate for a region known for its natural beauty. Tourism was considered by the society to be the salvation of the Hutsul region; it thought that tourism could be developed on a shoestring budget, whereas other projects for economic development would require the kind of investment that Depression-era Poland could ill afford.

At any rate, the work of many of the society's sections contributed to the furtherance of tourism in the region. There existed a section focused specifically on tourism, the Tourism and Health Resort Section. The Propaganda Section was to do whatever necessary to advertise the region and its strengths, as well as drum up interest in the Hutsul Route March and the multiday summer event known as the Hutsul Holiday, which presented aspects of Hutsul culture more fully to a broad audience. An Economic Section provided assistance with the construction and repair of roads and railways, the necessary routes for travel to and about the region; it also helped warehouse Hutsul handicrafts, made in the winter but having their greatest demand during the tourist season (for example, during the Hutsul Holiday).[28] There was even a Hygiene Section; in addition to helping fight diseases, such as syphilis, and caring for Hutsul mothers and children, the Hygiene Section helped to determine the most appropriate locations for sanatoriums and spas.[29] All told, these various sections suggest that the Society of Friends of the Hutsul Region thought Czarnohora worth seeing—and worth developing.

But could these sections—indeed, the work of the society as a whole—have been motivated by a Polish etatist self-interest in the region? The work of these sections served to integrate this remote area into the body of the Polish state. Their various projects necessitated an influx of outsiders—lowland Poles—to the region, thus helping to dilute the East Slavic element (although this could be felt mostly during the winter ski and summer vacation seasons). There is no denying that the activities of the society in some way preempted any move on the part of nationally conscious Ukrainian agitators, who might well have sought to gain ground in the region.[30] Even solicitude as to the state of health of the Hutsuls could be interpreted as simply fending off illnesses that might spread to the tourist population. Was this not simply a case of the society wishing to gain the upper hand in developing the region?

Recall, however, the second of the four aims of the society: to protect those characteristics of the region that comprised its distinctiveness. In the 1930s, the Hutsul population was under threat, the economic crisis making it difficult for them to maintain their customs and traditional lifestyle; simply put, they were not able to make a living, or even enough to ensure the close-to-subsistence levels to which they were accustomed. Such concerns led to the creation of another section of the Society of Friends of the Hutsul Region, one that sheds further light on Polish-style multiculturalism. This was the intriguingly named Section for the Preservation of Nativeness (Sekcja Obrony Swojszczyzny).

The concept of *swojszczyzna,* which I have rendered as nativeness, is key to the special kind of Polish multiculturalism seen in the interwar period. In terms of the people to whom it was applied—the highland folk—one might think of it as native cultural distinctiveness—that is, whatever made the region unique. *Swojszczyzna* could be applied to the natural environment, the distinctive highland environment, but it was most often used in reference to the human environment, to manifestations of culture. Poles in the interwar period were convinced that *swojszczyzna* was being threatened by encroaching modernity. That is, regions were losing their distinctive color. Not only was development—in the form of formless architecture—reaching the highlands, but it was also penetrating even the preserve of the Hutsul homestead. Highland village folk were becoming more and more like the nearby townsfolk, some purchasing their clothing ready-made. One could find incongruous sights, such as that of a Hutsul man, perhaps now working for a lumber mill, wearing his traditional shearling vest with ready-made trousers, or Hutsul women in purchased boots and not the soft leather *postoly* that traditionally were laced up over homespun woolen socks.[31] All of this spoke of a degree of leveling, of a reduction to a lowest common denominator of culture that threatened the Second Republic's diversity.

How, then, did the Section for the Preservation of Nativeness seek to preserve a nativeness that was already being undermined? (Although, to be sure, the still very isolated Hutsul region was much better off, insofar as the maintenance of traditional customs was concerned, than were other regions of the Polish highlands.) The society sought to instill in the Hutsuls an appreciation for their own handicrafts by helping with cottage industry. One of the first ideas of the society was to establish a museum in the largest of the Hutsul villages, Żabie. There, proper examples of authentic Hutsul handicrafts, both old and new, would serve as inspiration for the Hutsuls. At the same time, they would provide a standard against which their handiwork could be measured (to keep them from producing shoddy or cheap goods). The society also underscored the value of Hutsul distinctiveness by mandating that participants in the various contests and festivals sponsored by the society appear in proper Hutsul garb and on purebred Hutsul horses. It likewise produced a periodical and calendars in the Hutsul dialect—the first such publications ever attempted. Hutsuls were taught that their lifestyle was unique and exotic, and that only by maintaining the old ways could they expect to attract tourists to the region—tourists who often would seek to be housed in Hutsul huts, pay for accommodation and meals, and otherwise take an interest in things Hutsul. In other words, the past—their native traditions and customs—could bring them more fully into the future, a future characterized by increased prosperity and regional revitalization.

Here we see the perfect amalgamation of the aims of the society: to maintain what was valuable from the Hutsul past while steeling the Hutsuls for an encounter with modernity. Nativeness would be restored to its rightful—central—spot. Hutsuls were exhorted to "go [or remain] native" out of pride, not to reject what was traditionally theirs because of some inferiority complex or dilute it unthinkingly with cheap modern elements.

This positive assessment of the Society of Friends of the Hutsul Region is reinforced by yet another connection. Documents of the Society of Friends of the Hutsul Region attest to the fact that the head of the Section for the Preservation of Nativeness in Kołomyja was no less than the Polish literary figure and philosopher Stanisław Vincenz.[32] The limited extant papers of the society do not allow one to comprehend the full extent of his involvement in the society. Still, anyone writing about the region's "discovery" in the interwar period must write about Vincenz, who essentially initiated the "discovery" of the Hutsuls by illustrious individuals from outside Poland before the society was even founded. The Polish writer and philosopher was instrumental in bringing distinguished guests from the West to the region and showing them around. Visitors in the early 1930s included men like the Swiss sociologist Hans Zbinden, who published accounts of his visits to the region; the Italian anthropologist Lidio Cipriani, who came to study this fascinating primitive folk; and the rabbi of Stockholm, Marcus Ehrenpreis, who was planning to write a biography of Israel Baal Shem Tov, the founder of Hasidism, who himself hailed from the highland region.[33]

Stanisław Vincenz was famous for his deep appreciation of the Hutsuls, their language and customs, as well as the multicultural environment in which they found themselves. Although a scion of a Polish noble family (albeit descended likewise from an immigrant from France), he was a true son of the region. Vincenz had literally grown up there—he had even been given unto the care of a Hutsul nursemaid, thanks to whom he learned the dialect and many tales from the Hutsul past. As an adult, Vincenz had chosen to live in the isolated village of Bystrets rather than spend his time in a larger metropolis, where one might expect to find a thinker of his stature. (He claimed that the quiet was conducive to philosophical contemplation.)[34]

Himself the author of a veritable epic on the Hutsuls, *On the High Uplands,* Vincenz was concerned that Poles—indeed, that Europeans as a whole—come to appreciate this gift of the Hutsul region in their midst. This is evident from an interview with the Polish writer, significantly entitled "Europe and Poland vis-à-vis the Hutsul Region."[35] Vincenz began by relating a few details from a recent visit of the British consul general, who was able to see all the best the Hutsul region had to offer in the company of one who knew it intimately. He noted the reactions of the consul—of "Europe"—to the Hutsuls. The consul was impressed by the veritable noble courtesy of the Hutsuls, of the dignity with which they listened to tales from their past—tales that reminded the listener of Homeric ones. The visitor was likewise charmed by the "aristocratic" beauty of the Hutsul women. Also noteworthy was the old Polish hospitality of the Jewish innkeeper, a true example of a patriotic Pole of the Mosaic persuasion. Through the eyes of the consul, the intended audience for the interview saw the stock that "Europe" placed in this multicultural region: it valued the region's Jewish as well as Hutsul culture, wanted to visit its synagogues as well as acquire Hutsul souvenirs. In Vincenz's multicultural world, the world he described with such empathy and shared with his guests, Poles and Jews, Armenians and Roma, all had their place alongside the Hutsuls in the high uplands.

But the value of the Hutsul region for Europe was still greater, according to Vincenz. Besides being a place where various cultures lived together in harmony, it could be seen as providing clues to the origins of other folk cultures. Vincenz deemed the discovery of the "deposits of culture . . . hidden in the subconscious of the national spirit, that is, in folk culture" superior to the invention of psychoanalysis.[36] He likewise believed in the "unity of man in various cultures" and was convinced that "those nations that seize upon this and achieve knowledge about the subconscious and the internal current of the entire culture accessible to us w[ould] have control over the consciousness of the world."[37] In a seminal 1938 article entitled "Notes on Folk Culture," Vincenz discussed how an understanding of the way Hutsuls create epic songs could shed light on the same for, say, the Serbian epics or the Russian *byliny*. But he also argued for the fragility of folk culture, which by its very nature was spontaneous, nearly involuntary, and subconscious: any disruption or intrusion on the part of "foreign" civilization could destroy it forever. In that way, man would lose access to crucial information about himself as a human being, and would lose the reserve of values and energies not present in conscious culture. After all, the isolation in which Hutsul culture (for example) thrived did not breed barbarism or backwardness—Vincenz maintained—but rather the opposite: "it [could] foster the development and maturation of some kind of distinctness, very important and valuable for humanity."[38]

The Hutsul region was a treasury of distinctiveness, a distinctiveness all the more remarkable for its being unconscious. It was a world in which superstitions ruled, where legends of giants continued to excite the imagination, and where the old ways were still considered the best ways. The Hutsul region was the "Slavic Atlantis," an island of a pure folk, even primeval, culture, which resembled a world that had been long lost elsewhere. Were the Hutsul region to lose its distinctiveness, it would be a huge loss not only for interwar Poland but also for Europe and the world as a whole. After all, cultural richness and diversity was Europe's main virtue, according to Vincenz. He wrote that "to abandon differentiation is to abandon Europe and all its traditions and spiritual aspirations."[39] Doubtless he would maintain that Poles had a responsibility, as rulers of this land, to protect it, care for it, study it, and keep it as a treasury of the primitive for the world at large. Indeed, given the direction the world of interwar Europe was headed, perhaps Czarnohora would be the last oasis of culture: witness Vincenz's relation of the reaction of Hans Zbinden. After Hitler came to power, the Swiss writer reportedly declared that "most likely the Hutsul region will be the last haven of culture in a sea of frenzied waves of hatred and antagonism."[40] Yet another visitor to the region entreated that it should be turned into a national park so that its "fascinating distinctness not be destroyed."[41]

Doubtless Vincenz would have liked to see that happen. He feared that this "Slavic Atlantis" might be destroyed before it was ever thoroughly understood. The author of *On the High Uplands* agitated for more study of the region, for conditions in which Hutsul language, culture, and art could flourish, and for the creation of a Hutsul museum in Żabie. In this he was on the same wavelength as the Society of Friends of the Hutsul Region, which indeed set about studying the region as well as creating the museum Vincenz saw as very desirable.[42]

Vincenz's fears were justified. Before too long the second great war of the century would sweep through the region. In its wake, and in the wake of the Soviet regime that followed it, much of what was irreplaceable in the Hutsul region—the ubiquity of the highland dialect, the pious cultivation of traditions, even the Hutsul rhythm of life in a multiethnic environment (destroyed in the course of the war and the Holocaust)—was lost forever. What remained was but a shadow of the ancient cultural richness that had earlier characterized the region.

So, what can be learned from interwar Poland? First, that the spirit of Polish multiculturalism, although under siege on the part of integral nationalists, was still alive in parts of the multiethnic borderlands. There were Poles who fervently believed that the Polish nation was enriched by regional diversity, not lessened by it. They were a diverse bunch themselves (something I have only hinted at here), politicians and military men as well as philosophers and bureaucrats, seeking to foster tourism within the county. As we have seen, they functioned collectively and individually. Second, it was not outside the power of even ostensibly "nationalizing" states to support multiculturalism. Organizations such as the Society of Friends of the Hutsul Region clearly acted under the aegis of the Polish state, which—among other things—provided funding for many of their endeavors. Third, the role of influential individuals in all this should not be underestimated: they served as examples and catalysts for a broader engagement in and support of regional distinctiveness. As demonstrated here, the Polish writer Stanisław Vincenz (now much celebrated in post-1989 Poland and published likewise in Ukrainian translation) valued the Hutsul language and customs and advocated the serious study of this endangered culture. And he was not the only one to do so in interwar Poland. Fourth (and this may be a corollary to the second point), good work could sometimes be done by those who supported diversity not as a value in itself but rather for different reasons. Regardless of what motivated some of these actors to action (questions of economic development and national security clearly playing a role), the effect was still noteworthy: diversity was fostered within the region, and the nativeness of the regionally conscious highlanders was nurtured in ways that it had never been before, even under the benign multinationalism of Habsburg rule.

Notes

1. Use of the term "heart of Europe" in relation to Poland was popularized by Norman Davies, who thus titled one of his histories of the country. The citation from the introduction to this volume—Johannes Feichtinger and Gary B. Cohen, "Introduction. Understanding Multiculturalism: The Habsburg Central European Experience"—comes from page 13.
2. Andrzej Walicki, *The Enlightenment and the Birth of Modern Nationhood: Polish Political Thought from Noble Republicanism to Tadeusz Kościuszko,* trans. Emma Harris (Notre Dame, IN, 1989)'.
3. See, e.g., Tomasz Kizwalter, *O nowoczesności narodu: Przypadek Polski* (Warsaw, 1999), who is in agreement with Ernest Gellner on this point. For a discussion of this, see Patrice M. Dabrowski, "What Kind of Modernity Did Poles Need? A Look at Nineteenth-Century Nation-Making," *Nationalities Papers* 29, no. 3 (2001): 509–23.
4. The subject of this chapter will be covered much more thoroughly in the book I am preparing, which is tentatively entitled *"Discovering" the Carpathians: Episodes in Imagining and Reshaping Alpine Borderland Regions.*
5. During the period of Habsburg rule (1772–1918), this particular, heterogeneous piece of the Polish-Lithuanian Commonwealth was not only transformed into a loyal Habsburg province, known as Galicia, but also witnessed the creation of Galicians. According to Larry Wolff, both province and inhabitants should be viewed as "fundamentally provincial" and "fundamentally non-national." Larry Wolff, *The Idea of Galicia: History and Fantasy in Habsburg Political Culture* (Palo Alto, CA, 2010), 6.
6. An introduction to the views of both can be found in Patrice M. Dabrowski, "Uses and Abuses of the Polish Past by Józef Piłsudski and Roman Dmowski," *The Polish Review* 56, nos. 1–2 (2011): 73–110, which also cites much of the relevant literature.
7. Piłsudski has been cited by Eric Hobsbawm, *Nations and Nationalism Since 1870: Programme, Myth, Reality* (Cambridge, 1990), 44–45. In the Italian case, these were actually the words of Ferdinando Martino, the secretary of education, not Massimo d'Azeglio, according to Alon Confino, *Nation as a Local Metaphor: Württemberg, Imperial Germany, and National Memory, 1871–1918* (Chapel Hill, NC, 1997), 15.
8. Rogers Brubaker, *Nationalism Reframed: Nationhood and the National Question in the New Europe* (Cambridge, 1996), esp. 84–103.
9. Timothy Snyder, *Sketches from a Secret War: A Polish Artist's Mission to Liberate Soviet Ukraine* (New Haven, CT, 2005), 63.
10. Tadeusz Hołówko, "Kresy," *Gazeta Polska* 24 (August 1930), cited in Andrzej Chojnowski, *Koncepcje polityki narodowościowej rządów polskich w latach 1921–1939* (Wrocław, 1979), 164.
11. Snyder, *Sketches,* 64.
12. Rogers Brubaker, *Ethnicity without Groups* (Cambridge, MA, 2004).
13. I discuss an episode that gave impetus to the "discovery" of the Hutsuls and their artistry by the broader Galician and Austrian public circa 1880 in Patrice M. Dabrowski, "'Discovering'

the Galician Borderlands: The Case of the Eastern Carpathians," *Slavic Review* 64, no. 2 (Summer 2005): 380–402.
14. There was nonetheless a tremendously picturesque branch of the Habsburg railway system that, as of the nineteenth century, extended into the region, along the Prut River Valley. Yet the heart of Czarnohora was much harder to reach.
15. I address this subject in my present book-length project, *"Discovering" the Carpathians: Episodes in Imagining and Reshaping Alpine Borderland Regions.*
16. Wacław Jędrzejewicz, "Ś.p. Generał Tadeusz Kasprzycki," *Niepodległość* 8 (1980): 226–27. In July 1934, Kasprzycki was promoted to First Vice Minister for Military Affairs.
17. Derzhavnyj Arkhiv Ivano-Frankivskoï Oblasti (DAIFO) 370/1/42: 23.
18. Jan Kitleruk, "Jak wstąpiłem do Legjonów Polskich," *Żołnierz Polski* 16, no. 7 (1 March 1934): 136–38.
19. A similar myth—"the legend of the Polish-Ukrainian alliance for the independence of Ukraine," according to Józewski—was to provide the groundwork for Polish-Ukrainian cooperation; Snyder, *Sketches,* 78.
20. Jerzy K. Maciejewski, "Odkrywamy Huculszczyznę," in *Huculskim szlakiem II Brygady Legionów Polskich* (Warsaw, 1934), 33.
21. From his introduction to Maciejewski, *Huculskim szlakiem,* 7–8.
22. "Pierwszy etap marszu huculskiego Szlakiem II-ej Brygady," *Polska Zbrojna,* 18 February 1934; "Malinowski Tadeusz (1888–1980)," in *Słownik biograficzny generałów Wojska Polskiego 1918–1939* (Warsaw, 1994), 212.
23. Today the village is called Verkhovyna, and it is in present-day Ukraine.
24. DAIFO 370/1/42: 1, paragraph 4.
25. DAIFO 370/1/42: 2.
26. DAIFO 370/1/42: 1.
27. DAIFO 370/1/42: 22b.
28. DAIFO 370/1/42: 20ff.
29. DAIFO 370/1/42: 19–19b.
30. To the extent that a new Ukrainian journal, *Hutsul's'ke Slovo* (Hutsul Word), was founded in Kołomyja, which was to take up the cause of the Hutsuls.
31. Such sights were noticed by an Englishman pedaling his way through the region in the 1930s: Bernard Newman, *Pedalling Poland* (London: H. Jenkins, 1935). They have also been documented in an exhibition at the State Ethnographic Museum in Warsaw entitled "Image of the Hutsuls and the Hutsul Region in Archivalia and Photographs from the Nineteenth and Twentieth Centuries" (Wizerunek Hucułów i Huculszczyzny w archiwaliach i fotografiach z XIX i XX wieku), on display from 13 June through 17 September 2006.
32. DAIFO, 370/1/8: 2, cited by Mirosława Ołdakowska-Kuflowa, *Stanisław Vincenz pisarz, humanista, orędownik zbliżenia narodów: Biografia* (Lublin, 2006), 177.
33. Hans Zbinden, "Ostkarpatenland," *Der Bund,* nos. 23–25 (1933); Hans Zbinden, "Polenfahrt in stürmischer Zeit," *Der Bund,* nos. 427, 429, 431, 435, 437, 439, 441, 443 (1939). Lidio Cipriani took photographs of the Hutsuls and also wrote about them in *L'Illustrazione Italiana.* Unfortunately, Marcus Ehrenpreis never managed to include the promised biography of Israel Baal Shem Tov in his works on towering Jewish intellectual figures (per correspondence in May 2005 with Stephen Fruitman, author of *Creating a New Heart: Marcus Ehrenpreis on Jewry and Judaism,* PhD diss., University of Umea, 2001).
34. *Kurjer Lwowski,* 14 March 1934.
35. Simsund, "Europa i Polska wobec Huculszczyzny," *Gazeta Poranna,* 18 February 1934.
36. Stanisław Vincenz, "Uwagi o kulturze ludowej," *Złoty Szlak,* no. 2 (1938): 6.
37. Ibid., 6–7.

38. Ibid., 16.
39. Vincenz, cited in Marek Adamiec, "Polish Literature on the Internet," http://www.fpoma.strony.ug.edu.pl/Polish%20Literature%20on%20the%20Internet.pdf (accessed 5 August 2013).
40. Hans Zbinden, cited in Simsund, "Europa i Polska wobec Huculszczyzny."
41. Statement attributed to Lidio Cipriani, in Simsund, "Europa i Polska wobec Huculszczyzny."
42. That said, Vincenz had his (gentle) reservations about the society from its very outset. He noticed that it was hugely ambitious but had not yet harmonized its various strivings, some of which were bound to clash with others. Vincenz thought that it would take a delicate touch to achieve what was necessary in the region. Interestingly (if not surprisingly), he also thought that Ukrainian society and Ukrainian intellectuals should be included in these efforts. Simsund, "Europa i Polska wobec Huculszczyzny."

Chapter 5

MULTICULTURALISM AGAINST THE STATE
Lessons from Istria

Pamela Ballinger

Since its bloody disintegration, the former Yugoslavia has provided the material for many a cautionary tale about the challenges of maintaining peaceful coexistence within multiethnic, multinational, and multiconfessional societies, as well as the difficulties of reestablishing such coexistence in the aftermath of warfare and ethnic cleansing. Some prominent scholars have even gone so far as to draw the pessimistic (and highly controversial) conclusion from Bosnia-Herzegovina that preemptive partition of ethnically mixed countries and organized population transfers offer the best solution for avoiding or minimizing bloodshed.[1] Such a position implies that ethnic coexistence proves ephemeral at best and usually cannot survive once the logic of ethnonational war takes over. Other observers, however, have pointed to the experience of the small Istrian peninsula—lying to the east of Italy and today divided between Slovenia and Croatia—as a place where residents "have learned to tolerate different languages and nations, to live together irrespective of political borders and to put their region above nation or ideology."[2] Slavenka Drakulić asserts that "[t]he Istrian model has demonstrated that tolerance is possible, and that it works."[3]

Though more explicit than Drakulić regarding the ways in which Istrianism has been promoted as a consciously "multicultural" political project, scholars such as Frykman, Burstedt, and Cocco also look to Istria as a place where a "workable compromise—convivenza or *suživot*—[has existed] in the post-1945 era."[4] In keeping with the aims of this volume, I use the Istrian case to interrogate critically the editors' assertion (following Moritz Csáky) that "Habsburg Central Europe may be regarded as a 'laboratory' for the multicultural, or pluricultural experience . . . in which processes significant for the globalized character of society in the twenty-first century can be usefully explored." The chapters in this volume thus reflect a growing interest in Central European multiculturalisms, both on their own terms and in view of their relevance for broader critical and political debates about pluricultural societies.[5]

Istria has received attention for its experiment in multiculturalism since the early 1990s, when there arose in the Istrian peninsula a political movement that claimed to offer a model for coping with, and even celebrating, cultural diversity. The Istrian Democratic Assembly (Istarski Demokratski Sabor or Dieta Democratica Istriana, hereafter IDS-DDI) came into being in 1989, founded by Ivan Pauletta, and became a political party the following year.[6] In its origins, the IDS-DDI had close ties with the Gruppo '88, a group of reform-minded intellectuals within Yugoslavia's Italian minority. Several of the IDS-DDI's key and early proponents came from the Italian minority and, not surprisingly, respect and preservation of the small population of ethnic Italians in Istria (today estimated at thirty thousand persons) has proven a central part of the regionalist project.

The IDS-DDI has held power in Croatian Istria since 1992, winning county majorities in all subsequent elections. Through 1999, the IDS-DDI stood in opposition to the national government, headed by Franjo Tudjman and his Croatian Democratic Union (HDZ) party. The IDS-DDI rejected the militarization of Croatian society during the "homeland war" and protested the use of Istrian tax revenues to finance the conflict. Tudjman's ethnonational definition of Croatia as the state of Croats (and others)[7] further reinforced the Istrian sense of standing apart and offering an alternative model to the exclusive nationalisms that had destroyed the Yugoslav federation.

In the late Yugoslav era, as nationalist politicians came to dominate the scene in much of the country, they frequently drew upon historical grievances in order to propagate a sense of victimization, and hence a need for preemptive measures to prevent victimization (by the "other" group) in the future. In Istria, by contrast, the discussion of previously tabooed topics—such as the executions by partisans of civilians during and after World War II in the karstic pits known as the *foibe,* and the mass migration of the majority of the peninsula's Italians after the war—made for a narrative stressing the need to acknowledge and overcome the divisions that had torn Istria apart in the first half of the twentieth century. Although a sense of victimization was also central to the construction of a new narrative of Istrian history, in contrast to other parts of Yugoslavia the identities of victimizers and victims were not cast predominantly in ethnonational or religious terms, but rather in terms of state centers dominating and exploiting peripheries.[8] This narrative move portrayed all Istrians—whether ethnically identified as Italian, Slovene, Croat, Rumeni, Montenegrin, Albanian, or Serb—as members of a region whose cultural and linguistic intermixture had survived in spite of the heavy-handed policies of distant centers of power that failed to understand the Istrian reality.

Persons living in Istria, whether actively engaged in local politics or not, frequently tell the story of a grandparent or parent who possessed four or five passports (Habsburg, Italian, the area of Zone B contested by Italy and Yugoslavia after World War II, Yugoslav, Croatian, or Slovene) without ever changing residence.[9] This situation of rapidly changing state/political borders and the persistence of a regional identity (Istrian) becomes, in such accounts, symbolic of the region's fate in the past century. Political leaders and supporters of the regionalist movement have stressed this Istrian awareness of the noncongruence of political and sociocultural borders as an explanation for why Istria did not experience interethnic violence in the 1990s.

Peter Turčinović, head of the regionalist party in Rijeka, voiced a popular view when he told a reporter at the Triestine newspaper *Il Piccolo*:

> Almost every thirty years a new state and thus the Istrian adapts himself, giving primacy of place to the values of family and Man and only subsequently to the *patria* and to other values. This explains why in Istria all members of all nationalities are accepted, without extremism or episodes of intolerance.[10]

For Turčinović and other regionalists, Istrians cannot accept the monocultural state logic that asks citizens whether they are Italian, Croatian, or Slovene (or something else). The only feasible answer lies in declaring oneself "Istrian."

Though scholarly commentators have focused on what I deem the "multiculturalist" model promoted by the IDS-DDI in explaining the electoral success of the regionalist project, leaders of the party also stressed the need for a regional framework (that of a Euroregion) to address a host of issues created by the territorial division of the peninsula: the question of once-shared infrastructure (such as hospitals) and the practical problems for Istrians who lived in one state and worked in another, or who had close relatives or who owned property across the borders. Historian John Ashbrook has underscored the multiple reasons for which the majority of residents in Croatian Istria supported the regionalists, such as the IDS-DDI's aim of constituting Istria as a demilitarized zone, the protection of cultural minorities, the efforts to establish Istria as a Euroregion within the Council of Europe's Congress of Local and Regional Authorities, and a desire to determine Istria's economic fate. He argues, however, that these positions "most likely were not enough to sway Istrians into supporting the party, especially in the first few years of Croatian independence . . . the IDS, to compete with the HDZ, needed to politicize regional identity."[11]

A great deal of work on Istrianity has focused more on the discourses of multiculturalism deployed by the regionalists than on the lived realities of multiculturalism in contemporary Istria. Indeed, Driessen has critiqued my previous work[12] on precisely these grounds, arguing that I address only "the level of *identity discourse.*"[13] I agree with Driessen that we need further research on "the contexts in which Istrians evoke 'cosmopolitanism,' the meanings they attach to it, and how understandings of the term are assimilated into their daily lives."[14] Yet I have also sought to demonstrate how the discourse and understanding of Istrianity translates into material practice in everyday life, working both to draw new boundaries of inclusion (uniting "autochthonous" Istrians) and exclusion (differentiating genuine Istrians from newcomers, whether Croats from Zagreb or Herzegovina or recent property owners from other EU countries like Italy and Austria).

While we cannot claim identity discourse—particularly the top-down version promoted by the regionalists—as synonymous with practices on the ground, we also cannot falsely separate them. To do so risks reifying and idealizing an "authentic" realm of everyday life removed from the discursive constraints of politics. Understandings of Istria's multiethnic and multilingual character have a deep history in the region, even if the processes by which local peoples have interpolated and refracted such ideologies proves more difficult to map out. Understanding multiculturalism in contemporary Croatian Istria—a multiculturalism that defined itself (at least until 2000) as firmly *against the state*—requires examination of previous state-directed multiculturalisms in Istria: the "historical practice of diversity"[15] in the Habsburg Monarchy and the Yugoslav socialist experiment in multinationalism.

Genealogies of "Multiculturalism" in Istria

In excavating the multiple genealogies of Istrian multiculturalism, I use the term multicultural in the sense employed by the editors of the volume—discourses about difference utilized by governments "to solve the problems created by cultural diversity," even as they may actually sharpen those differences. After Istria's incorporation into the Habsburg Empire in 1797 (a process completed in 1815), the peninsula became part of a vast multiethnic polity. Areas in Istria had been under control of the multiethnic Venetian Empire for centuries, although Venice never maintained a hold over the entire peninsula (for example, the central area around Pazin/Pisino). In its eastern Adriatic possessions, the Venetian administration had recognized cultural diversity but more in terms of a marked divide between the urbane and urban "civilized" dwellers of the coast and the exotic, backward peoples of the interior.[16] Although the Venetians understood their subjects in terms of "nations," they did not conceptualize such nations in terms of ethnicity (qua language groups), as subsequent Habsburg officials and ethnographers would.

In the Venetian Empire, "nation" did not yet resonate as "national." The categories of identity employed by the Venetians in Dalmatia, for example, "did not recognize a national distinction between Serbs and Croats among the Slavs, and, in fact, Venice preferred to consider both Italians and Slavs of Dalmatia as amalgamated members of the same Dalmatian nation."[17] By the late Venetian period a sense of the Slavs of Dalmatia as belonging to a larger South Slav, or even pan-Slav, world had begun to emerge.[18] A "national question" did not yet exist, however, as the Venetians worried more about how to render the Dalmatian lands economically productive than about the loyalty of its *fedelissimi* subjects.[19] The question of particularistic identities and their relationship to putative national territories would instead become a key issue during the Habsburg period.

When Istria came under Habsburg control, the new rulers surveyed the territory (a process carried out between the years 1817 and 1825) and found it marked by poverty, as well as cultural difference:

> As [with] many other peripheral regions of the Habsburg territory, Istria, which appeared to an outsider as a multitude of microcosms (s. Apollonio, 1998; Ivetic, 2000 et al.), puzzled and intrigued the imperial observers and members of the rising national elites alike. Although the motivations were different, both of these tried to reinterpret and classify the cultural variety of Istria according to "national" categories.[20]

Imperial ("antinationalist") and nationalist understandings of this cultural difference competed throughout the Habsburg era.[21]

Ethnographers in service to the empire consciously filtered their interpretations of cultures and customs through a lens designed to promote a harmonious empire of peoples. As head of the Imperial and Royal Bureau of Statistics, Karl Freiherr von Czoernig helped establish a highly influential view (what Nikočević goes as far as to deem a "stereotype") of Istria as an exceedingly complex and mixed region, even by Habsburg standards.[22] In his three-volume ethnographic work mapping the broader monarchy, Czoernig identified 137 peoples and 22 linguistic categories.[23]

Aiming to forge an ethnographic paradigm that would underwrite a multicultural—rather than a nationally divided—polity, Czoernig viewed cultural difference

> through the prism of "tribes" (*Volksstämme*)—but not peoples and/or nations—which was to be one of the key words in the rhetoric of those who would attempt to reduce the importance of the emerging national identities in the coming decades, emphasizing supranational identity and patriotism on the level of the entire Monarchy.[24]

After the tumult of 1848, in particular, Czoernig became further convinced "that the 'national principle' as advocated by other states was not suitable for Austria-Hungary, where 'racial fighting' and attempts at mutual suppression amongst tribes within the same territory would result in raw violence and anarchy."[25] Czoernig instead envisioned an empire made up of many tribes, whose harmonious coexistence would be "based on rights to land and property granted by the crown."[26]

The work of Czoernig and other imperial ethnographers labored to overturn, even as it actually reinforced some aspects of, long-standing stereotypes about peoples in the monarchy. In the eighteenth century, German-speaking scholars and visitors to the Habsburg Adriatic had reworked Venetian hierarchies that placed civilized and cultivated coastal peoples (increasingly understood as "Italian") well above backward interior peoples (increasingly coded as "Slavs").[27] Images of Adriatic Slavs also echoed German-speaking scholars' classifications of Pannonian "Croats" and Romanians, often depicted by German-speaking scholars (particularly those in dialogue with the descriptive statistical school) as *"Naturmenschen*: hardened, lazy, wild, sensual, poor, extravagant, and drunken."[28] Slavs thus stood as "savage" in both negative and positive aspects: economically unproductive and irrational, yet also simple and in a "state of nature." Czoernig refracted such ideas with his deep interest in the Istrian interior peoples from Cicari(j)a known as the Ćići, who stood for him as the preeminent example of uncontaminated "savagery."[29]

The popular interest in the monarchy's peoples aroused by the work of Czoernig and others bore fruit in a series of initiatives aimed at using ethnographic work as a political instrument of (re)conciliation. Crown Prince Rudolf von Habsburg sponsored the encyclopedic project detailing the empire's people and cultures that became known as the *Kronprinzenwerk* (KPW), consisting of twenty-four volumes of ethnographic descriptions published between 1886 and 1902. The sponsorship of such projects by members of the imperial family represented a conscious effort to inculcate loyalty in and identification with the monarchy and hence the empire, rather than a specific nation or particularistic group.[30] Targeted at a popular (yet literate) audience, the KPW motto *Wissen ist Versöhnung* (knowledge is conciliation) sounds prescient of contemporary multicultural discourse, embodying the notion that greater awareness of diversity would foster tolerance among the monarchy's many peoples.[31] Ironically, the specific KPW texts dedicated to the Austrian Littoral actually flattened out some of the cultural complexities of the region. Vjekoslav Spinčić viewed Istria's Slavic groups through a Croatian prism, stressing similarities between different Croat and Slovene populations in the peninsula. Peter Tomasin's discussion of non-Slavic elements in the Austrian Littoral's popular culture reflected the tendency of Austrian ethnographers to view the urbanized Italianate groups as less pure or authentic and thus less interesting ethnographically.[32] This relative lack of attention to the urban residents "meant that Istrian Italians were interpreted too uniformly in the cultural sense, without consideration of the considerable differences between the everyday culture of the inhabitants."[33]

In practice, the KPW's publication in German and Hungarian also undercut its stated aim to harmonize differences by opening up questions about translations into other languages. For some of the authors of pieces contained within the KPW, writing in the "foreign" administrative language actually furthered the sense of distance and difference from the imperial center.[34] Conceived as a powerful means to combat the "land and peoples" model and demands from nationalists within the monarchy, the KPW instead "might have fueled nationalist fervor," though it "clearly also served as a source book for groups inclined to cherish 'their' traditional culture."[35]

The activities of bodies such as the Viennese Anthropological Society and the Society for Austrian Ethnology further contributed to the fashioning of persistent understandings of the monarchy's peoples in general and groups in particular, such as the "Istrians" and their constituent peoples. Even as the anthropological model shifted in the late nineteenth century away from Czoernig's theoretical framework toward an evolutionist paradigm associated with scholars like Michael Haberlandt, the image of Istria as home to a "multicultural, a-national and hybridised"[36] population endured. As employed by state-sponsored ethnographers like Haberlandt, the evolutionist framework was adapted to accommodate the "state idea." Alongside those Habsburg scholars and administrators who sought to reconcile the monarchy's peoples in an ethnographical and harmonious picture stood nationalistically minded observers who instead posited radically different histories and traditions that seemed to justify separate territorial arrangements (whether of autonomy or independent statehood). In Istria and Dalmatia, for example, Italian irredentists seeking union with the motherland after 1861 found equally insistent countervoices stressing Slovene or Croatian singularity, or a South Slav vision.

Despite the different aims and ethnographic biases associated with the Habsburg (imperial) and nationalist positions, the discourses of these groups interpenetrated and also informed (albeit incompletely and sometimes in unpredictable ways) the self-understandings of members of the putative groups. This, in turn, informed practices ranging from those of administration to everyday interactions, such as attending religious services or belonging to voluntary associations.[37] As Elke-Nicole Kappus notes,

> Not only nationalists, but the Empire's administrators as well classified the Istrian peoples in increasingly homogenised "national" groups and it is, in fact, hard to determine if the national movements had informed the administrative categories or vice versa. It is, however, certain that the very Habsburg bureaucracy institutionalized the categories in terms of which the people would increasingly model their sense of belonging, loyalty and identity well before the arrival of the "nation state."[38]

Thus, multiculturalism, understood here in terms of the monarchy's explicit efforts to create forms of solidarity across emerging ethnonational divisions, cannot be completely isolated from the more difficult to document issue of how (and whether) an Istrian pluricultural society operates in practice.

The particular genealogy of Habsburg multiculturalism I have outlined here informs contemporary Istrianism to a considerable degree. The Habsburg era serves as a source of nostalgia for many Istrians in Croatian Istria, even though Istrians also insist that current Istrian regionalism offers a homegrown (in contrast to the previous Viennese-imposed) solution to cultural difference.[39] Likewise, the model of a socialist multinational Yugoslavia in which minorities received official recognition and protection provokes nostalgia, especially when contrasted with the nationalizing regimes of fascist Italy (which controlled Istria from 1920 to 1943) and Tudjman's Croatia (1991–99). At the same time, in regionalist discourse the Yugoslav regime represents an example of Istria's domination by a distant center.

Memories and interpretations of the Yugoslav period prove more mixed than do those of the distant and seemingly halcyon Habsburg days. When Istrians express admiration for Yugoslav "Brotherhood and Unity," they often refer to the solidarity of the partisan war fought by Slavs and Italians against the Nazi and fascist forces, or to the period of liberalization in the 1960s and 1970s. The experience of Yugoslav socialism in the years immediately following World War II instead brings to mind the migration of the majority of Istria's Italians (what some now interpret as an episode of ethnic cleansing),[40] the persecution of Cominformists (real or imagined), and the imposition of a centralizing model patterned after Stalin's USSR. In the cultural realm, the model promoted in that first decade sought to forge a supranational Yugoslav nation with specific Yugoslav socialist values.[41] Moves toward a more decentralized and truly federalist model in the 1960s meant that the regime now sponsored "what could be called a multinational self-image. Instead of seeing national cultural particularities as something to be overcome by one means or another, Yugoslav leaders decided to embrace cultural difference and use it as a sign of strength."[42] As occurred with the policies promoted by the Habsburgs, the unintended consequence of this Yugoslav multiculturalism was to reinforce territorialized ethnonational identities. As Wachtel contends, "[i]t was the gradual victory of cultural particularism that laid the crucial groundwork for the ultimate political collapse of Yugoslavia."[43]

An alternative vision of pluricultural living together that some inhabitants of Istria invoke refers back to the prenational period under Venice. This particular genealogy links Istria to a larger maritime world, one in which borders proved literally fluid and yet one in which the architectural signs of Venice (campanili, the lions of St. Mark) linked together far-flung territories. Though this past would appear to exclude whole areas of Istria (such as Pazin/Pisino, which Venice never controlled), *who* invokes this past can prove surprising. Anthropologist Irena Weber, for instance, describes the relentless marketing of the Venetian heritage of Piran/Pirano, a town in Slovene Istria in which the majority of residents (the "heirs" of that Venetian past, so to speak) left en masse after World War II.

The marketing of Piran/Pirano as Venetian to outside tourists nonetheless also resonates within the town.

> The Venetian past is the main heritage narrative frame of reference used in Piran for tourists and local inhabitants alike. It is quite obvious why it is used for tourists—Venice sells well. As for the local inhabitants, it reflects a distant past that does not need to be contested since it is virtually nobody's past and can safely be "remembered." Interestingly, it is another imperial past, namely the Habsburg one that is being collectively forgotten here, in marked contrast to Trieste where it is much celebrated.[44]

The lack of interest in the Habsburg past in Piran/Pirano also contrasts with towns in Croatian Istria, such as Rovinj/Rovigno, which proudly celebrates its dual Venetian and Habsburg heritages. In Rovinj/Rovigno, the Venetian maritime past has received emphasis with the opening of a small museum dedicated to the traditional wooden boat known as the *batana*, which has become a symbol of both the town and of the larger Italian minority in Istria.[45] Emphasizing the Venetian past can thus simultaneously celebrate a specifically "Italian" past and a cosmopolitan past in which the empire's peoples lived together, as well as project a future of tolerant coexistence.[46]

The emphasis on a Venetian past also points to the Adriatic and, more broadly, the Mediterranean as symbolic resources employed in the construction of contemporary versions of multiculturalism.[47] The Austrian nostalgia that thrives in Trieste draws upon, for example, a specific kind of multiethnic experience in port cities that frequently becomes the object of idealization long after both empires ended and structural transformation in ports have rendered those societies less "cosmopolitan,"[48] understood here to encompass both cultural diversity and elements of tolerance. Although a rich body of work on Mediterranean port cities and their "cosmopolitan" qualities exists (for an introduction, see the special issue of *History and Anthropology* from 2005),[49] this literature often remains disconnected from work on the "Central European experience." In the former Yugoslavia, the relative lack of attention to the maritime aspects of the "Central European" experience reflects a political and scholarly ambivalence in socialist Yugoslavia and even contemporary Croatia about the place of Mediterranean elements in Croatian "national identity."[50]

In multinational socialist Yugoslavia, the so-called Adriatic orientation was downplayed in favor of cultural and political representations that stressed rural cultures and the peasantry as the essence of "traditional" culture. Writes anthropologist Dunja Rihtman-Auguštin,

> Although it is hard to understand today, in a country which had such a significant coastal belt with a highly indented and proportionally lengthy coast, the economic orientation towards the Adriatic Sea and the economic possibilities offered by the sea were regarded as treasonable by the central Yugoslav authorities . . . the central

Yugoslav authorities constantly opposed the *Adriatic Orientation* with the *Danubian Orientation*.[51]

Ethnographic museums and ethnographic studies mirrored these economic and political preferences, with an almost exclusive focus on rural life until the late 1980s.[52] The Istrian Ethnographic Museum founded in 1962, for example, contained scarce references to the peninsula's Italian populations and their specific cultural forms in the coastal towns.[53] Yugoslav anthropology thus refracted older biases of Habsburg ethnographers, who displayed little interest in the Italianized towns, whose urbanity and "cosmopolitanism" appeared to signify cultural inauthenticity or deracination.[54] In the Yugoslav case, understandings of what constituted authentic folk "culture" worked together with the political imperatives of a regime that had engaged after World War II in a decade-long territorial dispute with Italy over Trieste and Istria and replaced Istria's departing Italianate population with South Slav migrants. In Yugoslavia, then, the maritime past often stood not for a cosmopolitan past that could be invoked as a precursor of "Brotherhood and Unity" but rather as an imperial-nationalist history of "Italian" claims upon the eastern Adriatic.

Historian Maura Hametz has demonstrated how the Italian fascist regime that controlled Istria from 1922 until 1943 exploited the Adriatic's "cosmopolitan" maritime heritage to assert the essential Italianness of the sea and its territories. The regime transformed local festivals into state-sponsored marine exhibitions that glorified Trieste's links to "the maritime spirit of our [Italian] people who see the sea as the greatest factor in the welfare and prosperity of the nation."[55] The city and the broader region's ties to the Apennine peninsula and Venice received emphasis, even though Trieste had never been Venetian and had looked to its Central European hinterland since its declaration as a Habsburg free port in 1719. Nonetheless, the city became viewed through an imaginary that, in the words of one nationalist, "approached Trieste 'from the sea by way of Venice,'"[56] rather than by train from Vienna or Ljubljana.

Although the fascist regime's use of this maritime past for nationalist and expansionist aims proves quite transparent in its instrumentalism, other uses and invocations of cosmopolitan or multicultural pasts in ways that may draw boundaries of exclusion or foster intolerance sometimes prove more subtle and difficult to discern. A wide range of scholars, wary of the nostalgic and unproblematic uses to which concepts of cosmopolitanism and multiculturalism have been put of late, have urged the need to trace out the genealogies of specific or "local" cosmopolitanisms.[57]

Heeding Sant Cassia and Schäfer's warning that "the premises that underlie the term 'cosmopolitanism' in the contemporary era contain a different set of social assumptions [from its understanding in the past],"[58] I have tried to demonstrate the particular versions of cosmopolitanism that operated in Trieste and

Istria.[59] I contend, for example, that "nineteenth and early twentieth-century Trieste was economically and culturally controlled by a class-bound, politically restrictive bourgeois mercantile elite that was considerably less cosmopolitan than late-twentieth- and early-twenty-first century nostalgia would make out."[60] As I discuss in the next section, the limits of such cosmopolitanism echo the limits of contemporary Istrian multiculturalism.

Istrianity: Strengths and Weaknesses

Previous versions of political multiculturalism in Istria have often worked, albeit unintentionally (as in the Habsburg Monarchy or socialist Yugoslavia), to reinforce the separateness of ethnonational groups. When political conditions shift or crises occur, exclusivist identifications and intolerance can easily come to dominate politics and damage the fabric of diversity in pluralistic societies. The regionalist program and its concept of Istrianity instead claim to offer a homegrown model for a tolerant society that reflects and grows out of local pluricultural realities, rather than a top-down imposition by a distant state center. Does the Istrian experiment live up to its claims and go beyond its predecessors, even as it simultaneously draws strength from widespread nostalgia for those previous incarnations of multiethnic coexistence and cooperation?

In some aspects, the contemporary project of Istrianity reveals the same conceptual limits as its predecessors. Istrianness encodes a strong sense of regional and territorialized identity that draws new boundaries of both belonging and exclusion. The emphasis on being from a particular *place* (Istria) builds upon an intellectual tradition in the region that sees peoples as "belonging" to particular places and kinds of environments (think Jovan Cvijić and the "Dinaric Man").[61] By the same logic, then, migrations may take groups to environments in which they are deemed territorially incompatible.[62] Such notions run through the ways in which "Istrians" often describe their new neighbors (e.g., the Bosnian or Kosovar who has no experience of the coast and its lifeways). Equally deep-rooted ideas about Istria as historically part of a Western or European civilizational realm (drawing upon nostalgia for the "Western" Venetian and Habsburg heritage) in contrast to an "Eastern," Oriental (Ottoman) sphere further underscore the difference between civilized and "tolerant" Istrians and the "Balkan types" in their midst.

Building upon anthropological analyses that underscore the exclusionary potential of Istrianity,[63] sociologist Emilio Cocco has contended that "even though universal aspirations of multiculturalism and tolerance are put forward, the sense of Istrianity points at the maintenance of a fragile ethnic and social balance that is very likely to be lacerated by any ideological national hatred."[64] Yet Cocco also recognizes—as do I—that the forms such exclusion has taken in contemporary Istria, as opposed to other parts of the former Yugoslavia in the 1990s, differ dramatically. Violence and intolerance have not characterized life in Croatian Istria. Rather, a strong distinction between genuine Istrians (*Istriani patocchi, Istriani d.o.c.*) and "non-Istrians" now living in Istria (particularly Muslims from Bosnia and Kosovar Albanians) marks everyday life in Istria, where difference becomes visible in things such as residential patterns, cuisine, practices of home care, gender relations, and the *perceptions* of such things on the part of different groups.[65]

Language, specifically the ability to speak various Istrian patois, serves as a particularly strong marker of difference. Croats from Slavonia or Muslims from Sarajevo living in Istria can certainly find a common tongue with which to communicate with their Istrian neighbors, but they often find themselves excluded when Istrians shift between various forms of čakavski Croatian, distinct town or village dialects, and Istro-Veneto (an Italian variation). Likewise, Istrians may feel excluded when newcomers "speak amongst themselves," reinforcing ideas about the "clannishness" of these recent arrivals.

At the political level, the protection of Italian-Croatian bilingualism has been a crucial component of the regionalist project. The efforts of Tudjman's minister of education in the mid-1990s to prevent ethnic non-Italians from attending Italian language schools (themselves a product of the Yugoslav version of multiculturalism and its recognition of an official Italian minority with its own institutions and associations) galvanized the regionalists. The IDS-DDI thus rejected the nationalist logics of a regime that sought to map ethnic identity neatly onto linguistic identity. Bilingualism was seen as a feature of Istrianity, part of the refusal to accept one exclusive ethnic or national identity. In this sense, the regionalists would appear to have learned a lesson from the Habsburg state multiculturalism that used language as an (extremely contested) instrument for evaluating identity, as in the four censuses between 1880 and 1910 that measured identity (poorly) on the basis of *Umgangssprache* (language of use).[66]

In the language politics of everyday life, however, bilingualism often defines the boundary between authentic Istrians and others—that is, bilingualism and use of dialect become the markers of a regional identity from which many living in the region are effectively excluded. In practical terms, as well, the focus on bilingualism—so admirable when compared to the monolinguistic homogenizing policies of the Tudjman regime—may be fostering a sort of reductive multiculturalism that envisions Istrianity as an umbrella for Slavs (Croat and Slovene) and Italians. In her efforts to create a museum that reflects the multicultural history and realities of Istria, the Istrian Ethnographic Museum's director, Lidija Nikočević, has observed how the Italian-Slav binary that defined competing nationalisms/irredentisms in the late nineteenth century and the first half of the twentieth century may unwittingly be replicated by the "multicultural" celebration of Istrianism. When Istrians talk about the peninsula's cultural and linguistic differences, they increasingly think in terms of Italians and Slavs, to the neglect of other "minorities" such as the Montenegrins of Peroj, the Istro-Rumeni, Serbs, Albanians, and others.

Throughout the 1990s, the dangers of this reductivism were less apparent, as the Istrian model served as an effective form of opposition to Tudjman's party and its centralizing efforts. When Tudjman died in 1999 and a center-left democratic coalition came into power in 2000, the IDS-DDI suddenly became part of the governing coalition. It did not take long, however, for differences to surface, most notably over the article of the regional statute that recognized Italian-Croatian bilingualism in the county of Istria; the Constitutional Court of Croatia soon questioned the constitutionality of the statute.[67] The IDS-DDI later withdrew from the coalition. Although they established a good working relationship with the subsequent center-right (reformed HDZ) government, the IDS-DDI continued for several years to cherish an oppositional role, a role that suited the sense of Istrian difference (by way of its pluriethnic tolerance) and superiority to other areas of Croatia. To some degree, then, the regionalist project remained positioned *against* the state, even if the stance of the central government toward the EU has transformed completely since the days of Tudjman and as the IDS-DDI continues to insist that it represents the ("European") model for the rest of a Croatia that is now the EU's most recent new member.

The long-cherished goal of establishing an Istrian Euroregion, a proposal that Tudjman and his supporters had attacked as a sign of "secessionist" ambitions, has also come to pass (though Istria is now part of a larger Adriatic Euroregion rather than a more narrowly defined Istrian Euroregion). Despite this initiative, Istrian multiculturalism remained not just positioned "against the state" (to some extent), but paradoxically also contained "within the (Croatian) state." Notwithstanding the IDS-DDI's claims (and hopes) to have overcome the divisions created in 1991 by the drawing of a new political border between Slovenian and Croatian Istria, that border has dramatically altered the social fabric of life in Istria. The imperative to consolidate national identity on the Slovene side of the border, coupled with Slovenes' desire to distance themselves from their less prosperous neighbor, has meant that the IDS-DDI's early hopes of a transstate movement were frustrated. In 1996, the IDS-DDI disappeared altogether from the Slovene electoral lists.[68]

Anthropologist Borut Brumen's work in the Slovene village of Sv. Peter, three kilometers from the Dragogna River, suggests that along this part of the border social distance between inhabitants has increased since 1991. When Brumen asked his informants how they viewed their neighbors just across the border, they responded, "They were Istrians, just like us. We spoke the same language, the only difference being that they used more of the Croatian and we more of the Slovene words. It is only now that we call them Croatian Istrians. Before we were all just Istrians."[69] After the establishment of the new border, economic relationships and patterns of marriage between inhabitants on opposite sides of the Dragogna became increasingly rare. Sv. Peter lies at the heart of a contested area in which the maritime and land borders between Slovenia and Croatia remain in question over two decades after independence. As a consequence, the villagers of Sv. Peter "have now invented 'Others' who are not Istrian anymore but Croats from the other side of the border."[70] Though the regionalist project is not "responsible" for such a change, it also has not succeeded in overcoming these transformations. When viewed from Slovene Istria, the "Istrian" identity's capacity to embrace all the peninsula's inhabitants appears to have shrunk since 1991.

In two other communities on the Croatian side of the post-1991 border, anthropologist Lidija Nikočević likewise found that the border had severely disrupted previous patterns of reciprocity, labor, and kinship. The villagers in Pasjak and Gradinj viewed themselves as Istrians and resisted a strict ethnic definition as "Croats." Nikočević found greater "hesitancy" to identify with the putative ethnonational group on the Croat, as compared to the Slovene, side of the border. She explains this hesitancy not in terms of a greater (Croatian) Istrian tolerance or rejection of nationalism but as a result of "the deep dissatisfaction with the inferior economic status of the individuals and villages as a whole, which constantly compare themselves with examples across the border, and the general frustration with the border in all its aspects."[71] Here, then, Istrianness served as a symbolic resource with which villagers on the Croatian side of the border sought to maintain the sense of shared culture that once linked them with their now-divided "Slovene" counterparts, who no longer profess a sense of common Istrian identity.

The villages Nikočević studied do not lie astride major, manned border crossing points but rather small, often unmarked ones, which makes for a certain amount of flexibility in how villagers negotiate crossings with local authorities. The border station at the Dragogna, near Sv. Peter, by contrast represents a harder and more controlled border. Not surprisingly, the attitudes of inhabitants on both sides of the border hardened during the 1990s, as evidenced by Brumen's research. Just as once frequent relationships between the villages of Sv. Peter/S. Pietro (in Slovenia) and Kaštel/Castello (in Croatia) have diminished, so, too, have the once numerous contacts between residents in Piran/Pirano (in Slovenia) and Savudrija/Salvore (in Croatia). The imposition of customs when crossing the short distance across the Gulf of Piran meant that people living in and around Savudrija rarely traveled by boat to Piran anymore to go shopping or to go to the dentist.

The intermittent fishing war created during the last decade by the extended tensions over the maritime border inaugurated even more dramatic transformations. Fishers on either side of the contested maritime border held different visions of where to draw the demarcation line in the small Gulf of Piran. Slovene fishermen feared that their economic livelihoods would become unviable if the border were drawn evenly down the Gulf, as Croatian fishermen demanded and the Croatian government had long proposed. Such a demarcation risked denying Slovene fishers access to international waters, thereby "trapping" them in a narrow triangle of relatively unproductive waters. Croatian fishers, in contrast, resented what they perceived as Slovenia's territorial pretensions and the sense that Croatia had to "placate" its neighbor in order to win Slovene support for Croatia's EU candidacy during the accession period. Interviews I conducted between 2002 and 2008 with fishers on both sides of the contested border reveal the extent to which forms of solidarity and identification among fishers broke down.[72]

An obvious manifestation of this lack of shared feeling could be seen in July 2006, when a contingent of Slovene fishermen traveled to nearby Trieste to protest a plan to build offshore liquefied natural gas (LNG) platforms in the Gulf of Trieste. When I had spoken with fishers and other residents of Piran/Pirano in the weeks leading up to the protest, the urgency of defeating the proposed LNG project dominated our conversations. However, when I crossed the border and spoke with fishers in Croatia, I found little interest in the subject. The fishers hoped, of course, that the project would not go through, but they did not attend the protest in Trieste because the "border question" remained open. (Members of the non-Istrian Croatian environmentalist group Eko Kvarner did, however, attend the demonstration alongside representatives from different Slovene groups.) Throughout Croatian Istria, a sense of difference from and often resentment toward Slovenes proves acute.[73] The EU integration process and Croatia's candidacy sharpened, rather than diminished, this feeling of difference. Istrianity thus represents a sense of shared identity that increasingly differentiated Croatian Istria from Slovene Istria from 1991 on. This difference does not remain restricted to the level of discourse or sentiments. Rather, it represents a deep transformation in the forms of "inter-cultural communication"[74] or what Roth calls "inter-cultural competence . . . developed over a long period of time and integrated into the systems of interethnic coexistence."[75] Certain forms of multicultural practice are in sharp decline in Istria, even as multicultural discourse flourishes. The territorial dimensions of contemporary Istrian multiculturalism, heir to its Habsburg and Yugoslav predecessors, significantly constrain the structure and scope of this project. It remains to be seen whether the dismantling of the Slovene-Croatian border after Croatia's entry into the EU in 2013 renews practices of intercultural exchange truncated by Yugoslavia's dissolution.

Reflecting on his experiences living in the Istrian town of Rovinj/Rovigno, Russell Scott Valentino has noted a "rigidity" that haunts discursive (literary) constructions of Istrianness, one that reflects "a lack of fluidity in Istrian life itself, a cultural fixedness that distinguishes it from what is usually understood as multicultural in North American cultural debates." As Valentino's wife pointed out,

> "Yes, Istria is heterogeneous, that's clear," she said. "You see it as soon as you cross the border, even before. But it's only heterogeneous with regard to what's here already, what's been here for a long time. In that way it is homogeneous. It's homogeneously heterogeneous." She searched for the right word. "It's a melted pot."[76]

Given this, I remain skeptical of Cocco's hope that "an Istrian 'international' regionalism able to link local specificity and cosmopolitan rights"—at least in its present form—"could be envisaged as an original and progressive way to achieve a new form of international citizenship."[77]

Conclusion

The ongoing experiments in multiethnic living and multicultural governance in Croatian Istria represent an important alternative to the exclusivist nationalisms that dominated public life in much of the former Yugoslavia during the 1990s. As I have sought to demonstrate in this chapter, however, the Istrian regional identity contains its own exclusions and has not succeeded in maintaining certain forms of intercultural communication across the Istrian peninsula. The territorialized understanding of identity—of belonging to a *place,* as well as to a community of speakers of various linguistic variants—means that this multiculturalism does not entirely escape the logics of territorialized states, even when it positions itself against the state (and beyond the state, below the state, and so on).

In identifying the limits of Istrian multiculturalism, I do not mean to deny its strengths or to diminish the courage of the regionalists of the Tudjman era in providing an alternative to a narrow version of Croatian nationalism and belonging. I do, however, use the Istrian case to reflect upon the larger "Central European" experience by locating key elements of contemporary Istrian multiculturalism in previous experiments in governing pluralistic societies. Excavating those genealogies demands considering Habsburg or Yugoslav (or Venetian, for that matter) "cosmopolitanisms" or multiculturalisms on their own terms, not through the nostalgic lenses of the twenty-first century. Scholars have increasingly looked to the "transcultural past" in an effort to rethink what Hoerder has called the "monocultural nation-state paradigm."[78] The Ottoman and Habsburg experiences have received considerable attention,[79] particularly in light of the episodes of genocide and ethnic cleansing that devastated the lands of these pluralistic (former) empires in the twentieth century.

As scholars, however, we must examine our own theoretical genealogies and remember that previous generations also used the Central European "example" to "evaluate and influence political choices and strategies at local, international and national levels,"[80] even though the conclusions drawn then often differ starkly from the evaluations we make of the Habsburg experiment now. Glenda Sluga notes that the longevity of debates about whether pluralistic states like the Habsburg Monarchy or its Yugoslav successors proved artificial or unnatural "should encourage us to reflect on the kinds of metaphors and analogies implied in political assessments of the significance of diversity and identity in the present as well as in the past."[81] The contributions in this volume represent an important step toward doing so.

Notes

1. See Robert M. Hayden, "Schindler's Fate: Genocide, Ethnic Cleansing, and Population Transfers," *Slavic Review* 55, no. 4 (Winter 1996): 727–48; John J. Mearsheimer and Robert A. Pape, "The Answer: A Three-Way Partition Plan for Bosnia and How the US Can Enforce It," *The New Republic* 14 (June 1993): 22–28; John J. Mearsheimer and Stephen Van Evera, "When Peace Means War: The Partition that Dare not Speaks its Name," *The New Republic* 18 (December 1995): 16–21.
2. Slavenka Drakulić, *Café Europa: Life after Communism* (New York, 1999), 167.
3. Ibid.
4. Jonas Frykman, "Making Sense of Memory: Monuments and Landscape in Croatian Istria," *Ethnologia Europaea* 33, no. 2 (2002): 118; see also Anna Burstedt, "The Place on the Plate!" *Ethnologia Europaea* 32, no. 2 (2002): 145–58; and Emilio Cocco, *Metamorfosi dell'Adriatico orientale* (Faenza, 2002).
5. Dirk Hoerder, "Revising the Monocultural Nation-State Paradigm: An Introduction to Transcultural Perspectives," in *The Historical Practice of Diversity: Transcultural Interactions from the Early Modern Mediterranean to the Postcolonial World*, ed. Dirk Hoerder, Christiane Harzig, and Adrian Shubert (New York, 2003), 1–12; Glenda Sluga, "Bodies, Souls, and Sovereignty: The Austro-Hungarian Empire and the Legitimacy of Nations," *Ethnicities* 1, no. 2 (2001): 89–100.
6. Cocco, *Metamorfosi dell'Adriatico orientale*, 182.
7. On the "constitutional nationalism" characteristic of the Yugoslav successor states, see Robert Hayden, "Constitutional Nationalism in the Formerly Yugoslav Republics," *Slavic Review* 51, no. 4 (1992): 654–73.
8. The Istrian account also contrasts with the narratives of ethnic victimization common among Italians who left Istria after World War II and resettled in Trieste. Pamela Ballinger, *History in Exile: Memory and Identity at the Borders of the Balkans* (Princeton, NJ, 2003), 129–67.
9. Robert Gary Minnich, "At the Interface of the Germanic, Romance and Slavic Worlds: Folk Culture as an Idiom of Collective Self-Images in Southeastern Alps," *Studia ethnologica* (1990): 163–80; Pamela Ballinger, "'Authentic Hybrids' in the Balkan Borderlands," *Current Anthropology* 45, no. 1 (2004): 31–60.
10. *Il Piccolo,* 18 November 1996.
11. John Ashbrook, "Locking Horns in the Istrian Political Arena: Politicized Identity, the Istrian Democratic Assembly, and the Croatian Democratic Alliance," *East European Politics and Societies* 20, no. 4 (November 2006): 640.
12. Ballinger, *History in Exile;* Ballinger, "'Authentic Hybrids' in the Balkan Borderlands."

13. Hank Driessen, "Mediterranean Port Cities: Cosmopolitanism Reconsidered," *History and Anthropology* 16, no. 1 (2005): 138.
14. Ibid.
15. Dirk Hoerder, Christiane Harzig, and Adrian Shubert, eds., *The Historical Practice of Diversity: Transcultural Interactions from the Early Modern Mediterranean to the Postcolonial World* (New York, 2003).
16. Larry Wolff, *Venice and the Slavs: The Discovery of Dalmatia in the Age of Enlightenment* (Palo Alto, CA, 2001).
17. Wolff, *Venice and the Slavs*, 11.
18. Valentina Gulin, "Morlacchism between Enlightenment and Romanticism: Identification and Self-Identification of the European *Other*," *Narodna umjetnost* 34, no. 1 (1997): 92-93.
19. Wolff, *Venice and the Slavs*, 131-132.
20. Elke-Nicole Kappus, "Imperial Ideologies of Peoplehood in Habsburg—an Alternative Approach to Peoples and Nations in Istria," *Annales* 12, no. 2 (2002): 324.
21. Ibid., 322.
22. Lidija Nikočević, "State Culture and the Laboratory of Peoples: Istrian Ethnography during the Austro-Hungarian Monarchy," *Narodna umjetnost* 43, no. 1 (2006): 44.
23. Ibid., 42.
24. Ibid., 42-43.
25. Regina Bendix, "Ethnology, Cultural Reification, and the Dynamics of Difference in the *Kronprinzenwerk*," in *Creating the Other: Ethnic Conflict and Nationalism in Habsburg Central Europe*, ed. Nancy M. Wingfield (New York, 2003), 153.
26. Ibid. As late as the 1830s, there persisted alternative conceptualizations of difference within the monarchy that stressed class and occupational divisions, as well as ideas about civil society and the possession of civic "virtues" by specific groups. András Vári, "The Functions of Ethnic Stereotypes in Austria and Hungary in the Early Nineteenth Century," in Wingfield, *Creating the Other*, 39. These class divisions typically overlaid geographical-environmental distinctions, such as urban and rural, coastal or mountainous, more than ethnonational ones. As the nineteenth century progressed, however, these differentiations increasingly became understood in ethnic or national terms that examined criteria such as language and religion as key markers of identity; in nationalist imaginaries, these identities became wed to claims about peoples belonging to particular territories. Pieter Judson, "Inventing Germans: Class, Nationality and Colonial Fantasy at the Margins of the Hapsburg Monarchy," *Social Analysis* 33 (1993): 47–67.
27. Cathie Carmichael, "Ethnic Stereotypes in Early European Ethnographies: A Case Study of the Habsburg Adriatic c. 1770–1815," *Narodna umjetnost* 33, no. 2 (1996): 197–209.
28. Vári, "The Functions of Ethnic Stereotypes," 45.
29. Nikočević, "State Culture and the Laboratory of Peoples," 44; on the Ćići as the Istrian "pet group" of the Viennese anthropologists, see also Kappus, "Imperial Ideologies of Peoplehood in Habsburg," 326.
30. Kappus, "Imperial Ideologies of Peoplehood in Habsburg," 325.
31. Nikočević, "State Culture and the Laboratory of Peoples," 45.
32. Ibid., 47–48. See also Reinhard Johler, "A Local Construction—Or: What Have the Alps to do with a Global Reading of the Mediterranean?" *Narodna umjetnost* 36, no. 1 (1999): 95.
33. Nikočević, "State Culture and the Laboratory of Peoples," 48.
34. Bendix, "Ethnology, Cultural Reification, and the Dynamics of Difference in the *Kronprinzenwerk*," 157.
35. Ibid., 161.
36. Nikočević, "State Culture and the Laboratory of Peoples," 51.

37. See Vanni D'Alessio, "Istrians, Identifications and the Habsburg Legacy: Perspectives on Identities in Istria," *Acta Histriae* 14, no. 1 (2006): 15–39.
38. Kappus, "Imperial Ideologies of Peoplehood in Habsburg," 324.
39. Ballinger, *History in Exile,* 226–28, 248–49.
40. Who is doing the remembering and in which contexts remembering takes place (institutional, familial, spatial, etc.) obviously makes for considerable variation in the depiction of the Austrian and Yugoslav periods. Much of my previous work has focused on how self-described ethnic Italians from Istria, both those who left in the decade after World War II and settled across the border in Trieste and those who remained and became part of an official minority, remember the mass migration from Istria after World War II and how that contested past informs the present. On the experiences of Italians as a minority under Yugoslavia and then Croatia and Slovenia, see Guido Rumici, *Fratelli d'Istria, 1945–2000: Italiani Divisi* (Mursia, 2001).
41. Andrew Wachtel, *Making a Nation, Breaking a Nation: Literature and Cultural Politics in Yugoslavia* (Palo Alto, CA, 1998), 128–72.
42. Ibid., 174.
43. Ibid.
44. Irena Weber, "Heritage Narratives on the Slovenian Coast: The Lion and the Attic," in *Cultural Heritages as Reflexive Traditions,* ed. Ullrich Kockel and Mairead Nic Craith (Houndmills, 2007), 162.
45. Pamela Ballinger, "Lines in the Water, Peoples on the Map: Representing the 'Boundaries' of Cultural Groups in the Upper Adriatic," *Narodna umjetnost* 43, no. 1 (2006): 15–39.
46. Istria's population became much more diverse during the Venetian period, in part because refugees from Ottoman territory fled to Venetian-held areas and in part because the Venetians resettled various Slavic and Albanian groups in Istria after devastating plagues depopulated the peninsula. The Habsburgs likewise resettled parts of the peninsula in the wake of violence and epidemics.
47. See Dieter Haller, "The Cosmopolitan Mediterranean: Myth and Reality," *Zeitschrift für Ethnologie* 129 (2004): 34; Nataša Rogelja, "Sea Fetishism: On the Shore-Dwelling Population," in *Proceedings of Mediterranean Ethnological School,* ed. Bostjan Kavanja and Matej Vranjes (Ljubljana, 2005), 100–1, 109.
48. See Haller, "The Cosmopolitan Mediterranean."
49. *History and Anthropology* 16, no. 1 (2005): Special issue: Re-visioning the Mediterranean. Paul Sant Cassia and Isabel Schäfer, eds.
50. Jasna Čapo Žmegač, "Ethnology, Mediterranean Studies and Political Reticence in Croatia: From Mediterranean Constructs to Nation-Building," *Narodna umjetnost* 36, no. 1 (1999): 35–52.
51. Dunja Rihtman-Auguštin, "A Croatian Controversy: Mediterranean-Danube-Balkans," *Narodna umjetnost* 36, no. 1 (1999): 109.
52. Čapo Žmegač, "Ethnology, Mediterranean Studies and Political Reticence in Croatia."
53. The current director of the museum, Lidija Nikočević, has recognized the need to reorganize the museum in innovative ways that represent Istria's multicultural heritage. New exhibits, for example, examine Istria as seen through the eyes of Habsburg ethnologists and folklorists and focus on Istrian self-identification as expressed through tourist souvenirs. Lidija Nikočević, "Trying to Grasp Multiculturality: New Museological Practice in Istria," presented at the ICME sessions, ICOM Triennial Conference, Barcelona, July 2001, 4–5.
54. Johler, "A Local Construction," 95.
55. Cited in Maura Hametz, *Making Trieste Italian 1918–1954* (Woodbridge, 2005), 93–94.
56. Hametz, *Making Trieste Italian,* 89.

57. Pheng Cheah, "Introduction Part II: The Cosmopolitical—Today," in *Cosmopolitics: Thinking and Feeling Beyond the Nation,* ed. Pheng Cheah and Bruce Robbins (Minneapolis, 1998), 20–41; Bruce Robbins, "Actually Existing Cosmopolitanism," in Cheah and Robbins, *Cosmopolitics,* 1–19. On the contradictions of the "Odessan Myth" of tolerance and its limits, see Tanya Richardson, "Living Cosmopolitanism? 'Tolerance,' Religion, and Local Identity in Odessa," in *The Postsocialist Question: Faith and Power in Central Asia and East-Central Europe,* ed. Chris Hann and the "Civil Religion" Group (Berlin, 2006), 213–40; Tanya Richardson, *Kaleidoscopic Odessa: History and Place in Contemporary Ukraine* (Toronto, 2008).
58. Paul Sant Cassia and Isabel Schäfer, "'Mediterranean Conundrums': Pluridisciplinary Perspectives for Research in the Social Sciences," *History and Anthropology* 16, no. 1 (2002): 20.
59. In anthropological literature focused specifically on the "Mediterranean" as an object of analysis, discussions of cosmopolitanism have focused on its links with discourses of modernity and "questions of symbolic domination by the West." Sant Cassia and Schäfer, "'Mediterranean Conundrums,'" 22. See also Ilay Örs, "Coffeehouses, Cosmopolitanism, and Pluralizing Modernities in Istanbul," *Journal of Mediterranean Studies* 12, no. 1 (2002): 119–45.
60. Ballinger, *History in Exile,* 33.
61. Jovan Cvijić, *La Péninsule Balkanique: Géographie Humaine* (1918, Paris).
62. Carmichael, "Ethnic Stereotypes in Early European Ethnographies," 199. For Istria specifically, see also Ballinger, "Lines in the Water, Peoples on the Map."
63. Pamela Ballinger, "The Istrian *Esodo*: Silences and Presences in the Construction of Exodus," in *War, Exile, and Everyday Life,* ed. Maja Povrzanovic and Renata Jambresic Kirin (Zagreb, 1996), 117–32; Bojan Baskar, "Made in Trieste: Geopolitical Fears of an Istrianist Discourse on the Mediterranean," *Narodna umjetnost* 36, no. 1 (1999): 121–34.
64. Cocco, *Metamorfosi dell'Adriatico orientale,* 192.
65. Ballinger, "'Authentic Hybrids' in the Balkan Borderlands."
66. David Kertzer and Dominique Arel, "Censuses, Identity Formation, and the Struggle for Political Power," in *Census and Identity: The Politics of Race, Ethnicity, and Language in National Censuses,* ed. David Kertzer and Dominique Arel (Cambridge, 2002), 26. On the inadequacies of such language categories for nineteenth-century Istria, see D'Alessio, "Istrians, Identifications and the Habsburg Legacy." For the period immediately after World War II and the citizenship "options" in the 1947 Treaty of Peace with Italy, readers are referred to Pamela Ballinger, "Opting for Identity: The Politics of International Refugee Relief in Venezia Giulia, 1948–1952," *Acta Histriae* 14, no. 1 (2006): 115–40.
67. Cocco, *Metamorfosi dell'Adriatico orientale,* 63.
68. Prior to Croatia's entry into the EU, the most effective transstate political institution cutting across the border in Istria was that of the Italian minority, whose representatives share a common leadership in the Unione Italiana.
69. Borut Brumen, "The State Wants It So, and the Folk Cannot Do Anything against the State Anyway," *Narodna umjetnost* 33, no. 2 (1996): 146.
70. Ibid., 151.
71. Nikočević, "Negotiating Borders: Myth, Rhetoric, and Political Relations," *Focaal* 41: 102."State Culture and the Laboratory of Peoples: Istrian Ethnography during the Austro-Hungarian Monarchy," 102.
72. In June 2010, a referendum was held in Slovenia on whether to approve an agreement with Croatia to submit the border dispute to international arbitration. The measure passed by a narrow margin. The actual arbitration process is expected to take several years.
73. Pamela Ballinger, "Watery Spaces, Globalizing Places: Ownership and Access in Postsocialist Croatia," in *European Responses to Globalization,* ed. Janet Laible and Henri Barkey (Amsterdam, 2006), 153–78.

74. Brumen, "The State Wants It So," 152.
75. Klaus Roth, "Toward 'Politics of Interethnic Coexistence': Can Europe Learn from the Multiethnic Empires?" in *Europe: Cultural Construction and Reality,* ed. Peter Niedermüller and Bjarne Stoklund (Copenhagen, 2001), 41.
76. Russell Scott Valentino, "Me Bastard, You Bastard: Multiculturalism at Home and Abroad," *The Iowa Review* 33, no. 1 (2003): 98.
77. Cocco, *Metamorfosi dell'Adriatico orientale,* 195.
78. Hoerder, "Revising the Monocultural Nation-State Paradigm."
79. Fikret Adanir, "Religious Communities and Ethnic Groups under Imperial Sway: Ottoman and Habsburg Lands in Comparison," in Hoerder, Harzig, and Shubert, *The Historical Practice of Diversity,* 54–86; Michael John, "National Movements and Imperial Ethnic Hegemonies in Austria, 1867–1918," in Hoerder, Harzig, and Shubert, *The Historical Practice of Diversity,* 87–105.
80. Sluga, "Bodies, Souls, and Sovereignty," 227.
81. Ibid.

Chapter 6

MIGRATION IN AUSTRIA
An Overview of the 1920s to 2000s

Michael John

The Republic of Austria is located at a European crossroads, an intersection of developed and less-developed regions, the junction of East and West. For centuries its territory and the territory of the preceding state entities have been an attractive destination for migrants. The imperial capital of Vienna in 1900 was a focus of internal Austrian-Hungarian migration of nearly all the ethnic and national elements.[1] At the turn of the nineteenth century the multinational Habsburg Monarchy suffered through a deep crisis connected with national political tensions, and rising nationalist politics unquestionably affected the development of mass migration in the state. In the last quarter of the nineteenth century the political system did not succeed in reforming itself, and when the dynastic-corporatist state finally disintegrated at the end of World War I, the sole feasible alternative was a system of supposedly homogenous nation-states or, in the case of Czechoslovakia and Yugoslavia, new, smaller, and presumably less diverse multiethnic or multinational states.

This chapter examines the patterns of migration to the Republic of Austria since World War I, some of the social consequences, and the political debates that have arisen about migration and to what extent the Austrian society should be considered multicultural and have laws and regulations protecting the rights of culturally diverse elements in the population. This chapter employs several operating definitions of "multiculturalism," deriving from the popular and political discussions of migration, but those definitions are not the focus of this analysis per se. Here, multiculturalism is not perceived as a political or cultural dogma or as a political postulation, but more simply as a category describing the characteristic social conditions of societies that contain culturally heterogeneous individuals and groups. These individuals and groups live together in spaces confined by politically established frontiers and characterized by unpredictable and uncontrollable crossings in the practices of everyday life, as the introduction to this volume points out. This has resulted in many ambiguous and contradictory developments in twentieth-century Austria.[2]

Interwar Period: More Emigration than Immigration

After the collapse of the Habsburg Monarchy, the new Republic of (German) Austria was one of the successor states, with Vienna as its capital. In Vienna and other major cities of the former monarchy, multiculturality became a social category of lesser importance during the interwar period than previously. Nevertheless, the heritage of the monarchy was kept alive to some extent. The 1920 constitution of the First Republic protected the rights of minorities and, under Article 149, entitled children to be educated in their mother tongue without compulsion to learn a second language. In interwar Austria we can find the relevant national minorities, defined in law and government regulations by self-ascription and language: Slovenes in Carinthia and Styria, Croats in Burgenland, Hungarians in Vienna and Burgenland, Czechs and Slovaks in Vienna and Lower Austria, and Roma in Burgenland, the latter defined officially as "Gypsies" in 1934, not following an attribution by language or cultural criteria. Czechs were by far the largest minority population in Vienna, a consequence of their migration from Bohemia and Moravia during the last decades of the Habsburg Monarchy. When Milena Jesenska, a friend of Franz Kafka, remembered commuting between Vienna and Prague in the early 1920s, she reported that she regularly taught the Czech language to the daughters of liberal bourgeois Viennese families. Such instruction was still commonplace at that time.[3]

Additionally, there were other ethnonational minorities and a large Jewish population. Jews were officially regarded only as a religious denomination. Modernity and the Zeitgeist of the "roaring twenties" influenced Vienna and other major cities of Austria. In the early 1920s, the Jewish population reached a peak with 201,513 persons, or 10.8 percent of the total population of Vienna, many of them born outside Austria.[4] In 1923, 53.8 percent of the Viennese inhabitants were born in Vienna. Therefore, 556,000 persons, or 29.9 percent, were foreign-born.[5] Despite a wave of remigration of almost 200,000 persons back to their lands of origin, the language-defined Czech (and Slovak) population in Vienna was 81,353 individuals.[6] Even the results of the 1934 census show that, of the 794,155 migrants living in Vienna,[7] 349,133 had been born in Austria (the territory within the 1919 borders) and 445,022 in foreign countries, including 292,880 in Czechoslovakia, 52,986 in Poland, and 28,472 in Hungary.[8] Indeed, the number of those citing a language of everyday use (*Umgangssprache*) other than German in Vienna had dropped sharply, from 111,396 persons in 1923 to 56,314 in 1934.[9] Yet in the mid-1930s about 800,000 of Austria's residents, representing 12 percent of the population, had been born outside of Austria.[10] Taking the second generation and the autochthonous minorities into account, we can presume that of approximately 6.5 million Austrians, more than a million had a personal cultural and linguistic background that could not be referred to as "pure" German, to use the contemporary formulation of nationalists.

Vienna was able to maintain its position as the financial capital of East Central Europe in the 1920s. Czechoslovakia was then Austria's most important foreign trading partner. The Czech-speaking minority in Austria—individuals who lived in the country before 1919—was in a safe position as a result of bilateral treaties signed with Czechoslovakia, whereby this state assumed the formal role of protector of the Austrian Czechs.[11] Trade with Hungary, Poland, Yugoslavia, and Romania also made important contributions to the Austrian economy. Vienna was forced to undergo a certain reduction of its commercial importance, but it continued to be a key hub of trade with Eastern Europe. Contemporary publications show this very clearly.[12] *Mitteleuropa*, as an economically integrated region, remained a reality during the 1920s.[13] Not only for political reasons, but also as a result of the specific composition of Vienna's population and its economic function, developments in the federal capital were in increasing contrast to the generally more ethnically homogeneous Austrian provinces (*Bundesländer*). One exception to this generalization was the province of Burgenland, created in 1921 out of what was formerly the westernmost part of Hungary, which had over forty thousand Croats, defined by self-ascription, about ten thousand Hungarians, and many thousands of others who were at least to some extent bilingual or multilingual.[14]

Slovene minorities—defined by self-ascription—lived in Carinthia and Styria, provinces that were sites of contestation after World War I. Austrian and Yugoslavian experts made various suggestions for drawing new borders, since no clear linguistic boundaries separated ethnically homogenous territories. Three cities in predominantly Slovene Lower Styria had German-speaking majorities: according to 1910 statistics for the communities of Marburg/Maribor, Pettau/Ptuj, and Cilli/Celje, 78 percent of the population listed German as their language of everyday use and 16.3 percent cited Slovenian.[15] The Paris Peace Conference awarded all of Lower Styria to Yugoslavia. It implemented a plebiscite in Southern Carinthia to allow the population to decide whether to become part of Austria or Yugoslavia. Although Southern Carinthia was predominantly Slovenian speaking, residents favored incorporation into Austria at the plebiscite in 1920. Carinthia had an autochthonous Slovenian-speaking minority numbering over 35,000 in 1923.[16] In Austrian Styria, the population perceived the drawing of the border as *Die Zerreißung der Steiermark* (the rending asunder of

Styria). This led to a migration of Slovenian-speakers from Styria to Yugoslavia and a much stronger flow of people from Yugoslavia to Austria. This flow was obviously ethnically and politically motivated; it included individuals who saw themselves as Germans and some Slovenian speakers and Croatian speakers who were opposed to the southward-orientated structure of the new state with its capital in Belgrade. During the 1920s, 5,443 former Yugoslav citizens became Austrian citizens; they settled primarily in and near Graz.[17] The Styrian capital became even more a center of German nationalistic activities than it had been previously.[18]

One decisive paradigmatic change typical of this period was the enormous importance taken on for the first time by the "foreigners question." Following the collapse of the Habsburg Monarchy, many people who had previously been its subjects (*Untertanen*) suddenly found themselves in the position of now being "foreign citizens" in Austria. The question arose of belonging in the "new" Austria, the Republic of Austria.[19] New measures dealing with Polish Jewish refugees from the former Austrian crown land of Galicia were based upon provisions of the 1919 peace agreement, the Treaty of St. Germain, which established new rules for granting Austrian citizenship. Enforcement regulations issued by the Austrian government on 20 August 1920 stipulated that persons possessing the right of permanent residence in a successor state of the Austro-Hungarian Empire "and who differ racially and linguistically from the majority of the population of that state" may, within six months "elect Austrian citizenship, if they belong, racially and linguistically, to the German majority of the population of Austria."[20] In alignment with the views of Christian social and German nationalist organizations, as well as those of Minister of the Interior Leopold Waber, these regulations were interpreted unfavorably with respect to East European Jews.[21] For the first time in modern Austrian jurisdiction and administration, the biologically and culturally inspired term *Rasse*—which cannot simply be translated into English as "race"—was introduced. However, as a result of international interventions, the refugees were not pushed out of the country because of this law. Finally, many Jewish refugees were granted the right of permanent residence and Austrian citizenship by Vienna's Social Democratic municipal administration, 20,360 of them between 1920 and 1925.[22] All in all, during the years 1910 to 1923 more than 101,000 inhabitants of other successor states—primarily German-speaking, non-Jewish Old Austrians (*Altösterreicher*) and the above-mentioned Jewish refugees—opted for Austrian citizenship.[23]

The idea of exclusion by using the categories *Rasse* and *Volkszugehörigkeit* (ethnicity) did not end with the failure of Waber's regulations. In 1923 the Austrian census officially introduced the category *Rasse*.[24] Jewish organizations protested against this, as did Czech organizations in Austria. The press in Prague criticized the Austrian chancellor Ignaz Seipel, as well as the minister of interior Felix Frank, a German nationalist politician and a member of the Großdeutsche

Volkspartei (Greater German People's Party). He was seen as responsible for the implementation of the term.[25] The Christian socialist chancellor Seipel was not a supporter of an *Anschluss* (unification with Germany), but of a community of one people and one culture (*Volks- und Kulturgemeinschaft*).[26] The census data were eventually collected, but for several reasons the unclear and controversial category was not evaluated.[27]

The scandal concerning the use of the category *Rasse* in 1923 showed clearly that political motivations stood behind the framework of the census. From the beginning of official Austrian censuses in 1869 and 1880, political intentions dominated the surveys; for example, only one vaguely defined "language of daily use" could be indicated. In addition, the census kept the number of "foreigners" low by conducting the survey on December 31.[28] From 1890 to 1910 members of the Austrian parliament introduced more than twenty interpellations and proposals to change the timing of the census, without any lasting result.[29] There was also a desire to mask bilingualism during the interwar period. In particular, for the censuses of 1923 and 1934, categories were introduced to accept only the reporting of a single language and to diminish and simultaneously distinguish clearly "foreign" elements. The new Republic of Austria should be presented as a "German" state. These data should thus be handled with care, given the political circumstances of the surveys. They were part of the political debate concerning migration and foreignness, touching directly on the question of "Austrian" identity.[30]

The example of post–World War I Vienna shows, however, that the strategy of inclusion—to grant Austrian citizenship—was successful for the Social Democrats during the 1920s. A considerable number of Social Democratic delegates in parliament and the city council were Jewish. Aside from the Social Democrats, all other major parties were affected, in varying degrees, by anti-Semitic views, and it was a fact that ethnic voting lost its influence when the social and political conflicts between left-wing and right-wing parties intensified.[31] In Vienna, a Zionist-oriented party received 13,075 votes in 1919, 24,253 in 1923, and 13,075 in 1927. In 1932 it did not campaign. A Czecho-Slovak Party was very successful in 1919, too: the Czecho-Slovaks received 57,380 votes. Right before the next election in 1923 the Social Democratic Party announced that they would reserve two seats for Czech candidates. As a consequence, the Czecho-Slovak Party received only 7,603 votes, and in 1927 it did not campaign. From the mid-1920s the Social Democrats could count on Czech and Jewish electorates, mostly migrants.[32]

The provinces, as well as the higher-ranking chartered cities, had a certain degree of latitude in which to maneuver in dealing with the issues of "inclusion" and "integration." Linz, Wels, Krems, Graz, and Bregenz pursued policies aimed at exclusion, whereas the City Council of Vienna granted the right of domicile to many former migrants from the north and east of the Habsburg Monarchy.

After 1921 the Viennese Social Democrats changed their policy, which two years previously had called for strict regulations concerning "foreign" migrants (in the so-called *Sever-Erlass*). Municipal policy-making in Vienna in those days was more oriented toward inclusion than had been the case around 1900. Large parts of the middle and the lower classes were nevertheless characterized by distinct attitudes of antisemitism.[33]

The migration flow to Vienna during the years 1914–20 strengthened the Yiddish-speaking element of the Jewish population.[34] This had consequences concerning the relation between "assimilated" Viennese Jews and East European Jews, so-called *Ostjuden*. Already in the days of the Habsburg Monarchy, sharply defined contrasts had emerged between the "assimilated" Jews and the mostly orthodox, Yiddish-speaking East European Jews. This situation intensified during the interwar years. But it was primarily the aggressive antisemitism of the non-Jewish majority of the population, not the inner Jewish conflict, that had an important influence on society. In 1922 Austrian writer Hugo Bettauer had a bestseller in *Stadt ohne Juden* (City without Jews), a satire in which he played out the scenario of a Vienna without Jews; in the novel they were forced to emigrate by the chancellor and his government. The book was a big success and a film was produced. In 1925 Bettauer was shot by a young member of the already-existing Nazi Party and died from his wounds.[35]

From 1919 through the mid-1920s one could observe craftsmen and laborers from Czechoslovakia, Germany, Hungary, Poland, and Italy in the Austrian labor market. During the years of a short economic boom, Italian brick makers from Trentino and Friaul were employed in Upper Austria and the western parts of Austria. The demand for skilled labor combined with the hyperinflation in Austria made it possible for them to demand payment in foreign currency (lira or dollar) and receive it.[36] But as early as 1921 the Social Democratic trade union in Salzburg demanded the exclusion of Italian technicians and workers building a hydraulic power plant in the south of the province.[37] In the wake of more massive political pressure from the Social Democratic Party and workers' organizations, such as unions and the Chamber of Labor, the so-called Domestic Work Force Protection Act (*Inlandarbeiterschutzgesetz*) was passed in 1925 in order to regulate the position of foreigners in the Austrian labor market. Otto Bauer, the head of the Social Democratic Party, referred not only to the labor market when he argued for the new law in parliament. He reminded the other parliamentarians of the situation in East Prussia before World War I: "What did happen there? The Polish workers played a role similar to the Slovak workers [in Austria]. First they came as seasonal workers. But quite often they worked the whole year around, and settled down permanently . . . As a consequence whole districts became slavicized. Gentlemen, this influenced the European map; today these districts belong to Poland. One has to know these experiences to understand that what is now happening in the northeast of Lower Austria is a real danger."[38]

Otto Bauer, who, although a Marxist, never left the official Jewish religious community, was a decided supporter of a culturally "German"-oriented Austrian republic. During the 1920s he was a convinced supporter of the unification of post-Habsburg Austria with Germany.

The new law prohibited foreigners without work permits from working in Austria.[39] Czech migrants who stayed in Vienna for a long time but did not have Austrian citizenship were not seen as "foreigners." But they were not allowed to leave Austria for longer than eight days; otherwise they would lose their specific status. After protest by the trade unions and Czech organizations, the limit was extended in 1926 to three weeks.[40] For seasonal workers, who were expected to stay only for a short time, it was easier to get a work permit. Entrepreneurs intervened and asked for the possibility to engage foreign laborers. They were primarily Slovak workers and day laborers, who were hired for agricultural work, especially during harvest time, and who accepted the harsh conditions during their engagement. Newspapers reported on the bad housing, the long workdays, and the exhausting work of the laborers, especially for those who were involved in the sugar harvest.[41] While in some years 12,000 to 15,000 seasonal workers from Czechoslovakia were active in Lower Austria, in the south, in Styria and Burgenland, Slovene and Croat workers were rarely hired, even though this would have been possible.[42] Labor migration for regular jobs was at a very low level. In 1926, the first year the Domestic Work Force Protection Act was in effect, 3,871 foreign nationals were allowed to work in Austria: 1,223 from Germany, 892 from Czechoslovakia, and 751 from Hungary.[43] Only 172 labor migrants from Yugoslavia were registered.[44] The protectionist policies had thus won the day, not only within the Austrian labor movement, but in Austrian politics overall. By 1934, when the labor movement lost its influence, the size of the foreign workforce had grown, despite the unemployment rate in Austria remaining high: 10,266 new working permits were issued for foreign nationals, 4,127 for Czechoslovakian citizens, 1,714 for Hungarians, and 1,541 for Germans.[45] However, regular labor migration was still low compared to the years just before World War I or the years after World War II, and temporary labor migration dominated the situation in the labor market.

The Domestic Work Force Protection Act was part of a larger development concerning assimilation and immigration policies that led, on the whole, to an increase in normative pressure during the interwar period. The 1920s and 1930s in Austria were characterized by an accelerated process of "Germanization."[46] The fact that in the period 1920–36 a further 120,000 German-speaking Old Austrians assumed Austrian citizenship without opting for it might have contributed to this process, too.[47] These persons originated primarily from former Habsburg crown lands, now successor states, and preferred to stay in Austria, with its "German" orientation. In addition, one is confronted with a phenomenon that Oliver Rathkolb called "Austro-solipsism." This "solipsism" means a more or less subtle but continuous manifestation of provincialism and egocentrism, where a majority of the population opposed new migrations of "foreign" origin.[48]

Nevertheless, as a result of permanent economic crisis, during the interwar period Austria became a land in which for a certain period emigration exceeded immigration.[49] According to official statistics, 80,164 persons left Austria for other countries (including Turkey and the Soviet Union). Emigration to other European countries was not recorded exactly, but it certainly exceeded overseas emigration. We can differentiate three phases of emigration: (1) 1919–23: during this period, 50 percent of all interwar emigrants left Austria, with emigration growing in the years 1922 and 1923; (2) 1924–30: the figures for emigration dropped, but were still on a remarkable level; and (3) 1931–37: the lowest levels of emigration, with only 18.5 percent of the emigrants leaving Austria in these years.[50] A large proportion of emigrants came from the southeastern Austrian province of Burgenland (24,416 persons), followed by Vienna (22,021), Styria (10,543), and Lower Austria (10,179). Labor migration and chain migration was characteristic of the emigrants. Important destinations were the United States, Brazil, Argentina, and Canada.[51]

Unemployment and a tense labor market can be interpreted as the economic background of the Austrian emigration of the interwar period, but in many cases this was not the deciding factor for emigrating. This may have been especially true for the Jewish emigrants who left Austria between 1919 and 1937. The Jewish population reacted to what was at times massive antisemitism in various ways. One of them was emigration, especially between 1923 and 1934. The permanent political and economic crises of the society played a role as well. There were more than 200,000 Jews living in Vienna in 1923, as compared to 176,034 in 1934; the figure for the whole of Austria was 221,003 in 1934.[52] As the census of 1923 did not provide the relevant data for all provinces, the tendency toward more ethnic and religious homogeneity in the Austrian population can be illustrated with the Viennese figures (see table 6.1).

The massive decrease of Czech language use, recorded in 1934, indicates, on the one hand, progressive assimilation; on the other hand, the figures have to be viewed in the context of the political purposes and specific date of the census.[53] The decrease of the Jewish population before 1934 can be traced to low birth rates and a steady stream of emigration. During the 1930s, the Zionist movement won majorities in elections for the boards of directors in virtually all Austrian Jewish communities.[54] Adolf Hitler was in power in Austria's neighboring state Germany from February 1933. This encouraged Jewish emigration from Austria, as did the civil war in 1934. According to official registries, some 4,515 Jews emigrated from Austria between March 1934 and March 1938; of these individuals, 2,713 went to Palestine.[55] On the other hand, 4,815 Jews migrated into Austria, primarily from Germany and Romania; a second accounting recorded the number of Jewish immigrants as approximately 5,500.[56] The attempts of

Table 6.1. Place of Birth, Residents of Vienna, Language of Everyday Use, Religion, 1923–34

	1923		1934	
	in numbers	percent	in numbers	percent
Place of Birth				
Vienna	1,004,301	53.8	1,077,102	57.5
Austrian Provinces	304,737	16.3	349,133	18.6
Foreign Countries	556,742	29.9	445,022	23.7
Unknown	—	—	2,873	0.2
Languages				
Not German	111,396	6.2	56,314	3.1
Of these: Czech*	81,353	4.5	39,714	2.2
Religions				
Other than Catholic	347,450	18.6	398,386	21.3
Of these: Jewish	201,513	10.8	176,034	9.4
Inhabitants, Total	1,865,780	100	1,874,130	100

*including Slovak
Sources: *Statistisches Handbuch*, vol. 6 (1925), 14; *Statistisches Handbuch*, vol. 8 (1927), 14; *Die Ergebnisse der österreichischen Volkszählung vom 22. März 1934*, vol. 3 (1935), 7, 14–15.

Romanian Jews to flee to Austria in late 1937 were seen by several newspapers as a threat to the nation and to public security. Between 1933 and March 1938 the press frequently wrote of the "fear of the foreigner."[57]

Analyzing the contemporary public and scientific discourse concerning minority questions, one can see that there was a strong tendency to differentiate between "native" groups like Slovene, Croatian, and Hungarian speakers and migrant "foreign" groups. Jews and Roma (termed *Zigeuner* or Gypsies) were clearly seen as allochthonous minorities; sometimes the label "nomads" was used. In 1935 the anthropologist Viktor Lebzelter from the Natural History Museum of Vienna was allowed to work on a "race map" (*Rassenkarte*) of the Burgenland province. He launched a study of craniometry; 4,144 persons were examined using several methods.[58] During the 1930s, the years of the authoritarian *Ständestaat*, the category "race" and the idea of "dissimilation" increasingly came to the fore.[59]

National Socialism and the *Ostmark*

In March 1938 the *Anschluss* brought Austria's existence as a sovereign state to an end. Austria's territory became part of the German Reich as the *Ostmark*. The years of National Socialism in Austria caused, as we know, a massive discontinuity in many aspects of life, including migration and minority affairs. After Nazi Germany's annexation of Austria in 1938, the regulations on immigration, residence, employment, and emigration of both nationals and nonnationals were replaced by German legislation that continued to be in force long after the destruction of the Nazi regime. From the very start, the National Socialist authorities imposed severe restrictions on Jews in virtually all areas, including employment, social benefits, housing, and acquisition of property. Jews were immediately described as "foreign," as "Asian," and as "a danger." The pogroms against Jews in 1938 in Vienna and also in Innsbruck were later described as a "regression into barbarism."[60] The Austrian historian Gerhard Botz commented on the Viennese events of 1938: "The attacks consisted mostly of symbolic acts and historic rituals aimed at the destruction of a sense of identity—humiliations and arrests—but there were also physical attacks, beatings, murders, and also robberies on a mass scale. It was as if medieval pogroms had reappeared in modern dress."[61]

The massive aggression against Jews was accompanied by "spontaneous" and state-organized expropriation of property known as *Arisierung* (Aryanization). In Austria more than 65,000 apartments, houses, and villas and approximately 33,000 businesses and stores were "Aryanized" or liquidated.[62] Between 1938 and 1941, 128,000 Jews were forced to leave Austria, and through 1945 more than 65,000 Austrian Jews were murdered, both inside and outside death camps.[63] Quite early on, National Socialists started to compare Jews and Roma and claimed that they should be treated in the same way. Tobias Portschy, the governor of Burgenland, was the first to call for a radical National Socialist solution of the "Gypsy question" in June 1938. Nearly all Austrian Roma and Sinti were deported to camps; two-thirds of this minority were murdered in the concentration camps, particularly Auschwitz.[64] In the Mauthausen concentration camp complex, in the vicinity of Linz, approximately 105,000 of the 205,000 inmates died. All the camps in Upper Austria, Mauthausen, Gusen, and Ebensee, had high death rates compared to other concentration camps in the territory of the German Reich.[65]

During the period of "total war," more than 900,000 forced laborers, prisoners of war, and inmates of concentration camps from all over Europe had to work in industry and agriculture in the *Ostmark*. This represented a huge wave of forced mass migration involving individuals from Ukraine to France and Norway to Greece. Upper Austria and its capital Linz were notably affected by this development. Soon after the occupation of Austria in 1938, Linz received the status of Hitler's *Patenstadt* (adopted city). More than this, as one of the five cities of the Führer, Linz was to project the power of National Socialism to the Germans and the world. The other *Führerstädte* included Berlin, Hamburg, Nuremberg, and Munich, but not Vienna. The former Austrian capital now had a markedly negative image and was seen as a "contaminated" city because of the previous Jewish and Slav immigration.[66] During the war the National Socialists concentrated on the economic plans for Upper Austria and built huge new steelworks and armament industries in Linz (the Reichswerke Hermann Göring) and Steyr and tank production in nearby St. Valentin.[67] The population of Linz rose from 108,000 in 1934 to 195,000 in 1945, and that of Steyr rose from 25,000 in 1934 to more than 50,000 in 1945.[68]

A clear "race" hierarchy regulated the relations of the ethnicities involved in the system of forced labor. In the fall of 1944 approximately 990,000 foreign workers performed forced labor in the territory of present-day Austria. At the same time, only 1.7 million native laborers were registered.[69] Because a high percentage of the native male population was fighting in the war, the National Socialist program of forced labor became a central and strategic economic factor. The inhuman system doubtlessly prolonged the war.[70] German laws regulating the admission of a foreign workforce remained effective in Austria after 1945, with some changes, until a complete reorganization was arranged in the 1960s.[71]

Postwar Migration: "Displaced Persons" and Refugees

After World War II, approximately 1.4 million foreigners lived in Austria, including former slave laborers, displaced persons, prisoners of war, and war refugees, but the repatriation or resettlement of civilian foreigners started quickly. Separate camps were established for the Jewish refugees in Austria who were liberated from the concentration camps and those who had fled from Eastern Europe into the US-occupied zone of Austria. Many of these victims of National Socialism were either stateless or did not want to return to their home countries. Resettlement was a prolonged and complicated process until the founding of the state of Israel sped up the relocation of Central and East European Jews.[72] According to estimates, from 1945 to the early 1950s some 200,000 Jews were brought into the US-occupied zone and spent at least a short time in the area. Upper Austria (south of the Danube) and Salzburg became focal points of these migratory and refugee movements in the territory of the reestablished republic.[73] Only a few thousand of these Jewish "displaced persons" (DPs) remained permanently in Austria.[74] The most prominent DP was Simon Wiesenthal (1908–2006), born in Buczacz, Galicia, who was liberated in 1945 from the Mauthausen concentration camp. He lived in Linz until 1961 and afterward in Vienna.[75] In the southern parts of Austria, Graz was a focus for immigrants and refugees from Romania and Yugoslavia, the latter coming especially from Slovenia and Croatia.[76]

However, the largest groups of foreigners in Austria consisted of German-speaking refugees from Eastern Europe who were expelled from their countries in revenge for the years of National Socialist rule. Hundreds of thousands of these men and women, mostly so-called *Volksdeutsche* (ethnic Germans), stayed in Austria (in 1948, 465,000).[77] They served later as a substitute for a development that began to occur in Western European countries during the business cycle upswing of the 1950s. In Austria, however, it was not until the 1960s that there was any significant immigration of foreign laborers. Austria, because of its geographical situation bordering three East European states and its permissive asylum policy, became a major destination for refugees from communist-dominated countries. There were three major influxes resulting from political crises in the communist countries. In 1956, as a result of the political uprising and the ensuing repression in Hungary, over 180,000 Hungarian refugees entered Austria. They found themselves in a situation of which subsequent refugees and migrants could only dream.[78]

In 1956 many Austrians were convinced that the Hungarians who appealed for their help were innocent victims of communist persecution and thus highly deserving of all kinds of support. Hence, the authorities and the general populace joined forces to provide for the needs of the fugitives in an unbureaucratic way.[79] On 4 November 1956, the Soviet army finally crushed the uprising. Already on 26 October, the Austrian minister of the interior, Oskar Helmer, instructed his officials that all refugees from Hungary were to be granted political asylum, no matter the reason they had come to Austria.[80] While the large majority of these persons were quickly resettled in other Western countries and 7,700 returned to Hungary, some 18,000 Hungarian refugees were left to be integrated into Austria. Many of those were elderly and unfit to work, and a sizeable number were of school age. For the latter group, special schools were founded in which the Austrian curriculum was taught by Hungarian refugees (including former teachers and other professionals). The welcome and the opportunities for integration for Hungarian refugees in 1956 were unprecedented. The joint history of Austria-Hungary during the years of the dual monarchy and the shared experience might have also played a role in this specific case. It contrasted markedly with everything that came afterward, even with the influx of Czechoslovak refugees in 1968. In the aftermath of the "Prague Spring" of 1968, about 162,000 Czechoslovakians entered Austria, the vast majority traveling on to other Western states.[81] In that year, the Austrian ambassador in Prague, Rudolf Kirchschläger, issued exit visas to Czechoslovak citizens who tried to leave their country, despite orders not to do so from Kurt Waldheim, the Austrian foreign minister.[82] In 1980–81 martial law was declared in Poland. The crushing of the Solidarity movement at this time triggered an inflow of 120,000 to 150,000 Poles to Austria, but again the majority of these refugees moved on. Only 33,000 Polish citizens asked for political asylum in Austria.[83]

"Guest Workers" and the Rotation System

The so-called Raab-Olah Agreement between entrepreneurs and trade unions in 1961 authorized foreign workers to come to Austria. The decision to allow a massive "foreign" migration was not a result of a democratic discussion in society but a kind of deal between the so-called social partners (*Sozialpartner*), which formed the so-called *Sozialpartnerschaft,* the Austrian model of cooperation between employers' associations and trade unions, the Economic Chamber, and the Chamber of Labor.[84] The "guest worker" (*Gastarbeiter*) immigration, with fixed annual "contingents" of low-paid manual workers, was promoted by contract labor programs and organized by state agencies similar to those in Germany. The first contract was established in 1962 with Spain, followed by Turkey in 1964. Perhaps it was due to Austrian-Yugoslav history that a contract with the neighbor to the southeast was signed quite late. After 1966 Yugoslavia became the most important country for the recruitment of workers for the Austrian economy. Between 1961 and 1972, a total of 265,000 immigrants came to Austria, peaking between 1969 and 1973.[85] Yugoslav nationals formed the biggest share of the guest workers, approximately 80 percent, in 1973. The Yugoslavian federal state of Serbia was the main source of Yugoslav migrants to Austria.[86] The second important focus of recruitment was Bosnia-Herzegovina. Turkey sent the second largest group of foreign guest workers, 12 percent of the total. Compared to the turn of the century or the 1920s, when the majority of migrants originated in Central Europe, this represented a new pattern of migration.[87]

The period 1961–73 was the era of the classic *Gastarbeiter* policy. In accordance with the logic of a labor market policy of compensation, an effort was made year after year to close the gaps created by the drain of Austrian labor to countries like Germany, Sweden, and Switzerland. Foreign workers were brought in by recruitment bureaus or other systematic methods.[88] An article in the monthly magazine of the Austrian trade unions gave an impression of the situation back in the late 1960s, when the Austrian economy was booming. Even the coverage in the union-owned magazine, which tended to advocate policies to protect the interests of native Austrian workers, sought to foster a certain degree of understanding for the growing number of foreigners in the Austrian workforce:

> A large textile manufacturer located near Vienna employs 800 guest workers. We talked to the personnel manager. He recruits his workers in Yugoslavia and Turkey, with the respective government labor offices acting as intermediary. In Yugoslavia, he has to pay a commission of 700 schillings a head; in Turkey, it's 1,100. Private recruiting is forbidden, but people are constantly coming up with new tricks to try to get around the ban, and the authorities are constantly on the lookout for private recruiters trying to cheat them out of their commissions.... Our personnel manager has especially high praise for his Turks, repeatedly stressing how reliable they are.[89]

A study conducted at the time by Austria's Social Partnership, representing the interests of management and labor, shows that many companies were trying to hire foreign workers during the upswing in the business cycle. These efforts ranged from dealing with smugglers and private recruiters all the way to encouraging their current foreign workers about to go back home on vacation to bring any interested compatriots back to Austria with them.[90] This explains the enormous rise in foreign labor migrants. From 1967 to 1973 the number of guest workers in Austria tripled.[91]

A large proportion of the Austrian population, especially the lower classes, was in opposition to the recruitment of the guest workers. The yellow press in particular worked to stimulate xenophobic emotions.[92] In the early 1970s, the Viennese Chamber of Commerce financed a campaign in the interest of a group of entrepreneurs to do something about the growing xenophobia in the lower classes. In those days the economy needed a larger labor force. With this campaign a pressure group tried to strengthen the acceptance of the new migrants from southeastern Europe by calling on Austria's past as a multinational state: in posters a little Vienna-born boy whose family was apparently of Czech origin asked a Serbian slaughterhouse worker named Kolaric: "My name is Kolaric—yours also Kolaric—why do they call you names?"[93] With this campaign the irritating facets of a new and growing xenophobia in Austria did not disappear; the campaign was not very successful in stopping the xenophobic attitudes against the guest workers. Nevertheless, at the same time it was an expression of the still predominant paternalistic attitude toward the hard-working "guests" on the part of the elites in politics, culture, and the economy.[94]

When the international economic crisis of 1973 to 1974 ended the postwar business boom and many Austrians who had been working abroad or commuting to jobs in neighboring countries found themselves competing for work in the domestic labor market, Austria in turn reduced its own employment of migrant workers. More than 40 percent of the foreign migrants were let go, and it was not until 1991 that employment of foreigners again reached the level of 1973. The mid-1970s marked a turning point in Austrian immigration policy. As a consequence of economic crisis and oversupply in the Austrian labor market, Austrian politicians aimed to reduce the number of foreign workers. In 1976, the Foreign Workers' Employment Act (*Ausländerbeschäftigungsgesetz*) was introduced, which demanded the preferential hiring of Austrian nationals. This act provided for legal status for foreign workers, entitling all foreign workers with a continuous record of at least eight years of work to move freely in the Austrian labor market. Other foreign laborers remained bound to the employer or had to leave the country. The Employment Act of 1976 strengthened the position of the employer enormously.[95]

In Austria, the idea that the primarily male guest workers would leave again was essential to the labor market policy of the 1960s and 1970s. "Rotation" was the focus, meaning that immigrants were expected to stay and work for a couple of years and subsequently return to their home countries. New workers would be recruited if a larger workforce was needed. Despite the dramatic cutback in the employment of foreigners after 1974, it turned out over the course of the 1980s that the idealized conception of a rotation policy, whereby the number of foreigners was to be adjusted according to the country's economic and employment policy requirements, no longer functioned in reality. Male labor migrants who were originally "in transit," anticipating better opportunities in prosperous neighboring countries like Germany and Switzerland, rethought their position, established their legal right to remain in Austria, and began to send for the rest of their families.[96] During the 1970s the percentage of male laborers was 80–90 percent of the total foreign workforce; afterward it shrank to approximately 60 percent. The male-to-female ratio of the total foreign population, according to the 2001 Austrian census, was 53 percent male and 47 percent female.[97]

In discussing migration policy during the years of Bruno Kreisky's chancellorship, one has to mention minority politics. In 1976 the federal government passed a law on the rights of indigenous ethnic minorities, the *Volksgruppengesetz* (Ethnic Groups Act). Five groups—later extended to six—were recognized as ethnic minorities in different parts of Austria: Slovenes (in Carinthia), Croats (in Burgenland), Hungarians (in Burgenland and Vienna), and Czechs and Slovaks (in Vienna). The juridical commentaries to the law, which mentioned that only after three generations can one speak of *Volksgruppen,* showed a clear reference to Austria's history as part of the Habsburg Monarchy. From the 1970s onward there has been an ongoing debate among the "official" ethnic groups over the perception that the provisions meant to safeguard their cultural heritage are not being properly applied and executed. Immigrants, who have come to Austria since the 1960s as *Gastarbeiter,* are not officially recognized as cultural and ethnic minorities. Nevertheless, there are many more immigrants in Austria than members of the officially registered ethnic groups.[98]

In 1992, the comparatively small population of autochthonous Roma was recognized as an ethnic group in all nine Austrian *Bundesländer.* This group represents an exception, and the status of an official *Volksgruppe* was not extended to newcomers. The new migration of mostly Slovak and Romanian Roma to Graz, Styria, led to conflicts and controversy. In the media Graz was repeatedly described as the "European Capital of Begging."[99] In 1995, the ethnic group of Roma in Burgenland was deeply shocked when a pipe bomb killed four Roma, an assault motivated by xenophobia and racism.[100]

New Migration after the Dismantling of the Iron Curtain

As a result of new migration under changed macropolitical circumstances in the wake of the fall of the Iron Curtain, the proportion of foreigners among all Austrian inhabitants rose over the following ten years from under 5 percent to almost 10 percent. According to the statistics, the new wave of migration consisted primarily of (ex-)Yugoslavs, Turks, laborers from Eastern Europe, and more and more from Asia and Africa, a result of globalization.[101]

In the long run, one can see that during the last forty years ex-Yugoslavs made up the largest group of Austrian citizens of foreign origin; more than 40 percent of all foreign citizens and approximately 50 percent of the foreign workforce in Austria were ex-Yugoslavs. The percentage of citizens from Turkey, a group that, in recent years, has been surpassed by the category "others," was just under 20 percent and has stagnated since 1991. In reality, there was further migration that cannot be seen in the statistics, because every year some thousand Turkish citizens received Austrian citizenship. These individuals are no longer counted as foreign nationals. German employees have been increasing in the Austrian labor market since the late 1990s, so that the number of German employees in Austria has come to exceed significantly the number of Turkish employees (See figure 6.1). Many of those German nationals arriving most recently originate in eastern Germany. The category "others" consists primarily of immigrants from the Third World and Eastern Europe. The number of those coming from Central and East European postcommunist countries has risen since 1989. They work mainly in the construction sector, restaurants and hotels, agriculture and forestry, and textile, clothing, and leather industries. A specific group of Eastern European migrants is female and engaged in home care. Partly this "care drain" is organized informally and has historical connections in Central Europe.[102] Similarly, during the Habsburg Monarchy young women of Czech, Slovak, Hungarian, or Polish origin looked after children, the sick, and the elderly, but nowadays this specific workforce consists primarily of transnational migrants, individuals who belong to two or more societies at the same time.[103]

Between 1989 and 1993, the growing need for immigrants due to the economic upswing, the fall of the Iron Curtain, and the wars in Croatia and Bosnia-Herzegovina led to a doubling of the number of foreigners living in Austria, from 384,000 persons to 699,000. Despite the implosion of the communist regimes, 60 percent of these immigrants arrived from the traditional migration countries, Turkey and the former Yugoslavia. The government introduced a quota for work permits in 1990. The yearly fixed quotas vary between 8 and 10 percent of the total workforce. The proportion of both Eastern Europeans and immigrants from the Third World increased markedly over the 1990s; this was a result of the collapse of communist regimes in Eastern Europe as well as the subsequent globalization of the world economy. During the 1980s and 1990s the position of the Turkish migrants was also strengthened. The immigrant social networks in Austria and abroad (both in the sending countries and other destination countries) were probably the most important factor driving the perpetuation of migrant flows over the last twenty-five years.

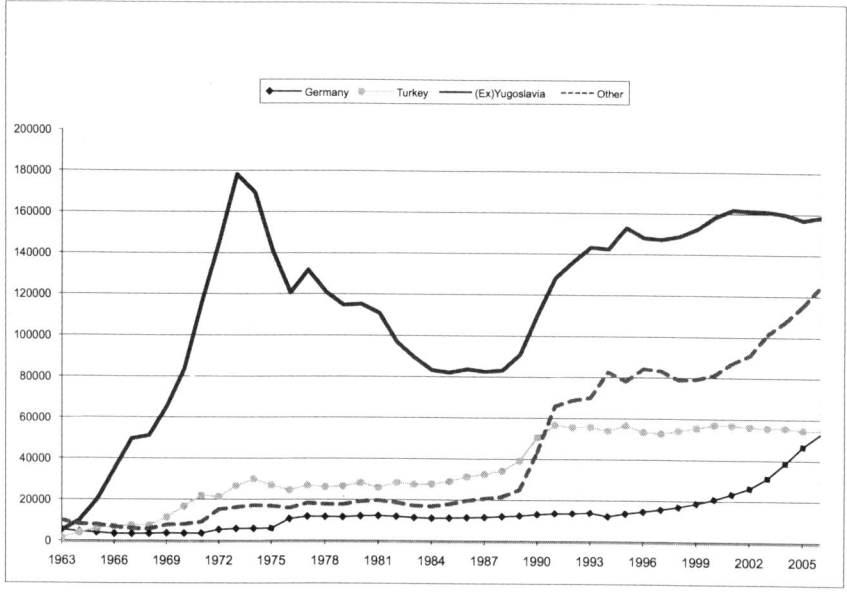

Figure 6.1. Workforce in Austria by Nationality, 1963–2006

Source: Austrian Statistical Yearbook

The number of unregistered immigrants—so-called illegals (illegal aliens)—played a major role in the public discussions of the 1990s, particularly when Austrian politician Jörg Haider's popularity at the polls was at its peak.[104] Haider and the Freedom Party broke taboos in Austrian politics by bringing in the topic of migration and active xenophobia into electoral campaigns. "Criminality," "limitation of immigration," a new national "patriotism" under the slogan "Austria first" (*Österreich zuerst*), and "foreign infiltration" (*Überfremdung*) were keywords in some campaigns. From 1986, the year Haider became head of the party, to 1999, the Freedom Party successfully raised its share of the votes in national elections from 5 percent to 27 percent, xenophobia being a very important motive for voters. The whole atmosphere in politics and in society changed.[105] In reaction to this change, liberals, engaged Christians, Social Democrats, and other left-wingers, Greens and Alternatives, organized and stood up against Haider's antiforeigner movement. In January 1993, the Sea of Lights (*Lichtermeer*) demonstration took place in Vienna. In the biggest demonstration held since World War II in Austria, far more than two hundred thousand, mostly younger, people holding candles and torches voiced their protest against xenophobia and for human rights and solidarity in the center of Vienna.[106]

There is no dispute about the fact that Austria experienced an enormous wave of immigration over the 1990s, and Vienna was the focus. But in the long run,

Table 6.2. Population Born Outside Austria by Province, 1951–2001

	1951		1971		2001	
	in numbers	percent	in numbers	percent	in numbers	percent
Vienna	302,224	17.1	208,698	12.9	366,289	23.6
Vorarlberg	25,347	13.1	33,234	12.2	53,938	15.4
Salzburg	44,548	13.6	37,337	9.3	72,627	14.1
Tyrol	55,436	13.0	50,743	9.4	83,406	12.4
Upper Austria	155,548	14.0	94,434	7.7	144,427	10.5
Lower Austria	93,223	7.5	80,904	5.7	135,489	8.8
Carinthia	45,135	9.5	30,624	5.8	44,754	8.0
Styria	112,374	10.1	72,476	6.1	83,748	7.1
Burgenland	15,133	5.5	10,406	3.8	18,721	6.7
Austria	848,968	12.2	618,174	8.3	1,003,399	12.5

Sources: Austrian census reports quoted in Weigl, *Migration und Integration,* 15.

compared to the last decades of the Habsburg Monarchy or the interwar period, or even compared with the year 1951, which still reflected the postwar situation, the 2001 census did not paint a dramatic picture. The total figures of those born outside Austria were nearly the same in 1951 and 2001. During the 1950s and part of the 1960s Austria experienced emigration and immigration only on a small scale. The 1971 census showed figures going down in all provinces. In 2001 the numbers in all provinces were on a similar level as in 1951, with the exception of Vienna and Upper Austria, which was *the* region (south of the Danube, in the US occupation zone) where the so-called displaced persons were concentrated (see table 6.2). In international comparisons Austria in 2001 was among the states with the highest percentage of immigrants, exceeding the percentage in the United States. In the European Union, the percentage of immigrants in the Austrian population was only exceeded by Luxemburg, Estonia, and Cyprus.[107]

The figures for Vienna showed a significant increase in immigration in 2001: of 1,550,123 inhabitants, 248,264 individuals (16.0 percent) had the status of foreign nationals; 76.4 percent of the population was born in Austria and 23.6 percent outside Austria. For language of everyday use, 75.3 percent reported German, and 24.7 percent reported other languages, partly in combination with German: 9.3 percent reported Serbian-Croatian-Bosnian, 4.7 percent Turkish, 1 percent Hungarian, 0.5 percent Czech, and 9.2 percent other languages and unknown. In terms of religion, 49.2 percent of the population declared the Roman Catholic religion, 25.6 percent were without a designated religion (*konfessionslos*), 7.8 percent proclaimed themselves Muslims, 6.0 percent Orthodox, 4.7 percent Protestants, and 0.5 percent Jews.[108] According to Austrian censuses, the Jewish population was on the rise for the first time since 1945. In Vienna, 6,988 Jews were registered in 2001, 8,140 in Austria altogether.[109] There is still verifiable antisemitism in Austria. Although the quality is quite different from the 1930s and 1940s, it is a prejudice that was passed on from older generations. In Austria the number of Jewish communities is now small as a consequence of National Socialism.[110] According to the 2001 census the composition of Vienna's population, however, shows at least as much or more diversity overall than in the days of the Austro-Hungarian Monarchy.

The geographical distribution of the diverse ethnic and religious population groups demonstrated that integration and exclusion, assimilation and multiculturalism, were simultaneous phenomena in fin de siècle Vienna. With the exception of localized concentrations, in 1900 Czech-speaking immigrants in Vienna tended not to live in ghettos. As opposed to United States cities, urban centers in Central Europe did not consist of exclusive ethnic or national neighborhoods in the past, and they do not today. The geographical distribution of population segments, ethnic minorities, and the overall population can be measured by the index of segregation,[111] which ranges between the extremes of zero and one hundred. Zero refers to an identical distribution of a population segment and the rest of the population; one hundred indicates an absolutely variant distribution (ghetto, complete segregation). In 2001 the index of segregation of citizens of former Yugoslavia was 34.1. Those coming from other destinations (other than Turkey, former Yugoslavia, Eastern Europe, and the European Union) had the low value of 21.0. As a leading urban metropolis, Vienna takes part in numerous international networks, such as the United Nations offices in Vienna. Many jobholders in this sector belong to the already mentioned group, "coming from other destinations"; sociologically they belong to the middle class. The Turkish population, however, partly forming an underclass, reached a value of 37.3. In Graz, the level of segregation was lower than in Vienna, but the Turkish segregation in Linz showed a result of 48.0, which is rather high.[112]

The spatial segregation finds an equivalent in the level of education. While in 2001, according to the census, 33.5 percent of the Austrian-born population attended only the compulsory schooling (primary and middle school) and 30.8 percent had some level of advanced education (academic secondary school, higher technical and vocational college, and universities and colleges), the figures for individuals born in former Yugoslavia and Turkey showed a completely different scenario: 60.8 percent of the Yugoslavian-born and 80.7 percent of the Turkish-born population attended only compulsory schools, and the figures for advanced education amounted to only 13.4 percent and 8.0 percent, respectively.[113] These results, and specifically the figures for segregation, recall in part the situation of one hundred years earlier, when in 1910 the Czech language group had a segregation index value of 21.2 and the Jews had a value of 44.2.[114] In 1923, the value for Czechs was still 20.1 and for Jews 42.3.[115] In this context, the present-day Jewish population still forms a highly distinct group. In 2001, partly because of their historic experiences, Viennese Jews retained a very high segregation index of 50.2.[116]

Recent History and the Current Situation

The years from 1997 to 2003 were characterized by a massive increase in asylum applications; 2000 was the only year with a decrease in the number of applications. In 1997, 6,719 persons applied for asylum; the number rose to 39,354 by 2002. The number of applications shows an ongoing increase in six years. Then, in 2003, the number of applications dropped to 32,364. The approval rate for the asylum applications climbed from 8.1 percent in 1997 to 28.4 percent in 2003. In 1999, this quota rose exceptionally to 50.7 percent, due to a large extent to the crisis in Kosovo.[117] During the late 1990s and the first decade of the twenty-first century, several scandals occurred because of police brutality against asylum seekers, including the widely known death of Marcus Omofuma, an African applicant for political asylum, in 1999. Police officers had to deport the twenty-five-year-old Nigerian immigrant; they strapped him to his airplane seat and taped his mouth and nose shut. He died during the flight. Other incidents show that the treatment of Omofuma cannot be seen as a solitary case.[118]

In 2000, after thirteen years of a "grand coalition" between the Austrian Social Democratic Party (SPÖ) and the Austrian People's Party (ÖVP), the ÖVP formed a coalition with the right-wing Freedom Party, which proposed a drastic cut in immigration to Austria and the end of the "excessive foreign presence" in Austria.[119] Slogans always played an important role in the populist electoral campaigns of the Freedom Party: "Vienna must not become Chicago" was a slogan used in the 1996 elections, bringing together migration and images of criminality, symbolized by the word "Chicago." Many Austrians connected "Chicago" with gangsterism and crime. *Daham statt Islam,* a play on words in Austrian dialect meaning "Home instead of Islam," and "Pummerin instead of Muezzin" ("Pummerin" is the name of the bell in Catholic St. Stephen's Cathedral in Vienna) were successfully used slogans during the electoral campaign of 2006. A variation of the 1996 slogan was also in use: "Vienna must not become Istanbul."[120]

During the last two years of the "grand coalition" government, approximately 300,000 foreign workers were officially registered in Austria. Despite the populist propaganda, the figure nevertheless rose under the new coalition after 2000 and reached a peak in September 2006 with 408,000 foreign workers.[121] The economy was booming and the number of foreign workers from EU member states had grown, as did the number of "third-country nationals," citizens of non-EU/EEA (European Economic Area) countries. The increase was partly due to the government facilitating the recruitment of seasonal workers, who were permitted to stay up to one year and to reapply after a two-month break.

Austria experienced an "absolute naturalization record" in its "population trend" for the year 2003: for the first time 44,694 foreign nationals were granted Austrian citizenship (a 6 percent naturalization rate).[122] Observers claim this is not due to a liberal policy in this field. The new record derived primarily from the long-lasting residence of migrants in Austria, who normally get citizenship after ten years.[123] From the late 1990s up to the present, two-thirds of the new Austrian citizens were former guest workers from Turkey and the former Yugoslavia. At the end of 2005 new laws made it more difficult to get Austrian citizenship, and at the same time marriages between Austrian citizens and foreigners were complicated enormously. Still, in 2005, 34,876 foreign nationals were granted Austrian citizenship. The strict new regulations did have an impact on the naturalization figures after 2005: the figure dropped to 26,259 in 2006, 14,041 in 2007, 7,978 in 2009, and finally 6,135 in 2010.[124] The number of binational marriages (one partner with non-Austrian citizenship) also significantly dropped because of new regulations, from 10,699 (27.9 percent of all marriages) in 2004 to 6,344 (17.9 percent) in 2009.[125]

Between 2005 and 2010 the number of foreigners grew by 16 percent. Regardless of small statistical adjustments, the components of this growth were an additional 47,689 in natural increase, an additional 212,159 in net migration, and minus 99,003 in naturalizations of foreigners. The strong natural increase derives from the massive excess of births over deaths among the foreign population in Austria, compared to the equilibrium for Austrian citizens, whose net population change was minus 36,259 during the same period.[126] The so-called total fertility rate (TFR; births per woman in childbearing years) of foreign women and Austrian women has differed significantly during the last twenty years. Women with Turkish citizenship reached 2.41 in 2009, and women coming from former Yugoslavia had a TFR of 1.87; at the same time the fertility rate for Austrian women was calculated at 1.27.[127]

As a result of the migration processes during the 1990s and 2000s, one can observe in Austria a new development: the relatively strong immigration to the western provinces of Tyrol, Salzburg, and Upper Austria (the percentage of foreign nationals on 1 January 2006 was 18.7 percent in Vienna, 12.8 percent in Vorarlberg, 12.3 percent in Salzburg, 10.2 percent in Tyrol, 7.5 percent in Upper Austria, and under 7 percent in all other provinces). In the cities the percentage of foreign nationals was much higher than the national and the respective regional averages. The city of Salzburg was on top with 20.2 percent, followed by Vienna with 18.7 percent, Bregenz (Vorarlberg) with 18.0 percent, Wels (Upper Austria) with 15.8 percent, Innsbruck (Tyrol) with 14.5 percent, and Linz (Upper Austria) with 13.1 percent.[128] During the last two decades, both migration and integration policies were primarily determined upon and implemented in the regions (*Bundesländer*). Federal laws tend to provide a general framework only.[129] In 2005, a new asylum law was adopted, which introduced new responsibilities in asylum matters and more regional competencies.[130] In 2010, altogether 18,779 asylum decisions were made, 16 percent thereof positive. In 2011, a total of 14,426 new asylum applications were filed.[131]

The European Union for some time has been seeking a common formula concerning migration and asylum politics. Antidiscriminatory EU Council directives, like 2003/109/EC or 2000/43/EC, were meanwhile implemented in Austria and were aimed at improving the conditions of the immigrant population. But altogether, recent developments meant in many cases deterioration, especially concerning asylum policy, binational marriages, and naturalization. Austria's Human Rights Advisory Board was established in 1999. It consists of eleven members who are appointed by the federal minister of the interior for a period of three years. The members of the board are not subject to governmental direction, they are fully independent, and they publish regularly critical reports on the situation in Austria. The "Comments and Suggestions Concerning the Austrian Laws Relating to Aliens and the Asylum Law," published in 2007, offered the criticism that the Austrian laws are not in accordance with the European Convention on Human Rights.[132] In 2003, 2005, 2007, 2009, and 2011, Austrian laws concerning asylum, migration, and integration were tightened again. This happened in several countries of the European Union, not only in Austria, and this development therefore must also be seen in the context of the general tendency toward a "Fortress Europe."[133]

Despite the world economic crises, several figures were quite high: compared to previous years, new peaks for the foreign workforce in Austria were reached in August 2008, with 469,200 persons in September 2010 and 516,000 persons in September 2011. The largest number of labor migrants originated in the former Yugoslavia, then Germany, Turkey, and Hungary. The statistics also show the continuous growth of non-European immigration.[134] According to the state-owned Statistik Austria (Statistics Austria), 951,429 foreign citizens were registered (11.3 percent of the population) on 1 January 2012 (see table 6.3).

A new figure, describing more precisely the composition of the Austrian population, was introduced recently: population with "migrant background" (*migrantischer Hintergrund*), including all foreign citizens, all foreign-born persons, and the second generation. On 1 January 2011, approximately 1,543,300 persons were defined with a "migrant" or "foreign background," 18.6 percent of the total population. In Vienna a level of 38.2 percent was reached.[135] In the context of these high percentages, there is still an ongoing public debate about even more restrictive laws. Polls show that antimigrant right-wing parties have a potential of attracting up to one-third of the votes; recently the Freedom Party in Vienna won more than 25.8 percent of the votes with an antiforeigner campaign, demonstrating that a significant minority of Austrians could

Table 6.3. Population in Austria, 1 January 2012, by Nationality and Birth

Country of Birth	Total	Nationality Austrian	Nationality Non-Austrian	Total in percent	Nationality Austrian	Nationality Non-Austrian
Total	8,408,121	7,456,692	951,429	100.0	88.7	11.3
Austrian	7,085,038	6,939,893	145,145	84.3	82.5	1.8
Non-Austrian	1,323,083	516,799	806,284	15.7	6.1	9.6

Sources: Statistik Austria Online, *Population Statistics, Population since 2001 by nationality and country of birth,* 2013. http://www.statistik.at/web_en/statistics/population/population_change_by_demographic_characteristics/population_by_citizenship_and_country_of_birth/index.html (accessed 9 August 2013)

be mobilized in a xenophobic way using migrants as scapegoats and hostile strangers.[136]

A specific category of migrants, "third-country nationals" (non-EU/EEA citizens) now have to pass a language exam. In 2009, for the first time migrants with foreign citizenship were deported because their knowledge of German was not sufficient.[137] In 2011 the regulations concerning "integration" were tightened again. All except highly skilled immigrants will have to learn German before they arrive (*Deutsch vor Zuzug,* German prior to immigration). Those immigrating before 30 June 2011 had to pass an exam showing their language knowledge. In case of violations of compulsory schooling, specific sanctions will be implemented against migrants.[138] The new regulations represent a normative and not a permissive orientation; any elements concerning "multiculturalism" or "diversity" are missing. The internationally recognized Migrant Integration Policy Index (MIPEX) shows that many highly industrialized states have left Austria behind. Austria and Poland rank, *ex aequo,* number twenty-four and twenty-five among thirty-one countries.[139]

Nevertheless, the attraction of Austria as a destination country is still high for the whole EU/EEA zone, including Eastern Europe, and for foreign nationals with origins in Asia or Africa. Austrian enterprises still emphasize the need for new, foreign workers. The Austrian economic chambers (*Wirtschaftskammer*), representing four hundred thousand member companies and the Federation of Austrian Industries, plead that more open-minded and cosmopolitan behavior is an important location factor in attracting foreign labor to Austria.[140] The Austrian national public service broadcaster ORF set up prizes to be awarded to whomever succeeded in advancing "integration" (*Integrationspreis*), and several Austrian municipalities and even smaller communes established their own specific, and quite often creative, integration policies.[141] A recent study, published in

2012, shows that discrimination in the labor market has diminished for several groups of migrants during recent years, but nonetheless, "Austria is among the few OECD countries that do not provide full and automatic labour market access to all permanent-type migrants upon entry."[142]

Assimilation Policies and a Land of Immigration

All in all, more than 1.5 million foreigners have been integrated into society under the so-called Second Austrian Republic (1945 to the present).[143] Foreign citizens make up today more than one-tenth of the resident population of Austria, which currently has about 8.4 million inhabitants. More than 16 percent of the present-day population was born outside the country, which is a higher proportion than in the United States. The statistics show that Austria is a country of immigration, while the official line continues to see Austria *not* as a traditional country of immigration, and the migration policy since 1991 reflects this ambiguity. One can observe the decline of the rights of foreign labor migrants and family reunification programs that followed public discontent and populist agitation against immigration in the 1990s. The situation for asylum seekers has also deteriorated.

The developments of the last two decades raise the question of whether the historical experience of the multinational Habsburg Monarchy plays a role today concerning migration, multiculturalism, and minority rights. Regarding the elites of society, the historical experiences and the historical traditions in several cases do play a role, as formerly existing social networks have been partly reestablished. For the mentality and the feelings of the majority of the Austrian population, the effects are probably different: the historical experience in many cases does not play a role regarding the acceptance of the otherness of migrants. People were trained for a long time in assimilation and adaptation to "Germanness" or a specific "Austrianness." At the same time, considerable segments of the population were trained in feelings of superiority over newcomers from the east or south. Old prejudices against "Slavs" and the former Yugoslavia are still intact. Up to the present the conflict over bilingual signposts in Carinthia—German and Slovene—remains unsolved and burdens the relationship between Austria and Slovenia.[144] As a consequence of migration, modern democracy, cultural plurality, and economic success, Austria's cities are today to some degree multicultural and colorful agglomerations.[145] But combined with globalization during the last fifteen years, xenophobia in large parts of the Austrian population is again on the rise, often combined with neoracism directed toward people coming from outside Europe.[146] Old religious prejudices, in particular against Islam, are visible in contemporary xenophobic attitudes.[147] For the year 2006 the monitoring of racism by the Austrian nongovernmental organization (NGO)

Zivilcourage und Anti-Rassismus-Arbeit (ZARA) listed 1,504 reported cases of discriminatory treatment, slander, or physical attacks.[148]

The historical background of the multinational Habsburg Monarchy and the development of immigration to Vienna and other parts of Austria led throughout the twentieth century to specific varieties of xenophobia and chauvinism. Under the given historical conditions, non-German components of cultural and national identity were for the most part rigorously repressed, including on the part of the individual actors themselves. National chauvinism on a massive scale can also be identified on the part of the majority of the Austrian population. The fact of overcompensation with respect to national identity, along with the repression of other components of identity among a considerable minority, however, led (not only in Austria but in other Central European states as well) to an intensification of the problem and to its manifestation in bizarre forms, such as German nationalists and National Socialists with Slavic names. The practice of unreflecting forced assimilation had consequences for the identity of considerable segments of the population. In the case of many immigrants and minority group members, prejudices were internalized into an individual's own self-image in the form of compensation for group or personal feelings of inferiority. In the historical context of fin de siècle Vienna, John Boyer has noted that antisemitism sometimes could have the function of a door opener into society for non-Jewish migrants.[149]

Norbert Elias and John Scotson's theory of "the established and the outsiders," an analytical approach focusing chiefly on "earlier" versus "later" settlement, can help to explain this phenomenon. This theory can be applied to the conflict between more or less assimilated settlers from the identical social class, as well as of the same regional origin (e.g., Bohemia and Moravia) in turn-of-the-century Vienna and Lower Austria. The findings of Elias and Scotson demonstrate the functioning of the following processes: locals who had been themselves migrants and could be categorized as belonging to the same social class assumed a higher position in the social hierarchy vis-à-vis the new arrivals. These longer-established individuals with strong intragroup ties resorted to methods of differentiation and exclusion. In this way, new immigrants were kept at a distance and established individuals were able to both maintain their positions and bolster their self-esteem.[150] Indeed, this process can be observed almost universally, at least in those countries that do not define themselves as immigration lands (in which, among other characteristics, immigrants are regarded as a welcome addition to their ethnic group), and is thus by no means a phenomenon typical of Vienna and Austria alone. During several decades of the twentieth century, personalities with an East European Slavic family background dating back to the Habsburg Monarchy were quite successful in Austrian politics. Descendants of new minorities (guest workers, East European refugees, non-European migrants, etc.), however, have never headed a ministry in recent Austrian history. These groups are definitely underrepresented in the Austrian parliament (1 out of 183 members in 2011) and in other representative political bodies.[151]

The Austrian history of migration during the twentieth century is to a certain degree a history characterized by discontinuities, especially concerning the patterns of migration (including origin, motivations, and recruitment). But one can find elements of continuity as well, and the strongest element in this respect is the social, economic, and political pressure to assimilate. As discussed above, Austria and Germany are territories in which the jus sanguinis has been operative for a longer period. This means that origin/descent was of chief relevance for group membership (acceptance/belonging), as opposed to France, the United States, Australia, etc., where diverse variations of the jus soli applied.[152]

For the most part, integration in Austria—politically, socially, economically—functioned quite well, particularly when a migrant assimilated to a high degree (more than would be necessary to function in the labor market). Austrian migration policy was, therefore, not only influenced by public interests in security, economic growth, and social welfare, but also by symbolic purposes. The "Austro-solipsism" concentrated in the small German-speaking *Kernland* (heartland) of the monarchy, which already was developed at the end of the nineteenth century, found success during the interwar period and again after World War II up to the present.[153] Despite the existence of certain strongly multicultural milieus, assimilation and strong pressure to assimilate have been characteristics of Austrian development for more than one hundred years.

While in the days of the emperor Czech-speaking migrants in Vienna seemed to be a threat to the German character of the city, recent immigrants, especially coming from Turkey, are assumed to oppose assimilation or integration and to live in a "parallel society."[154] In Austria, sometimes even the possibility of integration is not available because parts of the population block it. Examples of those affected by this are the Jewish population during the 1930s, as well as people with "foreign" appearance, "whose descent one can recognize," to quote a widely known dictum of an Austrian politician.[155] In November 2010, one month after the Freedom Party's success in Vienna's city parliament ballot, the Turkish ambassador Kadri Tezcan caused a scandal by criticizing the Austrian integration policy and the mental attitude against foreigners. He said in an interview: "The Turks (in Austria) . . . aren't happy. They don't want to be treated like a virus. (Austrian) society should help them integrate—and then it would benefit from them . . . What kind of problem does Austria have? . . . The Turks in Vienna are helping each other. They don't feel welcome here." Tezcan also stressed: "Turks aren't [Christians]. They are constantly being pushed to the corners of the society."[156] The undiplomatic approach of the ambassador stimulated an emotional discussion about assimilation, integration, and mental attitudes. Austria's largest newspaper carried the quite hostile headline "Türkei-Botschafter muss weg" (The Turkish Ambassador Must Go).[157] The incident showed that in the twenty-first century, traditional lines of argumentation are still in use.

Multiculturalism during the last twenty to twenty-five years was definitely not an issue that attracted a large proportion of people in Austria. In 1995–97 the most affirmative keywords for Austrian respondents were *Heimat* (home) and *Heimatverbundenheit* (attachment to the home region) with 72 percent consent, followed by *Sicherheit* (security) and *Ordnung* (order) with 65 and 63 percent, respectively. "Multicultural" was a sympathetic word for 19 percent and "foreigner" for 13 percent.[158] In 2010 "security" and "order" remained top-rated, along with "fairness." "Home" dropped significantly to 52 percent, but was still important. "Multicultural" now meant something positive for 17 percent and the acceptance of "foreigner" sank to 6 percent. Influenced by politics and politicians and by certain mass media, a majority of respondents felt "multicultural" to have unlikeable and negative connotations.[159] The role of the yellow press concerning the transmission of xenophobic and antiforeigner clichés has to be stressed at this point.[160]

Since the 1960s Austria has been characterized by growing immigration, and today it is a "land of immigration." Many different cultures and ethnicities are to be found in contemporary Austria, especially in the capital, Vienna. There have been several attempts to explain and make the present situation understandable for large proportions of the society by recalling the experiences and developments in the Habsburg dual monarchy. None of the attempts in politics, in the media, or in education projects were as successful as anticipated. The collective memory of current-day Austrians has marginalized the vast migration in the Austrian past, so that it is not an integral part of the "Austrian identity" and self-understanding among broad sections of the population.[161]

Multiculturalism as a strategy for "coping with diversity" was certainly a topic during the last decades of the Habsburg Monarchy. Later, during the interwar period, the years under National Socialist rule (1938–45), the postwar period, and the prosperous years of the 1950s, 1960s, and 1970s, over a long period and for differing reasons, it was no longer a topic under discussion. Changes in Europe during the late 1980s and early 1990s brought about a renewed discussion of multiculturalism. Antidiscrimination laws and the cultural opening toward Central and Eastern Europe following Austria's membership in the European Union and the EU's subsequent enlargement are proof of this development. Multiculturalism was then to some extent a topic of public debate, and Austrian society can now be described as a "plural society" with many diverse communities, as well as characterized by a tendency toward multiple or "patchwork" identities among parts of the population. Nevertheless, recent developments in politics and the climate of opinion fit into the inconsistent patterns of acceptance of migrants that have developed over the last one hundred years. In general, the processes of identity formation in Austria have not focused particularly on the objective cultural and religious diversity in society.[162]

Notes

Many thanks to Ad Futura Foundation, Ljubljana, the Scientific Center of the Slovenian Academy of Sciences and Arts, and the University of Nova Gorica, Slovenia, for supporting this research.

1. See Michael John, "'We Do Not Even Possess Our Selves': On Identity and Ethnicity in Austria 1880–1937," *Austrian History Yearbook* 30 (1999): 17–64; Andrea Komlosy, "Innere Peripherien als Ersatz für Kolonien? Zentrenbildung und Peripherisierung in der Habsburgermonarchie," in *Zentren, Peripherien und kollektive Identitäten in Österreich-Ungarn*, ed. E. Hars et al. (Tübingen, 2006), 55–78. For a short overview concerning the nineteenth and early twentieth centuries, see Sylvia Hahn, "Austria," in *The Encyclopedia of Migration and Minorities in Europe*, ed. K. Bade et al. (Cambridge, 2011), 83–89.
2. See Andreas Weigl, *Migration und Integration: Eine widersprüchliche Geschichte* (Innsbruck, 2009), 93–100.
3. See *Vivre Milena Jesenska: Wiener Festwochen* (Vienna, 1990), 1–8; see also J. Cerna, *Milena Jesenska* (Frankfurt, 1985), 32.
4. *Statistisches Jahrbuch der Stadt Wien für das Jahr 1929* (Vienna, 1930), 5.
5. *Statistisches Handbuch für die Republik Österreich*, vol. 8 (Vienna, 1927), 14.
6. The exact numbers were 79,278 Czechs and 2,066 Slovaks. *Vorläufige Ergebnisse der Volkszählung vom 7. März 1923: Beiträge zur Statistik der Republik Österreich*, vol. 12 (Vienna, 1923), 12. During the years of the Habsburg Monarchy there was only one category, "Bohemian-Moravian-Slovak"; afterward this was changed to "Czech" and Slovak." See V. Valeš, *Die Wiener Tschechen einst und jetzt* (Prague, 2004), 11.
7. Migrants are defined here as persons born outside Vienna. Otherwise, in this chapter the terms "immigration" and "immigrants" are used when migrants cross state borders.
8. *Statistisches Jahrbuch 1929* (Vienna, 1930), 5; *Ergebnisse der österreichischen Volkszählung vom 22. März 1934*, vol. 3 (Vienna, 1935), 14–15.
9. *Statistisches Handbuch*, vol. 8 (1927), 14; *Ergebnisse der österreichischen Volkszählung vom 22. März 1934*, vol. 3 (1935), 7 and 14–15.
10. See *Statistisches Handbuch*, vol. 15 (1935), 11.
11. Karl M. Brousek, *Wien und seine Tschechen* (Vienna, 1980), 84ff.
12. See Walther Federn, ed., *Almanach 1908-1918-1928: 10 Jahre Nachfolgestaaten*. Sonderausgabe zur 20-Jahrfeier des Oesterreichischen Volkswirts (Vienna, 1928).
13. See Stefan Karner, Ingrid Kubin, and Michael Steiner, "Wie real war 'Mitteleuropa'? Zur wirtschaftlichen Verflochtenheit des Donauraumes nach dem Ersten Weltkrieg," *Vierteljahresschrift für Sozial- und Wirtschaftsgeschichte* 74, no. 2 (1987): 153–85.
14. See Peter Haslinger, "Building a Regional Identity," *Austrian History Yearbook* 32 (2001): 105–24.
15. Emil Brix, "Zur untersteirischen Frage in der Nationalitätenstatistik," in *Als Mitteleuropa zerbrach: Zu den Folgen des Umbruchs in Österreich und Jugoslawien nach dem Ersten Weltkrieg*, ed. S. Karner and G. Schöpfer (Graz, 1990), 121.
16. Christian Promitzer, "The South Slavs in the Austrian Imagination," in *Creating the Other: Ethnic Conflict and Nationalism in Habsburg Central Europe*, ed. N. M. Wingfield (New York, 2004), 195.

17. For the figure referring to the years 1923 to 1930, see *Statistisches Handbuch*, vol. 14 (1933), 38.
18. Heidemarie Uhl, "'Bollwerk deutscher Kultur': Kulturelle Repräsentationen nationaler Politik in Graz um 1900," in *Kultur-Urbanität-Moderne: Differenzierungen der Moderne in Zentraleuropa um 1900*, ed. H. Uhl (Vienna, 1999), 39–82.
19. See Julie Thorpe, "Belonging in Austria: Citizens, Minorities and Refugees in the Twentieth Century," in *Europe: New Voices, New Perspectives: Proceedings from the Contemporary Europe Research Centre*, ed. M. Killingsworth (Melbourne, 2007), 99–100.
20. Austrian law StGBl. 397 ex 1920, par. 1.
21. See Beatrix Hoffmann-Holter, *"Abreisendmachung": Jüdische Kriegsflüchtlinge in Wien 1914 bis 1923* (Vienna, 1995), 248–57.
22. *Beiträge zur Statistik der Republik Österreich*, vol. 8 (Vienna, 1923), 139; *Statistische Nachrichten* 4 (1926): 122–30.
23. Andreas Weigl, "Demographic Transitions Accelerated: Abortion, Body Politics, and the End of Supra-Regional Labor Immigration in Post-War Austria," in *From Empire to Republic: Post-World War I Austria*, Contemporary Austrian Studies 19, ed. G. Bischof, F. Plasser, and P. Berger (Innsbruck, 2010), 145.
24. For more details see Alexander Pinwinkler, "'Bevölkerungssoziologie' und Ethnizität: Historisch-demografische Minderheitenforschung in Österreich, ca. 1918–1938," *ZfG Zeitschrift für Geschichtswissenschaft* 57, no. 2 (February 2009): 118.
25. See Brousek, *Wien und seine Tschechen*, 33.
26. Pinwinkler, "'Bevölkerungssoziologie' und Ethnizität," 114.
27. See G. Exner, J. Kytir, and A. Pinwinkler, *Bevölkerungswissenschaft in Österreich in der Zwischenkriegszeit (1918–1938): Personen, Institutionen, Diskurse* (Vienna, 2004), 170–72.
28. See John, "Identity and Ethnicity," 21–28.
29. See Emil Brix, "Die nationale Frage anhand der Umgangssprachererhebung in den zisleithanischen Volkszählungen 1880 bis 1910" (PhD diss., University of Vienna, 1979), 719–23.
30. For this reason Sylvia Hahn might have avoided the use of language statistics in her recent survey on Austrian migration history. See Hahn, "Austria," 86–89. On the other hand, language statistics, and the political background of their generating, are a useful tool for contextualized analysis.
31. See Marcus Gräser, "Mass Migration and Local Politics in Chicago and Vienna, 1850–1938: Some Questions, Some Hypotheses," *Bulletin of the German Historical Institute* (Washington DC) 40 (2007): 103.
32. M. Seliger and K. Ucakar, *Wien: Politische Geschichte 1740–1934*, vol. 2, *1896–1934* (Vienna, 1985), 1167–75.
33. See Wolfgang Maderthaner, "Die Juden und das Rote Wien," in *Wien, Stadt der Juden: Die Welt der Tante Jolesch*, ed. J. Riedl (Vienna, 2004), 144–46; Michael John, "Galician Jews in Austria from the 18th to the Early 20th Century," in Bade et al., *The Encyclopedia of Migration and Minorities in Europe*, 400–402.
34. See Thomas Soxberger, "Die jiddische Literatur und Publizistik im Wien der zwanziger Jahre," in *Berlin-Wien-Prag: Moderne, Minderheiten und Migration in der Zwischenkriegszeit*, ed. S. Marten-Finnis and M. Uecker (Bern, 2001), 243–54.
35. See M. G. Hall, *Der Fall Hugo Bettauer* (Vienna, 1978); Beth S. Noveck, "Hugo Bettauer and the Political Culture of the First Republic," in *Austria in the Nineteen Fifties*, Contemporary Austrian Studies 3, ed. Günter Bischof, Anton Pelinka, and Rolf Steininger (New Brunswick, NJ, 1995), 138–70.
36. See, e.g., ÖStA (Österreichisches Staatsarchiv/Austrian State Archive), AdR, Staatsamt f. soz. Verwaltung/Sozialpolitik, Box 61, Sek. IV. Dep. 15, SA 13.644-1921-1923, Magistrat der Stadt Linz an die Holzausfuhrstelle Wien, 21 November 1922.

37. See Eugene Sensenig-Dabbous, "Social Democracy in One Country: Immigration and Minority Policy in Austria," in *The European Union and Migrant Labour*, ed. G. Dale and M. Cole (New York, 1999), 214–15.
38. *Stenographisches Protokoll über die Sitzungen des Nationalrates (II. Gesetzgebungsperiode) der Republik Österreich: 1925 bis 1926* (Vienna, 1926), 3.266ff.
39. Ibid.
40. See Brousek, *Wien und seine Tschechen*, 68–69.
41. *Der Kuckuck*, no. 34 (24 November 1929), 8–9. See also the detailed article by Michael John, "Organisationsformen der Wanderminoritäten in Österreich 1867–1925: Thesen und Überlegungen," *Beiträge zur Geschichte der Arbeiterbewegung* 38, no. 2 (1996): 20–32.
42. *Statistisches Handbuch*, vol. 14 (1933), 36.
43. *Statistisches Handbuch*, vol. 8 (1927), 47.
44. Ibid.
45. *Statistisches Handbuch*, vol. 15 (1935), 35.
46. See Rainer Bauböck and Bernhard Perchinig, "Migrations- und Integrationspolitik," in *Politik in Österreich: Das Handbuch*, ed. H. Dachs et al. (Vienna, 2006), 726–42.
47. See Weigl, "Demographic Transitions Accelerated," 146.
48. See O. Rathkolb, *Die paradoxe Republik* (Vienna, 2006), 19–25.
49. See H. Fassmann and R. Münz, *Einwanderungsland Österreich? Historische Migrationsmuster, aktuelle Trends und politische Maßnahmen* (Vienna, 1995), 27–39.
50. See Michael John, "Die Auswanderung aus Österreich 1919–1937," in *Auswanderung aus Österreich: Von der Mitte des 19. Jahrhunderts bis zur Gegenwart*, ed. T. Horvath and G. Neyer (Vienna, 1996), 87.
51. Ibid., 87ff.
52. See *Die Ergebnisse der österreichischen Volkszählung vom 22. März 1934*, vol. 1(Vienna, 1935), 51.
53. The census was carried out in March 1934, after the socialist uprising (the civil war of 1934) and the elimination of parliamentary democracy in Austria. Viennese Czechs were suspected of sympathizing with the Social Democrats. The leadership of the now illegal Social Democratic Party found refuge in Brno, Czechoslovakia. Thousands of political opponents of the new Austrian regime were exiled in Czechoslovakia, a functioning democracy. In the climate of uncertainty in 1934 many inhabitants tended to respond to the question concerning language use with "German." The authoritarian Austrian *Staendestaat* (1934–38) presented itself as a "German" and "Catholic" state. One could declare only one language, and in 1934 Czech was indicated by 38,662 and Slovak by 2,052 persons. See Brousek, *Wien und seine Tschechen*, 34–35. Interestingly, under National Socialist rule the census of May 1939 showed a result of 62,260 Czechs and Slovaks in Vienna, although there was an ongoing migration from Vienna to Czechoslovakia in 1934–38. In 1939 the category "mother tongue" instead of "language of daily use" was used. *Statistisches Jahrbuch der Stadt Wien 1939–1942* (Vienna, 1946), 31.
54. See Lichtblau, "Juden in Österreich—Integration,Vernichtungsversuch und Neubeginn: Österreichisch-jüdische Geschichte 1848 bis zur Gegenwart," in *Geschichte der Juden in Österreich*, ed. Evelyn Brugger et al. (Vienna, 2006), 507–13.
55. The figure includes those coming by boat during the years 1933–37. See Gabriele Anderl and Angelika Jensen, "Zionistische Auswanderung nach Palästina vor 1938," in *Auswanderung aus Österreich*, ed. T. Horvath and G. Neyer (Vienna, 1996), 209.
56. J. Moser, *Demographie der jüdischen Bevölkerung Österreichs 1938–1945* (Vienna, 1999), 16.
57. See J. Thorpe, "Pan-German Identity and the Press in Austria, 1933–1938" (PhD diss., University of Adelaide, 2006).

58. See Viktor Lebzelter, "Eine rassenkundliche Übersichtsaufnahme des Burgenlandes," *Mitteilungen der Anthropologischen Gesellschaft in Wien* 67 (1937): 294–350; Verena Pawlowsky, "Profilierung im Mangel: Die Anthropologische Abteilung des Naturhistorischen Museums in Wien vor 1938," *Zeitgeschichte* 3 (May/June 2003): 157–58.
59. See Pinwinkler, "'Bevölkerungssoziologie' und Ethnizität," 131–32.
60. Quoted in R. Steininger, *Austria, Germany and the Cold War: From the Anschluss to the State Treaty 1938–1955* (New York, 2008), 15.
61. Ibid.
62. See C. Jabloner et al., *Schlussbericht der Historikerkommission der Republik Österreich: Vermögensentzug während der NS-Zeit sowie Rückstellungen und Entschädigungen seit 1945 in Österreich: Zusammenfassungen und Einschätzungen* (Vienna, 2003), 97, 116.
63. Florian Freund and Hans Safrian, "Die Verfolgung der österreichischen Juden 1938–1945: Vertreibung und Deportation," in *NS-Herrschaft in Österreich: Ein Handbuch*, ed. Emmerich Tálos et al. (Vienna, 2001), 783.
64. See G. Lewy, *The Nazi Persecution of the Gypsies* (Oxford, 2000), 57, 149.
65. Hans Maršálek, "Das KZ Mauthausen (Stammlager) 1938–1945," in *Oberösterreichische Gedenkstätten für KZ-Opfer*, ed. Land Oberösterreich (Linz, 2001), 51; Florian Freund and Bertrand Perz, "Zwangsarbeit von zivilen AusländerInnen, Kriegsgefangenen, KZ-Häftlingen und ungarischen Juden in Österreich," in Tálos et al., *NS-Herrschaft in Österreich*, 671.
66. See M. John and A. Lichtblau, *Schmelztiegel Wien—einst und jetzt*, 2nd ed. (Vienna, 1993), 292–93.
67. Kurt Tweraser, *National Socialism in Linz: English Summary*, ed. Fritz Mayrhofer and Walter Schuster (Linz, 2002), 24ff.
68. *Statistisches Jahrbuch der Stadt Linz 1951* (Linz, 1951), 28; K. H. Rauscher, "Die ökonomische und soziale Entwicklung von Steyr im Nationalsozialismus unter besonderer Berücksichtigung der lokalen Großindustrie" (PhD diss., University of Linz, 1998), 262ff.
69. According to Florian Freund and Bertrand Perz, "forced labor" was performed in Austria by civilians, prisoners of war, concentration camp inmates, and Hungarian Jews as a specific group. See F. Freund, B. Perz, and M. Spoerer, *Zwangsarbeiter und Zwangsarbeiterinnen auf dem Gebiet der Republik Österreich 1939–1945* (Vienna, 2004), 213–20.
70. See also *NS-Zwangsarbeit: Der Standort Linz der "Reichswerke Hermann Göring AG Berlin" 1938–1945*, vol. 1, ed. O. Rathkolb (Vienna, 2001); H. Feichtlbauer, *Zwangsarbeit in Österreich 1938–1945: Späte Anerkennung, Geschichte, Schicksale: Fonds für Versöhnung, Frieden und Zusammenarbeit* (Vienna, 2006).
71. See Eveline Wollner, "Die Reform der Beschäftigung und Anwerbung ausländischer Arbeitskräfte Anfang der 1960er Jahre in Österreich," *Zeitgeschichte* 4 (July/August 2007): 213–14.
72. See M. John, "Upper Austria, Intermediate Stop: Reception Camps and Housing Schemes for Jewish DPs and Refugees in Transit," *The Journal of Israeli History* 19, no. 3 (Autumn 1998): 24–25.
73. T. Albrich and R. Zweig, eds., *Escape through Austria: Jewish Refugees and the Austrian Route to Palestine* (London, 2002), 15.
74. After World War II large sections of the population, Austrian authorities, and politicians favored having the ethnic German refugees (so-called *Volksdeutsche*) stay in Austria, but not Jewish refugees and non-German-speaking DPs. The Austrian Ministry of Interior pursued a policy to clear the latter groups out of Austria and to complicate the process of gaining Austrian citizenship. In 1953, for example, the Jewish organization Agudas Israel asked the Austrian Ministry of Interior to ease the process of acquiring citizenship for Jewish refugees. Officials from the ministry rejected the appeal. See Tara Zahra, "'Prisoners of the Postwar':

Expellees, Refugees, and Jews in Postwar Austria," *Austrian History Yearbook* 41 (2010): 203–5.
75. See the autobiographical records of S. Wiesenthal, *Recht, nicht Rache: Erinnerungen*, 3rd ed. (Frankfurt, 1995).
76. See J. Corsellis and M. Ferrar, *Slovenia 1945: Memories of Death and Survival after World War II* (London, 2005), 87–111; Gabriela Stieber, "Volksdeutsche und Displaced Persons," in *Asylland wider Willen: Flüchtlinge im europäischen Kontext seit 1914*, ed. G. Heiss and O. Rathkolb (Vienna, 1995), 140–56.
77. See Brunhilde Scheuringer, "Szenarien zur Integration der volksdeutschen Flüchtlinge und Vertriebenen nach dem Zweiten Weltkrieg in Österreich," in *Österreichischer Zeitgeschichtetag 1993*, ed. I. Böhler and R. Steininger (Innsbruck, 1995), 225–28; H. Volkmer, *Die Volksdeutschen in Oberösterreich—ihre Integration und ihr Beitrag zum Wiederaufbau des Landes nach dem Zweiten Weltkrieg* (Grünbach, 2003).
78. G. Alföldy, *Ungarn 1956: Aufstand, Revolution, Freiheitskampf* (Heidelberg, 1997), 32; Brigitta Zierer, "Willkommene Ungarnflüchtlinge 1956?," in *Asylland wider Willen: Flüchtlinge im europäischen Kontext seit 1914*, ed. G. Heiss and O. Rathkolb (Vienna, 1995), 155–71.
79. See E. Stanek, *Verfolgt, verjagt, vertrieben: Flüchtlinge in Österreich von 1945–1984* (Vienna, 1985), 62–63; I. Murber and Z. Fónagy, *Die ungarische Revolution und Österreich 1956* (Vienna, 2006).
80. Ibid., 64.
81. Vlasta Valeš, "Die tschechoslowakischen Flüchtlinge 1968–1989," in *Asylland wider Willen: Flüchtlinge im europäischen Kontext seit 1914*, ed. G. Heiss and O. Rathkolb (Vienna, 1995), 172–81.
82. Klaus Eisterer, "The Austrian Legation in Prague and the Czechoslovak Crisis of 1968," *Contemporary Austrian Studies* 9 (2001): 214–35; Premysl Janyr, "Tschechoslowakei 1968— Charta 77," in *Asylland wider Willen: Flüchtlinge im europäischen Kontext seit 1914*, ed. G. Heiss and O. Rathkolb (Vienna, 1995), 182–83.
83. See R. Reiz, "Polnische Migration nach Österreich im 20. Jahrhundert" (Univ. Dipl. Arb., University of Linz, 2004), 34; United Nations High Commissioner for Refugees (UNHCR) in Austria, *A Long Tradition of Assisting Refugees* (Vienna, 2004), 1.
84. See E. Wollner, "Auf dem Weg zur sozialpartnerschaftlich regulierten Ausländerbeschäftigung in Österreich: Die Reform der Ausländerbeschäftigung und der Anwerbung bis Ende der 1960er Jahre" (Univ. Dipl. Arb., University of Vienna, 1996).
85. H. Fassmann and R. Münz, *Einwanderungsland Österreich? Historische Migrationsmuster, aktuelle Trends und politische Maßnahmen* (Vienna, 1995), 41–42.
86. Wolfgang Kos, "Winken zum Abschied, Winken zum Aufbruch," in *Gastarbajteri: 40 Jahre Arbeitsmigration*, ed. H. Gürses, K. Kogoj, and S. Mattl (Vienna, 2004), 14.
87. *Statistische Nachrichten—Statistische Übersichten* (ÖSTAT/WIFO Vienna, 1963–73).
88. See Hannes Wimmer, "Zur Ausländerbeschäftigungspolitik in Österreich," in *Ausländische Arbeitskräfte in Österreich*, ed. H. Wimmer (Frankfurt, 1986), 7–8.
89. *Solidarität: Zeitschrift des Österreichischen Gewerkschaftsbundes* (July/August 1969), 11.
90. Arbeitskreis für ökonomische und soziale Studien in Wien, ed., *Gastarbeiter: Wirtschaftliche und soziale Herausforderung* (Vienna, 1973), 25.
91. *Statistisches Handbuch Österreichs 1968* (Vienna, 1968), 259; *Statistisches Handbuch Österreichs 1974* (Vienna, 1974), 303.
92. See John and Lichtblau, *Schmelztiegel Wien*, 287.
93. See *Am Anfang war der Kolaric: Plakate gegen Rassismus und Fremdenfeindlichkeit*, ed. U. Hemetek (Vienna, 2002).
94. See Wladimir Fischer, "'I haaß Vocelka—du haaßt Vocelka': Der Diskurs über 'die Gastarbeiter' in den 1960er bis 1980er Jahren und der unhistorische Vergleich mit der Wiener

Arbeitsmigration um 1900," in *Wien und seine WienerInnen: Ein historischer Streifzug durch Wien über die Jahrhunderte,* ed. M. Scheutz and V. Valeš (Vienna, 2008), 224ff.
95. See Wimmer, "Ausländerbeschäftigungspolitik," 13–18.
96. See P. Fernandez de la Hoz, *Familienleben, Transnationalität und Diaspora,* ÖIF Materialien 21 (Vienna, 2004), 23–24.
97. *Statistisches Jahrbuch Österreichs 2007* (Vienna, 2007), 55.
98. Concerning the *Volksgruppenfrage,* the topic of "autochthonous" ethnic minorities in Austria, see G. Baumgartner, *6 x Österreich: Geschichte und aktuelle Situation der Volksgruppen* (Klagenfurt, 1995); see also C. Sulzbacher, "Österreich und seine Volksgruppen (ethnic groups)" (PhD diss., University of Salzburg, 2001).
99. See Stefan Benedik, "Define the Migrant, Define the Menace: Remarks on Narratives of Recent Romani Migrations to Graz," in *Mapping Contemporary History II,* ed. H. Konrad and S. Benedik (Vienna, 2010), 159–78.
100. Peter Wagner, "Gedenken an das Oberwarter Attentat," *Pannonia* 25, no. 2 (1997): 36–39; H. Samer, "Die Roma von Oberwart: Zur Geschichte und aktuellen Situation der Roma in Oberwart" (Univ. Dipl. Arb., University of Graz, 1997), 70–80.
101. International Organization for Migration (IOM), *Der Einfluss von Immigration auf die österreichische Gesellschaft* (Vienna, 2004), 14–15.
102. See, in general, *Global Women, Nannies, Maids and Sex Workers in the New Economy,* ed. A. R. Hochschild and B. Ehrenreich (New York, 2003); D. Pichler, "Grenzenlose Pflege: Eine quantitative und qualitative Analyse am Beispiel tschechischer und slowakischer Pflegekräfte in Österreich" (Univ. Dipl. Arb., University of Linz, 2005).
103. *Tschechen in Wie: Zwischen nationaler Selbstbehauptung und Assimilation,* ed. R. Wonisch (Vienna, 2010), 20, 200, 244.
104. See A. Pilgram, ed., *Grenzöffnung, Migration, Kriminalität: Jahrbuch für Rechts- und Kriminalsoziologie 1993* (Baden-Baden, 1993).
105. Fritz Plasser and Peter A. Ulram, "Rechtspopulistische Resonanzen: Die Wählerschaft der FPÖ," in *Das österreichische Wahlverhalten,* ed. F. Plasser and P. Ulram (Vienna, 2000), 228–30; Imma Palme, "Issue-Voting: Themen und thematische Positionen als Determinanten der Wahlentscheidung," in Plasser and Ulram, *Das österreichische Wahlverhalten,* 243–59.
106. For the documentation, the background, and the perspectives of the event see the anthology, M. Kargl and S. Lehmann, eds., *Land im Lichtermeer: Stimmen gegen Fremdenfeindlichkeit* (Vienna, 1994).
107. A. Weigl, *Migration und Integration: Eine widersprüchliche Geschichte* (Innsbruck, 2009), 14–15.
108. Statistik Austria (ed.), *Volkszählung 2001. Hauptergebnisse I – Wien* (Vienna, 2003), 18–19, 62, 72, 82.
109. *Statistisches Jahrbuch Österreichs 2007,* 54.
110. Experts call the phenomenon "antisemitism without Jews." See H. Weiss, *Nation und Toleranz: Empirische Studien zu nationalen Identitäten in Österreich,* with a contribution from Christoph Reinprecht (Vienna, 2004), 58–69.
111. The formula for the segregation index is $S = \sum_{i=1}^{n} \frac{|x_i - y_i|}{2}$ where x is the proportion of one population in a census tract, and y is the rest of the population, and the index (S) is the sum of the absolute values of the differences in the percentage of the two populations, divided by two. The index of segregation is a well-established measure of segregation in modern societies. For Viennese Jewry it has been used by Marsha L. Rozenblit, *The Jews of Vienna 1867–1914: Assimilation and Identity* (Albany, 1983), 225–26.
112. Weigl, *Migration und Integration,* 77.
113. Ibid., 73 (results for the population over fifteen).

114. *Statistisches Jahrbuch der Stadt Wien für das Jar 1912* (Vienna, 1914), 912; Lichtblau, "Juden in Österreich," 556.
115. *Statistisches Handbuch,* vol. 8 (1927), 12ff.; Lichtblau, "Juden in Österreich," 556.
116. Statistik Austria, ed., *Die Ergebnisse der Volkszählung 2001: Hauptergebnisse I—Wien* (Vienna, 2003), 82.
117. See IOM, *Der Einfluss von Immigration,* 15–16.
118. In this context, the cases of Seibane Wague, Yankuba Ceesay, and Richard Ebekwe have to be mentioned. See the racism monitoring website at http://www.no-racism.net (accessed 8 January 2012); see also Walter Sauer, "Afro-österreichische Dispora heute: Migration und Integration in der 2. Republik," in *Von Soliman zu Omofuma: Afrikanische Diaspora in Österreich 17. bis 20. Jahrhundert,* ed. W. Sauer (Innsbruck, 2007), 205–14.
119. See the theoretically oriented article by Christof Parnreiter, "Restriktive Migrationspolitik und ihr Scheitern an der Wirklichkeit," in *Herausforderung Migration: Beiträge zur Aktions- und Informationswoche der Universität Wien anlässlich des "UN International Migrant's Day,"* Abhandlungen zur Geographie und Regionalforschung 7, ed. S. Binder, G. Rasuly-Paleczek, and M. Six-Hohenbalken (Vienna, 2005), 35–49.
120. See *International Herald Tribune,* 1 October 2006, 3 October 2006, and 6 October 2006.
121. Statistik Austria Online, *Statistische Übersichten. Beschäftigung und Arbeitsmarkt,* 2007. https://www.statistik.at/web_de/services/stat_uebersichten/beschaeftigung_und_arbeitsmarkt/index.html (accessed 12 August 2013).
122. *Statistisches Jahrbuch Österreichs 2007,* 86.
123. Harald Waldrauch and Dilek Cinar, "Staatsbürgerschaft und Einbürgerungspraxis in Österreich," in *Österreichischer Migrations- und Integrationsbericht: Demographische Entwicklungen—sozioökonomische Strukturen—rechtliche Rahmenbedingungen,* ed. H. Fassmann and I. Stacher (Vienna, 2003), 282.
124. Statistik Austria Online, *Population Statistics, Naturalizations,* 1998–2010. http://www.statistik.at/web_en/statistics/population/naturalisation/index.html (accessed 26 August 2013).
125. Statistik Austria (ed.), *Demographisches Jahrbuch 2010* (Vienna, 2011), 145.
126. Ibid., 20.
127. Statistik Austria and Kommission für Migrations- und Integrationsforschung der Österreichischen Akademie der Wissenschaften, eds., *Migration and Integration: Zahlen, Daten, Indikatoren 2010* (Vienna, 2010), 36.
128. Statistik Austria Online, *Klassifikationen, Regionale Gliederungen, Bundesländer,* https://www.statistik.at/web_de/klassifikationen/regionale_gliederungen/bundeslaender/index.html (accessed 10 August 2013).
129. Gudrun Biffl, Système d'observation permanente des migrations *(SOPEMI) Report on Labour Migration Austria 2004–05* (Vienna, 2005), 83–84.
130. See IOM, *Der Einfluss von Immigration,* 15–16; Mathias Vogl, "Die jüngere Entwicklung im Bereich des Asyl und Fremdenrechts," in *2. Österreichischer Migrations- und Integrationsbericht 2001–2006,* ed. H. Fassmann (Klagenfurt, 2007), 24–26.
131. Statistik Austria and Kommission für Migrations- und Integrationsforschung der Österreichischen Akademie der Wissenschaften, eds., *Migration and Integration: Zahlen, Daten, Indikatoren 2011* (Vienna, 2011), 35; Republik Österreich, Bundesministerium für Inneres, *Asylstatistik Dezember 2011.* http://www.bmi.gv.at/cms/BMI_Asylwesen/statistik/files/2011/Asylstatistik_Dezember_2011.pdf (accessed 15 January 2012).
132. Menschenrechtsbeirat beim Bundesministerium für Inneres, *Bericht des Menschenrechtsbeirats über seine Tätigkeit im Jahr 2007* (Vienna, 2008), 27–28. http://www.bmi.gv.at/cms/BMI_MRB/mrb/jahresberichte/files/jahresbericht_2007.pdf (accessed 9 August 2013).

133. See Weigl, *Migration und Integration*, 96.
134. Statistik Austria Online, *Statistische Übersichten, Beschäftigung und Arbeitsmarkt*, 2011. http://www.statistik.at/web_de/services/stat_uebersichten/beschaeftigung_und_arbeitsmarkt/index.html (accessed 10 January 2012)
135. Statistik Austria and Kommission für Migrations, *Migration & Integration*, 21.
136. See SORA (Institute for Social Research and Consulting) and ISA (Institut für Strategieanalysen), *Wahltagsbefragung und Wählerstromanalyse: Gemeinderatswahl Wien 2010* (Vienna, 2010), 2, 16.
137. *Der Standard*, 7 October 2009, 8.
138. Staatssekretariat für Integration, Integrationsbericht. Expertenrat für Integration. *Das 20 Punkte Programm, Juli 2011*, 12–17. http://www.bmi.gv.at/cms/BMI_Service/STS/Vorschlaege_Langfassung.pdf (accessed 10 August 2013).
139. T. Huddleston and J. Niessen with E. N. Chaimh and E. White, *Migrant Integration Policy Index III* (Brussels, 2011), 11.
140. See Medienservicestelle Neue Österreicher/innen. Das Portal für JournalistInnen zu Migration und Integration, *Neues Fremdenrecht ab 1. Juli 2011 in Österreich*. http://medienservicestelle.at/migration_bewegt/2011/06/28/osterreichs-fremdenrecht-seit-20-jahren-immer-scharfer (accessed 15 January 2012).
141. See, in general, *Integration in Österreich: Sozialwissenschaftliche Befunde*, ed. H. Langthaler (Innsbruck, 2010); see also M. Gruber, *Integrationspolitik in Kommunen: Herausforderungen, Chancen, Gestaltungsansätze* (Vienna, 2010), 81–183.
142. OECD (Organization for Economic Co-operation and Development), *Jobs for Immigrants*, vol. 3, *Labour Market Integration in Austria, Norway and Switzerland* (Paris 2012), 109.
143. The Second Austrian Republic was founded in 1945 with the reestablishment of an independent Austrian state.
144. See Igor Grdina, "Gedanken zum Kärtner Schmerz Sloveniens," in *Die Kärntner Slovenen 1900–2000: Bilanz des 20. Jahrhunderts*, ed. A. Moritsch, 347–72. (Klagenfurt, 2000); W. Hauer, *Der Ortstafelstreit: Zum Verhältnis von Rechtsstaat und Demokratie* (Vienna, 2006); see also Robert Knight, "Liberal Values and Post-Nazi-Politics: The Slovenes of Carinthia," in *Demokratie: Modus und Telos: Beiträge für Anton Pelinka*, ed. A. S. Markovits and S. K. Rosenberger (Vienna, 2001), 143–58.
145. See, e.g., Binder, Rasuly-Paleczek, and Six-Hohenbalken, *Herausforderung Migration*, 10–34.
146. See Amnesty International, *Amnesty International Report 2004* (London, 2004); Weiss, *Nation und Toleranz*, 69–74; *Afrikaner in Wien: Zwischen Mystifizierung und Verteufelung: Erfahrungen und Analysen*, 3rd ed., ed. E. Ebermann (Münster, 2007).
147. See G. Lebhart and R. Münz, *Migration und Fremdenfeindlichkeit: Fakten, Meinungen und Einstellungen zu internationaler Migration, ausländischer Bevölkerung und staatlicher Ausländerpolitik in Österreich* (Vienna, 1999), 77–84; Österreichischer Rundfunk, *Der Islam und der Westen: Fakten, Ängste, Vorurteile*, 2 CDs (Vienna, 2007); see also N. Ornig, *Die Zweite Generation und der Islam in Österreich* (Graz, 2006), 25–60.
148. ZARA (Zivilcourage und Anti-Rassismus-Arbeit), ed., *Rassismus Report 2006: Einzelfall-Bericht über rassistische Übergriffe und Strukturen in Österreich* (Vienna, 2007), 6.
149. John Boyer, *Political Radicalism in Late Imperial Vienna: Origins of the Christian Social Movement 1848–1897* (Chicago, 1981), 105.
150. N. Elias and J. L. Scotson, *Established and the Outsiders*, 2nd ed. (London, 1994).
151. See Medienservicestelle Neue Österreicher/innen, *PolitikerInnen mit Migrationshintergrund*, 30 November 2011. http://medienservicestelle.at/migration_bewegt/2011/11/30/politik-erinnen-mit-migrationshintergrund (accessed 15 January 2012).

152. Jus soli ("right of the soil") is a legal principle by which citizenship is granted to any individual born in the territory of the related state.
153. Rathkolb, *Paradoxe Republik,* 19–28, 56–59.
154. See Leo Lucassen, "Is Transnationalism Compatible with Assimilation? Examples from Western Europe since 1850," *IMIS-Beiträge* 29 (2006): 15.
155. Josef Ratzenböck, former governor of Upper Austria, in a letter to the Austrian Ministry of Interior, 1990. Quoted in Peter Zuser, "Die Konstruktion der Ausländerfrage in Österreich: Eine Analyse des öffentlichen Diskurses 1990," *Political Science Series* 35 (1996): 34–35.
156. *Die Presse,* 10 November 2010, 3.
157. *Kronen Zeitung,* 11 November 2010, 1.
158. IMAS-Report, Umfrageberichte von IMAS-International, vol. 22 (October 1997), 1–3.
159. IMAS International Report, vol. 13 (June 2010), 1a–2a.
160. GfK Austria, *Integration in Österreich: Einstellungen, Orientierungen, und Erfahrungen von MigrantInnen und Angehörigen der Mehrheitsbevölkerung* (Vienna, 2009), 80–81; see also Karin Zauner, *Zuwanderung—Herausforderung für Österreichs Medien* (Vienna, 2012).
161. See Christiane Hintermann, "'that migration simply and really is the absolute normality': The Narration of Austrian Immigration History in Exhibitions," in *Migration and Memory: Representations of Migration in Europe since 1960,* ed. Christiane Hintermann and Christina Johannson (Innsbruck, 2010), 171–72.
162. See Bauböck and Perchinig, *Migrations- und Integrationspolitik,* 740–41.

Section III

IDENTITIES EXPRESSED, NEGOTIATED, AND CHALLENGED IN MULTICULTURAL SETTINGS

Chapter 7

THE SLICE OF DESIRE

Intercultural Practices versus National Loyalties in the Peripheral Multiethnic Society of Central Europe at the Beginning of the Twentieth Century

Oto Luthar

Introduction

Believing that not only speaking and writing but also desiring, whether for love, food, or success, represents forms of knowledge and communication, I have decided to discuss the historical circumstances and dynamics of the formation of intercultural practices of the late nineteenth and early twentieth century in Central Europe in a slightly different way from the other chapters in this volume. To discuss the cultural dynamics of a unique and continually changing region in northeastern Slovenia, where the four main sets of European linguistic groups (Hungarian, Slavic, Romance, and Germanic) meet, I have chosen to analyze two specific everyday practices: the mixture of ethnic cousins and the so-called interethnic ethnic consciousness. In this way, I hope to show that despite the breakup of old all-encompassing identity schemes caused by modernization, the people of that specific multicultural region still shared some transnational rhetoric for both their self-identification and recognition of others. Using multilingual diaries and recipe books, I will try to show that although they might have had a multiplicity of identities to sort out and to manage quite actively, people of the border areas were known for their strong intercultural habitus.

At the same time, I do not think that writing about food (or private memories) necessarily has to be as diverse as writing about any other part of life. On the contrary, since "food always condenses a happening, a plot," personal and cultural memories are integral to eating and speaking. Or, as the author of *A Slice of Life* would put it, simply to name a food is to invoke the lifetime of a person and a culture.[1]

Indeed, food has everything in the world to tell us about the mentalities of an age, its tropes of desire and want and geographies. Understood as part of the history of the world, the subject of food can be embraced as a history of a particular society. Or, as Countess Sybil Schönefeldt would put it, "food stands as the sensual basis of remembering" and "the courses" are like people: "they not only speak as symbolic illustrations like the still-life works of the Dutch painters, but they interact with us and help to create atmosphere."[2]

The Notion of Central Europe and Its Multicultural Character

Before giving the word to cooks, soldiers, lovers, and all those who are also involved in this story, I need to address the notion of Central Europe as an objective geographical, social, historic, and economic reality on the one hand and the historical formation of Central Europe as an imaginary concept and ideological construction on the other. By so doing, I have decided to focus on the "we" group construction based on assumed biology and the essentialist version of the past in northeastern Slovenia. There are several reasons for discussing this particular region. Prekmurje, as the region is called, is traditionally the most heterogeneous in Slovenia in cultural terms and one of the most multicultural regions in Central Europe in general.

Positioned between Austria to the north, Croatia to the south, and Hungary to the east, this is the only province where Slovene-speaking and Hungarian-speaking Protestant and Catholic communities and the Roma have lived together with little notable religious conflict since the Thirty Years' War. Before the Nazi deportation of the Jews in 1944, Prekmurje was also the home of two influential Jewish communities. And, finally, although the region is known today as the Roman Catholic "Bible Belt" of Slovenia (almost half of all Slovene Roman Catholic priests come from Prekmurje), religiously mixed marriages have always been very common there. In short, the region I am talking about has an interesting multicultural heritage based on the Habsburg tradition of the cohabitation of people of different cultural and religious characteristics and on the socialist Yugoslav emancipatory legal framework concerning the rights of ethnic minorities.

Since I am concentrating only on the Habsburg tradition vis-à-vis the traditional demands for loyalty and forms of legitimacy, I use two documents that offer an example of common intercultural practices of the late modern period. The first document is the diary of a soldier, a self-described Slovene, who served in Herzegovina at the beginning of the twentieth century. The diary is interesting because of the author's use of different narratives and languages. Surprisingly enough, he was—despite his limited education—quite confident in using three languages; when describing his military life he wrote in German, when referring to his family affairs he used Slovene, and his sexual fantasies were almost all written in Hungarian. The second document is a handwritten cookbook in Slovene, German, and Hungarian, also an interesting mixture of recipes and other household instructions for housewives, where in one sentence two and sometimes even three languages are used. Using these and some fragments from similar documents, I argue that this multicultural way of remembering and sharing professional expertise was the usual practice of everyday communication for many until the end of the Great War when, with the creation of the Kingdom of Yugoslavia and later socialist Yugoslavia, the three newly politicized national/ethnic identities, two religious identities, and (after 1945) one exclusive ideology produced a new set of practices of cohabitation and differentiation.

Between Exclusion and Intercultural Sociality

What concepts and theories of identification in multicultural settings are most helpful for understanding the two documents from Prekmurje? In considering this question, I must refer to the situation in Slovenia during the last twenty years, where multiculturalism can in no way be described as "a delayed antibiotic to the race trends of the 1970s and 1980s,"[3] but rather as a civic concept that celebrates cultural diversity while preserving a political core from being disrupted by this diversity. When discussing cultural diversity, one can rarely regard culture as simply unambiguous and noncontradictory, isolated from questions of history. At best it can be seen as a realm of individual attitudes in which diversity might lead to a reduction of prejudice but not to any change in the position of various groups. In other words, during the post-Yugoslav period in Slovenia, cultural diversity sometimes noted differences in values and outlooks while usually ignoring the differences in social position that influenced those values. In addition, after the period of tolerance toward ethnic groups that evidently would also vote for an independent Slovenia, plurality is increasingly perceived as a disturbing condition.

Like in some other parts of East Central Europe, in Slovenia the transitional period after 1989 was characterized by fragmentation, transformation, and the large-scale reorganization of economic, political, and cultural life. It was clearly a time of risk, of breaking down existing identities, and of the reemergence of marking differences and eroding intercultural sociality. Along with the new elective "postmodern" sociality in the new East Central Europe, earlier forms of exclusion were being reconstructed. Old ethnic certainties and a more culturally homogenous notion of collective identity based on biology and an essentialist version of the past were being reinvented.

It appears that each newly reconfigured state in this region went through a stage of the "'nationalizing' nationalism."[4] The concept implies that a core nation or nationality, defined in ethnocultural terms, distinguishes itself as the legitimate "owner" of the state. Despite its "ownership" of the state, this dominant or core nation conceives of itself as being weak in its cultural, economic, or demographic position within the state. The weak position—understood by interpreters of the national interest as a legacy of discrimination against that nation before it attained independence—is considered to justify "remedial" or "compensatory" projects using the state power to promote specific interests of the core nation. "We" group solidarity is based almost exclusively on ethnicity, obscuring or omitting other identities like class and gender. This form of nationalism is the consequence of the large-scale reorganization of political space along national lines and the dominant role of ethnicity at the expense of the notion of citizenship.

In addition to the construction of cultural and national difference and reliance on the negative definition of identity (that is, "different than"), the politics of exclusion involve the radical reinterpretation of the past and the rewriting of history.[5] This rewriting is to be understood as the mobilization of interpretative resources in the struggle over the present and the future, where the story of the past is presented as an unchanging truth waiting to be discovered.

As a result, historical representations have become a battlefield over meaning as well as over how the national interest will be defined. They also open up space where present and future political power may be gained. The struggle over the authentic version of the past has taken place during the last ten years in public discourse outside academia. The battle over the supposedly authentic version of the past is an articulation of the essentialist notion of history and national identity, based on the notion of the possibility of the homogenization of the "we" group, on a viewed notion of identity, and on a unified national subject.

An example of the "reinvention of the nation" at the local level is the invention of conflicting religious identities in otherwise traditionally multinational/multiethnic Prekmurje.

Despite a long history of transcultural practices before 1989, five Slovene Roman Catholic villages caused a local furor in the mid-1990s by demanding the establishment of new municipalities, arguing that they were "trapped" between the Slovene Protestant community and the Hungarian ethnic minority, an isolated island within "their own homeland."[6] It appears ethnicity once again became the determining force shaping all relationships. Or, to put it in a broader, Central European perspective, in the region that was always a space of intercultural sociality, as well as a space of exclusion, national identity more than ever became a product of political, religious, and historical discourse.

Therefore, using Charles Taylor's argument that people are also "culture-bearing" and that the cultures they bear differ depending on their past and present identification, I argue that before, and in many cases also for a decade after,

World War I Slovenes living in regions like Prekmurje bore multiple (i.e., at least three) identities. Or, to put it in terms of new cultural history, every member of a particular part of the monarchy marked by a strong multicultural character partook of at least two, if not three, cultural settings.

Multicultural "Mental Equipment" and Ethnicity

Before reconstructing the lives and identities of my "informants," I will concentrate on how both of my witnesses were using the "mental equipment" of their time, as Lucien Febvre termed it.[7] More precisely, I will try to show that although being simple people, they were able to use a great deal of the different mental equipment of their time. Or, to put it in Erwin Panofsky's terms, my intention is to conceptualize the variations among their mental habits as differences in modes of their formation. In doing so, I am trying to describe the hierarchy of levels of language and cultural universes to which they belonged. Only in this way might I be able to show the limits of their "modes of feeling and thought," as Marc Bloch would put it. According to this, my presentation can also be understood as a case study showing how the perception and representation of the world was organized for the people of the late nineteenth and early twentieth century in a typical multicultural environment in Central Europe. According to the theoretical and methodological framework that I am using, this contribution can be identified as a study in the history of mentalities. Or, to put it in a constructivist manner, I intend to reconstruct collective and individual identities by trying to find out what an individual or group shared with other men or women of the time.

Though I am using the inescapable term "identity," I am aware that it has been asked to do a great deal of analytical work. It simply tends to mean too much. Therefore, I agree with Rogers Brubaker that "the work done by identity might better be done by several clusters of less congested terms: identification and categorization, self-understanding and social location, commonality and connectedness."[8]

Working on the material for this chapter, I have come to appreciate the force of Eric Hobsbawm's dictum that nationhood and nationalism, while constructed from above, cannot be understood unless also analyzed from below, that is, in terms of the assumptions, hopes, needs, longings, and interests of ordinary people, which are not necessarily national or ethnic. Studying the everyday preoccupations and comprehensions of ordinary Prekmurians—to whom ethnicity was indeed largely irrelevant—helped make sense of certain puzzles, in particular the lack of popular mobilization due to the considerable popular indifference in the face of elite-level nationalist propaganda. Yet this nonresponsiveness to the appeals of ethnonational enterprises does not mean—as we are going to see—that ethnicity was insignificant in that multicultural region. Social life was pervasively, though unevenly, structured along ethnic lines, and ethnicity "happened" in a variety of everyday settings. Ethnicity was embodied and expressed not only in political projects and nationalist rhetoric, but also mainly in everyday encounters, practical categories, commonsense knowledge, cultural idioms, cognitive schemas, interactional cues, discursive frames, organizational routines, social networks, and institutional forms. Such everyday ethnicity—we might call it naive, apolitical nationalism—may be invisible to most of those who are interested in collective action, but it merits study in its own right.

On the other hand, this study tries to show the problematic aspect of those theories that stress a kind of ontological independence of the individual from her/his various roles. Individuals, thus, might experience "stress" based on the tensions among their roles. Yet I hope that it will become clear that in many situations only different rhetoric enabled intercultural communication or, as already stressed in the beginning, without attaining perfection, the members/actors of this multicultural environment had a "very high level of systematicity to their schemes of identity."[9]

Two Life Stories

Although belonging to the majority of the "less able," both of my informants would qualify as "typical" representatives of the late nineteenth- and early twentieth-century Habsburg mental habit. Both of them could speak and write in at least two languages, which is also why they both seemed to be well integrated in their social and/or professional environment(s). More importantly, according to the notes in his diary, the noncommissioned officer Jozsef Doncsecz could, despite his rural roots and the fact that he came from a backward region, turn his multilingualism to enormous advantage. In particular, this holds true for his knowledge of one Slavic language, Slovene, and its Prekmurian dialect. While serving in a garrison in the southeastern corner of newly colonized provinces (between 1899 and 1902), Doncsecz put it to good use in his everyday communication but could also learn with relative ease its kin languages, notably the Herzegovinian Serbian and/or Croatian dialect, and thus better understood the region's mixture of languages, religions, and cultures.

This is also recorded in several segments of his diary containing transcripts of Serbian songs with which he tried to illustrate certain situations or experiences. In a similar vein, as he most frequently used Hungarian to depict his sexual fantasies and almost exclusively employed German when referring to official matters, Doncsecz resorted to the local mixture of Croatian, Serbian, and Bosnian in his attempts to reproduce tavern tunes. Slovene, on the other hand, mainly served him to curry favor with a girl from his native Prekmurje. In this archaic, nowadays barely intelligible, dialect from the very edge of the Slovene- and

Croatian-speaking area, his beloved Etelka never appears as an object of desire. In Slovene, she is a kind friend and confidante who usually disappears from the story the very moment the author surrenders to sexual fantasies. The role of a sexual object is, as a rule, assumed by local prostitutes, whose services are catalogued in Slovene only when the author refers to their prices (e.g., sex in the bushes, one forint; hand in blouse, thirty kreuzer; hand in panties, sixty kreuzers, etc.). Apart from that, almost all other sexual fantasies are depicted in Hungarian. However, it is often the case that a text (usually written in the form of a letter or a poem) begins in German ("Ein Liebes Brief," "Jungfrau Lied," or a poem titled "O bleib bei mir"), continues in Hungarian or Slovene and its Prekmurian dialect, and, when the author starts to indulge in sexual fantasies, as a rule ends in Hungarian.

It appears that the Hungarian literary and popular tradition of the time allowed more possibilities for very emotional,[10] traumatic, or pornographic depictions of male sexual fantasies. Finally, however, it is quite clear that the author skillfully exploited the advantages of the language mixture in which he deemed German more appropriate in reference to official matters, which he made especially clear under titles and addresses such as "Abschied Lied," "Soldaten Lied," "Reservisten Lied," "Ein Anderer" or "Liebes Fräulein," "Ablösungsraport," or indications of posts and positions ("Francesi Jozef corpl.," "Commandant" of "k.u.k. Festungsartilerie," in "Companie No. 313") and dates (e.g., duration of military service; names of days and months). Slovene, on the other hand, was intended for semiofficial or familiar and, most notably, intimate but not too emotional communication with friends, family members, and a girl of his heart,[11] while Hungarian appeared to upgrade Slovene or, as already mentioned, served to describe sexual fantasies. For instance, the letter to his fiancée's parents, where Doncsecz discloses his feelings for their daughter, is followed by a rather detailed description of sexual intercourse between a Gypsy and a nun.

This, however, does not mean that the author devised any kind of hierarchy of languages in which he tried to express himself. However, by analyzing such sources, the very concept of "mother tongue" becomes questionable, especially when dealing with the so-called private use of different languages. To put it differently, the more we delve into this multicultural universe, the more we understand that it is impossible to claim it is the consequence of the inadequacy of a particular language. On the contrary, the fluidity of switching between languages has to be understood as a natural state of intercultural communication.

Therefore, I would agree with Bernard Lory, who, after doing his research on eighteenth- and nineteenth-century Bitola, concluded that people of this multicultural Macedonian city had just one, albeit multilingual and highly eclectic, culture.[12] Judging from the types of records, our soldier also uses Slovene as a means of self-identification (self-presentation) by raising "essential" questions, such as how many years would he like to live, what is his greatest desire, does he like to dance and drink wine, what is his favorite color, etc. He, furthermore, demonstrates his "national determination/awareness" through a collection of poems titled "Slovenske pesmi" (Slovene poems), where he talks about all sorts of things. Interestingly, he never refers to Slovene as Wendisch—a term with which the Hungarian administration attempted to identify the Prekmurian dialect as a special Slavic language having as much in common with Slovene as Croatian. The question arises as to what extent Doncsecz was able to identify with the national idea and also whether he referred to his home region by its contemporary name. The Prekmurians of that time more often referred to the region by the name of Slovenska krajina, whereas the name Prekmurje was in use in other Slovene regions.

Very little was actually known then about the lands in these parts of Central Europe, and it was not until 1918 that the Slovenes were first mentioned in *National Geographic*. The author of the article "The Races of Europe" describes them as a kind, exotic, interesting, and fairly cosmopolitan people who, judging by their "habits and purpose . . . are in sharp contrast to the Croats and Slavonians, their near kin." In the opinion of Edwin A. Grosvenor, they were "intermarrying with Germans, Hungarians, and Italians," "seemed very recently little affected by racial concerns," and were generally not "inclined to racist complaints." Perhaps in consequence, the Austrians "treated them with a moderation not shown to other subject Slavs."[13]

Knowing this, it is also easier to read Doncsecz's diary as an indicator of the contemporary internal Orientalization or the contemporary attitude toward particular "others" in this region who were, in this case, represented mainly as the Orthodox Christians and Muslims. His memoirs and diary notes demonstrate more than clearly the attitude toward the peripheral cultures that were, albeit part of the monarchy, defined as different. This only confirms the conclusion reiterated on several occasions in Slovene historiography that, at the turn of the century, Slovenes—despite voicing considerable enthusiasm for the Yugoslav idea—knew very little about Croats and Serbs. While they pursued slightly more direct contacts with the neighboring Croats, they knew Serbs only from what they heard or read in newspapers.[14]

As holds true for all other cases (from caricatures and political cartoons to failing language reforms), private reflections of everyday life in the monarchy reveal a subtle and finely nuanced palette of differentiation between various nations and cultures. Therefore, whenever we talk about transcultural connections, we should also thematize different practices of intercultural exclusion, as these counterprocesses both form a part of a dynamic cohabitation of different cultures. To put it more concretely, even though relations with Germans and Hungarians increasingly sharpened with the emerging idea of the trialistic reorganization of the monarchy, we cannot overlook the fact that up until its fall, the majority of the Slovene population lived in an environment influenced by Slovene, German, Italian, and Hungarian cultures. So, people such as Doncsecz actually belonged in bilingual, sometimes even trilingual, environments. According to this, one could answer Ernst Bruckmüller's question, "Was There a 'Habsburg Society'?" positively, since there clearly was a sort of integrated society under the Habsburg Monarchy, not in a sense of one, unified society of the Habsburg Monarchy, but in a sense of a Habsburg or at least of an Austrian society.[15] This was because—as Bruckmüller would put it—a sort of residual loyalty to or acceptance of the Habsburg Monarchy existed there until 1914. Whether or not this basic loyalty included Hungary is subject to doubt, given the large-scale popular expressions against Hungarians.[16] It remains clear, however, that despite the monarchy's many languages there certainly were Austro-Hungarian people whose numerous societies were not only locally bounded but also connected supraregionally, at least on the societal level of officers and higher bureaucrats, and alongside the national societies of the educated middle class and petty bourgeoisie.

The fact that active bi- or trilingualism was not only in the competence of soldiers, scholars, and public servants in general is proven by my great-great-aunt Marija Hujs, the author of a multilingual cookbook manuscript. She worked her entire life for different families in Murska Sobota, the provincial capital of Prekmurje, and in some smaller towns across the Hungarian part of the monarchy. Commuting from the suburbs to the city center or from the regional center to her hometown, she was a typical mediator in her time between the urban and rural/suburban, between socially competent and noncompetent, and between various languages. Her cookbook, containing 265 recipes, not only represents a mélange of various languages but also serves as a miniature language handbook. Consulting her cooking instructions on a daily basis, a regular user could not only discover the secrets of western Pannonian (or even Habsburg) cuisine but also learn all three measuring systems and the names of various cooking tricks.

This was the usual way of communicating cooking instructions. At the time, the Slovenes still had no culinary vocabulary of their own and, even in the central Slovene regions like Carniola, Carinthia, and lower Styria, names for some more exotic ingredients were derived/borrowed from vernacular German. The first cookbook was translated by a Franciscan priest, poet, and linguist, Valentin Vodnik (1758–1819), in the previous century (1799); the first genuine local cooking manual dates to 1905. Hence, it is not surprising that housewives relied on family cookbooks, which had just started to gain popularity in the period concerned. The variegated content of such a book, a "life manual," offering a wide range of advice to a young housewife, should not be too surprising. One would find not only food recipes but also instructions on how to organize the household, and quite often advice on how to take care of the "mental prosperity" and "physical wellness/welfare" of the entire family.[17]

Therefore, it is not surprising that the author of the manuscript, which has served at least three generations of housewives in my father's family, also teaches each new generation that an essential part of cooking is to keep the kitchen properly. Nevertheless, this is not just any part of the house. It is the separate universe full of elements of which we can create the world, "a world the size of a dinner plate."[18] And there is probably no need to point out that her advice addresses exclusively female readers, which is why I was, after my aunt gave me the cookbook, most likely the first male reader ever. This in no way means that men were not affected or influenced by this particular world. Quite the opposite; not only were they served a great variety of foods and desserts, but they also clearly profited from the general knowledge of their wives and cooks. They were provided with health instructions and many other practical matters; in cases the cookbook was also a sort of address book in which they were informed of crucial facts about their broader family. Finally, the economic situation of the families whose female parent was a renowned cook or author of a well-accepted cookbook was slightly, if not much, better than that in other peasant or suburban families. Women who could sell their cooking were also more independent, more knowledgeable, and more self-conscious.

According to the data I could gather from her and other relatives, my great-great-aunt Marija started to write her cookbook in her twenties, probably at the same time that Doncsecz finished his diary. Living in a similar "life world," as Alfred Schütz and Thomas Luckman would term it,[19] as Jozsef's imaginary fiancée, she would likely be very similar to Etelka. Just as Etelka, she lived in the world of three or four languages and assumed the then-customary role of a housewife. However, since I do not know much more of Etelka than her name, any further comparison is rendered impossible. What is possible to conclude is that the girl of Doncsecz's heart would surely not have any problem reading Marija's recipes. Etelka would most likely switch from one language to another with the same ease as Marija and—more than we could ever be able to—understand perfectly well why one recipe had a German title, continued with Hungarian names of measuring units, and concluded with Slovene instructions for preparation. Moreover, Etelka would most probably read the bi- or trilingual recipes with the same ease as Marija had written them, accordingly prepare *Judenteig, Butermasse,* or *Gernteig,* bake an *Omlet* or *Rotssild,* and in the end serve a *Kakao snite.* She would also consider it quite natural that the recipes included a long series of instructions for preserving fruit and vegetables, or making black currant wine and various jams. Among the recipes she would also surely find one for making sugar decorations for Christmas trees. Most likely she would not be bothered by Marija's authoritative instructions with regard to hygiene, especially in reference to annoying flies, and her respect for the author of the cookbook would even grow if she knew that Marija had collected the bulk of her cooking knowledge in the triangle of Vienna, Budapest, and Zagreb. Therefore, she also might not be bothered by the rigidity of instructions and would probably know that writing with an archaic pen can cause mistakes in spelling. The recipes, in a way, are similar to daily orders in the military: short and concrete and, in many cases, written in one single sentence.

Take, for example, my favorite recipe for *Kitolo fänk* (squeezed doughnut), for which one has to have "½ liter of milk[,] half a liter of flour together with 4 eggs and beaten egg whites." The mixture is then put into a special machine that forms finger-long pieces that have to be baked until "yellow" and finally decorated "with powdered sugar and grated chocolate." Or, consider a little longer "command/order/instruction" for the dessert called *Preznic:*

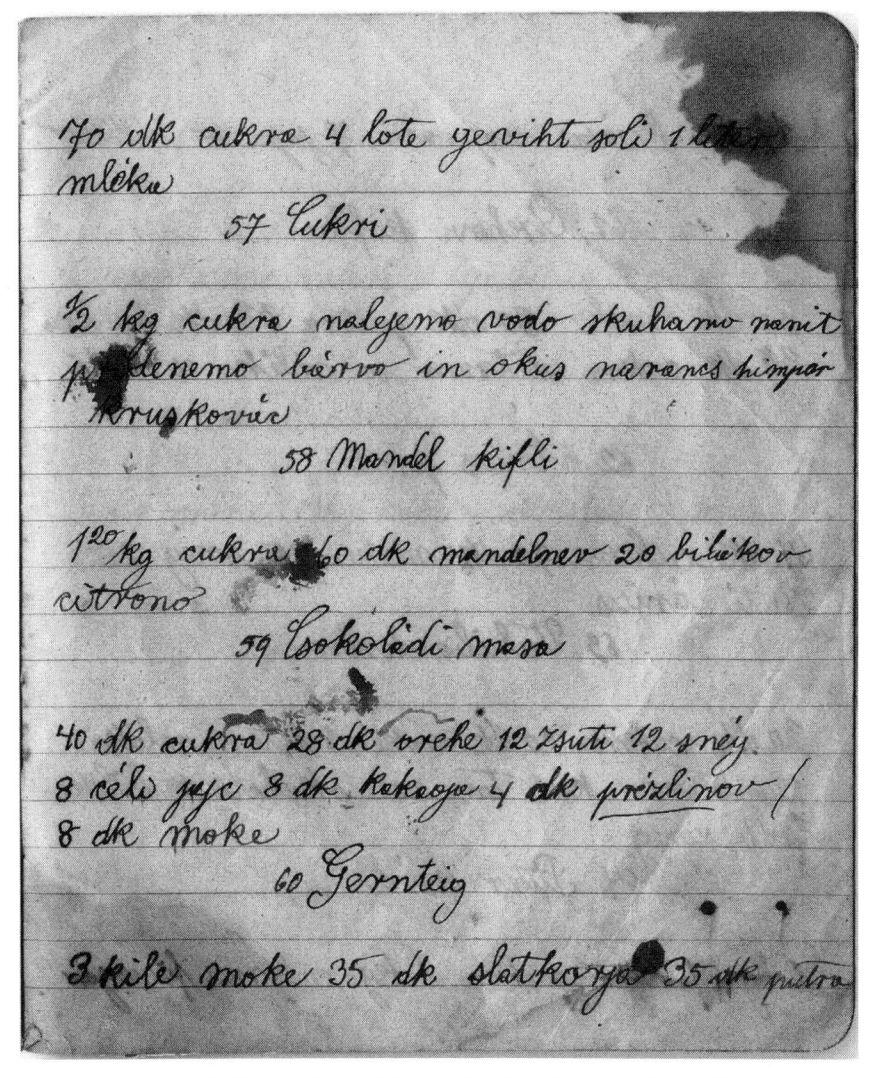

Figure 7.1. Recipe for *Preznic* from a Manuscript Cookbook by Marija Hujs, in the possession of Oto Luthar

Take ¾ kg flour and the same amount of butter and knead dough ready for baking, the stuffing contains ½ kg grained almonds and ½ nuts ½ kg raisins ½ kg dried grapes without seeds . . . two peeled oranges and lemons ⅛ kg sugar[,] everything mixed with juice of three oranges and three lemons ¼ liter of white wine[,] the stretched dough paste has to be greased with the nose thick filling and pieces of butter[,] from the whole quantity you can bake 4 *Preznic*s.

From Marija's fluid usages of languages and Jozsef's multilingual daydreaming we can imagine that, besides being a world of continuous metamorphosis, their lifeworld was also a life of belonging, roots, diversification, and, finally, a world of creating imagined communities. Being a part of a typical Central European latecomer society, however, they might as well still be part of a premodern cultural landscape of linguistic mobility and continuous metamorphosis instead of the modernist imaginary of fixed, differentiating roots intertwined in an identity that is striving for unitary belonging.

Notes

1. Bonnie Marranca, ed., *A Slice of Life* (New York, 2003), 24.
2. Sybil Gräfin Schönfeldt, *"Feine Leute kommen spät . . ." oder Bei Thomas Mann zu Tisch: Tafelfreuden im Lübecker Buddenbrookhaus* (Zurich, 2004), 10.
3. Avery F. Gordon and Christopher Newfield, "Introduction," in *Mapping Multiculturalism*, ed. Avery F. Gordon and Christopher Newfield (Minneapolis, 1996), 3.
4. See Rogers Brubaker, *Nationalism Reframed: Nationhood and the National Question in the New Europe* (Cambridge, 1996), 4.
5. On the rewriting of history, see Oto Luthar, "Possessing the Past: The Problem of Historical Representation in the Process of Reinventing Democracy in Eastern Europe—the Case of Slovenia," *Filozofski vestnik—Acta Philosophica* 18, no. 2 (1997): 233–56.
6. See the minutes of the Council of Commune of Moravske Toplice, which includes Bogojina, from 26–27 May 1996, as well as articles in *Delo,* Slovenia's most influential daily, in May 1996.
7. Lucien Febvre, "History and Psychology," in *A New Kind of History,* ed. Peter Burke (New York, 1973), 9–10.
8. Rogers Brubaker, *Ethnicity without Groups* (Cambridge, MA, 2004), 4.
9. Craig Calhoun, ed., *Social Theory and the Politics of Identity* (Oxford, 1995), 11.
10. In his diary a lot of quite emotional blueprints of letters to his parents and fiancée can be found that are usually written in Hungarian. Therefore, the impression remains that Slovene turns into Hungarian, even when he wanted to address his beloved with "My dear angel . . . tulip or may blossom, swan or dove." The same happens when he is trying to explain that his heart is going to explode or when he is blueprinting the letter to his fiancée's parents asking them for the hand of their daughter. Similarly, the author takes recourse to Hungarian whenever he tries to express fear and horror from cannons and shells that killed "many Hungarian lads."
11. In an imaginary conversation with his girl, Doncsecz frequently resorts to his newly acquired "Serbo-Croatian": "Tvoje suze na mom obrazu bitče duši mojoj lijek" (Your tears on my face will remedy my soul) or "Kucaj srce dok ne pukneš" (Beat, oh heart, until you break). This

provides yet more proof of his competence (and advantage) as a speaker of one of the Slavic languages.

12. Bernard Lory, "Religiöse und ethnische Minderheiten und Mehrheiten im Westlichen Balkan aus historischer Perspektive," presented at the 45th Internationale Hochschulwoche Inklusion und Exklusion auf dem Westbalkan, Akademie für politische Bildung, Tutzing, 10 October 2006.

13. Edwin A. Grosvenor, "The Races of Europe," *The National Geographic Magazine* 44, no. 6 (December 1918): 489.

14. See also Peter Vodopivec, *Od Pohlinove slovnice do samostojne slovenske države: Slovenska zgodovina od konca 18. stoletja do konca 20. stoletja* (Ljubljana, 2006), 153. According to the lecture given by one of the most important Slovene writers, Ivan Cankar, Slovenes started to become more acquainted with their "brothers" only at the beginning of the twentieth century. It was not until the time when Doncsecz served in Herzegovina that the idea emerged of kin ties between Slovenes, Croats, and Serbs, who were deemed "brothers in blood and cousins in language, while in culture as the fruit of a multi-centennial separate education" they appeared as "yet strangers to each other, as much as our farmer from Upper Carniola is a stranger to a Tyrolean or as much as a vinedresser from Gorica is a stranger to a Friulian." Taken from Ivan Cankar's lecture, "Slovenci in Jugoslovani" [The Slovenes and the Yugoslavs], 12 April 1913, reprinted in Cankar, *Izbrana dela*, vol. 10: *Kriticčni in polemični spisi. Krpanova kobila. Bela krizantema* (Ljubljana 1959), 391-402.

15. Ernst Bruckmüller, "Was There a 'Habsburg Society' in Austria-Hungary?," Twentieth Annual Robert A. Kann Memorial Lecture, *Austrian History Yearbook* 37 (2006): 1–16.

16. Judging from the echoes in Slovene literature of the time, the Hungarians were perceived by the Slovenes as "serious enemies," that is, as an object of a "negativistic haste." In the opinion of Slovene historian Igor Grdina, the Slovene elites regarded the "secessionist Hungarians" as the greatest threat to the monarchy. Therefore, it comes as no surprise that the most influential (yet not the best) Slovene poet, Jovan Vesel Koseski (1798–1884), called them the "poisonous tooth" that has for a thousand years threatened the Slavic heart. Surprisingly enough, the Hungarians were seen as the enemies also by poet Anton Aškerc (1856–1912) and writer Josip Stritar (1836–1923), who were both convinced that "the Hungarian . . . was never our friend." See Igor Grdina, *Med dolžnostjo spomina in razkošjem pozabe* (Ljubljana, 2006), 75–76.

17. Katharina Prato, *Nauk o gospodinjstvu, Založba umetniška propaganda,* 2nd ed. (Ljubljana, 1935), 9.

18. Schönfeldt,*"Feine Leute kommen spät,"* 142.

19. Alfred Schütz and Thomas Luckman, *Structures of the Life World,* vol. 1 (Evanston, IL, 1973).

Chapter 8

ON "NEIGHBORS" AND "STRANGERS"
The Literary Motif of "Central Europe" As *Lieu de Mémoire*

Andrei Corbea-Hoisie

In their derivation of the word *Nachbar* (neighbor), German etymological dictionaries refer to a combination of two words, namely, *nahe* (near) and *Bauer* (peasant). These are the semantic roots of a word in use by the Middle Ages: in the rustic community, *Nachbarn* were those persons whose properties were directly adjoining, or, in a wider sense, inhabitants of a space forming a unit that was determined by the category of nearness or adjacency. Thus, they were *Hiesige*[1] (locals), and in this rural world, primordially closed, shared an identity that was shaped by the collective symbolic frame of "big traditions."[2] Although this quality of being local was and remains a social and historical construct, it was frequently cloaked as an ostensibly "natural" condition, as an orderly configuration of "boundaries and stereotypes,"[3] given once and for all, and appeared to be fairly stable over the course of the centuries, forming a persistent opposition to the political-cultural pressure of various centers with universal claims (in the ecclesiastic and secular spheres).[4] In anthropology and sociology, models of the development or emergence in modernity of more extensive societal, political, and cultural identities emphasize the development of the mutual understanding of individuals within such primary units of social life, a mutual understanding that happens through a process of elemental exchange. Karl Deutsch, for instance, who referred to communication as an essential social connecting link, talks about behavior patterns of societal needs and objectives that are handed down and repeatedly learned, and that serve to keep individuals together and to distinguish them from others.[5]

In the course of this enormous, centuries-long, and pervasive change in terms of people, goods, and ideas—a change that was ignited and sustained by a continuous economically and politically determined competition, which, for example, Norbert Elias synthesized in the term *Zivilizationsprozesses* (civilizing process)—the boundaries and seclusion of such communities was continuously challenged, because the constitutive and formative *Kommen und Gehen*[6] (coming and going) rendered inevitable the increasingly complex interdependencies, that is, "mutual dependence between people."[7] The world of the "locals" was thus forced to take cognizance of this otherness, in the first place, through the presence of what Karl Deutsch calls "newcomers." Even if they were striving for quick *Assimilierung* (assimilation), these newcomers could not hope to be perceived as anything other than outsiders[8] in terms of the patterns mentioned earlier. George Simmel, in his famous "The Stranger," emphatically differentiates the wanderer who "comes today and goes tomorrow" from the one who "comes today and stays tomorrow." The latter causes discontent among the locals, because he, a stranger, intends to stay. Sure enough, they suspect "that he has not quite overcome the freedom of coming and going,"[9] which consequently results in his difference being perceived as a disaster and a threat to the environment. His gradual emergence as a neighbor does not change his status as an outsider yet; that is to say, he imports qualities into the circle of locals to which he does not belong from the beginning, or as Simmel says, qualities "which do not and cannot stem from the group itself." In other words, there are some among the neighbors, again quoting Simmel, who say "they are not like 'us!' . . . They are local but do not follow the stereotypes, which the locals themselves develop and maintain."[10]

Through its mobility, modernity changed the formerly exceptional circumstance into a standard: neighborhoods changed at an accelerated rate, the "civilizing process" led to "Western people . . . bring[ing] about in large areas of the world a change in human relationships and functions in line with their own standards."[11] Agents of the bourgeois habitus, with its liability to individualistic anonymity, permeated those primordial-peripheral communities and thus contributed to the creation of equal distances between individuals, such that either there were "no longer any strangers or all are strangers."[12] On the one hand, this alleged rationalization of society and its leveling made Norbert Elias feel optimistic, stating that, through the formation of the monopoly of force of the modern state and due to a progressive differentiation of social functions, there emerged "pacified social spaces . . . which are normally free from acts of violence."[13] On the other hand, this rationalization was reviewed critically, at least by Horkheimer and Adorno, who formulated an extreme judgment of the barbaric downside of enlightened modernity.[14] They criticized the theory of social development when it came to applying it concretely to those who fit poorly into the concept of identity formation that the equalization causes. The more the criteria appeared relative for an individual or collective exclusion of "neighbors" on the basis of an alleged "strangeness," the more the moral self-legitimation of the enlightening and civilizing perspective was questioned. Here it turned out that the category of the *Ethnischen* (ethnic), too often invoked, was actually a "political-bureaucratic construct" and not a "natural variable."[15] It is unclear how the formation of *Fremdstereotypen* (stereotypes of strangers), which at certain occasions change into *Feindbilder* (iconic images of enemies), determine those mechanisms that, within modern "civilization," can steer the "social construction of strangeness" toward either occasional "irritation" in the face of strangers or even toward repeated outbursts of violence and a revival of barbarism.

"The Cunning of Reason"

In the spirit of the well-known formula of Hegel,[16] postcolonial studies express criticism of Elias's dichotomy between the controlled space of civilization and barbarism, where violence is "diffuse, scattered, lawless, and therefore unpredictable and paralyzing."[17] However, this criticism points out that, for modern elites, "the barbarians" always served "as an instrument of the stratification and reproduction of cultural hegemony"; these elites reserved the right to determine "who the Barbarian [or the stranger] is."[18] Furthermore, for these elites, nonconformity to established categories was seen as a provocation against the "natural character" of their authority.[19] However, as Shmuel Noah Eisenstadt concluded in his reflection on the peculiarities of European civilization, "a victory of the periphery over the center, conceivable, even possible . . . —a victory in the sense that the periphery emancipates itself from the center or even overlays the center."[20] This is especially because modern centers, in their very construction, allow themselves to be infected by the autarchic spirit of peripheral-primordial communities through their acceptance of potential protest of a socialist or nationalist character: those inner forces were allowed to rebel "against the institutional realities of modern civilization in their own symbolism." As a consequence they forced "total exclusion of parts of the population, who used to form a common framework with those who now carry out the exclusion, but who now are defined completely differently and are excluded from any category of humanity."[21] One of the causes of this development was the fact that the self-critical modernity, which arose in universalist centers, discovered the allegedly *unentfremdeten Wilden* (unalienated savage) and projected onto him a paradisiacal natural *Erlösungsversprechen* (promise of salvation). This form of *Inklusion des Wilden* (inclusion of the savage), which embodied *romantische Transzendenz* (romantic transcendence) as a sign of modern culture, went so far that "no longer the center, but the periphery . . . promised identity and authenticity"; "seeming unreasonableness and insanity appear as deeper truth." As a consequence, modern order breaks down through a "falling back into making personal and arbitrary decisions over life and death."[22]

After the annexation of the northern Moldavian lands by Austria in 1775, and the gradual settlement of German and Jewish families in Romanian and Slavic villages and market towns of this province, a historically determined neighborhood emerged. This can be described in terms used by Elias, or Eisenstadt, or those who interpret Habsburg expansion from the perspective of "postcolonial studies":[23] the civilizing process brought together a socially and nationally colonizing upper class, controlled by a center constructed as being universal, and a lower class to be colonized, which was still tied to the primordial values of the periphery. This simultaneously implies a collision and a process of permeation and mixing, leading to a widespread network of interdependencies. The thesis whereby the orient as object of Western research is a discursive construction, dependent on miscellaneous colonial-utilitarian concepts,[24] corresponds to the context in which the old conception of Austria's cultural mission in the European (half-Asian) East[25] projected itself onto, as it were, an almost binary depiction of forces acting in the social field of the province: the Western side always takes the initiative of progress/enlightenment, accompanied by tolerance, whereas the recipients passively, yet often with a certain resistance, accept efforts to civilize them.

Urban Bukovina, whose provincial capital, Czernowitz, had no traditional base of an urban-bourgeois habitus of medieval origin, specifically deviated from other Cisleithanian examples in that its linguistic-cultural heterogeneity became one of the main criteria for the cohesion of those social groups living outside the urban milieu. In a contemporary analysis of social relations in nineteenth-century Bukovina, the author emphasizes one fact with remarkable sobriety: in the case of Czernowitz, there could be no talk of "organic exchange of population with the controlled region"; "rather than in the rural area itself and its villages, the new settlement area of the cities was located elsewhere, namely outside the rural area and in the cities again," with the consequence that this "does not permit assimilation to occur."[26] The well-known definition of the "stranger" by Simmel, which involves the seed of a bourgeois-capitalistic mobility by the fact that he "comes today and stays tomorrow,"[27] can easily be transferred to a collective urban identity of Czernowitz as a site of concentrated individual foreignness.

Many of the new and strange neighbors very quickly became the preferred bogeymen of nationalist protest. Of those new neighbors, the Jews, who were mostly merchants and not allowed to own land, personified "the specific character of the mobility of strangers," according to Simmel. "For, the fundamentally mobile person comes in contact, at one time or another, with every individual, but is not organically connected, through established ties of kinship, locality, and occupation, with any single one."[28] An example of these nationalist protests is the harangues of the Romanian national poet Mihai Eminescu, who bewailed conditions in Bukovina in the 1870s, where "the Galician Jews and the Bavarian Swabians became the masters over this land": "What did the Jews do to Bukovina? A swamp of thoroughly corrupt elements, a gathering place of those who could not live anywhere else in the Babylonian realm. . . . And that is called in Viennese journalistic-jargon, bringing civilization to the Orient."[29] The province's annexation with Romania after Austria-Hungary lost World War I was followed by a forceful "Romania-ization" policy in all public domains, which appeared as the vengeance of "autochthonic" rusticity on the abhorrent *Entfremdung* (estrangement, alienation) of urban enclaves. Almost twelve years after 1918, Romanian nationalism was on the verge of merging with the extreme xenophobia of fascist movements.

At the same time, the German-speaking Jewish writer Alfred Margul-Sperber (who later discovered Paul Celan) believed that he could oppose the symbolic figure of his wet nurse, "Bäurin Frosina," to this allegedly fatal polarity in order to affirm his own indigenousness as organic and individually legitimate: "It is a village destiny, with which my life begins / She was not allowed to keep her child and nursed the Jewish child / And her lot did not permit her to give her own child / The overwhelming love the farm maid gave me." Sperber's pathetic-sounding appeal to "Bäurin Frosina" as a witness ("She was nursing me with her longing for the village and the well and the lea / Now not only the blood of my ancestors courses through my veins / but also the dark brooding of the farmers, their rumbling and heavy tread / I carry in my blood from my wet nurse"),[30] which is intended to convince the intransigent neighborhood of the relativity of the strangeness constructed along ethnic/racial lines, along with a growing insecurity, finally reveals a sense of resignation toward the imminence of a catastrophe whose barbaric dimension is unpredictable.

What Does Rezzori's Kassandra Foretell?

The character of the autochthonic wet nurse—owing to whom the child belonging to a "colonist" family developed a special relationship to the language and customs of his/her environment—is no rarity in the German-speaking literature of Central Europe: Karl Emil Franzos remembered the Ruthenian Marinia ("She taught me how to walk, and how to talk, naturally Ruthenian, and a little Polish—she is my one and only").[31] Elias Canetti also remembered his Romanian wet nurse: "I always heard her praises, and even though I can't remember her, the word 'Rumanian' has always had a warm sound for me because of her."[32] Similarly, Norman Manea conjured up in his autobiographical novel the Romanian peasant woman Maria, who treated him in his childhood as if he were her own son.[33] On the other hand, the symbolic image of milk in its oxymoronic form of "black milk," alluding to earth, became apparent in the Bukovinian Paul Celan's famous *Todesfuge* and, prior to this, in Rose Ausländer's writing.[34] Therefore, it is reasonable to ask if it can be a coincidence that, in a certain period of time, several authors, who come from the same Eastern European cultural area, are concerned with this peculiar motif of a strange wet nurse and educator. It is apparent that the writers assume that the problematic encounter of the local and the stranger can best be understood in this specific geographic-historic space. Adorno repeatedly claimed that the "image character" of discourses of art, in contrast to scientific discourses, offers a more immediate approach to a "totality," "which appears more truly in the individual than in the syntheses of singularities."[35] Therefore, belles lettres as *lieu de mémoire* are able to "summon into appearance" "the essence that conceals itself in the factual," that is, in contrast to the "objective" sciences, which strive to tell the "truth" about the past, "otherwise obstructs."[36] In concert with the historical analyses and efforts to construct sociological models of the complex phenomenon of European environments barbarically destroyed, and the suffering inflicted on millions of people in the course of the last century, it is not advisable to regard the narrated fiction of this enormous overthrow of lives and environments as a mere reflection, a more or less successful linguistically staged reproduction of human existence, but rather as an expression "remote from psychology," "of which the sensorium was perhaps once conscious in the world and which now subsists only in artworks."[37] Two of such immaterial *lieux de mémoire* will be reconstructed in the following.

Kassandra was the name of the "foster mother" to whom Gregor von Rezzori refers in one of five "Portraits for an Autobiography," which he published as *The Snows of Yesteryear* in 1989.[38] After the young peasant woman—just like Sperber's Frosina—had given birth to an illegitimate child in a monastery, she was brought into the family of an Austrian civil servant employed in Czernowitz, where she played a symbolic dual role: she was the living indicator of a simultaneously near and distant environment of locals, to whom the von Rezzoris appeared as representatives of strange imperial rulers, although they had family locally. At the same time, within the familial sphere, which clung to its artificial segregation, she was expected to be the incarnation of a strangeness against which the center had to assert its authority everywhere in its peripheries. She, who used to be at home in the Carpathians, now walked around wearing a "sterilized" costume in the spacious house of the von Rezzoris in an exclusive residential area of Czernowitz, in order to reproduce, merely through her presence, the schizophrenic situation of this fictional and alienated localness of a strange caste that came and stayed, even without making the effort of learning the *Landessprache* (local idiom).[39] Not only does she appear as a numerical minority, but also, through her alleged cultural and even aesthetic inferiority (she is deemed "inhumanely ugly and primitive"), she confirms the delusion of the pseudofeudalistic "colonial gentry," including von Rezzori, whose trauma of 1918 was nourished by "the presumptuous feeling of belonging to another, superior civilization." No cliché referring to Kassandra is too crude for the civilized: she is "a beast" and "a barely tamed savage"; she belongs to an "old line of slaves" of "primitive people"; her "large simian face" is "grotesque and impish"; she is "foolishly dressed"; she is "like some exotic specimen from the sideshow of a traveling circus," etc. Therefore, she is "the distorted funhouse-mirror image of each of us" as well. This funhouse-mirror image also seems to be symptomatic in the peasant woman's reaction to the strangeness imposed upon her: she has alienated the estranged constellation of relationships in the house of the "masters" because she has "imitated, paraphrased, parodied, and derided" their habitus, "exploding any impending drama into absurd humor, shattering it in laughs."[40]

This effect, which leads to a disenchantment or disempowering of those fantasies solidified in the course of a civilizing mission, was reinforced still further by Kassandra's way of adjusting to the "language spoken by her masters," which remained the language of the "educated classes" even in the post-Austrian time: the "absurd lingua franca" that originated through her adjustments, of which "each second or third word was either Ruthenian, Romanian, Polish, Russian, Armenian, or Yiddish,"[41] challenged the sovereign implicitness of the language of culture, even if this challenge occurred unintentionally and unconsciously. The continuous skepticism, however, that the illiterate woman maintained toward books—heightened because she thought she saw in reading a process similar to black magic—derived from her mythic-primordial disposition against the abstract in general, which, in her view, obstructs one's natural view of things through illusion and fiction originating from the abstract, over which her masters also agonized. In this sense, *nomen est omen*: Kassandra, who wanted to convey the world of periphery to her strange neighbors from a distant and aspiring metropolis, remains unheard and misunderstood. The child, who discovers the world through her and "had suckled the milk of that soil, with all its light and dark powers, from which she . . . had sprung,"[42] will one day not be able to resist the temptation of culture. The historical catastrophe to be unleashed soon, which will also overtake the von Rezzoris, seems to be interconnected with a symbolic impossibility to overcome barriers of mutual understanding, which Kassandra had hoped to surmount through her love for the strange boy. During the relocation that will bring the mother to Germany as a refugee in 1940, she allows some time to delete photographic traces of the wet nurse, who in a way dared to challenge the motherliness of the biological mother. Having arrived in the West, where they themselves (as fugitives from the East) are treated disparagingly, the von Rezzoris will have to learn how relatively conferrable strangeness is—something they could have become aware of already in the case of Kassandra back in Bukovina.

A Symbolic Victory of a "Periphery"

The narrative weave of Aharon Appelfeld's novel *Katerina*,[43] which was published in Hebrew in the same year as *Blumen im Schnee,* is more complicated than in the case of von Rezzori, where the openly declared intention to memorialize makes it easy to identify the voice of the author as the voice of the narrator. In this case, the narrator, who originates from Bukovina and was, as a child, a victim of the persecution of Jews during World War II, narrates a story in which, concerning himself, a twofold alterity speaks: one is the alterity of the Christian, and one is the alterity of the woman. In addition to the brilliance of the author's psychological analysis, a complicated game becomes evident. Through the alienated reflections and mediations of contents in the various instances and identities that are present, the game provides an unconventional stimulus for thought, the figure of mediator between the worlds of neighbors and strangers not only being in the center of the plot, but also narrating it. The peasant woman Katerina, born in an isolated Bukowinian village, is a child of this primordial-patriarchal periphery, who is still living in intimate understanding with nature, being a part of it. For the human soul who comes to know familiar space as a dimension of eternity, existence means a cyclic repetition of birth, mating, and death in whose rituals the initial survival instinct is reproduced. It is not a coincidence that people in this apparently paradisiacal place, where the air smells of grass and water, command a secret language that connects them with animals. The generally prevailing silence, which occasionally is interrupted by howling, hides a latent seething, where stormy passion mingles with raw wiles and relentless ferocity, and where faith, whose universalist message still remains incomprehensible, had to adjust to these natural morals. The rhythm of this existence outside of history gets interrupted by an encounter one day, which for the community of locals will represent the immediate discovery of the stranger: on a footpath in the forest, Jews clad in black suddenly appear with suitcases full of colorful goods through which wafts a breeze of a different world. Those Jews come and stay. From now on they are going to constitute a part of the community: "Once an economy is somehow closed," according to Simmel, "the trader, too, can find his existence. For in trade, which alone makes possible unlimited combinations, intelligence always finds expansions and new territories, an achievement which is very difficult to attain for the original producer with his lesser mobility."[44] The village eyes the Jews curiously but also with a certain repulsion. In their absolute difference with regard to language and customs, their physical appearance, their fear of death (which constitutes their sense for history), they are regarded as messengers from a secular order from far away, which, with its dangerous alluring colorfulness, is a threat to the primordial community. "The farmers esteem them, fear them, and, when their envy of them becomes too great, kill them."[45]

At first Katerina becomes a victim of this unexpectedly encroaching civilization: her temptations pull her into sin and drive her among the losers, to the margins of the social structure. In her misery, despite quite a bit of reluctance, she accepts the offer of a Jewish woman to work in her house. Something fateful happens in this very moment: Katerina—perhaps like von Rezzori's

Kassandra—a stranger to the Jews, starts to acquire strangeness, *nolens volens,* as felt by the Jews themselves. This is not a sudden process, because she approaches the Jews with all the usual prejudices of her people, who imagined in the difference of the unloved neighbors the form of an ostensibly magical and devilish symbol. A Jewess rescued Katerina from her life on the street and even trusted her after Katerina gave birth to an illegitimate child. In retrospect, this Jewess appeared as an angel to Katerina, who not only saved her from physical decay but also gave her surprising access to a world where the miracle of human life was appreciated—especially because of the constant danger that the strangers had to fear from their neighbors. Kassandra experienced the stranger as a pathological fantasy of the masters. In contrast, Katerina's most important experience in Jewish households, in which she changes from being an outsider to a member of civilization, is most concisely recorded in Elias's elocution: "The conversion of 'alien' social constraints into self-restraints, into a more or less habitual and automatic individual self-regulation of drives and affects."[46] Katerina identified the Jews she got to know with rationality. She was impressed by this rationality less as an expression of technological progress than, first and foremost, as a means to overcome instincts and passion, to free human nature from a primeval element, and to break the spell of a myth, which paralyzed will power. One day she realized that the book, which is in the center of Jewish everyday life, can heal. The book contributed to seeing the profound background of things and to gaining calm assurance of salvation, with which it is possible to face the bitter fate of being a stranger. Thus, Katerina got to know a not-less-passionate form of love, which roots and protects people, a love that she will almost exclusively give to those strangers: to the Jewess Rosa and her husband, whose children she would like to bring up after the parents are killed by furious farmers; to the Jewish pianist Henny; to the Jew Sami.[47] Her own child, though, should be a stranger to the locals.

This civilization, however, did not bring the expected salvation. Those high walls, by which people are enclosed, will not allow them to escape their predetermined fate: Katerina is not allowed to keep Rosa's children because, as their aunt tells them, "it is forbidden to forget that you are Jewish";[48] the Jews who broke away from their community, such as Henny the pianist or her partner, will end up in deep despair. In addition, Katerina's "Jewish" child will be brutally killed by farmers filled with hatred. Katerina, who killed the murderer of her child in the heat of the moment, is sentenced to lifelong detention. Behind prison walls she hears the sound of railways, accompanied by the joy of local inmates, those railways the (symbolic) products of civilization in which Jews are barbarically transported to their deaths. The fateful alliance between highest technology and resentment determined at the periphery served to exterminate strangeness in this world, in which now primordial silence rules again. The strange neighbors are henceforth—and for how long?—only allowed to exist in Katerina's memory:

the dire dystopia that seems to install itself by the end of the novel, as Appelfeld imagined it, could illustrate, in the last resort, the perverted effect of this "dialectical" mechanism, described by Shmuel Noach Eisenstadt,[49] that symbolically establishes the possible victory of the monologism of the patriarchal "periphery" over the dialogism of a civilization that carries in itself the seed of its doom.

Another Word on Multiculturalism

A debate focused on the failure of that distinct model of multiculturalism that was associated with the status quo of religious, linguistic, and national plurality in Habsburg Bukovina,[50] and especially in the provincial metropolis Czernowitz, should not be restricted to the evaluation of political confrontations nourished by the identity-related and forced conflictual ideology that became increasingly virulent in its manifestations in Habsburg Central Europe before World War I.[51] The type of urban civilization imported here from the west of the Habsburg Monarchy during the "process of civilization" has since the beginning been marked by that fundamental semantic incongruity between "nature brute et nature humaine,"[52] foreseen by Michel de Certeau, together with its consequences for the social construction of the stereotype of the "other" on both sides of the "hostility" front separating the "nomad" colonizers from the "sedentary" colonized.[53] The urban identity of Czernowitz, founded first of all on the conversion of "nomad" foreigners to the sedentary life, has preserved the contradiction in its very essence: the "socio-dynamics of stigmatization," to use Norbert Elias's words,[54] have radically reversed here the traditional hierarchy between "locals" and "foreigners," in the sense that the locals felt marginalized and treated as such by the newcomers.[55] The consequences of the clash between the urban center of Bukovina and its periphery became even more obvious, the source of a deep social crisis, disguised in the appearance of the religious, linguistic, or national conflict.[56] This crisis subsisted in a latent form, with intermittent violent acts, and became evident much later in comparison with other regions of the Habsburg Monarchy, when the intelligentsia of the "small nations"[57] was sufficiently developed to contest directly the supremacy of the German enclave of the settlers. This centrifugal dynamic was built in such a way that the potential communicative space,[58] resulting from the pluralism de facto of the Bukovina population, has been exposed especially to the collision between the autonomous and rival cultural fields,[59] functioning in a complete parallelism and separated by inexpugnable frontiers; Bukovina's multiculturalism has never meant more than their simple addition that, without the chance of viable founding contact points of interculturality, are illustrated in the universe of esthetic experience as a never to be accomplished *promesse du bonheur* by the two fictional wet nurses, Gregor von Rezzori's Kassandra and Aharon Appelfeld's Katerina.

Notes

This work was supported by CNCSIS-UEFISCSU, project number PNII-IDEI, code 2207/2008.

1. Ulrich Beck, "Wie Nachbarn Juden werden: Zur politischen Rekonstruktion des Fremden in der reflexiven Moderne," in *Modernität und Barbarei,* ed. Max Miller and Hans-Georg Soeffner (Frankfurt am Main, 1996), 318–44.
2. Shmuel Noah Eisenstadt, "Die Konstruktion nationaler Identitäten in vergleichender Perspektive," in *Nationale und kulturelle Identität: Studien zur Entwicklung des kollektiven Bewußtseins in der Neuzeit,* ed. Bernhard Giesen (Frankfurt, 1991), 23.
3. Beck, "Wie Nachbarn Juden werden," 324.
4. Eisenstadt, "Die Konstruktion nationaler Identitäten in vergleichender Perspektive," 23.
5. Karl W. Deutsch, *Nationalism and Social Communication: An Inquiry into the Foundation of Nationality* (Cambridge MA, 1978), 37–38; see also Otto Dann, "Der moderne Nationalismus als Problem historischer Entwicklungsforschung," in *Nationalismus und sozialer Wandel,* ed. Otto Dann (Hamburg, 1978), 18.
6. Norbert Elias, *Über den Prozeß der Zivilisation,* vol. 2 (Frankfurt, 1980), 324. Cf. Norbert Elias, *The Civilizing Process* (Oxford, 1994).
7. Elias, *Über den Prozeß der Zivilisation,* 2: 324.
8. Deutsch, *Nationalism and Social Communication,* 127.
9. Georg Simmel, "Exkurs über den Fremden," in *Soziologie: Untersuchungen über die Formen der Vergesellschaftung* (Frankfurt, 1992), 764–65; Georg Simmel, *The Sociology of Georg Simmel,* trans., ed., and with an introduction by Kurt H. Wolff (Glencoe, IL, 1950), 402.
10. Beck, "Wie Nachbarn Juden werden," 323.
11. Elias, *The Civilizing Process,* 463.
12. Beck, "Wie Nachbarn Juden werden," 323.
13. Elias, *The Civilizing Process,* 447.
14. See Max Horkheimer and Theodor W. Adorno, *Dialektik der Aufklärung: Philosophische Fragmente* (Frankfurt, 1969).
15. Sighart Neckel, as quoted in Beck, "Wie Nachbarn Juden werden," 339.
16. The expression "the cunning of reason" (*List der Vernunft*) was introduced by the philosopher Georg Friedrich Hegel, *Vorlesungen über die Philosophie der Geschichte* (Frankfurt, 1986), 46; see also the English version, *The Philosophy of History,* trans. J. Sibree, with a preface by Charles Hegel (Kitchener, 2001), 47.
17. Zygmunt Bauman, "Gewalt—modern und postmodern," in Miller and Soeffner, eds., *Modernität und Barbarei,* 41–42.
18. Bauman, "Gewalt—modern und postmodern," 43–44.
19. Zygmunt Bauman, as quoted in Beck, "Wie Nachbarn Juden werden," 326.
20. Eisenstadt, "Die Konstruktion nationaler Identitäten in vergleichender Perspektive," 31.
21. Shmuel Noah Eisenstadt, "Barbarei und Moderne," in Miller and Soeffner, eds., *Modernität und Barbarei,* 96.
22. Bernhard Giesen, "Die Struktur des Barbarischen," in Miller and Soeffner, eds., *Modernität und Barbarei,* 120–21.
23. Johannes Feichtinger, Ursula Prutsch, and Moritz Csáky, eds., *Habsburg Postcolonial* (Innsbruck, 2003).
24. Edward Said, *L'Orientalisme: L'Orient crée par l'Occident* (Paris, 1980).
25. The expression was coined by Karl Emil Franzos, *Aus Halb-Asien, Culturbilder aus Galizien, der Bukowina, Südrußland und Rumänien* (Leipzig, 1876).

26. Marie Mischler, *Soziale und wirtschaftliche Skizzen aus der Bukowina* (Vienna and Leipzig, 1893), 3–4.
27. Simmel, *Sociology of Georg Simmel*, 402.
28. Ibid., 404.
29. Mihai Eminescu, *Opere*, vol. 9, ed. Petru Cretia (Bucuresti, 1980), 430–31.
30. The poem dates from the year 1931, but it was first published in Alfred Margul Sperber, *Zeuge der Zeit, Staatsverlag für Kunst und Literatur* (Bucharest, 1951), 38.
31. Karl Emil Franzos, "Mein Erstlingswerk: 'Die Juden von Barnow,'" in *Die Geschichte des Erstlingswerks*, ed. Karl Emil Franzos (Leipzig, 1894), 221–22.
32. Elias Canetti, *Die gerettete Zunge* (Munich, 1977), 16–17; Canetti, *The Tongue Set Free: Remembrance of a European Childhood*, trans. Joachim Neugroschel (New York, 1979), 9.
33. Norman Manea, *The Hooligan's Return: A Memoir*, trans. Angela Jianu (New York, 2003). Similarly, the motif of the Czech maidservant is said to have been present in German literature from Bohemia and Prague. See Georg Escher, "Ghetto und Großstadt. Die Prager Judenstadt als Topos," in *Die Besetzung des öffentlichen Raumes. Politische Plätze, Denkmäler und Strassennamen im europäischen Vergleich*, ed. Rudolf Jaworski and Peter Stachel (Berlin, 2007), 353–73.
34. See the poem "Ins Leben" from *Der Regenbogen* (Czernowitz, 1939), 9.
35. Theodor W. Adorno, *Ästhetische Theorie* (Frankfurt, 1970), 130; Adorno, *Aesthetic Theory*, ed. and trans. Gretel Adorno and Rolf Tiedemann, with an introduction by Robert Hullot-Kentor (Minneapolis, 1997), 84.
36. Adorno, *Aesthetic Theory*, 105.
37. Ibid., 112.
38. Gregor von Rezzori, *Blumen im Schnee* (Munich, 1989); Gregor von Rezzori, *The Snows of Yesteryear: Portraits for an Autobiography*, trans. H. F. Broch de Rothermann (New York, 1989).
39. H. F. Broch de Rothermann translates *Landessprache* as "local language" or "official idiom"; in the context of von Rezzori's narrative, however, "official idiom" would seem to be the more appropriate gloss. While Kassandra does not speak the *Landessprache* in this sense, she does speak the *Landessprache* in another sense, discussed later.
40. All quotes are from von Rezorri, *The Snows of Yesteryear*, 5, 8, 10–13, 15, and 35–36.
41. Ibid., 43–44.
42. Ibid., 7.
43. Aharon Appelfeld, *Caterina* (Bucharest, 2002); Aharon Appelfeld, *Katerina*, trans. Jeffrey M. Green (London, 1995).
44. Simmel, *Sociology of Georg Simmel*, 403.
45. Appelfeld, *Katerina*, trans. Mirjam Pressler (Berlin, 2011), 152.
46. Elias, *The Civilizing Process*, 461.
47. The character of Maria in Manea, *The Hooligan's Return*, displays striking similarities to Appelfeld's fictional character Katerina.
48. Appelfeld, *Katerina*, trans. Pressler, 52.
49. Eisenstadt, "Die Konstruktion nationaler Identitäten in vergleichender Perspektive," 31.
50. Emanuel Turczynski, *Geschichte der Bukowina in der Neuzeit* (Wiesbaden, 1993).
51. Philipp Menczel, *Trügerische Lösungen: Erlebnisse und Betrachtungen eines Österreichers* (Stuttgart, 1932).
52. See Michel de Certeau, *Art de faire: Invention du quotidien* (Paris, 1980); Michel de Certeau, *The Practice of Everyday Life*, trans. Timothy J. Tomasik (Minneapolis, 1998).
53. Simmel, "Exkurs über den Fremden," 760.

54. Norbert Elias and John Scotson, *Etablierte und Aussenseiter,* trans. Michael Schröter (Frankfurt, 2002), 13. Originally published as Norbert Elias and John Scotson, *The Established and the Outsiders* (London, 1965).
55. Elias and Scotson, *Etablierte und Aussenseiter,* 9.
56. Eugen Ehrlich, *Die Aufgaben der Sozialpolitik im österreichischen Osten* (Czernowitz, 1909).
57. Miroslav Hroch, "Das Bürgertum in den nationalen Bewegungen des 19. Jahrhunderts: Ein europäischer Vergleich," in *Bürgertum im 19. Jahrhundert: Deutschland im europäischen Vergleich,* vol. 3, ed. Jürgen Kocka (Munich, 1988), 337–59.
58. Moritz Csaky, "Kultur, Kommunikation und Identität in der Moderne," in *Moderne: Kulturwissenschaftliches Jahrbuch,* ed. Helga Mitterbauer and Johannes Feichtinger, vol. 1 (2005), 110, 115.
59. See Pierre Bourdieu, *Les règles de l'art. Genèse et structure du champ littéraire* (Paris, 1992); Pierre Bourdieu, *The Rules of Art: Genesis and Structure of the Literary Field* (Palo Alto, CA, 1996).

Chapter 9

Culture as a Space of Communication

Moritz Csáky

With the end of World War I, the Habsburg Monarchy dissolved into a variety of nation-states. Thus, a development that had become increasingly predictable in the Central European region since the nineteenth century drew to its close: it had aimed at granting the various ethnic-linguistic "nationalities" autonomous, national rights. Up to the present day it is fairly usual to describe this historical development, which apparently culminated in 1918, from the perspective of a "national teleology." Historiography thus remains predicated upon the national narrative of the nineteenth century; it rarely tries to see the constitutive linguistic and cultural differences of the region, which nationalist movements exploited for their ends from a point of view that is not indebted to the category of the nation-state. A different perspective would clearly be rewarding. After 1918 the various successor states were forced to grapple with problems similar to those the monarchy had to tackle before its demise. Despite the stipulations of the Parisian peace negotiations, which prescribed that the principle of nationality (*Nationalitätenprinzip*) should guide the formation of new states, their territories were by no means linguistically or culturally homogenous, and each of them comprised minorities. The same pluralist condition had been symptomatic of the old monarchy. My aim in this concluding chapter, then, is not to perpetuate the national narrative in explaining these ostensibly "national" differences, but rather to approach the issue from the angle of *Kulturwissenschaft* (culture studies).

Central Europe: Modernization and Crisis

The Central European region, which, according to Milan Kundera, should not be perceived as a geographically or politically confined space, but rather as a "non-intentional entity"[1] comparable to the Braudelian *Méditerranée,* was a linguistically and culturally heterogeneous, differentiated region. This region was always marked by a situation of pluriculturality, which retained differences, in contrast to multiculturality, which purports to remove cultural differences. Recognized for centuries, this *traditional horizontal differentiation* acquired its contentious edge only in the nineteenth century, when it became conspicuous in the quickly growing cities and was attacked by national ideology. This situation reinforced the symptoms of crisis caused by modernization, industrialization, and mechanization.

Initially, modernization had a standardizing, "globalizing" function. Simultaneously, however, the increasing differentiation (*Ausdifferenzierung*) of economy resulted in a growing differentiation of society. This means that an accretive *vertical social differentiation* accompanied the acceleration of economic development. New individual and collective systems of reference emerged, which became noticeably more complex, multifarious, and apparently arbitrary. In this very situation, old routines of legitimization lost their integrative power. This process left, as Jean-François Lyotard laconically observed, merely a "longing for the lost narrative [*récit*]," a narrative "lost for the vast majority of people." According to Lyotard, the experience of delegitimization is not merely a hallmark of postmodernism. It was a phenomenon of the fin de siècle, typical of Vienna and Central Europe during the decades around 1900. It was, Lyotard maintains, impossible to cope with the overwhelming consequences of delegitimization, and this incapacity in turn instilled pessimism and the specific kind of mourning work (*travail de deuil*) that "raised the generation of the Viennese fin de siècle: the artists Musil, Kraus, Hofmannsthal, Loos, Schönberg, Broch, but also the philosophers Mach and Wittgenstein. Without any doubt, they widened as far as possible the conscience, as well as the theoretical and artistic responsibility, of delegitimization." Wittgenstein, Lyotard continues, "opened up a perspective on a species of legitimacy that differed from performativity in his investigations of language games."[2] Does this reference to Vienna make sense? If this is the case, how can it be explained? Is it possible to explain this connection in reference to an overarching sociocultural and historical context and at the same time to situate it therein?

The symptoms described did not surface for the first time in fin de siècle modernism; they date back at least to the *Vormärz,* the decades before 1848, when they aroused general disquiet and increasingly dominated public discourse, literature, and the arts. The Bohemian writer Alfred Meißner deplored this situation in explicit terms:

> This inner conflict [*Zerrissenheit*] is not feigned [*erheuchelt*]. *Zerrissenheit* is the disease of our time. We are torn apart in faith, in writing, in philosophy, in morals. The old unity of the world, of Antiquity and the Middle Ages, is gone. We know

that liberty must come, and we are manacled and held in captivity like schoolboys, it hurts, it tears us apart . . . We float between heaven and earth, we do not know what to believe, the split between religion and philosophy is too wide, it tears us apart . . . Plenty of rifts [*Risse*] for the man of the nineteenth century.[3]

Modern mass movements, which promised to solve the impending social questions, can be seen as a response to this tension-ridden differentiation, and the same applies to the *grands récits* of national ideology, which purported to eliminate social, linguistic, and cultural varieties in the name of a homogeneous nation.

The Heterogeneity of the Central European Region

In what follows I shall offer a thumbnail sketch of two aspects of Central Europe's characteristic heterogeneity. In my opinion this heterogeneity was constituted by two components, *endogenous* plurality, traceable in the history of the region, and *exogenous,* transregional, "global" plurality. As a signifier *endogenous plurality* denotes the "ethnic," linguistic, and cultural heterogeneity typical of the entire region. For centuries, the essence of Central Europe was its variety of peoples, languages, and cultures.[4] This is the salient feature of the region, and one might say that the region's unity rested upon this inner, endogenous *heterogeneity*. This heterogeneity is also conspicuous in other fields. One of the sources of cultural diversity is the copresence of all three monotheist, world religions, Judaism, Christianity, and Islam, in their various denominations. Another source of diversity was constituted by the different political and administrative traditions of the kingdoms and hereditary territories, which were unified under the aegis of the Habsburgs—a plethora of traditions that, frequently at loggerheads with each other, resisted centralizing efforts. The pluralist situation created a milieu that permitted intercultural exchange and acculturation, but it also was characterized by the permanent existence of irreconcilable tensions—these tensions gave rise to contradictions and conflicts that came to the fore particularly in the era of increasingly "nationalizing" policies.

In this chapter, the *exogenous plurality* denotes the sum of extrinsic elements inserted from abroad, which came to exert power in the region and contributed to its specific cultural and linguistic configuration. These "transfers" transmitted cultural codes from extraregional cultural contexts. I shall restrict myself to two brief examples: from at least the sixteenth century there was a notable, significant Spanish influence in Central Europe. The Habsburgs of the sixteenth century, particularly Ferdinand I, Maximilian II, Rudolf II, and Mathias, received a Spanish education. The initial resistance to the rule of Ferdinand I in the Austrian lands also originated in fears of Spanish "infiltration"—not only did the Spanish style of administration hold sway in Central Europe, but a flock of

Spanish councillors were also firmly established in the emperor's court. In the context of the Counter-Reformation there also was a decisive Spanish input; the Jesuits were imbued with Spanish spirituality. Their religious work firmly established elements of the Spanish Baroque, which broadly shaped mentality, percolating to the lowest orders of society and lastingly affecting political culture, which is still characterized by a certain ingrained obedience to authority (*Autoritätshörigkeit*). "Historically," as Joseph Roth put it incisively, "Spain borders on Austria . . . there is no classic [*Klassiker*] of German literature who stems from Spain but Grillparzer. He originates from Spain, like the Habsburgs. He derives from Calderón."[5]

The gateway by which Ottoman cultural elements poured into the region seems almost forgotten: the region's eastern and southeastern countries, occupied by the Sublime Porte, were exposed to Ottoman culture for centuries. This influence can be pinpointed in Hungarian traditional dress (shepherd's costume, magnate's costume), in architecture (minarets, "Magyar" style of the late nineteenth century, peasant architecture in the Balkans), in music (reception of Janissary music in the military bands of imperial regiments, "alla turca" in Viennese Classicism), as well as in regional cuisine (stuffed cabbage, strudel, *tarhonya,* coffee) and traced to the present, although it is rarely recognized as such.

A Region of Contrasts

The plurality or heterogeneity of the region was a constant theme of numerous scholarly accounts, not only in the nineteenth century. This heterogeneity acquired a reputation as a source of irritation in the course of "nation building"; it was held responsible for increasingly violent conflicts and crises, particularly in urban milieus. A late eighteenth-century *Statistik*[6] of the kingdom of Hungary explicitly draws attention to the "diversity of the people in Hungary," which corresponds to a diversity of languages.[7] Almost a hundred years later, the Viennese geographer Friedrich Umlauft described the monarchy as a state of contrasts: "As our fatherland lies at the passage between the differentiated and mountainous West of the European continent and its homogeneous and level East, it encompasses, as a consequence of its remarkable extension in longitude and latitude, the most glaring differences of physical condition, population, and intellectual [*geistig*] culture, and this is why we are permitted to call it a state of contrasts." From an ethnographic point of view, Umlauft continues, "all main groups of peoples are represented on the soil of the Austro-Hungarian Monarchy in significant quantities: Germans in the West, Romans in the South, Slavs in the North as well as in the South; and this is complemented by the entity of the Magyars couched between these main peoples." This fact,

Umlauft maintains, is important for "historical memory," being determined not by one, but by several histories: "Thus Austria's history is a confluence of histories—German, Hungarian, and Polish—similar to the pouring [*Vereinigung*] of various fluids into a majestic riverbed, which carries further the water masses received." The diverse peoples living in this area partially intersect, which subjects them to dynamic processes of ethnogenesis: "As the peoples mentioned do not live in sharply demarcated, secluded regions but rather interpenetrate, a singularly mixed population is to be found in these frontier areas. Nowhere in Europe can the intermingling of nationalities be observed in such conspicuous a manner as in our fatherland."[8] In 1841, Rotteck's and Welcker's famous *Staats-Lexikon* mentions this condition of plurality as an obvious feature of the region and draws the following conclusion: "The prominence and size of the several main nations of the monarchy led to the idea that it should be viewed as Europe in a nutshell [*Europa im Kleinen*] and to presuppose, apart from the European, a specific Austrian balance."[9]

The same can be said of the monarchy's subregions: "Europe in a nutshell" was anticipated twenty years before, in 1820, by Johann Csaplovics, who described the pluricultural kingdom of Hungary:

> But it is not only with respect to the physical quality and natural products that Hungary is Europe *in nuce;* this contention also holds true regarding the country's population: almost all European races [*Volksstämme*] find their home here. Several larger and smaller peoples significantly distinguished by their provenance, their language as well as their physical and moral properties, live here, and despite their ever-intensifying intermingling each retains its specific way of life, customs, and branches of trade.[10]

The Hungarian polyhistor Csaplovics himself, who became acutely aware of his Slovakian descent but composed most of his oeuvres in German or Latin, epitomizes the pluralist condition. Kume Kunitake, a Japanese diplomat, perceived the monarchy of the late nineteenth century in strikingly similar terms, pondering over politics' responses to the structural heterogeneity of the region:

> Among Europe's countries [the monarchy] is seen as [a] multiethnic state [*Vielvölkerstaat*], a home to many different peoples mutually intermingled to the highest degree. Russia and Prussia predominantly consist of one people only, so the [desired] equality of peoples proves a rather simple issue. But in Austria there is no province exclusively inhabited by members [*Angehörige*] of one people. Hence follows the immense intricacy faced by attempts at implementing politically uniform objectives in the [monarchy's] various countries.[11]

As late as 1915, during World War I, Hugo von Hofmannsthal justified his idea of Europe by referring to the specific experience of the monarchy, whose reconciliatory mission among nations is also rooted in its pluricultural tradition. "More than all the others, Austria requires Europe—after all, it is Europe on a small scale."[12] Hofmannsthal's ideal probably encapsulates a kernel of what today is referred to as the "multination."[13]

Of course, there are diametrically opposed, inherently negative, and derogatory appraisals of Central Europe's pluralist condition. Casting "national identity" as the ultimate end of any political community, the French historian Jean-Pierre Rioux consequently characterizes Central Europe as "doomed to the cacophony of languages and peoples." The consciousness of a national identity as epitomized by France, Rioux emphasizes with an air of condescending commiseration, could never have developed under these conditions. The formation of the French nation, Rioux continues, is both solitary and worthy of emulation: "Above all, France was a political and moral construction: cultural in the most noble sense of the term."[14] Bearing testimony to the national narrative of the nineteenth century, this account's epistemic predicates are strongly reminiscent of this very pattern. It is surprisingly similar to the "national" categories that shaped the attitudes toward the heterogeneity of Central Europe in the second half of the nineteenth century. Here in particular, the difference of spoken languages came to be seen as inescapable and insurmountable. Departing from one's concrete, nonmetaphorical language, national independence, self-reliance, and "authenticity" were asserted in dissociation from the respective "other." The militant emphasis on a specific language—at the expense of the other languages spoken in the respective pluricultural milieu—remained a constant issue of high politics since the Reichstag of Kremsier (1848/49).[15]

Disagreement culminated in the crisis over Badeni's language decrees (1897), which allotted equal rights to Czech and German in the Bohemian and Moravian provincial administration. These debates constantly revolved around the reinforcement of national difference by means of emphasizing linguistic difference. Against the backdrop of political symbiosis provided by the monarchy, language was heavily instrumentalized for political ends, probably more so than elsewhere. Today we need to ask whether this perspective, indebted to the nationalist narrative of the nineteenth century, is at all sufficient for a description and explanation of the Habsburg Monarchy's past and its crises—a past shaped, as it were, by the symbiosis of various linguistic-cultural currents *and* those currents contending for preeminence. "Cultural transfer," a concept briefly mentioned above, might lend itself as an alternative. But is it not also inappropriate in perpetuating the "essentialist" notion of culture, which is the very core of the nationalist imagery, thereby also reaffirming its key practices of inclusion and exclusion? We need a completely different perspective to get rid of this binary worldview, a perspective not encumbered by the nationalist encoding of culture, if we wish to analyze the characteristic developments of the Central European region and its set of preconditions.

Nationalization of Culture

This proposal should not be discarded: it is still common to perceive culture in these implicitly nationalist, straitjacketing categories and to assume that the nation constitutes a homogeneous or necessary entity. This perspective is prevalent in political parlance—I think of the discourses of identity in postsocialist countries, but also of the ongoing discussion about the cultural coherence and unity of Europe as defined by a set of ostensibly shared values; the latter is no less a reiteration of the national narrative than the former.[16] It is difficult to deny that this implicit perpetuation of national narratives reinforces nationalist tendencies. Evidently there is some inherent value in the well-reflected and critical application of national narrative: this exception applies to the reconstruction of historical developments or literary corpora, situating these sources in their original context with its circumstantial conventions.

In this case the nationalist pattern is critically applied to make sense of how nineteenth-century authors, subscribing to their "imagined community," envisaged the nation as an objective yet to be achieved or actively wielded key topoi to forge a national discourse. The application of the nationalist pattern is indispensable if we try to retrieve the self-conception of nationalist ideology, the gestation of its ideals of nationalization and territorialization. Its application is justifiable whenever we aim at describing "national society" as a cultural idea whose flourishing became possible only by virtue of the nineteenth-century appropriation of traditions, which, in turn, were transmitted and made *accessible* by the historiography of the time. To give but one example: the "territorialization" of culture was achieved by means of transforming the nation into a pattern of political entity or statehood and by regarding the nation as equivalent to this very entity. Niklas Luhmann, among others, established this connection and drew attention to its implications for "national" identities:

> To convert what a nation should be from imagination to reality one needs to ensure by political means the religious, cultural, and organizational uniformity [*Vereinheitlichung*] of the territory claimed by the nation-state. In this respect language, culture, and statehood are amalgamated into a political agenda distinguished only by the circumstances of its origins [*Ausgangslage*]. National identity is not a "given," it needs to be defined, achieved, and secured.[17]

We need to be cautious, however, whenever the very presuppositions that served a "national" cultural idea are still employed as dominant criteria of historical narrative without being subjected to any critical, deconstructivist analysis. This caveat applies all the more whenever sociocultural processes are classified in terms of national criteria, and wherever these criteria are retrospectively grafted onto a past in which neither national nor ethnic parameters, products of the nineteenth century, played any role. We should be no less skeptical when contemporary processes are explained by authors who resort to national categories and criteria: neither the economy nor the shareholder markets operate within national confines, and the same transnational condition applies to broad segments of today's societies, globally connected by means of increasingly perfect technologies of communication and participating in a world of knowledge that is no longer indebted to an "indigenous," "local," let alone "national" lifeworld.

Realms of (National) Memory

Some tenets of today's memory studies present us with instances of the ill-reflected, anachronistic application of the national criteria discussed. A prominent current of memory studies aims at retrieving *lieux de mémoire*—sites of memory—relevant for a given nation. But the historical reconstruction of sites of memory from this perspective—instead of subjecting them to a critical deconstructivist analysis—not only perpetuates the national narrative; it also runs the risk of myth building, thereby constructing and lending credence to realms of memory relevant for today's nation-state. Paraphrasing Nietzsche, the introductory essay of the three-volume oeuvre *Deutsche Erinnerungsorte* emphasizes that the volumes have not been designed to see life "'atrophy and degenerate [*entartet*],'" but as "a call to 'action' [*Tat*] and 'life.' Far from being restricted to 'simple instruction' [*Belehrung*], they aim at contributing to a process of 'animation' [*Belebung*]."[18] In other words, if we fail to strive for deconstruction we unconsciously remain entrapped by the essentialist, holistic notion of (national) culture—Herder likens nations or *Volkskulturen* to spheres in a state of mutual repulsion[19]—and accept the idea of a teleological development of different, nationally encoded cultures, which are characterized by a continuum of "coherence" and formalized (national) order. But coherence is not, as Clifford Geertz insists, "the major test of validity for a cultural description."[20] It is by no means astonishing but rather logical that studies of the *lieux de mémoire* also subdivide their territorial scenes of inquiry along national frontiers. The respective research agendas typically focus on "German," "French," "Italian," or "Austrian" sites of memory; they adhere to national "formal orders" and refrain from analyzing those of potential translocal, transterritorial, or transnational importance.[21] Clifford Geertz justly stresses that "nothing has done more . . . to discredit cultural analysis than the construction of impeccable depictions of formal order in whose actual existence nobody can quite believe."[22]

Culture and Communication

We need to pay sufficient attention to the "fields" (Pierre Bourdieu) and "frames" (Erving Goffman) of culture if we wish to grasp the complexity of identity.

I would suggest perceiving culture, as the ethnologist Bronislaw Malinowski did, "as the widest context of human behaviour."[23] According to Malinowski, culture is "the integral whole consisting of implements and consumers' goods, of constitutional charters for the various social groupings, of human ideas and crafts, beliefs and customs."[24] Yet, Clifford Geertz alludes to the functional component of culture, referring to the significance of mechanisms of control: we are advised not to see culture as "complexes of concrete behavior patterns—customs, usages, traditions, habit clusters—as has, by and large, been the case up to now but as a set of control mechanisms—plans, recipes, rules, instructions (what computer engineers call 'programs')—for the governing of behavior."[25] According to Simon Frith, these mechanisms of control are constantly negotiated, because social groups do not necessarily rely on prescribed cultural sets of values but rather repeatedly acquire and renew values—inner coherence—by means of social practices: "What I want to suggest, in other words, is not that social groups agree on values which are then expressed in their cultural activities (the assumption of the homology models) but that they only get to know themselves *as groups* (as a particular organization of individual and social interests, of sameness and difference) *through* cultural activity, through aesthetic judgment."[26] Stephen Greenblatt's notion of culture also relies on Malinowski's but modifies it in significant ways: "A culture is a particular network of negotiations for the exchange of material goods, ideas, and—through institutions like enslavement, adoption, or marriage—people. . . . In any culture there is a general symbolic economy made up of the myriad signs that excite human desire, fear, and aggression."[27]

I endorse these definitions but suggest going a step further: I propose to see culture as a repertoire of scripts of behavior, best described from the perspective of communication. To reciprocally *act* in an understandable fashion means to communicate. This is a version of culture as a "spontaneous process, free of administrative or guiding centers."[28] Culture should thus be defined as a repertoire of elements, signs, symbols, or codes by means of which individuals communicate with each other. Culture is a space of communication in which lifeworlds are constituted and power relations are reconfigured by the establishment and dislocation of signs. Culture is a space of communication with permeable frontiers, new elements are continuously inserted, others are divested of their significance (or meaning), or are recoded or discarded. Thus, culture is a fabric of orienting threads, of linguistic as well as mimetic forms of conduct and patterns of expression; in short, of meanings by which individuals and social groups try to maneuver within an all-encompassing social space. The inculcation of a cultural system of signs, which refers to distinct codes or contents, is managed—in *Schriftkulturen*—not by means of rites but via performative, scriptorial, or "visual" medial realizations. Communicated contents are not simply medially transmitted or created (Marshall McLuhan), they are exposed to permanent creative redesign, appropriation, or renunciation, for example, by means of subversive, carnivalesque positions described by Bakhtin.[29]

Culture as a space of communication is dynamic, performative, not "authentic"; it is hybrid and polyvalent. On the basis of his Indian experience, Salman Rushdie has sharply repudiated the idea of homogeneous, authentic culture. He emphasized the complexity, heterogeneity, and polysemic structure of cultural practices and "contents." Rushdie also pours opprobrium on the Eurocentric notion of national culture:

> One of the most absurd aspects of this quest for national authenticity "is that . . . it is completely fallacious to suppose that there is such a thing as a pure, unalloyed tradition from which to draw. The only people who seriously believe this are religious extremists. The rest of us understand that the very essence of Indian culture is that we possess a mixed tradition, a *mélange* of elements as disparate as ancient Mughal and contemporary Coca-Cola American. To say nothing of Muslim, Buddhist, Jain, Christian, Jewish, British, French, Portuguese, Marxist, Maoist, Trotskyist, Vietnamese, capitalist, and of course Hindu elements."[30]

The Polish composer Krzysztof Penderecki articulates a similar view in a European context: "I am a hybrid," he said in one of his interviews. "My family comes from the Kresy [historical Eastern Poland]. My grandmother on my father's side was an Armenian, my grandfather—a polonized German . . . My father came from Ukraine. He was Orthodox." And further: "For example, I always felt drawn to Orthodoxy; on the other hand I was fascinated by Western culture with its rationalism, but also with its art of articulating the most complex feelings."[31] This implies—in Walter Benjamin's terms—that what we tend to regard as an authoritative and binding tradition, as continuum and stable cultural heritage, is a construal. Reliance on this construal, then, might constitute a fatal and prejudicial historical misperception ("there is a tradition which is catastrophe"[32]) because it reflects the position of the rulers and not the history of the oppressed. This implies that the "subject of history must be blasted out of history,"[33] a continuum that we, its accredited and subscribed believers, inscribe into the past.

The broad notion of culture I have sketched has further advantages. First, it resists the neat distinction between high and "low" culture and encompasses the entirety of the lifeworld and its circumstantial contexts.

Second, it resolutely eschews an essentialist notion of culture—cultural spaces of communication are systems of signs, "texts" that are repeatedly "read," reappraised, and reinterpreted, that are not self-contained but agglutinate at fluid transitory stages between spaces of communication, leaving their traces within these spaces and being dynamically entangled in multifarious ways: think of the permanent, dynamic transformation of a concrete spoken language with its neologisms, sense ascriptions, changes in semantic morphology, etc., a process that comprises borrowings from other concrete languages. This dynamic process is all the more important regarding nonverbal communication. Similar signs and symbols surface in different cultural contexts, and this renders the presumption of self-contained, clearly demarcated spaces of communication obsolete. Individuals and groups communicate daily with traffic signals, for example, with traffic lights. They find their way through a city, in a constant dialogue with the arrangement of streets and squares, signposts, the nomenclature of streets, with edifices like churches, palaces, shopping arcades, monuments, or sculptures attached to buildings. They communicate with the church tower, which serves as a landmark. In his literary semiotics of the city, *Wien und die Wiener,* Adalbert Stifter compares the tower of St. Stephen's Cathedral to a poplar; the top of the tower serves as a beacon for the "poor countryman," a stranger in the city: "[a]n infinite lane swallows" the traveller, "a stream in which dirty and shining things drift is incessantly getting denser and noisier, the more he approaches the poplar he fails to see now—yes, there she appears, a dark tall pole in the glittering air—no, it is not her; more to the right there suddenly towers a bigger one, more tranquil, grey-blue dusk bearing the eagle on the top—there she is, one almost sees the delicate foliage climbing up her shaft."[34] To put it more concisely, readers interpret the "text" of a city; they communicate with different signs, which refer to something, for instance, a tower that gives them security that they try to keep an eye on. In a crowd one tries to map one's surroundings by "reading" the movement of the other pedestrians as they pass by, coordinating one's movement with the movement of the others and readjusting it to their respective pace. In the case of rain one tries to adjust one's movement with the umbrella in order not to collide with other pedestrians' umbrellas, to accelerate one pace or prepare to strike a new path. One might also silently follow a crowd that presumably heads in the direction one also aims for, such as a festive occasion one wishes to participate in.

Nonverbal, mimetic forms of expressions like gazes, gestures, and different postures accompany verbal communication that can be supported by the uttering of phonemes. One example is the polyvalent expression "aha," typical for several Central European languages, which, according to phrasing and pitch, can signify a question, a reluctant response, or a renunciation. The application of different folklore rhythmic elements in music, such as in the Viennese operetta, can establish connections that could not materialize on the theater stage. With the intonation of a waltz, the image of Vienna surfaces—or a wedding in the countryside is evoked. With a czardas, the imagination immediately turns to the Hungarian plains—or another piece containing a czardas or czardas motif readily springs to mind. The sound of a polka may evoke a Bohemian landscape, or allude to a part of the ballet at the end of the second act of Johann Strauß's *Fledermaus*. The cancan of Léhar's *Lustige Witwe* must not simply serve as a signifier of Parisian society, but can also refer to Jacques Offenbach, whose operetta *La Vie Parisienne* it is borrowed from.

Those who promote the construction of an authentic national culture, an either/or culture if I am permitted the expression, encounter considerable difficulties if confronted with these polysemic constellations, with this configuration of either *and* or. Signs or symbols, which prevail in several national spaces of communication, need to be reinterpreted, rewritten, and recoded under national auspices; they must be incorporated into an "imaginary national context." Symbols with a specific representative communicative function are subjected to nationalist instrumentalization. The same symbol may thus serve diametrically opposed collective national identities: the double cross in the Slovak coat of arms is taken to signify the Slovak nation, whereas the same double cross acts as a representative signifier for the Magyar nation in the Hungarian coat of arms. What had originally been a universalist symbol of the pluricultural kingdom of Hungary is now appropriated for opposed national agendas. "As nationalism had been the dominant paradigm since the nineteenth century," Jan Nederveen Pieterse judiciously observes, "cultural accomplishments have been recurrently claimed for the 'nation,' culture was 'nationalized' and 'territorialized.' A quite different account could be reconstructed on the basis of what Diaspora, migration, nonnatives, and intermediators contributed to the formation and dissemination of culture."[35]

A third advantage of this concept of culture as a space of communication is that it enables us to resist the temptation to diminish specific cultural configurations, *differences;* it is not prone to make these differences dissolve into vague "transculturality." Both dynamic interaction and the "open" but always tangible differences between cultural spaces of communication are taken into account. I do not intend to explain away the very real differences that originate between concrete languages and enduringly shape cultural contexts, but there was a time when these very differences were not conceived in ideological terms, and there is sufficient reason to try to scrutinize and destabilize the categories superimposed by various nationalist legacies.

Fourth, this broad conception of culture means that individuals and groups are able to communicate in two or more "languages" at the same time. They are able to participate simultaneously in different spaces of communication (in Malinowski's terms, "institutions"), thus transcending communicative boundaries. Concrete language is not the crucial distinguishing characteristic; it does not occupy the place nationalist ideology attaches to it. According to Yuri Lotman, "each culture possesses mechanisms for the creation of an internal polyglotism . . . each culture exists . . . only in the context of other cultures . . . the mastering of [these cultures'] languages constitutes" a situation of "external polyglotism."[36]

Fifth, it allows us to get a sense of "open" or "blurred frontiers" if we take into account the fact that individuals and social groups act in several spaces of communication at the same time and are able to "switch" between given contexts. Evidently, this potential to operate in a pluricontextual, "polyglot" setting applies also to individuals in a comparably homogeneous linguistic context. Both forms of polyglotism suggested by Lotman indicate hybrid cultural configurations that escape "racial," "ethnic," or "national" reifications. These cultural constellations are often discarded or even attacked for precisely this reason, for the fact that they fail to dovetail with prescribed "national" categories. It is obvious that those who destabilize clear-cut national and cultural realignments and ascriptions "become a problem of social organization [*Ordnungsproblem*] by virtue of their mere existence. They are a stumbling block . . . as it is impossible to map them according to received, simple, and unambiguous categories."[37] Culture as a space of communication is always a hybrid *mélange;* it does not imply an epistemology of multiculturality as a total entity, which supersedes or diminishes differences. Our approach has further corollaries: individuals and groups can share common experiences and remember key historical events similarly. But their memories may also diverge sharply. Different memories may not only occur in the minds of those who belong to different spaces of communication, but these discrepancies can also be observed when we critically examine the "collective" memory within one selected space of communication. Endorsing the notion of *histoire croisée*,[38] we realize that history is essentially polyvalent, as there is no such thing as a binding memory that enshrines and perpetuates historical experience and thus prescribes a binding historical narrative (in the singular), but rather memories, histories, and narratives (in the plural); this suggests a variety of different—contradictory—but equally valid narratives.

Edward Said made an eloquent case for the recognition of a heterogeneous, polyvalent narrative of the past in the Palestinian case: "There are many kinds of Palestinian experiences, which cannot all be assembled into one. One would therefore have to write parallel histories of the communities in Lebanon, the occupied territories, and so on. That is the central problem. It is almost impossible to imagine a single narrative."[39] These plural pasts consist of histories of interstices, of diasporas, of continuous migration and mobility. Clifford Geertz emphasized that a history of polyvalent cultural experiences and processes must consist of "guessing at meanings, assessing the guesses, and drawing explanatory conclusions from the better guesses, not discovering the Continent of Meaning and mapping out its bodiless landscape."[40] In Central Europe, constellations of hybridity primarily occur in urban milieus—in milieus where people from different spaces of communication intermingle and interact. Boundaries are transcended in a series of "creolizations" that epitomize the regional polycentrism at the heart of the city. The center of the city is constantly destabilized through assimilationist tendencies, tendencies that imply subversive protest against ostensible stable constructions of power. Culture is essentially hybrid, a creolizing ensemble and at the same time transnational, translocal, transterritorial, fluid, and not homogeneous or essentialist. If we refrain from reiterating the rigid dispensations of ethnicity and nationalist categories, a wealth of antagonistic discourses and correlations resurfaces—we are able to grasp processes that betray retrospectively imposed frontiers. I would like to argue that these processes shaped the consciousness of individuals and social groups in a manner at least as pervasive and durable as artificially imposed nationalist presuppositions.

Finally, the notion of culture as a space of communication does not exclude economic aspects. Initially, communicative "behavior" aims at enabling the individual to survive in a group as well as to persist as a group in a broader social context. "The final motive or drive in all this was primarily biological survival."[41] If we harness Marx's suggestions for a theory of culture, we might characterize the abovementioned elements, signs, symbols, and codes as commodities that circulate in society. On the one hand, the "fetishism of commodities" alludes to the fact that these commodities' value hinges on social conditions and reflects these premises. Commodities thus act as "material relations between persons and social relations between things."[42] On the other hand, some of these commodities are divested of their original "utility value," their communicational exchange value. Within the fabric of culture, within the process of circulation of goods, they are susceptible to overestimation and ideological overstatement. This applies, for example, to symbols instrumentalized for national identity formation, thus being shrouded in an emotionally charged myth. In Walter Benjamin's terms, these symbols are transformed into "phantasmagorias." Spaces of communication are formed by individuals and groups guided by economic and social aims and agendas. The rivalry of different personae and groups, their contending for pre eminence, is always inscribed into the organizing structure of spaces of communication. "Culture as communication" thus also encapsulates the antagonism between the victorious and the defeated, between those who manage to acquire and harness economic as well as symbolic capital, and those who fail to do so.

Urban Milieus

If we return to the Central European context, we need to address the issue of the possible benefits of the proposed notion of culture in contrast to the nationalist pattern. Obviously it allows us to resist and transcend artificial differences like nation, ethnic group, national culture, and national history. Cultural processes are reappraised as transnational and transterritorial constellations: they are not primarily determined by the topography of political or national frontiers. Furthermore, the proposed notion enables us to perceive the linguistic-cultural heterogeneity of Central Europe as a plurality of different, antagonistic, and overlapping spaces of communication. This insight yields further conclusions: the permanent fluctuation of verbal and nonverbal elements, signs, and codes gives rise to a communicative metaspace, a "texture" that remains recognizable and legible throughout the region notwithstanding the distinctions imposed by concrete languages and their vocabularies. A Central European city, even if the traveler does not know the township he traverses, may be "read" according to its architectonic structure, due to similar or analogous architectonic "codes." The concrete spoken languages constitute the most obvious distinguishing features. If someone fails to understand a neighbor who speaks a different language, he or she feels different. If someone moves in a linguistic environment dominated by a language the respective person does not speak, he or she feels a "stranger," without necessarily converting this experience of "strangeness" into an ideological statement. It was precisely at this point that national narratives began to operate, where they began to perpetuate and appropriate differences and enshrine national "authenticity." It is by no means surprising, then, that this contending for preeminence and preponderance in the region often culminated, and indeed still culminates, in conflicts over language: I have already drawn attention to the crisis sparked by Badeni's language decree, but another immediately relevant example is the protracted and acrimonious argument over bilingual *Ortstafeln,* place-name signs, in Carinthia.

This regional macrocosm is reflected in the microcosm of urban milieus. A history of these microcosms, as proposed by Pieterse, would require "a historiography of the formation of hybrids [*Hybridbildung*]" typical of "metropolitan cultures, this means an alternative historiography" that confronts the imperial fabrication of history.[43] I shall briefly dwell on a few selected examples to clarify this point: the bifurcating, factual, and metaphorical polyglotism of the region exerted a lasting influence on the mentality of its inhabitants. This might be illustrated by referring to the sheer percentage of Vienna's "nonnative," migrant population, which amounted to 60 percent in 1900, when the city's population totaled 1.7 million. The rival spaces of communication were tangible in the city; they gave rise to tensions, crises, and conflicts. This "polyglotism" kindled the scorn of those who subscribed to nationalist positions, like the poet Eduard von Bauernfeld: "I feel much more the compatriot of Lessing and Goethe . . . than of any 'Wenceslaus' or 'Janos' or any other man whose name ends on 'inski,' 'icki,' and 'vich,' with whom I am united [*zusammengeschweißt*] by political destiny, and who in principle cares as little for me as I do for him."[44] The elements by which individuals communicate in the urban milieu—both in verbal and nonverbal "language"—coalesce and are knit together, they form a "creolizing" language.

Maria Hornung notes that the intensity of foreign language influences at play in the Viennese colloquial vernacular is unique. She maintains that it is remarkable how Vienna manages to incorporate these influences in past and present; "think of the immense influx of Czech residents setting in during the second half of the last century and continuing until World War I . . . a perfunctory glance at the Viennese phone directory shows an abundance of foreign names: the Czech, Slovak, Polish, Hungarian, Croatian, Italian, and Friulian family names have no foreign connotation," and the citizens all speak an "unadulterated [*unverfälscht*] Viennese dialect."[45] This specific vernacular is, Hofmannsthal explained, "among all German the most mixed [*gemengteste*]," interspersed with foreign words, but "they are *our* foreign words [*Fremdwörter*], at home with us for centuries," so much so "that they thereby lost their citizenship in their proper homeland [*Heimat*]."[46] Richard Reichensperger has traced Johann Nestroy's appropriation of foreign words, his borrowings from the vocabulary and his appropriation of syntactic elements, both derived from languages spoken in Vienna, languages that had been intermingling with German and had agglutinated components and formed new mixed languages—for instance, the characteristic *Böhmakeln* or the *Mauscheln*. Nestroy's use of these words was designed to mirror both the linguistic-cultural heterogeneity of Vienna, but also the copresence of different social, economic, and cultural realities in the city: applied to the semiotics of the city, this means "that Nestroy not only provides us with a syntactic cross-section of the city structure, but also offers a longitudinal section, in etching into relief different linguistic layers. He does not simply emphasize—as Stifter did—the syntactic axis of the city's structure, but also its paradigmatic axis. In the inner polyglotism of his plays, where linguistic levels from dialect to the exaggerated stage parlance [*Bühnensprache*]," and a range of languages including Czech, Italian, French, and German, "as well as various specialist jargons [*Fachsprachen*] are applied, Nestroy converts the 'external polyglotism' (Lotman) of the modern city, its mixture of language, into a literary, linguistic form."[47]

Stefan Simonek's recent impressive book *Distanzierte Nähe: Die slawische Moderne der Donaumonarchie und die Wiener Moderne*[48] elucidates that this representation of Vienna's multiple realities in fin de siècle writing was by no means restricted to German-language literature. Similar concerns informed autochthonous Czech (Josef Svatopluk Machar), Slovene (Ivan Cankar), Polish (Tadeusz Rittner), and Ukrainian literature (Marko Čeremšyna). Theodor W. Adorno noted that ostensibly "alien" elements remained an integral part of Viennese language; they became a constitutive part of a tradition, which also aroused jaundice and fanaticism:

> Given the circumstances of this case it is quite correct, that . . . [the] foreign words this dialect teems with are divested of [*entragen*] the exterritorial and aggressive character [*Wesen*] which is usually intrinsic to them in German. It is entirely sufficient to hear a concierge speak of a "rekommendierten Brief" to become aware of the difference, of a linguistic atmosphere in which the foreign is at the same time foreign and familiar.[49]

It is in this setting of hybridity that Adorno locates Vienna's impulse of musical creativity. He alludes to the symbiosis of different, heterogeneous national (*nationeller*) elements, which serves as a medium of Viennese music making: Mozart's explicit Italian borrowings reveal that "[t]he national [*nationellen*] moments . . . relate dialectically to each other."[50] Schubert's "à la Hongroise . . . bears that untouched, unintentional stamp of noncompliance with the civilizational side of integral music, with the side that is too culture-immanent and estranged from the living subject."[51] Adorno insists that this observation is also valid for the decades around 1900:

> The central musical tradition that aims at integral form and is profoundly akin to the idea of universality, the antithesis of the nineteenth century's national schools, itself acquired a national [*nationellen*] imprint from Vienna. Many of Mahler's and Berg's themes speak in Viennese; even Webern secretly—and therefore all the more emphatically—speaks the idiom . . . The Viennese dialect was the true world language of music, and what it conveyed was the craftsmanlike tradition of motivic-thematic compositional work.[52]

One might adduce other examples. In Prague, for instance, Franz Kafka and his friends moved in exceedingly hybrid, antagonistic, and, again, strongly intersecting cultural spaces of communication. This hybridity was pivotal for identity constitution: "Franz Kafka is, like no one else, a child of three cultures: Czech, German, and Jewish."[53] His command of German did not exclude a proficiency in Czech, the language he spoke with his *Fräulein,* the governess; he conversed in Czech with relatives (e.g., with the family of Ottla), colleagues, and friends from the workers' accident insurance agency, spoke a "gewähltes Schrifttschechisch,"[54] read Czech books and newspapers, and wrote letters in that language.[55] Kafka's closest confidant Max Brod wrote: "I am overcome by the desire to prove . . . that one can scarcely speak of a pure German and a pure Czech nation in Prague, but rather solely of Praguers."[56] Furthermore, Kafka's life forms a linchpin of several cultural spheres that became relevant for his multiple identities. Besides his role in Czech- and German-speaking spaces of communication, I restrict myself to referring to his notion of "uns allen gemeinsame[n] Judentum" (Judaism common to all of us).[57] Kafka's interests revolved around Jewish religion, Yiddish culture (e.g., theater), the Hasidic tradition of Eastern Jewry, and, increasingly so, the Zionist movement, which he regarded with growing sympathy. He learned Hebrew ("and probably chemistry will leave [some time] for Hebrew," noting how arduously slow his progress was) and read Hebrew texts ("I read a little Hebrew, mainly a novel by Brenner," and "besides that I read little and only Hebrew").[58] This "polyglotism" could also be the furnace of crises and conflicts, primarily so in a time of national ideologies striving to squash or eradicate these multifaceted identities: "I stand between German and Polish," Tadeusz Rittner—based in Vienna and publishing in both languages—noted with an air of resignation, this means: I know and feel both. My descent, my innermost strivings and sentiments are Polish. And frequently I find it much easier to think in this language rather than in the other one. But sometimes it is the other way round. Of some of my writings the Germans say it's Polish, and the Poles say it's German. On both sides, I am often treated as a guest. And I see so much, here and there, with the dispassionate and unprepossessing gaze of the stranger.[59]

Rittner's fate, a good example of a multipolar identity in a hybrid, complex cultural system, was shared by many others, for example, by the author Ödön von Horváth:

You ask me for my *Heimat* [homeland], I answer: I was born in Fiume, grew up in Belgrade, Budapest, Preßburg, Vienna, and Munich and have a Hungarian passport—but *Heimat*? I don't know it. I am a typical Austro-Hungarian mixture: Magyar, Croatian, German, Czech . . . But: the concept, "fatherland," a nationalist counterfeit, is alien to me. My fatherland is the people.[60]

Conclusion

The proposed notion of "culture as a space of communication" presents a reappraisal of cultural processes that unfolds in complex constellations. The history of Central Europe provides us with a set of privileged starting points for this kind of investigation. The concept constitutes an alternative model of explanation opposed to nationalist categories, which continue to inform—be it implicitly or explicitly—much historical work. This kind of work reiterates nationalist parlance; it extenuates or belittles cultural differences and thus perpetuates the elusive quest for a coherent national culture. It uncritically reproduces the eminently political language designed to foster the nineteenth-century process of nation building. Our proposed concept enables us to perceive the cultural heterogeneity of Central Europe as a plurality of coexisting and intersecting, overlapping and antagonistic spaces of communication, as a series of dynamic processes of interaction and dislocation. This set of problems is comparable to the very challenges today's societies are forced to face: attempts at explaining contemporary processes that point to the "age of globalization" gave rise to various theoretical impulses that can be fruitfully applied to similar problems in the past. Concepts like cultural networks, globalization, cultural transfer, hybridization, mélange, or creolization furnish us with a theoretical armamentarium conducive to the explanation of present and past processes alike. Taking the past as point of departure, we might offer the following conclusion: Central Europe may be regarded as a "laboratory" in which processes of global relevance emerged.

Notes

Translated by Franz Leander Fillafer. All translations are by the translator unless otherwise indicated.

1. Milan Kundera, "Einleitung zu einer Anthologie oder Über drei Kontexte," in *Die Prager Moderne: Erzählungen, Gedichte, Manifeste,* ed. Květoslav Chvatík (Frankfurt, 1991), 22.
2. Jean-François Lyotard, *La condition postmoderne* (Paris, 1979), 68. "Ce pessimisme est celui qui a nourri la génération début-de-siècle à Vienne: les artistes, Musil, Kraus, Hofmannsthal, Loos, Schönberg, Broch, mais aussi les philosophes Mach et Wittgenstein. Ils ont sans doute porté aussi loin que possible la conscience et la responsabilité théorique et artistique de la déligitimation. On peut dire aujourd'hui que ce travail de deuil a été accompli. Il n'est pas à recommencer. Ce fut la force de Wittgenstein de ne pas en sortir du côté du positivisme que développait le Cercle de Vienne et de tracer dans son investigation des jeux de langage la perspective d'une autre sorte de légitimation que la performativité. C'est avec elle que le monde postmoderne a affaire. La nostalgie du récit perdu est elle-même perdue pour la plupart des gens."
3. Letter from Alfred Meißner to Moritz Hartmann, 24 August 1839, in Otto Wittner, ed., *Briefe aus dem Vormärz: Eine Sammlung aus dem Nachlaß Moritz Hartmanns,* Bibliothek deutscher Schriftsteller aus Böhmen, Mähren und Schlesien 30 (Prague, 1911), 20.
4. See Herwig Wolfram, *Die Geburt Mitteleuropas: Geschichte Österreichs vor seiner Entstehung* (Vienna, 1987); Herwig Wolfram, *Grenzen und Räume: Geschichte Österreichs vor seiner Entstehung* (Vienna, 1995).
5. "Spanien grenzt historisch an Österreich . . . Es gibt keinen Klassiker deutscher Sprache, der vom Spanischen herkäme, außer Grillparzer. Er stammt aus Spanien—wie die Habsburger. Er stammt von Calderón." Joseph Roth, "Grillparzer: Ein Porträt," in *Joseph Roth Werke,* vol. 3, *Das journalistische Werk 1929–1939,* ed. Klaus Westermann (Cologne, 1989), 746.
6. *Statistik,* literally "statistics," in its eighteenth-century connotation, designates the broadly conceived cameralist science of the state. A statistical handbook of the time would thus comprise a narrative, surveys, and registers of data on the most diverse subjects, ranging from agriculture to ecclesiastical affairs. It was designed to provide the outlines for the administration, amelioration, and advancement of the respective state or conglomerate of territories.
7. Martin Schwartner, *Statistik des Königreichs Ungern* (Pest, 1798), 87–107.
8. "Wie unser Vaterland den Uebergang vom gegliederten und gebirgigen Westen des europäischen Continents zu dessen ungegliedertem und ebenen Osten bildet, so schließt es in Folge seiner bedeutenden Längen- und Breitenausdehnung auch die grellsten Gegensätze in Beziehung auf physische Verhältnisse, Bevölkerung und geistige Cultur in sich, weshalb man die Monarchie auch einen Staat der Contraste zu nennen berechtigt ist." Friedrich Umlauft, "Einleitung," in *Die Oesterreichisch-Ungarische Monarchie: Geographisch-statistisches Handbuch* (Vienna, 1876), 1.
9. "Oestreich," in *Staats-Lexikon oder Encyklopädie der Staatswissenschaften,* vol. 12, ed. Carl von Rotteck and Carl Welcker (Altona, 1841), 143.
10. Johann Csaplovics, "Das Königreich Ungern [sic] ist Europa im Kleinen," *Erneuerte Vaterländische Blätter für den Österreichischen Kaiserstaat* 13 (1820): 410.
11. Peter Pantzer, ed., *Die Iwakura-Mission: Das Logbuch des Kume Kunitake über den Besuch der japanischen Sondergesandtschaft in Deutschland, Österreich und der Schweiz im Jahre 1873* (Munich, 2002), 250.

12. Hugo von Hofmannsthal, "Krieg und Kultur," in *Gesammelte Werke in zehn Einzelbänden*. [IX]: *Reden und Aufsätze II: 1914–1924*, ed. Bernd Schoeller and Rudolf Hirsch (Frankfurt, 1979), 417.
13. See Stéphane Pierré-Caps, *La multination: L'avenir des minorités en Europa centrale et orientale* (Paris, 1995).
14. Jean-Pierre Rioux, "La mémoire culturelle," in *Pour une histoire culturelle*, ed. Jean Pierre Rioux and Jean-François Sirinelli (Paris, 1997), 343.
15. Stefan Malfèr, "Die Sprachenfrage und der verstärkte Reichsrat von 1860," in *Jenseits und diesseits der Leitha: Elektronische Festschrift für Éva Somogyi zum 70 Geburtstag*, ed. Imre Ress and Dániel Szabó (Budapest, 2007), 101.
16. See Moritz Csáky and Johannes Feichtinger, eds., *Europa—geeint durch Werte? Die europäische Wertedebatte auf dem Prüfstand der Geschichte* (Bielefeld, 2007).
17. Niklas Luhmann, "Der Staat des politischen Systems: Geschichte und Stellung der Weltgesellschaft," in *Perspektiven der Weltgesellschaft*, ed. Ulrich Beck (Frankfurt, 1998), 365.
18. Etienne François and Hagen Schulze, eds., *Deutsche Erinnerungsorte*, vol. 1 (Munich, 2001), 24. A similar argument is developed in Pierre Nora, "Comment écrire l'histoire de France?" in *Les Lieux de mémoire*, vol. 2, ed. Pierre Nora (Paris, 1997), 2219–39.
19. See Wolfgang Welsch, "Transkulturalität: Zur veränderten Verfassung heutiger Kulturen," in *Hybridkultur: Medien, Netze, Künste*, ed. Irmela Schneider and Christian W. Thomsen (Cologne, 1997), 67–90.
20. Clifford Geertz, "Thick Description: Toward an Interpretive Theory of Culture," in *The Interpretation of Cultures* (New York, 1973), 17.
21. Cf. Moritz Csáky, "Gedächtnis, Erinnerung und die Konstruktion von Identität: Das Beispiel Zentraleuropas," in *Nation und Nationalismus in Europa: Kulturelle Konstruktion von Identitäten: Festschrift für Urs Altermatt*, ed. Catherine Bosshart-Pfluger, Joseph Jung, and Franziska Metzger (Frauenfeld, 2002), 25–49; Moritz Csáky, "Die Mehrdeutigkeit von Gedächtnis und Erinnerung," in *Erinnern und Verarbeiten: Zur Schweiz in den Jahren 1933–1945*, Itinera 25, ed. Georg Kreis (Basel, 2004), 7–30.
22. Clifford Geertz, "Thick Description," 18.
23. Pierre Bourdieu, *Distinction: A Social Critique of the Judgement of Taste* (London, 1984); Bourdieu, "The Genesis of the Concepts of *habitus* and of *field*," *Sociocriticism*, 2, no. 2 (1985): 11-24; Bourdieu, *The Field of Cultural Production* (Cambridge, UK, 1993); Erving Goffman, *Frame Analysis: An Essay on the Organization of Experience* (Cambridge, MA, 1974); Bronislaw Malinowski, *A Scientific Theory of Culture and other Essays* (Chapel Hill, NC, 1944), 5.
24. Ibid., 36.
25. Clifford Geertz, "The Impact of the Concept of Culture on the Concept of Man," in *The Interpretation of Cultures*, 44.
26. Simon Frith, "Music and Identity," in *Questions of Cultural Identity*, ed. Stuart Hall and Paul du Gay (London, 1996), 111.
27. Stephen Greenblatt, "Culture," in *Critical Terms for Literary Study*, 2nd ed., ed. Frank Lentricchia and Thomas McLaughin (Chicago, 1995), 229–30.
28. Zygmunt Bauman, "Gesetzgeber und Interpret: Kultur als Ideologie von Intellektuellen," in *Sozialstruktur und Kultur*, ed. Hans Haferkamp (Frankfurt, 1990), 479.
29. See Marshall McLuhan, *Understanding Media: The Extensions of Man* (New York,1964); and Mikhail Bakhtin, *Rabelais and his World* (Bloomington, IN, 1984).
30. Salman Rushdie, "Commonwealth Literature Does Not Exist," in *Imaginary Homelands: Essays and Criticism 1981–1991* (London, 1991), 67.

31. Mieczysław Tomaszewski, "Der Schaffensweg des Krzysztof Penderecki," *Silesia Nova: Vierteljahrsschrift für Kultur und Geschichte* 5, no. 1 (2008): 53.
32. Walter Benjamin, "Das Passagenwerk: Aufzeichnungen und Materialien," in *Gesammelte Schriften*, vol. 5, ed. Rolf Tiedemann (Frankfurt, 1982), 591.
33. Ibid., 594.
34. Adalbert Stifter, "Aussicht und Betrachtungen von der Spitze des St. Stephansturmes," in *Wien und die Wiener = Adalbert Stifter, die Mappe meines Urgroßvaters, Schilderungen, Briefe* (Munich, 1968), 282.
35. Jan Pieterse, "Der Melange-Effekt: Globalisierung im Plural," in *Perspektiven der Weltgesellschaft*, ed. Ulrich Beck (Frankfurt, 1998), 119.
36. Jurij M. Lotman, "Zur Struktur, Spezifik und Typologie der Kultur," in *Aufsätze zur Theorie und Methodologie der Literatur und Kultur*, ed. Karl Eimermacher (Kronberg, 1974), 431.
37. Elisabeth Beck-Gernsheim, "Schwarze Juden und griechische Deutsche: Ethnische Zuordnung im Zeitalter der Globalisierung," in *Perspektiven der Weltgesellschaft*, ed. Ulrich Beck (Frankfurt, 1998), 127.
38. See Michael Werner and Bénédicte Zimmermann, "Penser l'histoire croisée: Entre empirie et réflexivité," in *De la comparaison à l'histoire croisée*, ed. Michael Werner and Bénédicte Zimmermann (Paris, 2004), 15–49.
39. Salman Rushdie, "On Palestinian Identity: A Conversation with Edward Said," in *Imaginary Homelands*, 179.
40. Clifford Geertz, "Thick Description," 20.
41. Malinowski, *A Scientific Theory of Culture*, 10.
42. "[A]ls sachliche Verhältnisse der Personen und gesellschaftliche Verhältnisse der Sachen." Karl Marx, "Der Fetischcharakter der Ware und sein Geheimnis," in *Das Kapital: Kritik der politischen Ökonomie*, vol. 1 (Berlin, 1989), 86.
43. Pieterse, "Der Melange-Effekt," 119.
44. Eduard von Bauernfeld, "Aus Alt- und Neu-Wien (1873)," in *Bauernfeld's ausgewählte Werke in vier Bänden*, vol. 4, ed. Emil Horner (Leipzig, 1905), 90.
45. Maria Hornung, "Sprache," in *Die Stadt Wien*, ed. Peter Csendes, Ferdinand Opll, and Friederike Goldmann (Vienna, 1999), 85.
46. Hugo von Hofmannsthal, "Unsere Fremdwörter (1914)," in Schoeller and Hirsch, *Reden und Aufsätze II*, 363 and 364.
47. Richard Reichensperger, "Zur Wiener Stadtsemiotik von Adalbert Stifter bis H. C. Artmann," in *Literatur als Text der Kultur*, ed. Moritz Csáky and Richard Reichensperger (Vienna, 1999), 174.
48. Stefan Simonek, *Distanzierte Nähe: Die slawische Moderne der Donaumonarchie und die Wiener Moderne* (Berlin, 2000).
49. Theodor W. Adorno, "Notizen zur Literatur," in *Gesammelte Schriften*, vol. 11, ed. Rolf Tiedemann (Darmstadt, 1998), 220.
50. Die "nationellen Elemente [verhalten] sich dialektisch zueinander." Theodor W. Adorno, "Einleitung in die Musiksoziologie," in *Gesammelte Schriften*, vol. 14, ed. Rolf Tiedemann (Darmstadt, 1998), 356; Theodor W. Adorno, *Introduction to the Sociology of Music*, trans. E. B. Ashton (New York, 1988), 160–61.
51. "Schuberts à la Hongroise . . . trägt aber zugleich jenes Unberührte, Intentionslose, das dem Zivilisatorischen, allzu Kulturimmanenten, dem lebendigen Subjekt Entfremdeten der integralen Musik nicht sich fügt." Adorno, *Introduction to the Sociology of Music*, 163; Adorno, "Einleitung in die Musiksoziologie," 359.
52. "Jene zentrale Tradition der Musik, die auf integrale Form geht und der Idee von Universalität aufs tiefste verwandt ist, die Antithese zu den nationalen Schulen des neunzehnten

Jahrhunderts, hatte durch Wien selbst nationellen Einschlag. Wienerisch reden noch viele Themen von Mahler, Berg; insgeheim, und darum nur um so nachdrücklicher, spricht selbst Webern das Idiom . . . Das Wienerische, als Dialekt, war die wahre Weltsprache der Musik. Vermittelt ist das durch die handwerkliche Überlieferung der motivisch-thematischen Arbeit." Adorno, "Einleitung in die Musiksoziologie," 357–58; Adorno, *Introduction to the Sociology of Music,* 161–62. The published translation is slightly altered here to render the original more precisely.

53. Leopold B. Kreitner, "Der junge Kafka," in *"Als Kafka mir entgegenkam . . .": Erinnerungen an Franz Kafka,* ed. Hans-Gerd Koch (Berlin, 2005), 52.
54. V. K. Krofta, "Im Amt mit Franz Kafka," in Koch, *"Als Kafka mir entgegenkam . . . ,"* 98.
55. Franz Kafka, letter to Dr. Josef David, May 1921, in *Briefe 1902–1924* (Frankfurt, 1966), 327–28. See also pp. 80, 92, 127, 169ff., 180, 297ff., 308, 324, 328, 392, 401, 402, 416, and 426.
56. Max Brod, *Der Prager Kreis,* with an afterword by Peter Demetz (Frankfurt, 1979), 61.
57. Franz Kafka, letter to Robert Klopstock, early March 1924, in *Briefe,* 478.
58. Franz Kafka, letter to Max Brod, 25 October 1923, in *Briefe,* 453; Franz Kafka, letter to Robert Klopstock, October 1923, in *Briefe,* 459.
59. *Das Literarische Echo* 19, no. 7 (1 January 1917): 400–1, cited in Gabriela Giel, "Das zweisprachige Schaffen von Thaddäus Rittner in den Augen polnischer Literaturhistoriker," in *Transitraum Deutsch: Literatur und Kultur im transnationalen Zeitalter,* ed. Jens Adam et al. (Wrocław, 2007), 283. See Stefan Simonek, "Tadeusz Rittners literarisches Debüt im Rahmen der Wiener Moderne," in *Distanzierte Nähe: Die slawische Moderne der Donaumonarchie und die Wiener Moderne* (Bern, 2000), 19–62.
60. Cited in Antal Mádl, *Nikolaus Lenau und sein kulturelles und sozialpolitisches Umfeld* (Munich, 2005), 314.

Selected Bibliography

Acham, Karl, ed. *Geschichte der österreichischen Humanwissenschaften.* 6 vols. Vienna: Passagen Verlag, 1999–2006.
Acham, Karl. "Volk, Nation, Europa—bezogen auf ältere und neuere Formen Österreichs und des Österreichischen." In *Volk—Nation—Europa: Zur Romantisierung und Entromantisierung politischer Begriffe,* edited by Alexander von Bormann, 245–62. Würzburg: Königshausen & Neumann, 1998.
Adamiec, Marek. "Polish Literature on the Internet." http://monika.univ.gda.pl/-fpoma/Polish%20Literature%20on%20the%20Internet.pdf (accessed 15 June 2006).
Adanir, Fikret. "Religious Communities and Ethnic Groups under Imperial Sway: Ottoman and Habsburg Lands in Comparison." In *The Historical Practice of Diversity: Transcultural Interactions from the Early Modern Mediterranean to the Postcolonial World,* edited by Dirk Hoerder, Christiane Harzig, and Adrian Shubert, 54–86. New York: Berghahn Books, 2003.
Adas, Michael. "Contested Hegemony: The Great War and the Afro-Asian Assault on the Civilising Mission Ideology." *Journal of World History* 15, no. 1 (March, 2004): 31–64. Online access provided by the History Cooperative at http://www.historycooperative.org/journals/jwh/15.1/adas.html.
Adorno, Theodor W. *Aesthetic Theory.* Edited and translated by Gretel Adorno and Rolf Tiedemann, with an introduction by Robert Hullot-Kentor. Minneapolis: University of Minnesota Press, 1997.
———. *Ästhetische Theorie.* Frankfurt: Suhrkamp Taschenbuch, 1970.
———. "Einleitung in die Musiksoziologie." In *Gesammelte Schriften,* vol. 14, edited by Rolf Tiedemann, 169–436. Darmstadt: Wiss. Buchges, 1998.
———. *Introduction to the Sociology of Music.* Translated by E. B. Ashton. New York: Continuum, 1988.
———. "Notizen zur Literatur." In *Gesammelte Schriften,* vol. 11, edited by Rolf Tiedemann, 216–32. Darmstadt: Wiss. Buchges, 1998.
Albrecht, Andrea. *Kosmopolitismus: Weltbürgerdiskurse in Literatur, Philosophie und Publizistik um 1800.* Berlin: de Gruyter, 2005.
Albrecht, Catherine. "The Rhetoric of Economic Nationalism in the Bohemian Boycott Campaigns of the Late Habsburg Monarchy." *Austrian History Yearbook* 32 (2001): 47–67.
Albrich, Thomas, and Ronald Zweig. *Escape through Austria: Jewish Refugees and the Austrian Route to Palestine.* London: Frank Cass, 2002.
Alföldy, Geza. *Ungarn 1956: Aufstand, Revolution, Freiheitskampf.* Heidelberg: C. Winter, 1997.

Ali, Shaheen Sardar. "Religious Pluralism, Human Rights and Muslim Citizenship in Europe: Some Preliminary Reflections on an Evolving Methodology for Consensus." In *Religious Pluralism and Human Rights in Europe: Where to Draw the Line*, edited by Titia Leonon and J. E. Goldschmidt, 57–79. Antwerp: Intersentia, 2007.

Amin, Samir. *Capitalism in the Age of Globalization: The Management of Contemporary Society*. London: Zed Books, 1997.

———. "Economic Globalism and Political Universalism: Conflicting Issues." *Journal of World-Systems Research* 6, no. 3 (Fall/Winter 2000): 581–622.

———. *Spectres of Capitalism: A Critique of Current Intellectual Fashions*. New Delhi: Rainbow Publishers, 1999.

Amnesty International. *Amnesty International Report 2004*. London: Amnesty International Publications, 2004.

Anderl, Gabriele, and Angelika Jensen. "Zionistische Auswanderung nach Palästina vor 1938." In *Auswanderung aus Österreich*, edited by Traude Horvath and Gerde Neyer, 187–209. Vienna: Böhlau, 1996.

Appelfeld, Aharon. *Caterina*. Bucharest: Univers, 2002.

———. *Katerina*. Translated by Jeffrey M. Green. New York: Norton, 1994.

———. *Katerina*. Translated by Miriam Pressler. Berlin: Rowohlt Tasschenbuch, 2011.

Arbeitskreis für ökonomische und soziale Studien in Wien, ed. *Gastarbeiter: Wirtschaftliche und soziale Herausforderung*. Vienna: Europaverlag, 1973.

Arendt, Hannah. "Aufklärung und Judenfrage." In *Hannah Arendt: Die Verborgene Tradition: Acht Essays*, 108–26. Frankfurt: Suhrkamp, 1976.

———. "Creating a Cultural Atmosphere." In *The Jew as Pariah: Jewish Identity and Politics in the Modern Age*, edited by Ron H. Feldman, 91–95. New York: Grove Press, 1978.

Ash, Timothy Garton. "Freedom and Diversity: A Liberal Pentagram for Living Together." *New York Review of Books* 59, no. 18 (22 November 2012): 33.

Ashbrook, John E. "Locking Horns in the Istrian Political Arena: Politicized Identity, the Istrian Democratic Assembly, and the Croatian Democratic Alliance." *East European Politics and Societies* 20, no. 4 (November 2006): 622–58.

Ausländer, Rose. *Der Regenbogen*. Czernowitz: Literaria, 1939.

Austrian Statistical Yearbook. 1963–2006. Vienna: Statistics Austria, published annually.

Bachtin, Michail. *Rabelais and his World*. Bloomington: Indiana University Press, 1984.

Bahr, Hermann. *Österreichischer Genius: Grillparzer, Stifter, Feuchtersleben*. Vienna: Bellaria-Viel, 1906.

Ballinger, Pamela. "'Authentic Hybrids' in the Balkan Borderlands." *Current Anthropology* 45, no. 1 (2004): 31–60.

———. *History in Exile: Memory and Identity at the Borders of the Balkans*. Princeton, NJ: Princeton University Press, 2003.

———. "The Istrian *Esodo*: Silences and Presences in the Construction of Exodus." In *War, Exile, and Everyday Life*, edited by Maja Povrzanovic and Renata Jambresic Kirin, 117–32. Zagreb: Institute of Ethnology and Folklore, 1996.

———. "Lines in the Water, Peoples on the Map: Representing the 'Boundaries' of Cultural Groups in the Upper Adriatic." *Narodna umjetnost* 43, no. 1 (2006): 15–39.

———. "Opting for Identity: The Politics of International Refugee Relief in Venezia Giulia, 1948–1952." *Acta Histriae* 14, no. 1 (2006): 115–40.

———. "Watery Spaces, Globalizing Places: Ownership and Access in Postsocialist Croatia." In *European Responses to Globalization*, edited by Janet Laible and Henri Barkey, 153–78. Amsterdam: Elsevier Press, 2006.

Baskar, Bojan. "Made in Trieste: Geopolitical Fears of an Istrianist Discourse on the Mediterranean." *Narodna umjetnost* 36, no. 1 (1999): 121–34.
Battafarano, Italo Michele. "Bilingualismus und Simultaneum: Marginalia zu einem aktuellen Problem, das vor mehr als drei Jahrhunderten im barocken Sulzbach schon gelöst wurde." *Morgen-Glantz: Zeitschrift der Christian Korr von Rosenroth-Gesellschaft* 10 (2000): 333–46.
Battersby, Christine. *The Sublime, Terror and Human Difference*. London: Routledge, 2007.
Bauböck, Rainer, and Bernhard Perchinig. "Migrations- und Integrationspolitik." In *Politik in Österreich: Das Handbuch*, edited by Herbert Dachs, Peter Gerlich, and Helmut Kramer, 726–42. Vienna: Mainz, 2006.
Bauernfeld, Eduard von. "Aus Alt- und Neu-Wien (1873)." In *Bauernfeld's ausgewählte Werke in vier Bänden*, vol. 4, edited by Emil Horner. Leipzig: Hesse, 1905.
Bauman, Zygmunt. "Gesetzgeber und Interpret: Kultur als Ideologie von Intellektuellen." In *Sozialstruktur und Kultur*, edited by Hans Haferkamp, 452–82. Frankfurt: Suhrkamp, 1990.
———. "Gewalt—modern und postmodern." In *Modernität und Barbarei*, edited by Max Miller and Hans-Georg Soeffner, 36–67. Frankfurt: Suhrkamp Taschenbuch, 1996.
Baumgartner, Gerhard. *6 x Österreich: Geschichte und aktuelle Situation der Volksgruppen*. Klagenfurt: Drava, 1995.
Bayley, C. A. *Empire and Information: Intelligence Gathering and Social Communication in India, 1780–1870*. Cambridge: Cambridge University Press, 1996.
———. *Imperial Meridian: The British Empire and the World, 1780–1830*. London: Longman, 1989.
Beck, Ulrich. "Wie Nachbarn Juden werden: Zur politischen Rekonstruktion des Fremden in der reflexiven Moderne." In *Modernität und Barbarei*, edited by Max Miller and Hans-Georg Soeffner, 318–44. Frankfurt: Suhrkamp Taschenbuch, 1996.
Beck-Gernsheim, Elisabeth. "Schwarze Juden und griechische Deutsche: Ethnische Zuordnung im Zeitalter der Globalisierung." In *Perspektiven der Weltgesellschaft*, edited by Ulrich Beck, 125–67. Frankfurt: Suhrkamp, 1998.
Beiträge zur Statistik der Republik Österreich, vol. 8. Vienna: Österr. Staatsdruckerei, 1923.
Bendix, Regina. "Ethnology, Cultural Reification, and the Dynamics of Difference in the *Kronprinzenwerk*." In *Creating the Other: Ethnic Conflict and Nationalism in Habsburg Central Europe*, edited by Nancy M. Wingfield, 149–66. New York: Berghahn Books, 2003.
Benedik, Stefan. "Define the Migrant, Define the Menace: Remarks on Narratives of Recent Romani Migrations to Graz." In *Mapping Contemporary History II*, edited by H. Konrad and S. Benedik, 159–78. Vienna: Böhlau, 2010.
Benjamin, Walter. "Das Passagenwerk: Aufzeichnungen und Materialien." In *Gesammelte Schriften*, vol. 5, edited by Rolf Tiedemann. Frankfurt: Suhrkamp, 1982.
Bhatti, Anil. "Kulturelle Vielfalt und Homogenisierung." In *Habsburg Postcolonial: Machtstrukturen und kollektives Gedächtnis*, edited by Johannes Feichtinger, Ursula Prutsch, and Moritz Csáky, 55–68. Innsbruck: Studien Verlag, 2003.
———. "Sprache, Übersetzung, Kolonialismus." In *Kulturelle Identität: Deutsch-indische Kulturkontakte in Literatur, Religion und Politik*, edited by Horst Turk and Anil Bhatti, 3–19. Berlin: E. Schmidt, 1997.
———. "'. . . zwischen zwei Welten schwebend . . .': Zu Goethes Fremdheitsexperiment im West- östlichen Divan." In *Goethe: Neue Ansichten*, edited by Hans-Jörg Knobloch und Helmut Koopmann, 103–21. Würzburg: Königshausen & Neumann, 2007. Available

online at http://www.goethezeitportal.de/fileadmin/PDF/kk/df/postkoloniale_studien/bhatti_divan. pdf.
Birus, Hendrik. "The Goethean Concept of World and Comparative Literature." In *Comparative Literature and Culture* 2, no. 4 (2000). Available online at http://clcwebjournal.lib.purdue.edu/clcweb00-4/birus00.html.
Bjork, James. *Neither German nor Pole: Catholicism and National Indifference in a Central European Borderland*. Ann Arbor: University of Michigan Press, 2008.
Bloch, Ernst. *Erbschaft dieser Zeit*. Frankfurt, 1977.
———. *Tübinger Einleitung in die Philosophie*. 2 vols. Frankfurt: Suhrkamp, 1969.
Blumenberg, Hans. *Arbeit am Mythos*. Frankfurt: Suhrkamp Verlag, 1996.
Bottomore, Tom, and Patrick Goode. *Austro-Marxism*. Oxford: Clarendon Press, 1978.
Bourdieu, Pierre. *Les règles de l'art: Genèse et structure du champ littéraire*. Paris: Editions du Seuil, 1992.
———. *The Rules of Art: Genesis and Structure of the Literary Field*. Palo Alto, CA: Stanford University Press, 1996.
Boyer, John. *Political Radicalism in Late Imperial Vienna: Origins of the Christian Social Movement, 1848–1897*. Chicago: University of Chicago Press, 1981.
Brix, Emil. *Die Umgangssprachen in Altösterreich zwischen Agitation und Assimilation: Die Sprachenstatistik in den zisleithanischen Volkszählungen 1880 bis 1910*. Vienna: Böhlau, 1982.
Brod, Max. *Der Prager Kreis*. With an afterword by Peter Demetz. Frankfurt: Suhrkamp, 1979.
Brousek, Karl M. *Wien und seine Tschechen: Integration und Assimilation einer Minderheit im 20. Jahrhundert*. Vienna: Verlag für Geschichte und Politik, 1980.
Brubaker, Rogers. *Ethnicity without Groups*. Cambridge, MA: Harvard University Press, 2004.
———. "Ethnicity without Groups." In *Ethnicity without Groups*, 7–27. Cambridge, MA: Harvard University Press, 2004.
———. *Nationalism Reframed: Nationhood and the National Question in the New Europe*. Cambridge: Cambridge University Press, 1996.
Brubaker, Rogers, Margit Feischmidt, John Fox, and Liana Grancea, eds. *Nationalist Politics and Everyday Ethnicity in a Transylvanian Town*. Princeton, NJ: Princeton University Press, 2008.
Bruckmüller, Ernst. "Was There a 'Habsburg Society' in Austria-Hungary?" Twentieth Annual Robert A. Kann Memorial Lecture. *Austrian History Yearbook* 37 (2006): 1–16.
Brumen, Borut. "The State Wants It So, and the Folk Cannot Do Anything Against the State Anyway." *Narodna umjetnost* 33, no. 2 (1996): 139–55.
Brunner, José Joaquín. *Un espejo trizado: Ensayos sobre cultura y políticas culturales*. Santiago de Chile: FLACSO, 1988.
Bugge, Peter. "Czech Nation-Building, National Self Perception and Politics 1780–1914." PhD diss., University of Aarhus, 1994.
Burger, Hannelore. *Sprachenrecht und Sprachgerechtigkeit im österreichischen Unterrichtswesen 1867–1918*. Vienna: VOAW, 1995.
Burke, Peter. "Language and Identity in Early Modern Italy." In *The Art of Conversation*, 66–88. Cambridge: Polity Press, 1993.
Burstedt, Anna. "The Place on the Plate!" *Ethnologia Europaea* 32, no. 2 (2002): 145–58.
Calhoun, Craig, ed. *Social Theory and the Politics of Identity*. Cambridge, MA: Harvard University Press, 1995.

Canclini, Néstor García. *Culturas híbridas: Estrategias para entrar y salir de la modernidad.* México: Grijalbo, 1990.

Canetti, Elias. *Die gerettete Zunge.* Munich: C. Hanser, 1977.

———. *The Tongue Set Free: Remembrance of a European Childhood.* Translated by Joachim Neugroschel. New York: Seabury Press, 1979.

Čapo Žmegač, Jasna. "Ethnology, Mediterranean Studies and Political Reticence in Croatia: From Mediterranean Constructs to Nation-Building." *Narodna umjetnost* 36, no. 1 (1999): 33–52.

Carmichael, Cathie. "Ethnic Stereotypes in Early European Ethnographies: A Case Study of the Habsburg Adriatic c. 1770–1815." *Narodna umjetnost* 33, no. 2 (1996): 197–209.

Carpentier, Alejo. "The Baroque and the Marvelous Real." In *Magical Realism: Theory, History, Community,* edited by Lois Parkinson Zamora and Wendy B. Faris, 89–108. Durham, NC: Duke University Press, 1995.

Cerná, Jana. *Milena Jesenská.* Frankfurt: Neue Kritik, 1985.

Certeau, Michel de. *Art de faire: Invention du quotidian.* Paris: Gallimard, 1980.

———. *The Practice of Everyday Life.* Translated by Timothy J. Tomasik. Minneapolis: University of Minnesota Press, 1998.

Chakrabarty, Dipesh. *Provincializing Europe: Postcolonial Thought and Historical Difference.* Princeton, NJ: Princeton University Press, 2000.

Chang-Rodríguez, Raquel. "Coloniaje y conciencia nacional: Garcilaso de la Vega Inca y Felipe Guamán Poma de Ayala." *Caravelle: Cahiers du monde hispanique et luso-brésilien* 38 (1982): 29–43.

Chatterjee, Margaret. *Hinterlands and Horizons: Excursions in Search of Amity.* Lanham, MD: Lexington Books, 2002.

Chatterjee, Partha, ed. *Wages of Freedom: Fifty Years of the Indian Nation-State.* Delhi: Oxford University Press, 1998.

Cheah, Pheng. "Introduction Part II: The Cosmopolitical—Today." In *Cosmopolitics: Thinking and Feeling Beyond the Nation,* edited by Pheng Cheah and Bruce Robbins, 20–41. Minneapolis: University of Minnesota Press, 1998.

Chojnowski, Andrzej. *Koncepcje polityki narodowościowej rządów polskich w latach 1921–1939.* Wrocław: Ossolineum, 1979.

Cocco, Emilio. *Metamorfosi dell'Adriatico orientale.* Faenza: Homeless Book, 2002.

Cohen, Bernard, and Luc Rosenzweig. *Der Waldheim- Komplex.* Vienna: Verlag für Gesellschaftskritik, 1987.

Cohen, Gary B. *The Politics of Ethnic Survival: Germans in Prague, 1861–1914.* 2nd ed., rev. West Lafayette, IN: Purdue University Press, 2006.

Cohn, Bernhard. "The Command of Language and the Language of Command." In *Subaltern Studies IV,* edited by Ranajit Guha, 276–329. Delhi: Oxford University Press, 1985.

Confino, Alon. *Nation As a Local Metaphor: Württemberg, Imperial Germany, and National Memory, 1871–1918.* Chapel Hill: University of North Carolina Press, 1997.

Conrad, Sebastian, and Shalini Randeria, eds. *Jenseits des Eurozentrismus: Postkoloniale Perspektiven in den Geschichts- und Kulturwissenschaften.* Frankfurt: Campus Verlag, 2002.

Corsellis, John, and Marcus Ferrar. *Slovenia 1945: Memories of Death and Survival after World War II.* London: I. B. Taurus, 2005.

Crampton, Jeremy W., and Stuart Elden, eds. *Space, Knowledge and Power: Foucault and Geography.* Aldershot: Ashgate, 2007.

Csáky, Moritz. "Gedächtnis, Erinnerung und die Konstruktion von Identität: Das Beispiel Zentraleuropas." In *Nation und Nationalismus in Europa: Kulturelle Konstruktion von Identitäten: Festschrift für Urs Altermatt,* edited by Catherine Bosshart-Pfluger, Joseph Jung, and Franziska Metzger, 25–49. Frauenfeld: Huber, 2002.

——. *Das Gedächtnis der Städte: Wien und die urbanen Milieus in Zentraleuropa.* Vienna: Böhlau, 2010.

——. "Kultur, Kommunikation und Identität in der Moderne." *Moderne: Kulturwissenschaftliches Jahrbuch* 1 (2005): 110–15.

——. "Die Mehrdeutigkeit von Gedächtnis und Erinnerung." In *Erinnern und Verarbeiten: Zur Schweiz in den Jahren 1933–1945,* Itinera 25, edited by Georg Kreis, 7–30. Basel: Schwabe, 2004.

Csáky, Moritz, and Johannes Feichtinger, eds. *Europa—geeint durch Werte? Die europäische Wertedebattenauf dem Prüfstand der Geschichte.* Bielefeld: Transcript, 2007.

Csáky, Mortiz, Johannes Feichtinger, Peter Karoshi, and Volker Munz. "Pluralitäten, Heterogenitäten, Differenzen. Zentraleuropas Paradigmen für die Moderne." In *Kultur—Identität—Differenz: Wien und Zentraleuropa in der Moderne,* Gedächtnis—Erinnerung—Identität 4, edited by Moritz Csáky, Astrid Kury, and Ulrich Tragatschnig, 13–43. Innsbruck: Studien Verlag, 2004.

Csáky, Moritz, and Klaus Zeyringer, eds. *Ambivalenz des kulturellen Erbes: Vielfachkodierung des historischen Gedächtnisses: Paradigma.* Innsbruck: Studien Verlag, 2000.

Csaplovics, Johann. "Das Königreich Ungern [sic] ist Europa im Kleinen." *Erneuerte Vaterländische Blätter für den Österreichischen Kaiserstaat* 13 (1820): 410.

D'Alessio, Vanni. "Istrians, Identifications and the Habsburg Legacy: Perspectives on Identities in Istria." *Acta Histriae* 14, no. 1 (2006): 15–39.

Dallmayr, Fred, and G. N. Devy, eds. *Between Tradition and Modernity: India's Search for Identity: A Twentieth Century Anthology.* New Delhi: Sage Publications, 1998.

Dann, Otto. "Der moderne Nationalismus als Problem historischer Entwicklungsforschung." In *Nationalismus und sozialer Wandel,* edited by Otto Dann, 12–22. Hamburg: Hoffmann und Campe, 1978.

Deleuze, Gilles, and Felix Guattari. *A Thousand Plateaus: Capitalism and Schizophrenia.* Translated by Brian Masumi. London: Athlone Press, 1988.

Derrida, Jacques. *Monolingualism of the Other: Or the Prosthesis of Origin.* Translated by Patrick Mensah. Palo Alto, CA: Stanford University Press, 1998.

Derzhavnyi Arkhiv Ivano-Frankivs'koï Oblasti—The State Archive of the Ivano-Frankiv'sk Region, Ukraine (DAIFO). Fond 370: Papers of the Society of Friends of the Hutsul Region, Stanisławów Main Branch.

Deschaumes, Ghislaine Glasson, and Rada Ivekovic, eds. *Divided Countries, Separated Cities: The Modern Legacy of Partition.* New Delhi: Oxford University Press, 2003.

Deutsch, Karl W. *Nationalism and Social Communication: An Inquiry into the Foundations of Nationality.* Cambridge, MA: MIT Press, 1978.

Die Ergebnisse der österreichischen Volkszählung vom 22. März 1934 [1]. 1935. Wien: Druck und Verl. der Österr. Staatsdruckerei.

Die Ergebnisse der österreichischen Volkszählung vom 22. März 1934 [3]. 1935. Wien: Druck und Verl. der Österr. Staatsdruckerei.

Doderer, Heimito von. *Roman no. 7. 752 part 1. Die Wasserfälle von Sunj.* Munich: Deutscher Taschenbuch Verlag, 1971.

Drakulić, Slavenka. *Café Europa: Life after Communism.* New York: Penguin Books, 1999.

Driessen, Hank. "Mediterranean Port Cities: Cosmopolitanism Reconsidered." *History and Anthropology* 16, no. 1 (2005): 129–41.

Dünne, Jörg, and Stephan Günzel, eds. *Raumtheorie: Grundlagentexte aus Philosophie und Kulturwissenschaften*. Frankfurt: Suhrkamp Taschenbuch, 2006.

Ebermann, Erwin, ed. *Afrikaner in Wien: Zwischen Mystifizierung und Verteufelung. Erfahrungen und Analysen*. 3rd ed. Münster: Lit, 2007.

Eisenstadt, Shmuel Noah. "Barbarei und Moderne." In *Modernität und Barbarei*, edited by Max Miller and Hans-Georg Soeffner, 96–118. Frankfurt: Suhrkamp Taschenbuch, 1996.

———. "Die Konstruktion nationaler Identitäten in vergleichender Perspektive." In *Nationale und kulturelle Identität: Studien zur Entwicklung des kollektiven Bewußtseins in der Neuzeit*, edited by Bernhard Giesen, 21–38. Frankfurt: Suhrkamp Taschenbuch, 1991.

Eisterer, Klaus. "The Austrian Legation in Prague and the Czechoslovak Crisis of 1968." *Contemporary Austrian Studies* 9 (2001): 214–35.

Elias, Norbert. *The Civilizing Process*. Oxford: Blackwell Publishers, 1994.

———. *Über den Prozeß der Zivilisation*. Vol. 2. Frankfurt: Suhrkamp Taschenbuch, 1990.

Elias, Norbert, and John L. Scotson. *The Established and the Outsiders*. 2nd ed. London: Sage, 1994.

———. *Etablierte und Aussenseiter*. Translated by Michael Schröter. Frankfurt: Suhrkamp Taschenbuch, 2002.

Eminescu, Mihai. *Opere 9*. Bucharest: Ed. Acad. R.S.R., 1980.

Escher, Georg. "Ghetto und Großstadt. Die Prager Judenstadt als Topos." In *Die Besetzung des öffentlichen Raumes. Politische Plätze, Denkmäler und Strassennamen im europäischen Vergleich*, ed. Rudolf Jaworski and Peter Stachel, 353-73. Berlin: Frank & Timme, 2007.

Essen, Gesa von, and Horst Turk, eds. *Unerledigte Geschichten: Der literarische Umgang mit Nationalität und Internationalität*. Göttingen: Wallstein, 2000.

Exner, G. J. Kytir, and A. Pinwinkler. *Bevölkerungswissenschaft in Österreich in der Zwischenkriegszeit (1918–1938): Personen, Institutionen, Diskurse*. Vienna: Böhlau, 2004.

Fassmann, Heinz, and Rainer Münz. *Einwanderungsland Österreich? Historische Migrationsmuster, aktuelle Trends und politische Maßnahmen*. Vienna: Jugend & Volk, 1995.

Federn, Walter, ed. *Almanach 1908-1918-1928: 10 Jahre Nachfolge-Staaten*. Vienna: Verlag "Der Oesterreichischen Volkswirts," 1928.

Feichtinger, Johannes, and Moritz Csáky, eds. *Schauplatz Kultur—Zentraleuropa: Transdisziplinäre Annäherungen*. Innsbruck: Studien Verlag, 2006.

Feichtinger, Johannes, Ursula Prutsch, and Moritz Csáky, eds. *Habsburg Postcolonial: Machtstrukturen und kollektives Gedächtnis*. Gedächtnis—Erinnerung—Identität 2. Innsbruck: Studien Verlag, 2003.

———. "Habsburg (Post)-colonial: Anmerkungen zur Inneren Kolonisierung in Zentraleuropa." In *Habsburg Postcolonial*, edited by Johannes Feichtinger, Ursula Prutsch, and Moritz Csáky, 13–31. Innsbruck: Studien Verlag, 2003.

Feichtinger, Johannes, and Peter Stachel, eds. *Das Gewebe der Kultur: Kulturwissenschaftliche Analysen zur Geschichte und Identität Österreichs in der Moderne*. Innsbruck: Studien Verlag, 2001.

Feichtlbauer, Hubert. *Zwangsarbeit in Österreich 1938–1945: Späte Anerkennung, Geschichte, Schicksale: Fonds für Versöhnung, Frieden und Zusammenarbeit*. Vienna: Österreichischer Versöhnungsfonds: Braintrust, 2006.

Fischer, Wladimir. "'I haaß Vocelka—du haaßt Vocelka': Der Diskurs über 'die Gastarbeiter' in den 1960er bis 1980er Jahren und der unhistorische Vergleich mit der Wiener Arbeitsmigration um 1900." In *Wien und seine WienerInnen: Ein historischer Streifzug durch Wien über die Jahrhunderte,* edited by Martin Scheutz and Vlasta Valeš, 327–54. Vienna: Böhlau, 2008.

Foucault, Michel. *Power/Knowledge: Selected Interviews and Other Writings,* edited by Colin Gordon. Sussex: Harvester Press, 1980.

François, Etienne, and Hagen Schulze, eds. *Deutsche Erinnerungsorte.* Vol. 1. Munich: Beck, 2001.

Franzos, Karl Emil. *Aus Halb-Asien, Culturbilder aus Galizien, der Bukowina, Südrußland und Rumänien.* Leipzig: Duncker & Humblot, 1876.

Freund, Florian, and Bertrand Perz. "Zwangsarbeit von zivilen AusländerInnen Kriegsgefangenen, KZ-Häftlingen und ungarischen Juden in Österreich." In *NS- Herrschaft in Österreich: Ein Handbuch,* edited by Emmerich Tálos, Ernst Hanisch, Wolfgang Neugebauer, and Reinhard Sieder, 644–95. Vienna: öbv & hpt, 2001.

Freund, Florian, Bertrand Perz, and Mark Spoerer. *Zwangsarbeiter und Zwangsarbeiterinnen auf dem Gebiet der Republik Österreich 1939–1945.* Vienna: Oldenburg, 2004.

Freund, Florian, and Hans Safrian. "Die Verfolgung der österreichischen Juden 1938–1945: Vertreibung und Deportation." In *NS-Herrschaft in Österreich: Ein Handbuch,* edited by Emmerich Tálos, Ernst Hanisch, Wolfgang Neugebauer, and Reinhard Sieder, 767–94. Vienna: öbv & hpt, 2001.

Frith, Simon. "Music and Identity." In *Questions of Cultural Identity,* edited by Stuart Hall and Paul du Gay, 108–27. London: Sage, 1996.

Frykman, Jonas. "Making Sense of Memory: Monuments and Landscape in Croatian Istria." *Ethnologia Europaea* 33, no. 2 (2002): 107–19.

———. "Place for Something Else: Analysing a Cultural Imaginary." *Ethnologia Europaea* 32, no. 2 (2002): 47–68.

Gauss, Karl-Markus. *Ins unentdeckte Österreich: Nachrufe und Attacken.* Vienna: P. Zsolnay, 1998.

Geertz, Clifford. "The Impact of the Concept of Culture on the Concept of Man." In *The Interpretation of Cultures,* 33–54. New York: Basic Books, 1973.

———. "Thick Description: Toward an Interpretive Theory of Culture." In *The Interpretation of Cultures,* 3–30. New York: Basic Books, 1973.

Gellner, Ernest. *Language and Solitude: Wittgenstein, Malinowski, and the Habsburg Dilemma.* Cambridge: Cambridge University Press, 1998.

GfK Austria. *Integration in Österreich: Einstellungen, Orientierungen, und Erfahrungen von MigrantInnen und Angehörigen der Mehrheitsbevölkerung.* Vienna: GfK-Austria, 2009.

Giel, Gabriela. "Das zweisprachige Schaffen von Thaddäus Rittner in den Augen polnischer Literaturhistoriker." In *Transitraum Deutsch. Literatur und Kultur im transnationalen Zeitalter,* edited by Jens Adam, Hans-Joachim Hahn, Lucjan Puchalski, and Irena Światłowska, 275–84. Wrocław: Oficyna Wydawnicza ATUT—Wrocławskie Wydawnictwo Oświatowe, 2007.

Giesen, Bernhard. "Die Struktur des Barbarischen." In *Modernität und Barbarei,* edited by Max Miller and Hans-Georg Soeffner, 118–30. Frankfurt: Suhrkamp Taschenbuch, 1996.

Goetel, Walery. "Zagadnienia regjonalizmu górskiego w Polsce." Kraków: Wydawn. Zwiasku Ziem Górskich, 1936.

Goethe, Johann Wolfgang von. *Goethes Anschauen der Welt: Schriften und Maximen zur wissenschaftlichen Methode.* Compiled with an afterword by Ekkehard Krippendorff. Frankfurt: Insel Verlag, 1994.

———. *Goethes Werke,* edited by Erich Trunz. Hamburger Edition. 14 vols. Hamburg: Christian Wegner Verlag, 1953.

Gordon, Avery F., and Christopher Newfield. "Introduction." In *Mapping Multiculturalism,* edited by Avery F. Gordon and Christopher Newfield, 1–16. Minneapolis: University of Minnesota Press, 1996.

Grdina, Igor. *Med dolžnostjo spomina in razkošjem pozabe.* Ljubljana: Zalozba ZRC, ZRC SAZU, 2006.

Greenblatt, Stephen. "Culture." In *Critical Terms for Literary Study,* 2nd ed., edited by Frank Lentricchia and Thomas McLaughin, 225–32. Chicago: University of Chicago Press, 1995.

Grillparzer, Franz. *Franz Grillparzer, Sämtliche Werke: Ausgewählte Briefe, Gespräche, Berichte,* edited by Peter Frank and Karl Pörnbacher. 4 vols. Munich: Carl Hanser, 1960.

Grosvenor, Edwin A. "The Races of Europe." *The National Geographic Magazine* 44, no. 6 (December 1918): 431–536.

Gruber, M. *Integrationspolitik in Kommunen: Herausforderungen, Chancen, Gestaltungsansätze.* Vienna: Springer Verlag, 2010.

Gulin, Valentina. "Morlacchism between Enlightenment and Romanticism: Identification and Self-Identification of the European *Other.*" *Narodna umjetnost* 34, no. 1 (1997): 77–100.

Habermas, Jürgen. *Die postnationale Konstellation: Politische Essays.* Frankfurt: Suhrkamp Verlag, 1998.

Hall, M. G. *Der Fall Bettauer.* Vienna: Löcker, 1978.

Hall, Stuart. "The Spectacle of the 'Other.'" In *Representation: Cultural Representations and Signifying Practices,* edited by Stuart Hall, 223–90. London: Sage, 1997.

Haller, Dieter. "The Cosmopolitan Mediterranean: Myth and Reality." *Zeitschrift für Ethnologie* 129 (2004): 29–47.

Hametz, Maura. *Making Trieste Italian 1918–1954.* Woodbridge: The Royal Historical Society; Suffolk: Boydell Press, 2005.

Hammer-Purgstall, Joseph Freiherr von. *Vortrag über die Vielsprachigkeit: Festvortrag zur feierlichen Eröffnungssitzung der kaiserl: Akademie der Wissenschaften.* Vienna: Akademie der Wissenschaften, 1852.

Hasan, Mushirul, ed. *Inventing Boundaries: Gender, Politics and the Partition of India.* New Delhi: Oxford University Press, 2000.

Haslinger, Peter. "Building a Regional Identity." *Austrian History Yearbook* 32 (2001): 105–24.

———. *Nation und Territorium in tschechischen politischen Diskurs 1880–1938.* Munich: Oldenbourg, 2010.

Hauer, Wolfgang. *Der Ortstafelstreit: Zum Verhältnis von Rechtsstaat Demokratie.* Vienna: Linde, 2006.

Hayden, Robert M. "Schindler's Fate: Genocide, Ethnic Cleansing, and Population Transfers." *Slavic Review* 55, no. 4 (Winter 1996): 727–48.

Hegel, Georg Friedrich. *Vorlesungen über die Philosophie der Geschichte.* Frankfurt: Suhrkamp Taschenbuch, 1986.

Hemetek, Ursula. *Am Anfang war der Kolaric: Plakate gegen Rassismus und Fremdenfeindlichkeit.* Vienna: Südwind, 2002.

Hentges, Gudrun. "Minderheiten- und Volksgruppenpolitik in Österreich." In *Zuwanderung im Zeichen der Globalisierung: Migrations-, Integrations- und Minderheitenpolitik,* edited by Cristoph Butterwegge and Gudrun Hentges, 149–77. Opladen: Leske & Budrich, 2003.

Herder, Johann Gottfried. "Bekehrung der Juden." In *Adrastea,* edited by Günter Arnold, 628–42. Frankfurt: Deutscher Klassiker Verlag, 2000.

———. *Ideen zur Philosophie der Geschichte der Menschheit.* Edited by Martin Bollacher. Frankfurt: Deutscher Klassiker Verlag, 1989.

Hintermann, Christiane. "The Narration of Austrian Immigration History in Exhibitions." In *Migration and Memory: Representations of Migration in Europe since 1960,* edited by Christiane Hintermann and Christina Johannson, 162–81. Innsbruck: Studien Verlag, 2010.

Hobsbawm, Eric. *Nations and Nationalism Since 1870: Programme, Myth, Reality.* Cambridge: Cambridge University Press, 1990.

Hochschild, Arlie Russel, and Barbara Ehrenreich, eds. *Global Women, Nannies, Maids and Sex Workers in the New Economy.* New York: Metropolitan Books, 2003.

Hoerder, Dirk. "Revising the Monocultural Nation-state Paradigm: An Introduction to Transcultural Perspectives." In *The Historical Practice of Diversity: Transcultural Interactions from the Early Modern Mediterranean to the Postcolonial World,* edited by Dirk Hoerder, Christiane Harzig, and Adrian Shubert, 1–12. New York: Berghahn Books, 2003.

Hoerder, Dirk, Christiane Harzig, and Adrian Shubert, eds. *The Historical Practice of Diversity: Transcultural Interactions from the Early Modern Mediterranean to the Postcolonial World.* New York: Berghahn Books, 2002.

Hoffmann-Holter, Beatrix. *"Abreisendmachung": Jüdische Kriegsflüchtlinge in Wien 1914 bis 1923.* Vienna: Böhlau, 1995.

Hofmannsthal, Hugo von. "Krieg und Kultur." In *Gesammelte Werke in zehn Einzelbänden.* [IX]: *Reden und Aufsätze II: 1914–1924,* edited by Bernd Schoeller and Rudolf Hirsch, 417–20. Frankfurt: Fischer-Taschenbuch Verlag, 1979.

———. "Die Österreichische Idee." In *Gesammelte Werke in zehn Einzelbänden,* [IX]: *Reden und Aufsätze II: 1914–1924,* edited by Bernd Schoeller and Rudolf Hirsch, 453–58. Frankfurt: Fischer-Taschenbuch Verlag, 1979.

———. "Wir Österreicher und Deutschland." In *Gesammelte Werke in zehn Einzelbänden.* [IX]: *Reden und Aufsätze II: 1914–1924,* edited by Bernd Schoeller and Rudolf Hirsch, 390–96. Frankfurt: Fischer-Taschenbuch Verlag, 1979.

———. "Unsere Fremdwörter (1914)." In *Gesammelte Werke in zehn Einzelbänden,* [IX]: *Reden und Aufsätze II: 1914–1924,* edited by Bernd Schoeller and Rudolf Hirsch, 360–66. Frankfurt: Fischer-Taschenbuch Verlag, 1979.

Hölz, Karl. *Das Fremde, das Eigene, das Andere: Die Inszenierung kultureller und geschlechtlicher Identität in Lateinamerika.* Berlin: Erich Schmidt Verlag, 1998.

Horkheimer, Max, and Theodor W. Adorno. *Dialektik der Aufklärung: Philosophische Fragmente.* Frankfurt: S. Fischer, 1969.

Hornung, Maria. "Sprache." In *Die Stadt Wien,* edited by Peter Csendes, Ferdinand Opll, and Friederike Goldmann, 85–95. Vienna: VOAW, 1999.

Hroch, Miroslav. "Das Bürgertum in den nationalen Bewegungen des 19. Jahrhunderts: Ein europäischer Vergleich." In *Bürgertum im 19. Jahrhundert: Deutschland im europäischen Vergleich,* vol. 2, ed. Jürgen Kocka, 337–59. Munich: Dt. Taschenbuch- Verlag, 1988.

Hoz, Paloma Fernandez de la. *Familienleben, Transnationalität und Diaspora*. ÖIF Materialien 21. Vienna: OIF, 2004.
Huddleston, T., and J. Niessen, with E. N. Chaimh and E. White. *Migrant Integration Policy Index III*. Brussels, 2011.
Humboldt, Wilhelm von. "Ueber die Verschiedenheiten des menschlichen Sprachbaues [1827–1829]." In *Werke in fünf Bänden: Bd. III: Schriften zur Sprachphilosophie*, 3rd ed., ed. Andreas Flitner and Klaus Giel, 144–367. Darmstadt: Wissenschaftliche Buchgesellschaft, 1963.
Hyndman, Jennifer. "Border Crossings." *Antipode* 29, no. 2 (1997): 149–76.
International Organization for Migration (IOM). *Der Einfluss von Immigration auf die österreichische Gesellschaft*. Vienna: IOM, 2004.
Jabloner, Clemens, and der Historikerkommission der Republik Österreich. *Schlussbericht der Historikerkommission der Republik Österreich: Vermögensentzug während der NS-Zeit sowie Rückstellungen und Entschädigungen seit 1945 in Österreich: Zusammenfassungen und Einschätzungen*. Vienna: Oldenburg, 2003.
Jaffrelot, Christophe. *Les nationalistes hindous: Idéologie, implantation et mobilisation des années 1920 aux années 1990*. Paris: Presses de Sciences Politique, 1993.
Janyr, Premysl. "Tschechoslowakei 1968—Charta 77." In *Asylland wider Willen: Flüchtlinge im europäischen Kontext seit 1914*, edited by Gernot Heiss and Oliver Rathkolb, 182--87. Vienna: J & V Edition, 1995.
Jestaedt, Mathias, and the Hans-Kelsen-Institut, eds. *Hans Kelsen im Selbstzeugnis: Sonderpublikation anlässlich des 125. Geburtstages von Hans Kelsen am 11. Oktober 2006*. Tübingen: Mohr Siebeck, 2006.
Joklík, František. *O poměrech českého národního školství a učitelstva v kralovství českem*. Prague: V. Praze, 1900.
Johler, Reinhard. "A Local Construction—Or: What Have the Alps to do with a Global Reading of the Mediterranean?" *Narodna umjetnost* 36, no. 1 (1999): 87–102.
John, Michael. "Die Auswanderung aus Österreich 1919–1937." In *Auswanderung aus Österreich: Von der Mitte des 19. Jahrhunderts bis zur Gegenwart*, edited by Traude Horvath and Gerde Neyer, 83–110. Vienna: Böhlau, 1996.
———. "National Movements and Imperial Ethnic Hegemonies in Austria, 1867–1918." In *The Historical Practice of Diversity: Transcultural Interactions from the Early Modern Mediterranean to the Postcolonial World*, edited by Dirk Hoerder, Christiane Harzig, and Adrian Shubert, 87–105. New York: Berghahn Books, 2003.
———. "Organisationsformen der Wanderminoritäten in Österreich 1867–1925: Thesen und Überlegungen." *Beiträge zur Geschichte der Arbeiterbewegung* 38, no. 2 (1996): 20–32.
———. "Upper Austria, Intermediate Stop: Reception Camps and Housing Schemes for Jewish DPs and Refugees in Transit." *The Journal of Israeli History* 19, no. 3 (Autumn 1998): 21–46.
———. "Von der Anwerbung der 'Gastarbeiter' bis zu den Folgen der Globalisierung: Arbeitsmigration in Österreich." In *Migration—eine Zeitreise nach Europa. Ausstellungskatalog*, edited by Michael John and Manfred Lindorfer, 5–26. Linz, 2003.
———. "'We Do Not Even Posses Our Selves': On Identity and Ethnicity in Austria 1880–1937." *Austrian History Yearbook* 30 (1999): 17–64.
John, Michael, and Albert Lichtblau. *Schmelztiegel Wien—einst und jetzt*. 2nd ed. Vienna: Böhlau, 1993.
Joyce, James. *The Critical Writings of James Joyce*. Edited by Ellsworth Mason and Richard Ellmann. New York: Viking Press, 1959.

Judson, Pieter M. *Exclusive Revolutionaries: Liberal Politics, Social Experience, and National Identity in the Austrian Empire.* Ann Arbor: University of Michigan Press, 1996.

———. *Guardians of the Nation: Activists on the Language Frontiers of Imperial Austria.* Cambridge, MA: Harvard University Press, 2006.

Kafka, Franz. *Briefe 1902–1924.* Frankfurt: Fischer, 1966.

Kappus, Elke-Nicole. "Imperial Ideologies of Peoplehood in Habsburg—An Alternative Approach to Peoples and Nations in Istria." *Annales* 12, no. 2 (2002): 321–30.

Kargl, M., and S. Lehmann, eds., *Land im Lichtermeer: Stimmen gegen Fremdenfeindlichkeit.* Vienna: Picus, 1994.

Karner, Stefan, Ingrid Kubin, and Michael Steiner. "Wie real war 'Mitteleuropa'? Zur wirtschaftlichen Verflochtenheit des Donauraumes nach dem Ersten Weltkrieg." *Vierteljahresschrift für Sozial- und Wirtschaftsgeschichte* 74, no. 2 (1987): 153–85.

Kelly, T. Mills. "'Taking It to the Streets': Czech National Socialists in 1908." *Austrian History Yearbook* 29 (1998): 93–112.

Kertzer, David, and Dominique Arel. "Censuses, Identity Formation, and the Struggle for Political Power." In *Census and Identity: The Politics of Race, Ethnicity, and Language in National Censuses,* edited by David Kertzer and Dominique Arel, 1–42. Cambridge: Cambridge University Press, 2002.

Khundmiri, Alam. *Secularism, Islam and Modernity: Selected Essays of Alam Khundmiri.* Edited and with an introduction by M. T. Ansari. New Delhi: Sage, 2001.

King, Jeremy. *Budweisers into Czechs and Germans: A Local History of Bohemian Politics 1848–1948.* Princeton, NJ: Princeton University Press, 2002.

———. "The Nationalization of East-Central Europe: Ethnicism, Ethnicity, and Beyond." In *Staging the Past: The Politics of Commemoration in Habsburg Central Europe, 1848 to the Present,* edited by Maria Bucur and Nancy Wingfield, 112–52. West Lafayette, IN: Purdue University Press, 2001.

King, Robert D. *Nehru and the Language Politics of India.* Delhi: Oxford University Press, 1998.

Kitleruk, Jan. "Jak wstąpiłem do Legjonów Polskich." *Żołnierz Polski* 16 no. 7 (1 March 1934): 136–38.

Kizwalter, Tomasz. *O nowoczesności narodu: Przypadek Polski.* Warsaw: Wydawnictwo naukowe Semper, 1999.

Klabouch, Jiri. *Die Gemeindeselbstverwaltung in Österreich, 1848–1918.* Vienna: Verlag für Geschichte und Politik, 1968.

Klemperer, Victor. *Lingua Tertii Imperii, Notizbuch eines Philologen.* Leipzig, 1990.

Knight, Robert. "Liberal Values and Post-Nazi-Politics. The Slovenes of Carinthia." In *Demokratie: Modus und Telos: Beiträge für Anton Pelinka,* edited by Andrei S. Markovits and Sieglinde K. Rosenberger, 143–58. Vienna: Böhlau, 2001.

Komlosy, Andrea. "Innere Peripherien als Ersatz für Kolonien? Zentrenbildung und Peripherisierung in der Habsburgermonarchie." In *Zentren, Peripherien und kollektive Identitäten in Österreich-Ungarn,* edited by E. Hars and Fonds zur Förderung der Wissenschaftlichen Forschung (Austria), 55–78. Tübingen: Francke, 2006.

Kos, Wolfgang. "Winken zum Abschied, Winken zum Aufbruch." In *Gastarbajteri: 40 Jahre Arbeitsmigration,* edited by Hakan Gürses, Cornelia Kogoj, and Sylvia Mattl-Wurm, 12–17. Vienna: Mandelbaum, 2004.

Köves, Margit. "Jumping on to the Moving Train: Hungarian Responses to European Integration." In *Yearbook of the Goethe Society of India,* edited by Rajendra Dengle, 35–53. New Delhi: Madras German Book Centre, 2005.

Kreitner, Leopold B. "Der junge Kafka" In *"Als Kafka mir entgegenkam . . .": Erinnerungen an Franz Kafka*, edited by Hans-Gerd Koch, 45-54. Berlin: K. Wagenbach, 2005.

Krofta, V. K. "Im Amt mit Franz Kafka" In *"Als Kafka mir entgegenkam . . .": Erinnerungen an Franz Kafka*, edited by Hans-Gerd Koch, 92-94. Berlin: K. Wagenbach, 2005.

Kundera, Milan. "Einleitung zu einer Anthologie oder Über drei Kontexte." In *Die Prager Moderne: Erzählungen, Gedichte, Manifeste*, edited by Květoslav Chvatík, 7–22. Frankfurt: Suhrkamp, 1991.

Langthaler, H., ed. *Integration in Österreich: Sozialwissenschaftliche Befunde*. Innsbruck: Studien Verlag, 2010.

Lebhart, Gustav, and Rainer Münz. *Migration und Fremdenfeindlichkeit: Fakten, Meinungen und Einstellungen zu internationaler Migration, ausländischer Bevölkerung und staatlicher Ausländerpolitik in Österreich*. Vienna: IOAW, 1999.

Lebzelter, Viktor. "Eine rassenkundliche Übersichtsaufnahme des Burgenlandes." *Mitteilungen der Anthropologischen Gesellschaft in Wien* 67 (1937): 294–350.

Lenin, V. I. *Collected Works*, vol 19. Moscow: Progress Publishers, 1977. 503–7.

———. *Lenin on Language*. Moscow: Raduga Publishers, 1983.

Lewy, Guenter. *The Nazi Persecution of the Gypsies*. Oxford: Oxford University Press, 2000.

Lichtblau, Albert. "Juden in Österreich—Integration, Vernichtungsversuch und Neubeginn: Österreichisch-jüdische Geschichte 1848 bis zur Gegenwart." In *Geschichte der Juden in Österreich*, edited by Evelyn Brugger, Martha Keil, Albert Lichtblau, Christoph Lind, and Barbara Staudinger, 449–91. Vienna: Ueberreuter, 2006.

Lichtenberger, Elisabeth. *Gastarbeiter: Leben in zwei Gesellschaften*. Vienna: H. Böhlaus, 1984.

Lory, Bernard. "Religiöse und ethnische Minderheiten und Mehrheiten im Westlichen Balkan aus historischer Perspektive." Paper presented at the 45th Internationale Hochschulwoche Inklusion und Exklusion auf dem Westbalkan, Akademie für politische Bildung, Tutzing, 10 October 2006.

Lotman, Juriji M. "Zur Struktur, Spezifik und Typologie der Kultur." In *Aufsätze zur Theorie und Methodologie der Literatur und Kultur*, edited by Karl Eimermacher, 320–436. Kronberg: Scriptor, 1974.

Lovoziuk, Petr. "Karlov/Libindsorf: A Village in Discourse, a Discourse in a Village: Preliminary Research Report." *Fieldwork and Local Communities: Prague Occasional Papers in Ethnology* 7 (2005): 146–73.

Lucassen, Leo. "Is Transnationalism Compatible with Assimilation? Examples from Western Europe since 1850." *IMIS-Beiträge* 29 (2006): 15–35.

Luhmann, Niklas. "Der Staat des politischen Systems: Geschichte und Stellung der Weltgesellschaft." In *Perspektiven der Weltgesellschaft*, edited by Ulrich Beck, 345–80. Frankfurt: Suhrkamp, 1998.

Luthar, Oto. "Possessing the Past: The Problem of Historical Representation in the Process of Reinventing Democracy in Eastern Europe—the Case of Slovenia." *Filozofski vestnik—Acta Philosophica* 18, no. 2 (1997): 233–56.

Lützeler, Paul Michael, ed. *Europa: Analysen und Visionen der Romantiker*. Frankfurt: Insel, 1982.

Lyotard, Jean-François. *La condition postmoderne*. Paris: Éd. de minuit, 1979.

Maass, Christiane, and Anette Volmer, eds. *Mehrsprachigkeit in der Renaissance*. Heidelberg: Universitätsverlag Winter 2005.

Mach, Ernst. "Auszüge aus den Notizbüchern 1871–1910." In *Ernst Mach: Werk und Wirkung*, edited by Rudolf Haller and Friedrich Stadler, 167–211. Vienna: Hölder-Pichler-Tempsky, 1998.

Maciejewski, Jerzy K. "Odkrywamy Huculszczyznę." In *Huculskim szlakiem II Brygady Legionów Polskich*, 28-34. Warsaw: Wydawnictwo Towarzystwa Przyjaciół Huculszczyzny, 1934.

Maderthaner, Wolfgang. "Die Juden und das Rote Wien." In *Wien, Stadt der Juden: Die Welt der Tante Jolesch*, edited by Joachim Riedl, 144–46. Vienna: Zsolny, 2004.

Mádl, Antal. *Nikolaus Lenau und sein kulturelles und sozialpolitisches Umfeld*. Munich: IKGS- Verlag, 2005.

Mähner, Peter. "Grenze als Lebenswelt: Gnadlersdorf (Hnanice), ein südmährisches Dorf an der Grenze." In *Grenze im Kopf: Beiträge zur Geschichte der Grenze in Ostmitteleuropa*, edited by Peter Haslinger, 67–102. Frankfurt: Peter Lang, 1999.

Malfèr, Stefan. "Die Sprachenfrage und der verstärkte Reichsrat von 1860." In *Jenseits und diesseits der Leitha. Elektronische Festschrift für Éva Somogyi zum 70. Geburtstag*, edited by Imre Ress and Dániel Szabó, 93–118. Budapest: MTA Történettudományi Intézet, 2007.

Malinowski, Bronislaw. *A Scientific Theory of Culture and other Essays*. Chapel Hill: University of North Carolina Press, 1944.

Manea, Norman. *The Hooligan's Return: A Memoir*. Translated by Angela Jinau. New York: Farrar Straus and Giroux, 2003.

Marranca, Bonnie, ed. *A Slice of Life*. New York: Duckworth, 2003.

Marsalek, Hans. "Das KZ Mauthausen (Stammlager) 1938-1945." In *Oberösterreichische Gedenkstätten für KZ-Opfer*, edited by Siegfried Haider, 45–51. Linz: Oö. Landesarchiv, 2001.

Marx, Karl. "Der Fetischcharakter der Ware und sein Geheimnis." In *Das Kapital: Kritik der politischen Ökonomie*, vol. 1, 85–98. Berlin: [DDR]: Dietz, 1989.

Martín-Barbero, Jesús. *Communication, Culture, and Hegemony: From the Media to Mediations*. Translated by Elizabeth Fox and Robert A. White with an introduction by Philip Schlesinger. London: Sage, 1993.

Massey, Doreen. "Politics and Space/Time." In *Place and the Politics of Identity*, edited by Michael Keith and Steve Pile, 141–62. London: Routledge, 1993.

Massiczek, Albert. *Ich war Nazi: Faszination—Ernüchterung—Bruch: Ein Lebensbericht: Erster Teil (1916–1938)*. Vienna: Junius, 1988.

Mauthner, Fritz. *Der letzte Deutsche von Blatna*. Berlin: Ullstein & Co., 1913.

McLuhan, Marshall. *Understanding Media: The Extensions of Man*. New York: McGraw Hill, 1964.

Mearsheimer, John. J., and Robert A. Pape. "The Answer: A Three-Way Partition Plan for Bosnia and How the US Can Enforce It." *The New Republic* 14 (June 1993): 22–28.

Mearsheimer, John J., and Stephen Van Ever. "When Peace Means War: The Partition that Dare not Speaks its Name." *The New Republic* 18 (December 1995): 16–21.

Meinecke, Friedrich. *Weltbürgertum und Nationalstaat*. Edited by Hans Herzfeld. Munich: R. Oldenbourg, 1962.

Meißners, Alfred. Letter to Moritz Hartmann, 24 August 1839. In *Briefe aus dem Vormärz: Eine Sammlung aus dem Nachlaß Moritz Hartmanns*, Bibliothek deutscher Schriftsteller aus Böhmen, Mähren und Schlesien 30, ed. Otto Wittner. Prague: J. G. Calve, 1911.

Menczel, Phillipp. *Trügerische Lösungen: Erlebnisse und Betrachtungen eines Österreichers*. Stuttgart: Deutsche Verlags-anstalt, 1932.

Minnich, Robert Gary. "At the Interface of the Germanic, Romance, and Slavic Worlds: Folk Culture As an Idiom of Collective Self-Images in Southeastern Alps." *Studia ethnologica* (1990): 163–80.

Mischler, Marie. *Soziale und wirtschaftliche Skizzen aus der Bukowina*. Vienna and Leipzig: L. Weiss, 1893.
Moravske Toplice. Council of Commune Minutes. 26–27 May 1996.
Moretti, Franco. "Conjectures on World Literature." *New Left Review* 1 (January/February 2000): 54–68.
Morley, David, and Kevin Robins. *Spaces of Identity: Global Media, Electronic Landscapes and Cultural Boundaries*. London: Routledge, 1995.
Moser, Jonny. *Demographie der jüdischen Bevölkerung Österreichs 1938–1945*. Vienna: Dokumentationsarchiv des Österreichischen Widerstandes (DÖW), 1999.
Mozetič, Gerhard, ed. *Austromarxistische Positionen*. Vienna: Böhlau, 1983.
Müller-Funk, Wolfgang, Peter Plener, and Clemens Ruthner, eds. *Kakanien Revisited: Das Eigene und das Fremde der österreichisch- ungarischen Monarchie*. Tübingen: Francke, 2002.
Murber, Ibolya, and Zoltán Fónagy. *Die ungarische Revolution und Österreich 1956*. Vienna: Czernin, 2006.
Musil, Robert. "Nation als Ideal und Wirklichkeit (1921)." In *Robert Musil, Tagebücher, Aphorismen, Essays und Reden,* edited by Adolf Frisé. Hamburg: Rowohlt Verlag, 1955.
Nadas, Peter. "The Citizen of the World and the Buck Goat." Translated by Tim Wilkinson. *Common Knowledge* 11, no. 1 (Winter 2005): 8–17. Available online at http://muse.jhu.edu/login?uri=/journals/common_knowledge/v011/11.1nadas.html.
Naumann, Friedrich. *Mitteleuropa*. Berlin: Reimer, 1915.
Nehru, Jawaharlal. *An Autobiography*. New Delhi: Oxford, 1989.
———. *The Discovery of India*. New Delhi: Oxford University Press, 1997.
Neumann, Johann. *Tschechische Familiennamen in Wien*. Vienna: Holzhausen, 1972.
Newman, Barbara. *Pedaling Poland*. London: H. Jenkins, 1935.
Nikočević, Lidija. "Negotiating Borders: Myth, Rhetoric, and Political Relations." *Focaal* 41 (2003): 95–105.
———. "State Culture and the Laboratory of Peoples: Istrian Ethnography during the Austro- Hungarian Monarchy." *Narodna umjetnost* 43, no. 1 (2006): 41–57.
———. "Trying to Grasp Multiculturality: New Museological Practice in Istria." Paper presented at the ICME sessions, ICOM Triennial conference, Barcelona, July 2001.
Nimni, Ephraim J. "Introduction for the English-Reading Audience." In *Otto Bauer: The Question of Nationalities and Social Democracy,* edited by Ephraim J. Nimni, xv–xlvii. Minneapolis: University of Minnesota Press, 2000.
Nora, Pierre. "Comment écrire l'histoire de France?" In *Les Lieux de mémoire,* vol. 2, edited by Pierre Nora, 2219–39. Paris: Gallimard, 1997.
Noveck, Beth S. "Hugo Bettauer and the Political Culture of the First Republic." In *Austria in the Nineteen Fifties,* Contemporary Austrian Studies 3, edited by Günter Bischof, Anton Pelinka, and Rolf Steininger, 138–70. New Brunswick, NJ: Transaction, 1995.
Ogris, Werner. "Die Entwicklung des österreichischen Gemeinderechts im 19. Jahrhundert." In *Die Städte Mitteleuropas im 19. Jahrhundert,* edited by Wilhelm Rausch, 85–90. Linz: Der Arbitskreis, 1983.
Ołdakowska-Kuflowa, Mirosława. *Stanisław Vincenz pisarz, humanista, orędownik zbliżenia narodów: Biografia*. Lublin: Towarzystwo Naukowe Katolickiego Uniwersytetu Lubelskiego Jana Pawła II, 2006.
Ornig, Nikola. *Die Zweite Generation und der Islam in Österreich*. Graz: Leykam, 2006.
Örs, Ilay. "Coffeehouses, Cosmopolitanism, and Pluralizing Modernities in Istanbul." *Journal of Mediterranean Studies* 12, no. 1 (2002): 119–45.

Österreichischer Rundfunk. *Der Islam und der Westen: Fakten, Ängste, Vorurteile.* 2 CDs. Vienna: 2007.
Palme, Imma. "Issue-Voting: Themen und thematische Positionen als Determinanten der Wahlentscheidung." In *Das österreichische Wahlverhalten,* edited by F. Plasser and P. Ulram, 243–59. Vienna: Signum, 2000.
Pandey, Gyanendra. *The Construction of Communalism in Colonial North India.* Delhi: Oxford University Press, 1992.
Pannikar, K. N. *Culture, Ideology, Hegemony: Intellectuals and Social Consciousness in Colonial India.* New Delhi: Tulika, 1995.
Pantzer, Peter, Kunitake Kume, and Matthias Eichorn, eds. *Die Iwakura-Mission: Das Logbuch des Kume Kunitake über den Besuch der japanischen Sondergesandtschaft in Deutschland, Österreich und der Schweiz im Jahre 1873.* Munich: Iudicium, 2002.
Parnreiter, Christof. "Restriktive Migrationspolitik und ihr Scheitern an der Wirklichkeit." In *Herausforderung Migration: Beiträge zur Aktions- und Informationswoche der Universität Wien anlässlich des "UN International Migrant's Day,"* Abhandlungen zur Geographie und Regionalforschung 7, edited by Susanne Binder, Gabriele Rasuly-Paleczek, and Maria Six-Hohenbalken, 35–49. Vienna: Institut für Geographie und Regionalforschung, 2005.
Patnaik, Prabhat. *The Retreat to Unfreedom: Essays on the emerging World Order.* New Delhi: Tulika, 2003.
Pawlowsky, Verena. "Profilierung im Mangel: Die Anthropologische Abteilung des Naturhistorischen Museums in Wien vor 1938." *Zeitgeschichte* 3 (May/June 2003): 150–62.
Perchinig, Bernhard. "Migration Studies in Austria—Research at the Margins." *KMI Working Paper Series* 4 (2002).
Pichler, D. "Grenzenlose Pflege: Eine quantitative und qualitative Analyse am Beispiel tschechischer und slowakischer Pflegekräfte in Österreich." Univ. Dipl. Arb., University of Linz, 2005.
Pierré-Caps, Stéphane. *La multination: L'avenir des minorités en Europa centrale et orientale* Paris: O. Jacob, 1995.
Pieterse, Jan Neverdeen. "Der Melange-Effekt. Globalisierung im Plural." In *Perspektiven der Weltgesellschaft,* edited by Ulrich Beck, 87–124. Frankfurt: Suhrkamp, 1998.
Pilgram, Arno, ed. *Grenzöffnung, Migration, Kriminalität: Jahrbuch für Rechts- und Kriminalsoziologie 1993.* Baden-Baden: Nomos Verlagsgesellschaft, 1993.
Pinwinkler, Alexander. "'Bevölkerungssoziologie' und Ethnizität: Historisch-demografische Minderheitenforschung in Österreich, ca. 1918–1938." *ZfG Zeitschrift für Geschichtswissenschaft* 57, no. 2 (February 2009): 101–33.
Plasser, Fritz, and Peter A. Ulram. "Rechtspopulistische Resonanzen: Die Wählerschaft der FPÖ." In *Das österreichische Wahlverhalten,* edited by F. Plasser and P. Ulram, 225–42. Vienna: Signum, 2000.
Prato, Katharina. *Nauk o gospodinjstvu, Založba umetniška propaganda.* 2nd ed. Ljubljana: Umetniska propaganda, 1935.
Prochasko, Jurko. "Die Sarmatische Zivilisation." In *Sarmatische Landschaften: Nachrichten aus Litauen, Belarus, der Ukraine, Polen und Deutschland,* edited by Martin Pollack, 233–48. Frankfurt: Fischer Verlag, 2005.
Promitzer, Christian. "The South Slavs in the Austrian Imagination." In *Creating the Other: Ethnic Conflict and Nationalism in Habsburg Central Europe,* edited by N. M. Wingfield, 183–215. New York: Berghahn Books, 2004.
Rahman, Tariq. *Language and Politics in Pakistan.* Karachi: Oxford University Press, 2003.

Rai, Alok. *Hindi Nationalism*. Delhi: Orient Blackswan Pvt Ltd, 2001.
Rathkolb, Oliver. *Die paradoxe Republik*. Vienna: Zsolnay, 2006.
———, ed. *NS-Zwangsarbeit: Der Standort Linz der "Reichswerke Hermann Göring AG Berlin" 1938–1945*. Vol. 1. Vienna: Böhlau, 2001.
Raudaschl, Hannes. "Zur Wirtschafts- und Sozialgeschichte des Skisports in Österreich: Die Firma Fischer-Ski." Univ. Dipl. Arb., University of Linz, 2003.
Rauscher, K.H. "Die ökonomische und soziale Entwicklung von Steyr im Nationalsozialismus unter besonderer Berücksichtigung der lokalen Großindustrie." PhD diss., University of Linz, 1998.
Ravikant and Tarun K. Saint, eds. *Translating Partition: Essays, Stories, Criticism*. New Delhi: Katha, 2001.
Redlich, Josef. *Das Wesen der österreichischen Kommunal-Verfassung*. Leipzig: Duncker & Humboldt, 1910.
Reichensperger, Richard. "Zur Wiener Stadtsemiotik von Adalbert Stifter bis H. C. Artmann." In *Literatur als Text der Kultur,* edited by Moritz Csáky and Richard Reichensperger, 159–83. Vienna: Passagen, 1999.
Reiz, R. "Polnische Migration nach Österreich im 20. Jahrhundert." Univ. Dipl.Arb., University of Linz, 2004.
Republik Österreich, Bundesministerium für Inneres Asylstatistik. *Migration and Integration: Zahlen. daten. indikatoren 2011* (Vienna: Statistik Austria 2011). http://www.bmi.gv.at/cms/BMI_Asylwesen/statistik/files/2011/Asylstatistik_Dezember_2011.pdf (accessed 15 January 2012).
Retamar, Robert Fernández. *Calibán*. Mexico City: Ed. Diógenes, 1971.
Rezzori, Gregor von. *Blumen in Schnee*. Munich: C. Bertelsmann, 1969.
———. *The Snows of Yesteryear: Portraits for an Autobiography*. Translated by H. F. Broch de Rotherman. New York: Knopf, 1989.
Richardson, Tanya. *Kaleidoscopic Odessa: History and Place in Contemporary Ukraine*. Toronto: University of Toronto, 2008.
———. "Living Cosmopolitanism? 'Tolerance,' Religion, and Local Identity in Odessa." In *The Postsocialist Question: Faith and Power in Central Asia and East-Central Europe,* edited by Chris Hann and the "Civil Religion" Group, 213–40. Berlin: LIT, 2006.
Rihtman-Auguštin, Dunja. "A Croatian Controversy: Mediterranean-Danube-Balkans." *Narodna umjetnost* 36, no. 1 (1999): 103–19.
Rioux, Jean-Pierre. "La mémoire culturelle." In *Pour une histoire culturelle,* edited by Jean Pierre Rioux and Jean-François Sirinelli, 325–53. Paris: Editions du Seuil, 1997.
Robbins, Bruce. "Actually Existing Cosmopolitanism." In *Cosmopolitics: Thinking and Feeling Beyond the Nation,* edited by Pheng Cheah and Bruce Robbins, 1–19. Minneapolis: University of Minnesota Press, 1997.
Rodó, José Enrique. *Ariel*. Montevideo, 1900.
Rogelja, Natasa. "Sea Fetishism: On the Shore-Dwelling Population." In *Proceedings of Mediterranean Ethnological School,* vol. 6, edited by Bostjan Kavanja and Matej Vranjes, 89–114. Ljubljana: Filozofska fakulteta, 2005.
Rojas, Ricardo. *"Eurindia. Ensayo de estética sobre las culturas americanas."* Buenos Aires, 1951.
Rössner, Michael. "Barock als Element mitteleuropäischer und lateinamerikanischer Identität— Überlegungen zur Konstruktion und 'Innenausstattung' von Gedächtnisorten." In *Barock: Ein Ort des Gedächtnisses: Interpretament der Moderne/Postmoderne,* edited by Moritz Csáky, Federico Celestini, and Ulrich Tragatschnig, 47–64. Vienna: Böhlau, 2007.

———. " Ein Blick auf Weltordnungen und Zwischenwelten vom 16. bis zum 20 Jahrhundert." In *Andersheit: Von der Eroberung bis zu New World Borders: das Eigene und das Fremde: Globalisierungs-und Hybriditätsstrategien in Lateinamerika*, edited by Alfonso de Toro, 41-60. Hildesheim: Olms, 2008.

Rössner, Michael, ed. *Literarische Kaffeehäuser: Kaffeehausliteraten*. Vienna: Böhlau, 1999.

Roth, Joseph. "Grillparzer: Ein Porträt." In *Joseph Roth Werke*, vol. 3, *Das journalistische Werk 1929–1939*, edited by Klaus Westermann. Cologne: Kiepenheuer & Witsch, 1989–91.

Roth, Klaus. "Toward 'Politics of Interethnic Coexistence': Can Europe Learn from the Multiethnic Empires?" In *Europe: Cultural Construction and Reality*, edited by Peter Niedermüller and Bjarne Stoklund, 37–51. Copenhagen: Museum Tusculanum Press (University of Copenhagen), 2001.

Rotteck, Carl von, and Carl Welcker, eds. "Oestreich." In *Staats-Lexikon oder Encyklopädie der Staatswissenschaften*, vol. 12, 125-235. Altona: Hammerich, 1841.

Rozenblit, Marsha. *The Jews of Vienna 1867–1914: Assimilation and Identity*. Albany: SUNY Press, 1983.

———. "Sustaining Austrian 'National' Identity in Crisis: The Dilemma of the Jews in Habsburg Austria, 1914–1919." In *Constructing Nationalities in East Central Europe*, edited by Pieter Judson, 178–91. New York: Berghahn Books, 2005.

Rudigier, Andreas. "Ein Beitrag zur rechtlichen Stellung der trentinischen und italienischen Migranten: Staatsbürgerschaft und Heimatrecht: Theorie und Praxis mit besonderer Berücksichtigung von Bludenz." In *Auswanderung aus dem Trentino—Einwanderung nach Vorarlberg: Die Geschichte einer Migrationsbewegung mit besonderer Berücksichtigung der Zeit von 1870/1880 bis 1919*, edited by K. H. Burmeister and R. Rollinger, 151–88. Sigmaringen: Thorbecke, 1995.

Rudolf, Crown Prince of Austria, ed. *Oesterreichisch-Ungarische Monarchie in Wort und Bild: Auf Anregung und unter Mitwirkung weiland seiner kaiserl. und königl. Hoheit des durchlauchtigsten Kronprinzen Erzherzog Rudolf begonnen, fortgesetzt unter dem Protectorate Ihrer kaiserl. und konigl. Hoheit der durchlauchtigsten Frau Kronprinzessin-Witwe Erzherzogin Stephanie*, 24 vols. Vienna, 1886–1902.

Rudolf, Crown Prince of Austria. "Einleitung." In *Die Österreichisch-Ungarische Monarchie in Wort und Bild*, vol. 1, edited by Rudolf, 5. Vienna, 1886.

Rumici, Guido. *Fratelli d'Istria, 1945–2000: Italiani Divisi*. Milan: Mursia, 2001.

Rushdie, Salman. "Commonwealth Literature Does Not Exist." In *Imaginary Homelands: Essays and Criticism 1981–1991*, 61–70. London: Granta, 1991.

———. "On Palestinian Identity: A Conversation with Edward Said." In *Imaginary Homelands: Essays and Criticism 1981–1991*, 166–84. London: Granta, 1991.

Ruthner, Clemens. "'K.(u.)K. Postcolonial?' Für eine neue Lesart der österreichischen (und benachbarter) Literatur/en." In *Kakanien revisited: Das Eigene und das Fremde (in) der österreichisch-ungarischen Monarchie*, Kultur—Herrschaft—Differenz 1, edited by Wolfgang Müller-Funk, Peter Plener, and Clemens Ruthner. Tübingen: Francke, 2002.

Said, Edward. *Orientalism*. London: Chatto and Windus, 1978.

———. *L'Orientalisme: L'Orient crée par l'Occident*. Paris: Editions du Seuil, 1980.

Salgado, Cesar Augusto. "Hybridity in New World Baroque Theory." *The Journal of American Folklore* 112, no. 445 (Summer 1999): 316–31.

Sandner, Günther. "Zwischen Anerkennung und Differenz: Die Nationalitätentheorien von Karl Renner und Otto Bauer im Kontext." In *Eigene und andere Fremde: "Postkoloniale" Konflikte im europäischen Kontext*, edited by Wolfgang Müller-Funk and Brigitte Wagner, 20–104. Vienna: Turia and Kant, 2005.

Sant Cassia, Paul, and Isabel Schäfer. "'Mediterranean Conundrums': Pluridisciplinary Perspectives for Research in the Social Sciences." *History and Anthropology* 16, no. 1 (2002): 1–23.
Sarlo, Beatriz. *Una modernidad periférica: Buenos Aires 1920 y 1930.* Buenos Aires: Nueva Visión, 1988.
Sarmiento, Domingo Faustino. "Facundo: Civilización y Barbarie." *El Progreso* (1845).
Sauer, Walter. "Afro-österreichische Dispora heute: Migration und Integration in der 2. Republik." In *Von Soliman zu Omofuma: Afrikanische Diaspora in Österreich 17. bis 20. Jahrhundert,* edited by W. Sauer, 189–233. Innsbruck: Studien Verlag, 2007.
Savarkar, Vinayak D. "Some of the Basic Principles and Tenets of the Hindu Movement." In *Between Tradition and Modernity: India's Search for Identity: A Twentieth Century Anthology,* edited by Fred Dallmayr and G. N. Devy. New Delhi: Sage Publications, 1998.
Scheuringer, Brunhilde. "Szenarien zur Integration der volksdeutschen Flüchtlinge und Vertriebenen nach dem Zweiten Weltkrieg in Österreich." In *Österreichischer Zeitgeschichtetag 1993,* edited by Ingrid Böhler and Rolf Steininger. Vienna: Österreichischer Studien Verlag, 1995.
Schlegel, Friedrich. *Friedrich Schlegel: Kritische Ausgabe.* 35 vols. Edited by Ernst Behler. Munich: Ferdinand Schöningh, 1967.
Schmitt, Carl. *Staat, Bewegung, Volk: Die Dreigliederung der politischen Einheit.* Hamburg: Hanseatische Verlagsanstalt 1933.
———. *Verfassungslehre.* 4th ed. Berlin: Duncker & Humblot 1965.
Schönfeldt, Sybil Gräfin. *"Feine Leute kommen spät . . ." oder Bei Thomas Mann zu Tisch: Tafelfreuden im Lübecker Buddenbrookhaus.* Zürich: Arche, 2004.
Schwartner, Martin. *Statistik des Königreichs Ungern.* Pest: Gedruckt bey M. Trattner, 1798.
Seliger, Maren, and Karl Ucakar. *Wien: Politische Geschichte 1740–1934,* vol. 2, *1896–1934.* Vienna: Jugend und Volk, 1985.
Sensenig-Dabbous, Eugene. "Social Democracy in One Country: Immigration and Minority Policy in Austria." In *The European Union and Migrant Labour,* edited by G. Dale and M. Cole, 203–28. New York: Berg, 1999.
Simmel, Georg. "Exkurs über den Fremden." In *Soziologie: Untersuchungen über die Formen der Vergesellschaftung,* 764–71. Frankfurt: Suhrkamp 1992.
———. *The Sociology of Georg Simmel.* Translated, edited, and with an introduction by Kurt H. Wolff. Glencoe, IL: Free Press, 1950.
Simonek, Stefan. *Distanzierte Nähe: Die slawische Moderne der Donaumonarchie und Die Wiener Moderne.* Bern: P. Lang, 2000.
———. "Tadeusz Rittners literarisches Debüt im Rahmen der Wiener Moderne." In *Distanzierte Nähe: Die slawische Moderne der Donaumonarchie und die Wiener Moderne,* 19–62. Bern: P. Lang, 2000.
Simsund. "Europa i Polska wobec Huculszczyzny." *Gazeta Poranna,* 18 February 1934.
Sluga, Glenda. "Bodies, Souls, and Sovereignty: The Austro-Hungarian Empire and the Legitimacy of Nations." *Ethnicities* 1, no. 2 (2001): 89–100.
Smith, Anthony D. *Nationalism in the Twentieth Century.* New York: New York University Press, 1979.
Snyder, Timothy. *Sketches from a Secret War: A Polish Artist's Mission to Liberate Soviet Ukraine.* New Haven, CT: Yale University Press, 2005.
Solidarität. Zeitschrift des Österreichischen Gewerkschaftsbundes. July/August 1969.
Sosa, Aurelio Miro Quesada. "El Inca Garcilaso de la Vega: El mestizaje racial y cultural." In *Encuentro de dos mundos,* edited by Germán Peralta Rivera, 27–49. Lima: Banco de la Nación, Departamento de Comunicación Social y Relaciones Institucionales, 1991.

Soxberger, Thomas. "Die jiddische Literatur und Publizistik im Wien der zwanziger Jahre." In *Berlin-Wien-Prag: Moderne, Minderheiten und Migration in der Zwischenkriegszeit*, edited by S. Marten-Finnis and M. Uecker, 243–54. Bern: Lang, 2001.
Stachel, Peter. "Alfred Ilg und die 'Erfindung' des Barocks als österreichischer 'Nationalstil.'" In *Barock: Ein Ort des Gedächtnisses: Interpretament der Moderne/Postmoderne*, edited by Moritz Csáky, Federico Celestini, and Ulrich Tragatschnig, 101–51. Vienna: Böhlau, 2007.
———. "Übernationales Gesamtstaatsbewusstsein in der Habsburgermonarchie: Zwei Fallbeispiele." Available online at http://www.kakanien.ac.at/beitr/fallstudie/Pstachel1.pdf.
Stanek, Eduard. *Verfolgt, verjagt, vertrieben: Flüchtlinge in Österreich von 1945–1984*. Vienna: Europaverlag, 1985.
Statistische Nachrichten 4 (1926): 122–30.
Statistische Nachrichten—Statistische Übersichten (Vienna: ÖSTAT/WIFO, 1963–73).
Statistisches Handbuch für die Republik Österreich. Vol. 6. Vienna, 1925.
———. Vol. 8. Vienna, 1927.
Statistisches Handbuch Österreichs 1968. Vienna, 1968.
Statistisches Handbuch Österreichs 1974. Vienna, 1974.
Statistisches Jahrbuch der Stadt Wien für das Jahr 1912. Vienna, 1914.
Statistisches Jahrbuch Österreichs 2007. Vienna, 2007.
Statistik Austria, ed. *Die Ergebnisse der Volkszählung 2001: Hauptergebnisse I—Wien*. Vienna, 2003.
Statistik Austria and Kommission für Migrations- und Integrationsforschung der Österreichischen Akademie der Wissenschaften, eds. *Migration and Integration: Zahlen. daten. indikatoren 2010*. Vienna: Statistik Austria 2010.
Statistik Austria Online, *Klassifikationen, Regionale Gliederungen, Bundesländer* https://www.statistik.at/web_de/klassifikationen/regionale_gliederungen/bundeslaender/index.html (accessed 10 August 2013).
———. *Statistische Übersichten, Beschäftigung und Arbeitsmarkt*, (Statistical Tables, Employment and Labor Market), 2007. http://www.statistik.at/web_de/services/stat_uebersichten/beschaeftigung_und_arbeitsmarkt/index.html (accessed 10 January 2012) https://www.statistik.at/web_de/services/stat_uebersichten/beschaeftigung_und_arbeitsmarkt/index.html (accessed 12 August 2013).
———. *Statistische Übersichten, Beschäftigung und Arbeitsmarkt*,(Statistical Tables, Employment and Labor Market), 2011. http://www.statistik.at/web_de/services/stat_uebersichten/beschaeftigung_und_arbeitsmarkt/index.html (accessed 10 January 2012).
———. *Population Statistics, Naturalizations*, 1998–2010. http://www.statistik.at/web_en/statistics/population/naturalisation/index.html (accessed 26 August 2013).
———. *Population Statistics, Population by nationality and country of birth*, 2011. http://www.statistik.at/web_en/statistics/population/population_change_by_demographic_characteristics/population_by_citizenship_and_country_of_birth/index.html (accessed 9 August 2013).
Steiniger, Rolf. *Austria, Germany and the Cold War: From the Anschluss to the State Treaty. 1938–1955*. New York: Berghahn Books, 2008.
Stieber, Gabriela. "Volksdeutsche und Displaced Persons." In *Asylland wider Willen: Flüchtlinge im europäischen Kontext seit 1914*, edited by Gernot Heiss and Oliver Rathkolb, 140–56. Vienna: J & V Edition, 1995.
Stifter, Adalbert. "Aussicht und Betrachtungen von der Spitze des St. Stephansturmes." In *Wien und die Wiener = Adalbert Stifter, die Mappe meines Urgroßvaters, Schilderungen, Briefe*, 281–301. Munich: Winkler, 1986.

Stourzh, Gerald. *Die Gleichberechtigung der Nationalitätenin der Verfassung und Verwaltung Österreichs, 1848–1918.* Vienna: VOAW, 1985.

———. "Ethnic Attribution in Late Imperial Austria: Good Intentions, Evil Consequences (1994)." In *From Vienna to Chicago and Back: Essays on Intellectual History and Political Thought in Europe and America,* edited by Gerald Stourzh, 157–76. Chicago: University of Chicago Press, 2007.

Subhramanyam, Sanjay. "Connected Histories: Notes towards a Reconfiguration of Early Modern Eurasia." *Modern Asian Studies* 31, no. 3 (1997): 735–61.

Sulzbacher, Cornelia. "Österreich und seine Volksgruppen (ethnic groups)." PhD diss., University of Salzburg, 2001.

Tagore, Rabindranath. "Nationalism in India." In *Between Tradition and Modernity: India's Search for Identity: A Twentieth Century Anthology,* edited by Fred Dallmayr and G. N. Devy. New Delhi: Sage Publications, 1998.

———. "National Language of India." In *The English Writings of Rabindranath Tagore,* vol. 3, *A Miscellany,* edited by Sisir Kumar Das, 736. New Delhi: Sahitya Akademi 1996.

Tezcan, Levent. "Operative Kultur und die Subjektivierungsstrategien in der Integrationspolitik." In *Wider den Kulturzwang: Migration, Kulturalisierung und Weltliteratur,* edited by Özkan Ezli, Dorothee Kimmich, Annette Werberger, with Stefanie Ulrich, 47–80. Bielefeld: Transcript, 2009.

Thapar, Romila. *History and Beyond: Interpreting Early India, Time as a Metaphor of History, Cultural Transaction and Early India and from Lineage to State.* New Delhi: Oxford University Press, 2000.

Thieleking, Sigrid. *Weltbürgertum: Kosmopolitische Idee in Literatur und politischer Publizistik seit dem achtzehnten Jahrhundert.* Munich: Fink Verlag, 2000.

Thorpe, J. "Pan-German Identity and the Press in Austria, 1933–1938." PhD diss., University of Adelaide, 2006.

Tönnies, Ferdinand. *Gemeinschaft und Gesellschaft, Grundbegriffe der reinen Soziologie.* Darmstadt: Wissenschaftliche Buchgesellschaft, 1991.

Trabant, Jürgen. *Mithridates im Paradies: Kleine Geschichte des Sprachdenkens.* Munich: C. H. Beck, 2003.

Tweraser, Kurt. *National Socialism in Linz: English Summary,* edited by Fritz Mayrhofer and Walter Schuster. Linz: Archiv der Stadt Linz, 2002.

Turczynski, Emanuel. *Geschichte der Bukowina in der Neuzeit.* Wiesbaden: Harrassowitz, 1993.

Turk, Horst, Brigitte Schultze, and Roberto Simanowski, eds. *Kulturelle Grenzziehungen im Spiegel der Literaturen: Nationalismus, Regionalismus, Fundamentalismus.* Göttingen: Wallstein, 1998.

Umlauft, Friedrich. *Die österreichisch-ungarische Monarchie: Geographisch-statistisches Handbuch mit besonderer Rücksicht auf politische und Cultur-Geschichte.* Vienna: Hartleben, 1883.

Valentino, Russell Scott. "Me Bastard, You Bastard: Multiculturalism at Home and Abroad." *The Iowa Review* 33, no. 1 (2003): 89–100.

Valeš, Vlasta. "Die tschechoslowakischen Flüchtlinge 1968–1989." In *Asylland wider Willen: Flüchtlinge im europäischen Kontext seit 1914,* edited by Gernot Heiss and Oliver Rathkolb, 172–81. Vienna: J & V Edition, 1995.

———. *Die Wiener Tschechen einst und jetzt.* Prague: Praha Scriptorium, 2004.

Van de Veer, Peter. *Religious Nationalism: Hindus and Muslims in India.* Delhi: Oxford University Press, 1996.

Vári, András. "The Functions of Ethnic Stereotypes in Austria and Hungary in the Early Nineteenth Century." In *Creating the Other: Ethnic Conflict and Nationalism in Habsburg Central Europe,* edited by Nancy M. Wingfield, 39–55. New York: Berghahn Books, 2003.

Vasconcelos, José. *La Raza Cósmica: Misión de la raza iberoamericana. Noras de viajes a la América del Sur.* Mexico D.F: Espasa Calpe, 1948.

Vega, Garcilaso de la. *Royal Commentaries of the Incas and General History of Peru.* Part I. Translated by Harold V. Livermore. Indianapolis, IN: Hackett, 2006.

Verdery, Katherine. *Transylvanian Villagers: Three Centuries of Political, Economic, and Ethnic Change.* Berkeley: University of California Press, 1984.

Vincenz, Stanisław. "Uwagi o kulturze ludowej." *Złoty Szlak,* no. 2 (1938).

Vivre Milena Jesenska. Exhibit, Wiener Festwochen. Vienna, 1990.

Vodopivec, Peter. *Od Pohlinove slovnice do samostojne slovenske države: Slovenska zgodovina od konca 18. stoletja do konca 20. Stoletja.* Ljubljana: Modrijan, 2006.

Vogl, Mathias. "Die jüngere Entwicklung im Bereich des Asyl und Fremdenrechts." In *Österreichischer Migrations- und Integrationsbericht 2001–2006,* edited by Heinz Fassmann, 19–40. Vienna: Verlag Drava, 2007.

Volkmer, Herman. *Die Volksdeutschen in Oberösterreich—ihre Integration und ihr Beitrag zum Wiederaufbau des Landes nach dem Zweiten Weltkrieg.* Grünbach: Steinmaßl 2003.

Wachtel, Andrew. *Making a Nation, Breaking a Nation: Literature and Cultural Politics in Yugoslavia.* Palo Alto, CA: Stanford University Press, 1998.

Wagner, Peter. "Gedenken an das Oberwarter Attentat." *Pannonia* 25, no. 2 (1997): 36–39.

Waldrauch, Harald, and Dilek Cinar. "Staatsbürgerschaft und Einbürgerungspraxis in Österreich." In *Österreichischer Migrations- und Integrationsbericht: Demographische Entwicklungen—sozioökonomische Strukturen—rechtliche Rahmenbedingungen,* edited by Heinz Fassmann and Irene Stacher, 261–84. Vienna: Verlag Drava, 2003.

Walicki, Andrzej. *The Enlightenment and the Birth of Modern Nationhood: Polish Political Thought from Noble Republicanism to Tadeusz Kościuszko.* Translated by Emma Harris. Notre Dame, IN: University of Notre Dame Press, 1989.

Wandruscka, Adam, and Peter Urbanitsch, eds. *Die Habsburger Monarchie 1848–1918,* vol. 3, *Die Völker des Reiches.* Vienna: VOAW, 1980.

Weber, Irena. "Heritage Narratives on the Slovenian Coast: The Lion and the Attic." In *Cultural Heritages As Reflexive Traditions,* edited by Ullrich Kockel and Mairead Nic Craith, 158–70. Houndmills: Palgrave Macmillan, 2007.

Wefelmeyer, Fritz. "Glück und Aporie des Kulturtheoretikers: Zu Johann Gottfried Herder und seiner Konzeption der Kultur." In *Naturplan und Verfallskritik: Zu Begriff und Geschichte der Kultur,* edited by Helmut Brackert and Fritz Wefelmeyer, 94–121. Frankfurt: Suhrkamp, 1984.

Weigl, Andreas. "Demographic Transitions Accelerated: Abortion, Body Politics, and the End of Supra- Regional Labor Immigration in Post-War Austria." In *From Empire to Republic: Post-World War I Austria,* Contemporary Austrian Studies 19, edited by G. Bischof, F. Plasser, and P. Berger, 142–70. Innsbruck: Innsbruck University Press, 2010.

———. *Migration und Integration: Eine widersprüchliche Geschichte.* Innsbruck: Studien Verlag, 2009.

Weiss, Hilde. *Nation und Toleranz: Empirische Studien zu nationalen Identitäten in Österreich.* With a contribution by Christoph Reinprecht. Vienna: Braumüller, 2004.

Weiss, Peter. *Notizbücher, 1960–1971.* 2 vols. Frankfurt: Suhrkamp, 1982.

———. *Rapporte.* Frankfurt: Suhrkamp, 1968.

Wiesenthal, Simon. *Recht, nicht Rache: Erinnerungen*. 3rd ed. Frankfurt: Ullstein, 1995.
Wimmer, Hannes. "Zur Ausländerbeschäftigungspolitik in Österreich." In *Ausländische Arbeitskräfte in Österreich*, edited by Hannes Wimmer, 5–32. Frankfurt: Campus, 1986.
Wittgenstein, Ludwig. *Philosophische Untersuchungen*. 3rd ed. Frankfurt: Suhrkamp 1975.
Wolf, Eric. *Europe and the People without History*. Berkeley: University of California Press, 1982.
Wolff, Larry. *Venice and the Slavs: The Discovery of Dalmatia in the Age of Enlightenment*. Palo Alto, CA: Stanford University Press, 2001.
Wollner, E. "Auf dem Weg zur sozialpartnerschaftlich regulierten Ausländerbeschäftigung in Österreich: Die Reform der Ausländerbeschäftigung und der Anwerbung bis Ende der 1960er Jahre." Univ. Dipl. Arb., University of Vienna, 1996.
Wonisch, Regina, ed. *Tschechen in Wien: Zwischen nationaler Selbstbehauptung und Assimilation*. Vienna: Löcker, 2010.
Zahra, Tara. "Imagined Non-Communities: National Indifference as a Category of Analysis." *Slavic Review* 69 (Spring 2010): 93–119.
———. *Kidnapped Souls: National Indifference and the Battle for Children in the Bohemian Lands, 1900–1948*. Ithaca, NY: Cornell University Press, 2008.
ZARA (Zivilcourage und Anti.Rassismus-Arbeit), ed. *Rassismus Report 2006: Einzelfall-Bericht über rassistische Übergriffe und Strukturen in Österreich*. Vienna: ZARA, 2007.
Zbinden, Hans. "Ostkarpatenland." *Der Bund,* nos. 23–25 (1933).
———. "Polenfahrt in stürmischer Zeit." *Der Bund,* nos. 427, 429, 431, 435, 437, 439, 441, 443 (1939).
Zea, Leopoldo. *En torno a una filosofía Americana* (Mexico, 1945).
Zemmrich, J. *Sprachgrenze und Deutschtum in Böhmen*. Braunschweig: F. Vieweg & Sohn, 1902.
Zierer, Brigitta. "Willkommene Ungarnflüchtlinge 1956?" In *Asylland wider Willen: Flüchtlinge im europäischen Kontext seit 1914,* edited by Gernot Heiss and Oliver Rathkolb, 157–71. Vienna: J & V Editions, 1995.
Žižek, Slavoj. *Ein Plädoyer für die Intoleranz*. Vienna: Passagen-Verlag, 1998.
Zuser, Peter. "Die Konstruktion der Ausländerfrage in Österreich: Eine Analyse des öffentlichen Diskurses 1990." *Political Science Series* 35 (1996): 1–89.

Contributors

Pamela Ballinger is Fred Cuny Professor of the History of Human Rights and Associate Professor of History at the University of Michigan. She is the author of *History in Exile: Memory and Identity at the Borders of the Balkans* (2003). She has published on topics such as refugees, displacement, ethnic cleansing, human rights, and the Adriatic seascape in journals that include *Comparative Studies in Society and History, Contemporary European History, Current Anthropology, History and Memory, Journal of Modern Italian Studies, New Global Studies,* and *Past and Present.*

Anil Bhatti is Professor Emeritus, Centre of German Studies, at the Jawaharlal Nehru University, New Delhi (India), where he served as dean of the School of Language, Literature and Culture Studies and of the School of Arts and Aesthetics. He has published widely on cultural plurality and multilinguality, cultural homogenization, diversities and similarities, and authenticity. He was a fellow of the Kulturwissenschaftliches Kolleg, Konstanz, in 2010–12. In 2011 he received the Research Award of the Alexander von Humboldt Foundation.

Gary B. Cohen is Professor of Modern Central European History at the University of Minnesota, Twin Cities, where he has also served as director of the Center for Austrian Studies (2001–10) and chair of the Department of History (2010–13). He is the author of *The Politics of Ethnic Survival: Germans in Prague, 1861–1914* (1981; 2nd ed., rev., 2006) and *Education and Middle-Class Society in Imperial Austria, 1848–1918* (1996); of articles on social development, ethnic group relations, and education in modern Austria and the Czech lands in *The Journal of Modern History, Central European History, The Austrian History Yearbook, Český časopis historický, The East European Quarterly, Jewish History,* and *The Social Science Quarterly;* and of many book chapters.

Andrei Corbea-Hoisie is Professor of German Literature at the University of Iași, Romania. From 2005 to 2007 he served as Ambassador of Romania in Austria. He is a member of the Academy of Sciences of Erfurt. Corbea-Hoisie is a leading expert on multiculturalism in the historical landscape of Bukovina, and author of *Czernowitzer Geschichten* (2002) and *La Bucovine: Éléments d'histoire politique et culturelle* (2004). He has also published widely on Paul Celan and on the urban culture of Central Europe, and has translated writings of Theodor W. Adorno. In 2000 he received the Jacob and Wilhelm Grimm Award.

Moritz Csáky is Professor of Austrian and Central European History at the University of Graz, Austria (retired). In Graz, he headed the Special Research Program of the Austrian Science Fund (FWF), "Modernity: Vienna and Central Europe around 1900" (1994–2004). He is a member of the Austrian and the Hungarian Academies of Sciences, and the founding director of the Institute of Culture Studies and Theatre History of the Austrian Academy. He is the author of *Das Gedächtnis der Städte: Kulturelle Verflechtungen—Wien und die urbanen Milieus in Zentraleuropa* (2010).

Patrice M. Dabrowski is the author of *Commemorations and the Shaping of Modern Poland* (2004) as well as numerous articles on aspects of Polish history. She has just completed the text of a popular, thousand-year history of Poland to be published by Northern Illinois University Press. Dabrowski is also working on a book-length study tentatively entitled *"Discovering" the Carpathians: Episodes in Imagining and Reshaping Alpine Borderland Regions*. Currently affiliated with the Minda de Gunzberg Center for European Studies at Harvard, she has taught at Harvard, Brown, and the University of Massachusetts, Amherst, and has served as the director of the Harvard Ukrainian Summer Institute.

Johannes Feichtinger is a senior researcher at the Institute of Culture Studies and Theatre History of the Austrian Academy of Sciences (OeAW), and he teaches history at the University of Vienna. He has specialized in intellectual history and studies of culture. His publications include *Wissenschaft zwischen den Kulturen: Österreichische Hochschullehrer in der Emigration 1933–1945* (2001) and *Wissenschaft als reflexives Projekt: Von Bolzano über Freud zu Kelsen: Österreichische Wissenschaftsgeschichte 1848–1938* (2010).

Michael John is Professor at the Institute of Social and Economic History of the Johannes Kepler University of Linz, Austria. He has published widely on multiculturalism in Central Europe, and is the author of many works on the history of urban migration, migration and popular culture, and identity in different regions of Austria. He is also the author of *Vom nationalen Hort zur postmodernen City: Zur Migrations- und Identitätsgeschichte der Stadt Linz im 20. Jahrhundert* (2013), and the coeditor of *Schmelztiegel Wien* (1993, 2nd ed.).

Pieter M. Judson is Professor of History at the European University Institute in Florence and editor of the *Austrian History Yearbook*. His books include *Guardians of the Nation: Activists on the Language Frontiers of Imperial Austria* (2006), *Exclusive Revolutionaries: Liberal Politics, Social Experience, and National Identity in the Austrian Empire, 1848–1914* (1996), *Wien Brennt! Die Revolution von 1848 und ihr liberales Erbe* (1998), and, with Marsha L. Rozenblit, *Constructing Nationalities in East Central Europe* (2005). He has held fellowships from the Fulbright, Guggenheim, and Marshall programs; the National Endowment for the Humanities; the American Academy in Berlin; and the Internationales Forschungszentrum Kulturwissenschaften in Vienna.

Oto Luthar serves as the director of the Research Centre (SAZU) of the Slovenian Academy of Sciences and Arts in Ljubljana. He is also a professor at the University of Nova Gorica, where he is the head of the graduate program in cultural studies. He has published extensively on cultural history, interculturality, and national identities. Luthar is the editor of *The Land Between: A History of Slovenia* (2008), and the author of *The Margins of Memory: Anti-Semitism and the Destruction of Prekmurje Jews* (2012).

Michael Rössner is Professor of Romance Languages and Literature at the University of Munich, Germany, a member of the Austrian Academy of Sciences, and since 2009 director of its Institute of Culture Studies and Theatre History (OeAW), where he established a new research focus on cultural translation. He has published widely on cultural studies, and is the editor and translator of the *Complete Works of Luigi Pirandello* (16 vols., 1997–2001) and the editor of *Lateinamerikanische Literaturgeschichte* (2007, 3rd ed.).

Index

Adorno, Theodor W., 175, 179, 184n14, 185nn35–36, 202–3, 207nn49–51, 208n52
Adriatic Sea, 104, 106, 109, 110, 113, 117n4, 117n6, 118n27, 119n45, 120n64, 120n67, 121n77
Albanian, 102, 112–13, 119n46
anthropology, 14n8, 32, 95, 107–11, 113–14, 117n9, 117n13, 118n29, 120n59, 130, 152n58, 174
    ethnographic museums, 99n31, 110, 112, 119n53
    ethnography, 57, 104–7, 110, 118n22, 118n27, 120n62, 120n71, 190
    ethnology, 81n24, 107, 117n4, 117n9, 118n25, 118n34, 119n47, 119n50, 119n52, 195
    imperial ethnography, 106–10, 118n20, 118nn29–30, 118n38, 121n79
    Viennese Anthropological Society, 107
Appelfeld, Aharon, 13, 180, 183, 185n43, 185n45, 185nn47–48
Arendt, Hannah, 35, 45n66
Armenian
    language, 180
    people, 88, 96, 196
Ashbrook, John, 103, 117n11
assimilation
    cultural, 21, 23, 25, 79, 199
    forced, 146–47
    geographic and spatial, 140, 175, 177
    Jews, 127, 129, 154n111
    linguistic, 31, 67, 81n15, 129
    national (multiethnic and multicultural), 87, 89, 104, 154n103, 157n154
    policy, 128, 145
Ausländer, Rose, 178
Austria, 20–21, 25, 30–31, 177–78, 180, 189–92
    Lower Austria, 123, 127–29, 139, 146
    Republic of, 12, 122–57, 150n23, 150n30
    Second Austrian Republic, 145, 156n143
    Upper Austria, 127, 131–32, 139, 142, 152n72, 152n74, 157n155
Austrian Social Democratic Party (SPÖ), 125–27, 141, 151n53
Austro-Hungarian Monarchy. *See* Habsburg Monarchy
Austro-Marxists, 21, 28, 42n18, 43nn35–36

Baal Shem Tov, 95, 99n33
backwardness
    barbarism, 96, 131, 176, 178–79, 182, 184n1, 184n17, 184n21, 184n22
    highlanders, 88–89, 104, 106
    rural, 72–77, 166
    savagery, 49, 106, 176, 179
Baroque, Spanish, 19, 190
Bauer, Otto, 8, 14n13, 21, 27–28, 44n36, 127–28
Bauernfeld, Eduard von, 201, 207n44
Belgrade, 5, 125, 204

Benjamin, Walter, 46n85, 196, 200, 207n32
Berg, Alban, 203, 208n5
bilingualism, 30, 32, 41n7, 63–64, 68, 73, 75–76, 81n14, 112–13, 124, 126, 145, 169, 201
Bloch, Ernst, 36–38, 40, 42n11, 45nn72–73, 45n76
Bloch, Marc, 165
Bohemia, 66–67, 69, 71, 74, 80n11, 123, 146, 185n33, 197. *See also* Czech
 people, 81n16, 149n6, 188
 politics, 14n10, 80n8, 80n11, 192
borders (or boundaries)
 borderlands, 14n10, 87–89, 97, 98n4, 98n13, 99n15, 117n9, 117n12, 120n65
 territorial, nation-state, 11–35, 25, 27, 29, 59n10, 69–71, 86–89, 101, 103, 108, 113–16
 political relations, 120n68, 120nn71–72, 123–24, 161
 linguistic, 33, 61, 87, 124
 religious, 34
 inclusion, exclusion, belonging, 9–11, 17, 104, 110–12, 114–15, 168, 174–75
 cultural identity, 7, 17–20, 28, 35, 39–40, 45n75, 60n25, 61, 76, 87, 119n45, 199
Bosnia-Herzegovina, 101, 104, 134, 137, 162, 173n14
Bosnia, 69, 112, 117n1
Bosnian (language), 139, 166
Bosnian war, 23
Bourdieu, Pierre, 54, 186n59, 186n59, 194, 206n23
Braudel, Fernand, 188
Brenner, Yosef Haim, 203
Britain. *See also* colonialism
 British Empire, 21–22, 32, 41n8, 48, 50
  Britishness, 10, 28, 34, 49
  Europeanness, 49, 95, 196
Broch, Hermann, 188, 205n2
Brod, Max, 203, 208n56, 208n58
Brubaker, Rogers, 14n7, 62, 80n3, 87, 98n8, 98n12, 165, 172n4, 172n8

Budapest, 48, 170, 204
Bukovina, 12–13, 69, 80n2, 177–78, 180–81, 183
Burke, Peter, 7, 9, 14n11, 172n7

Calderon de la Barca, Pedro, 190, 205n5
Canetti, Elias, 178, 185n32
Cankar, Ivan, 173n14, 202
Carinthia, 81n25, 123–24, 136, 139, 145, 156n144, 169, 201
Carpathian, 86, 89–91, 98n4, 98n13, 99n15, 179
Celan, Paul, 178
census, 68–71, 73, 75–76, 81nn14–16, 81nn25–26, 112, 120n66, 123, 125–26, 129, 136, 139–40, 151n53, 154n111
 decennial, 68–71
Čeremšyna, Marko, 202
Cilli/Celje, 124
Cipriani, Lidio, 95, 99n33, 100n41
citizenship, notions of
 Austrian, 12, 63, 74, 125–26, 128, 133, 137, 140–44, 150n19, 152n74, 157n152, 202
 ethnic, 164
 international, 116
 Istrian, 120n66, 103
 jus soli, 147, 157n152
 Muslim, 41n2
 Poland, 87
 world, 27–28
Cocco, Emilio, 101, 111, 116, 117n4, 117n6, 120n64, 120n67, 121n77
coexistence
 cultural, 9–10, 13, 17, 19, 21, 37, 204, 332
 ethnic, 2, 101, 206, 111, 115, 120n75
 linguistic, 32, 69, 79
Cold War, 48, 54, 136–27, 152n60
colonialism
 anticolonial struggle, 17–18, 23, 25–34
 British rule, 21–22, 25–34
 colonial rule, 10, 19, 21–38, 41n8, 44n56, 48, 78, 118n26, 177, 179
 Spanish colonies, 49–52, 59n7

cosmopolitanism, 27, 104, 109–11, 116, 117n13, 119nn47–48, 119n57, 120n59, 144, 168
Counter-Reformation, 190
Croatia, 11–12, 57, 102–4, 109, 112–16, 117n4, 119n40, 119nn50–52, 120n68, 120nn72–73, 132, 137, 162. *See also under* Istria
    Croatian Democratic Union (HDZ), 102–3, 113, 117n11
    Croatian speakers, 102–7, 112–14, 123–25, 128, 130, 132, 136, 139, 166–68, 172n11, 173n14, 202, 204
Crown Prince Rudolf, 56–57, 59n22, 60n23, 106
Csáky, Moritz, 3–4, 12–13, 32, 41n8, 42n12, 44n46, 44n52, 46n84, 79n1, 82n28, 101, 184n23, 187–208
Csaplovics, Johann, 191, 205n10
Cuban Revolution, 50
culture
    concept of, 1–3, 5–9, 14n6, 18–21, 24–25, 27–28, 31–33, 35–40, 42n12, 43n31, 44n56, 45n66, 46n83, 62–66, 69–70, 78–79, 80n2, 163–65, 173n14, 176, 187, 192–204, 206n14, 206n20, 106nn23–27, 207n41
    folk culture, 90, 94–96, 109–10, 117n9, 119n53, 197
    urban milieus, 12, 19, 31, 65, 67, 71–75, 79, 104, 106, 109–10, 117n13, 118n26, 123–24, 150n18, 177–78, 183, 188, 190, 199–204
Cvijić, Jovan, 111, 120n61
Czarnohora (Hutsul region), 88, 92–93, 96, 99n14
Czech
    language/origin, 14n10, 61–63, 66–69, 72, 81n16, 123–24, 128–30, 133, 135–37, 139–40, 147, 149n6, 151n53, 185, 192, 201–4
    nationalism/movement, 66–67, 69–70, 75, 79, 80nn8–10, 81n24, 125–26

Czecho-Slovak Party, 126
Czechoslovakia, 48, 81n26, 88, 122–24, 127–28, 133, 151n53, 153n82
Czernowitz, 177, 179, 183, 185n34, 186n56
Czoernig, Karl Freiherr von, 105–6

Dalmatia, 104, 105, 107, 118n16
Derrida, Jacques, 33, 44n53
diversity
    cultural, multiculturalism, 1–12, 13n2, 20–28, 36, 79, 96, 104, 109, 117, 117n5, 118n15, 144, 148, 163
    ethnic, 3, 12, 18, 56, 85–88, 94, 97–98, 111, 140
    heterogeneity, 5–12, 17, 20, 23–25, 27–28, 53, 57, 61–68, 70–71, 73–79, 80n2, 89, 104–8, 112–15, 118nn25–26, 118n34, 163–64, 187–92, 195, 198–204
    internal European difference, 20–28, 35, 198
    linguistic, 3, 19, 29–32, 36, 62, 190
    religious, 18, 34, 79, 121n79, 149, 189
    right to diversity, similarity in diversity, 39–40
Dmowski, Roman, 86, 89, 98n6
Doderer, Heimito von, 19, 41n6
Domestic Work Force Protection Act, 127–28
Drakulić, Slavenka, 101, 117n2

education, schooling, 28, 62–64, 66–75, 77–79, 80nn11–12, 92, 112, 133, 140, 144, 148, 163, 173n14, 189, 203
Ehrenpreis, Marcus, 95, 99n33
Eisenstadt, Shmuel Noach, 176–77, 183, 184n2, 184n4, 184nn20–21, 185n49
Eminescu, Mihai, 177, 185n29
Enlightenment, 5, 17, 98n2, 118n16, 11n18
ethnopluralism, 9
European Union (EU), 47–48, 104, 113, 115, 120n68, 139–141, 143–144, 148, 151n37

fascism, 34, 108, 110, 178
Febvre, Lucien, 165, 172n7
Ferdinand I, Habsburg Emperor, 189–90

Fiume, 204
food, recipe, cuisine, 4, 12, 112, 161–172, 190, 195
Foreign Workers' Employment Act of 1976, 135–136
foreignness, 17, 22, 31, 33–34, 66, 90, 107, 126, 130–31, 145–47, 177, 183, 201–2
    foreigners, 123–48, 183
France, Frenchness, 4, 10, 20–22, 25, 33, 35, 147, 192, 194, 196, 202
Franzos, Karl Emil, 178, 184n25, 185n31
Freedom Party (and Haider, Jörg), 138, 141, 143, 147
Frith, Simon, 195, 206n26
Friulian, 173n14, 202
fundamentalism, 18, 20, 23, 28, 32, 34, 36, 41n8

Galicia
    Austrian crown lands, 80n2, 86, 88, 90, 98n5, 98n13, 125, 132
    Jews, 125, 132, 150n33, 177
Garton Ash, Timothy, 1, 13n2
Geertz, Clifford, 194–95, 199, 206n20, 206n22, 206n25, 207n40
Gellner, Ernest, 42n12, 89, 98n3
German, 85, 88, 106, 117n9, 118n26, 123–32, 134–39, 143–47, 151n53, 152n74, 163, 166–70, 174, 177–78, 183, 191, 192, 194, 196, 202–4
    Germanness, 4, 10, 14n10, 20–21, 25, 27, 28, 31, 33–35, 61–62, 66, 68–72, 75–79, 80n4, 80n8, 80n12, 81n16, 128
Globalization, 43n35, 44n38, 120n73, 137, 145, 188, 204
Goethe, 17, 19–20, 24–25, 30, 34, 41nn4–5, 41n9, 42n20, 42n22, 43n83, 43n85
Goffman, Erving, 194, 206n23
Greenblatt, Stephen, 195, 206n27
Grillparzer, Franz, 27, 43n32, 190, 205n5
Gypsies, 123, 130, 131, 152n64, 167

Habsburg Central Europe, ix, 3–5, 7, 9–13, 14n15, 19, 62, 69, 80n5, 82n28, 98n1, 101, 183
    defined, 3–5

Habsburg Monarchy, ix, 3–6, 10, 19–21, 35, 42n12, 43n30, 48–58, 79n1, 80n8, 80n13, 81n16, 85–86, 88, 98, 98n5, 99n14, 101, 103–11, 116–17, 118n20, 118n22, 118nn29–30, 118nn37–38, 120n71, 121n79, 122–23, 125–28, 136–39, 145–46, 148, 149n1, 149n6, 149n16, 169, 177, 183, 187, 190, 192, 204
    break-up of monarchy, 25, 27–28, 42n18, 43n30
    citizenship (successor states), 125, 128
    defined, 4
    ethnicities, 56
    identity, 58
    Istrian ethnography, 118n22, 120n71
    migration, 12–13, 31, 140
    multilingualism, 11, 14n10, 30–33, 169
    pluriculturality, 5, 21, 56, 58, 118n20, 190, 204
Habsburg tradition, 162, 166, 169, 189–90, 205n5
Hall, Stuart, 5, 13n6, 206n26
Hammer-Purgstall, Joseph von, 29–31, 44n42
Hebrew, 180, 203
Hegel, 38, 176, 184n16
Herder, Johann Gottfried, 2, 19, 21, 23–26, 33, 42n13, 42n16, 42n17, 42n19, 194
heterogeneity, 1–13, 17, 20, 23, 25–29, 35–37, 39–40, 53, 55, 57, 60n26, 89, 98n5, 116, 123, 162, 177, 188–92, 196, 199–204
Hindi, 32–33, 41n7, 44n40
    Hindu culture, 10, 28, 32, 34–35, 44n56, 45n59, 196
historical narratives, 7, 13, 37, 119n40
    collective memory, 14n15, 148, 191–96, 199
    cultural models of European and Latin American development, 47–58, 179, 191
    Habsburg past, 21, 116, 192–93
    invocations of the past, 98n6, 108–10, 135, 163–64, 172n5 (*see also* Sarmatian myth)

memory of traditions, 19, 91, 94–95, 174
Venetian heritage and past, 108–11
Hobsbawm, Eric, 98n7, 165
Hofmannsthal, Hugo von, 25, 31, 43n24, 44n41, 44n47, 57, 60n24, 188, 191, 192, 202, 205n2, 206n12, 207n46
Hołówko, Tadeusz, 87, 98n10
homogenization, homogeneity, 2, 5–6, 10, 13, 17, 19–20, 23–24, 27–29, 31–37, 39–40, 41n8, 50, 52, 55, 57, 77, 79, 79n1, 107, 112, 116, 122, 124, 129, 163–64, 187, 189–90, 193, 196, 199
Horkheimer, Max, 175, 184n14
Hornung, Maria, 201, 207n45
Horváth, Ödön von, 204
Humboldt, Wilhelm von, 24, 34, 44n54
Hungarians, 42n14, 106, 123–24, 128, 130, 133, 136–37, 139, 152n69, 161–64, 166–70, 172n10, 173n16, 190, 191, 197, 198, 202, 204
 Hungary, Hungarian, 12, 56, 81n14, 123–24, 127–28, 133, 143, 162, 169, 190–91, 198
Hutsul region (Huculszczyzna, Hutsul'shchyna, Czarnohora, Charnohora), tourism in, 88–97
Hutsuls, artistry of; fighting in World War I (Polish Legions, Zolnierz Polski), 89, 91, 93, 99n18, 99n20

identity
 Austrian, 56–57
 continental, transnational 50, 52, 54–55, 57
 cultural difference, 5–7, 9, 12
 ethnonational, 11, 101–2, 107–8, 111–12, 114, 118n26, 123, 161, 163, 165, 176
 European, 9, 47–50, 55, 58
 identity discourse, 8–10, 104, 193
 Istrian, 11, 114–16, 117n4, 117n8, 117n11
 Jewish, 45n66
 Kakanian, 58
 Latin American, 50–58
 linguistic, 11–12, 14n11, 64, 69, 112, 118n26, 192
 local, 14n10, 61–79, 80n2, 98n7, 103–4, 109–11, 116, 118n32, 119n54, 120n57, 140, 146, 150n31, 164, 166–69, 174–79, 181–83, 199
 mestizaje, 47–57
 and memory, 7–8, 10, 13, 19, 60n25, 98n7, 117n4, 117n8, 117n11, 157n161, 182
 mixed, hybrid, 51–52, 57–58, 107, 199, 203–4
 national, 2, 6–9, 28, 38, 43n25, 47–48, 55–58, 61–62, 66–70, 73–74, 78, 86, 104–7, 109, 113, 164, 189, 192–93, 200
 politicized, politics of 117n11, 120n66, 172n9
 regional, 6–7, 11, 41n8, 48, 62, 69, 74, 88, 97–98, 98n5, 102–6, 111–16, 118n26, 149n14, 150n23, 155n128, 190, 201 (*see also* identity: Istrian)
 religious, 118n26, 62
 spaces of identity, 45n75, 194, 206
India, 18–20, 25–29, 31–37, 41n7, 42n14, 43n25, 44n40, 44n50, 45n56, 45n64, 45n67. *See also* colonialism: anticolonial struggle
indifference, ethnic and national, 2, 7, 14n10, 72–75, 80n11, 82n26, 90, 165
interwar period, 11, 62–63, 77, 81n26, 85–98, 123–29, 139, 147–48, 150n23
Istria, 11–12, 101–17n4, 117n8, 117n11, 118n20, 117n29, 118n37, 119n40, 119n46, 119n53, 120nn62–63, 120n66, 120n68, 120n71. *See also* migration
 Croatian Istria, 102–4, 108, 112
 Istrian Democratic Assembly (IDS-DDI), 102–3, 112–13, 117n11
 Istrian Ethnographic Museum, 110, 112
 Istrianity, 103–4, 111–12
Italy, 101, 103, 104, 108, 110, 120n66
 Italian, 194, 203, 202

Jesenska, Milena, 123, 149n3
Jesuit, 190
Jews, 12, 35, 86, 88, 96, 99n20, 123,
    125–32, 139–41, 146–47, 150n33,
    153n74, 154nn110–11, 162, 177–78,
    181–82, 196, 203
    East European (*Ostjuden*), 125–27,
        129, 132, 140, 177–78
    Hungarian, 152n69
    Viennese, 123, 127, 129, 131, 141,
        154n111
Józewski, Henryk, 87, 89, 99n19

Kafka, Franz, 123, 203, 208nn53–55,
    208nn57–58
Kappus, Elke-Nicole, 107, 118n20,
    118nn29–30, 118n38
Kasprzycki, Tadeusz, 89, 91, 99n16
Kelsen, Hans, 8, 21, 42n12
King, Jeremy, 11, 14n10, 14n15, 63, 80n5,
    80n8, 80n13
Kohn, Hans, 85
Kosambi, D.D., 36
Kraus, Karl, 188, 205n2
Kreisky, Bruno, 136
Kremsier, 192
Kronprinzenwerk (KPW), 56, 106, 107,
    118n25
Kundera, Milan, 187, 205n1
Kunitake, Kume, 191, 205n11

Latin America, 10, 47–60
Latin, 21, 191
Lebanon, 199
Legionnaires Club, 91–92
Lehár, Franz, 197
Lenin, Vladimir, 21, 28, 44n37
Loos, Adolf, 188, 205n2
Lotman, Jurij, 199, 202, 207n36
Luckman, Thomas, 170, 173n19
Luhmann, Niklas, 193, 206n17
Lyotard, Jean-François, 57, 60n27, 188,
    205n2

Mach, Ernst, 6, 14n9, 42n12, 188
Machar, Josef Svatopluk, 202
Mahler, Gustav, 203, 208n52

Malinowski, Brigadier General Tadeusz,
    91, 99n22
Malinowski, Bronislaw, 195, 198, 206n23,
    207n41
Manea, Norman, 178, 185n33, 185n47
Mannheim, Karl, 37
Marburg/Maribor, 124
Marx, Karl, 25, 196, 200, 207n42
Marxists, 27, 128, 196. *See also*
    Austro-Marxists
Mathias, Habsburg Emperor, 189
Maximilian II, Habsburg Emperor, 189
McLuhan, Marshall, 195, 206n29
Mediterranean, 109, 117n5, 117n13,
    118n15, 118n32, 119nn47–52,
    120nn58–59, 120n63
Meißner, Alfred, 188, 205n3
memory. *See also under* identity
    "collective" memory, 7, 148, 199
    "historical" memory, 13, 191
    lieux de mémoire (sites of memory),
        56, 174, 179, 194, 206n18
mestizo, 49–60. *See also* identity: *mestizaje*
Mexican Revolution, 52–53
migration. *See also* foreigners; minority
    across Latin America, 50, 55
    after the civil war of 1934, , 151n53
    Austro-Hungarian, 31, 122–57
    contemporary migration in Austria,
        12, 157n161
    diasporic, 155n118, 198–99
    displaced persons, 132, 139,
        153n76
    European, 21, 23
    Gastarbeiter (guest worker), 134,
        136, 153n86
    globalized connections, 20, 33, 38
    immigrants, 63, 95, 129, 132–48,
        149n7, 151n37, 153n83,
        154nn99–101, 155n119, 156n139,
        156n142, 157n160, 117n8
    integration, 149nn1–2, 149n7,
        150nn30–31, 150nn33–34,
        151n46, 151n49, 154nn107–12,
        156nn134–47
    Italians in Istria, 50, 108, 111
        119n40, 120n69

labor, 18, 150n23, 153n86, 154n102, 155n129
mass migration after the World Wars, 29, 102, 119n40, 122
policy, 127, 133–34, 151n37, 156nn134–39
Slovenian-speakers, 123–25
Turkish migrants, 129, 134, 137–40, 142, 147
unregistered immigrants, illegal aliens, 138
minority, minorities, 1–2, 8, 23, 25
census numbers, 81n25
Czech-speaking, 123–24
German-speaking, 69
Hungarian, 154
Italian, 102, 109, 112, 117n8, 119n40, 120n68
linguistic, 179
migration policy, 37, 136, 143, 145–46, 151n37
rights, 2, 8, 12, 23, 87, 103, 108, 123, 130–31
Roma and Sinti, 130–31
schools, 65, 74
Mitteleuropa, 4, 13n4, 59n17, 80n7, 81n24, 124, 149n13, 149n15, 205n4
Moldavia, 177
monoglossia, polyglossia, 28–31
monolingualism (linguistic purity), 4, 30–36, 44n53, 112
Moravia, 66, 69, 72, 74, 81n16, 123, 146, 149n6, 192
Mozart, Wolfgang Amadeus, 203
multiculturalism, 101, 17–19, 24, 40, 85–87, 93–97, 99n1, 122–23, 144–45, 148, 183
Bukovinian model, 13
defined, 2
discourse, 101–4, 107–12
Istrian, 104, 111–12
policies, 2, 12
Yugoslav, 108–9
multiethnicity, 3–4, 97, 101, 104, 109, 111, 116, 120n75
multilingualism, 3–4, 6, 11–12, 19, 29–30, 32–33, 36–37, 48, 61–62, 64, 77, 79, 104, 124, 161, 166–69, 172

multinationalism, 19, 28
borderland, Galicia, 86–88
European empires, 43n35
Habsburg Monarchy, 3–4, 122, 135–36, 145–46
Poland, Polish Commonwealth, 86
Prekmurje, 164
Yugoslavia, 98, 101, 104, 108–9
Munich, 131, 204
Musil, Robert, 25, 43n24, 188
Muslim, 1, 32, 35, 41n2, 44n56, 112, 139, 168, 196

Nadas, Peter, 22–23, 42n15
nation, nationality, nationalization, 187, 189, 193–94, 199, 204
National Socialists, 80n8, 130–33, 140, 146, 148, 151n53, 152n67, 152n68
nationalism, 25, 27, 34, 41n8, 43nn24–25, 44n40, 44n56, 96, 98nn7–8, 102
civic, 85
ethnic, 85 (*see also* identity: ethnonational)
Hindu, 34, 41, 44n40
and language, 65–72
multinationalism, 98, 104
nation-building, 11, 48, 80n10, 98n3
nationalist narratives, 7–8. *See also* backwardness: rural
to explain national differences, 187–88, 192–93, 201, 204
German and Czech nationalists, 65–70
language frontier, 65–72
multiculturalism, 97
nationality, national group, 2, 4–5, 13n6, 23, 61–62, 68, 118n26, 184n5, 190. *See also* identity: national; multinationality
ethnocultural terms, 164
language as proxy for, 80n13
nationality conflict, 63, 71
nationality principle (*Nationalitätenprinzip*), 8, 187
nationality question, 21, 27, 67
nationalization process, 6–13, 14nn12–15

neighbor, 13, 35, 111, 113, 175–77. *See also* foreignness
nachbar, 174, 184n1, 184n3, 184n10
Nestroy, Johann, 202
Nietzsche, Friedrich, 194
Nikočević, Lidija, 105, 112, 114, 118n22, 118n29, 118n31, 118n33, 118n36, 119n53, 120n71
Nimni, Ephraim, 8, 14n13
nobility, Polish, 85–86, 90, 95, 98n2
non-EU/EEA citizens, 141, 144
Norbert, Elias, 146, 156n150, 175–77, 182–83, 184nn6–7, 184n11, 184n13, 185n46, 186n54
nostalgia, 108–11, 116, 205n2

Offenbach, Jacques, 197
Ottoman empire, 4–5, 111, 116, 119n46, 121n79, 190

Palestinian
 diaspora, plural histories, 199
 identity, 207n39
 Jewish migration, 129, 152n73
Panofsky, Erwin, 165
Paris Peace Conference, 86, 124, 187
peasants, 66, 71–78, 86, 88, 90, 109, 170, 174, 178–81, 190
Penderecki, Krzysztof, 196, 207n31
Pettau/Ptuji, 124
Pieterse, Jan Nederveen, 198, 201, 207n35, 207n43
Piłsudski, Józef, 86–87, 89, 91, 98nn6–7
Piran/Pirano, 108–9, 114–15
pluriculturalism, 3, 8–10, 18–21, 29, 31, 34–37, 39–40, 42n12, 61, 79n1, 101–2, 107–8, 111, 188, 191–92, 198
Poland
 Polish (or Pole), 11, 81n16, 85–98, 99n19, 99n31, 100n39, 123–25, 127, 133, 137, 144, 180, 191, 196, 202–4
 Polish Commonwealth (Commonwealth of Two Nations, Polish-Lithuanian Commonwealth), 85–86, 98n5

Polish Second Republic (interwar Poland), 11, 86–88, 90, 92–94, 96–97
Portugal (or Portuguese), 35, 196
postcolonial
 era, 19, 21, 35, 52, 117n5, 118n15, 184n23
 theory, 10, 31, 40, 41n8, 44n36, 46n83, 55, 57, 60n28, 78, 79n1, 82n28, 176–77
postmodernism, 7, 163, 184nn17–18, 188, 205n2
Prague, 5, 62, 71, 80n4, 81n15, 81n24, 123, 125, 133, 153n82, 185n33, 203
Prekmurje, 12, 162–69
Preßburg, 204
Prussia, 5, 127, 191

Raab-Olah Agreement, 134
Radical Party, 90
Rasse, 125–26, 130, 152n58
Reichensperger, Richard, 202, 207n47
Renner, Karl, 8, 27, 42n18, 44n36
Rezzori, Gregor von, 13, 178–81, 183, 185nn38–40
Rijeka, 103
Rioux, Jean-Pierre, 192, 206n14
Rittner, Tadeusz, 202–4, 208n59
Roma and Sinti, 88, 96, 123, 130–31, 136, 154n100, 162. *See also* minority, minorities
Romania, Romanian, 88, 106, 124, 129, 132, 136, 177–78, 180
Roth, Joseph, 190, 205n5
Rotteck, Carl von, 191, 205n9
Rovinj/Rovigno, 109, 115
Rudolf II, Hapsburg Emperor, 189
rural life, 61–64, 67, 71–79, 81n23, 109–10, 118n26, 166, 169, 174, 177, 197
Rushdie, Salman, 46n83, 196, 206n30, 207n39
Russia, 25, 43n35, 88–90, 180, 191

Said, Edward, 59n1, 184n24, 199, 207n39
Sarmatian, myth of origins, 86
Schlegel, Friedrich, 24, 42n19
Schmitt, Carl, 34–35, 45n57, 45n63
Schönberg, Arnold, 188, 205n2

Schubert, Franz, 203, 207n51
Scotson, John, 146, 156n150, 186nn54–55
Second Brigade (of the Polish Legions),
    Hutsul Route March of, 89–91, 93
secular spheres, 73, 174, 181
    secularism, 17–18, 32, 35, 40,
        44n55, 45n64
segregation, 10, 24, 28, 140–41, 154n111,
    179
    liberal apartheid, 21
    racial apartheid, 24
Seipel, Ignaz, 125–26
Serbia, 5, 96, 134
    Serbs, 102, 105, 113, 135, 139, 166,
        168, 172n11, 173n14
Simmel, George, 175, 177, 181, 184n9,
    185n27, 185n44, 185n53
Simonek, Stefan, 202, 207n48, 208n59
Slav, Slavic people, 105–8, 110, 112–13,
    118nn16–18, 119n46, 127, 132, 145–46,
    149n16, 161, 166, 168, 173n16, 177, 190
Slovak or Slovakian (people, descent), 123,
    127–28, 130, 136–37, 149n6, 151n53,
    191, 198, 202
Slovenia, x, 11–12, 61, 81n25, 119n40,
    119n44, 120n72, 153n76, 161–63,
    172nn5–6. See also Istria
    as ethnic minorities, 123–25, 128,
        130, 132, 136, 156n144, 162–70,
        172n10
    Slovene literature, 173n14, 173n16,
        202
    Slovene movement, nationalists, 61,
        66, 72, 75–76, 79
    Slovenian-speakers, 81n16, 101–17,
        124–25, 145
Snyder, Timothy, 87, 98n9, 98n11
Sobota, Murska, 169
sociality, 163–64
soldier, 12, 89–91, 162, 167, 169. See also
    Second Brigade (of the Polish Legions);
    Hutsul, artistry of
    Austro-Hungarian army, 90
Spain (Spanish), 4–5, 22, 134, 189–90,
    205n5
Sperber, Alfred Margul, 178–79, 185
Spinčić, Vjekoslav, 106
Stifter, Adalbert, 197, 202, 207n34, 207n47

Stourzh, Gerald (ethnicizing process), 4,
    13n3, 14n10, 80n6, 81n15
Strauß, Johann, 197
Styria, 81n16, 81n25, 123–25, 128–29,
    136, 139, 169
Sv. Peter, 113–14
swojszczyzna (nativeness)
    Society for the Preservation of,
        93–95, 98
    Society of Friends of the Hutsul
        region (*Towarzystwo Przyjaciół
        Huculszczyzny*), 89–95, 97,
        100n42
    Tourism and Health Resort Section
        (Society of Friends of the Hutsul
        Region) 89, 91–95, 97

Tagore, Rabindranath, 25–27, 32, 34,
    36, 43nn24–28, 43nn31–32, 44n50,
    45n70
Taylor, Charles, 164
Trieste, 25, 81n16, 109–11, 115, 117n8,
    119n40, 119nn55–56, 120n63
Trotsky, Leon, 196
Tudjman, Franjo, 102, 108, 112–13, 116
Turčinović, Peter, 103

Ukraine, Ukrainians
    ethnicity and nationality, 57, 60n25,
        85, 87–91, 93, 98n9, 99n19,
        99n23, 100n42, 119n57, 131, 196
    language, 81n16, 97, 99n30, 202
Umgangssprache (language of everyday use),
    81n15–16, 112, 124, 150n29
Umlauft, Friedrich, 13n5, 56, 59n21,
    190–91, 205n8

Venetian Empire, 104–6, 116, 119n46. See
    also historical narratives
Vienna, 71, 110, 170, 188, 190, 197, 203, 204
    site of diversity and hybrid identities,
        5, 13n3, 19, 31, 57, 108, 140, 202
    site of migration, 122–32, 134–36,
        138, 141–43, 146–57, 201
    Viennese culture, 53, 56
Vietnamese, 196
Vincenz, Stanislaw, 95–97, 99n32, 99n36,
    100n39, 100n42